Elementary Education
in
Rural Areas

CLIFFORD P. ARCHER

PROFESSOR OF EDUCATION
UNIVERSITY OF MINNESOTA

THE RONALD PRESS COMPANY • NEW YORK

Library of Congress Catalog Card Number: 58–5632

To

**Myrtle, Blair Philip
Helen and Stephen**

PREFACE

Modern education is not simply a matter of training children; rather, it is a problem of helping to build a school and community environment in which children, under guidance, can grow up to be democratic in social relationships, familiar with the ways of collecting facts to solve problems, eager to carry a share of community responsibilities, appreciative of the best in life, and free to exercise the functions of responsible citizenship. The school, as part of the community, must share in community problems and community enterprises. Any other kind of education lacks vitality and usefulness and tends to be abstract and meaningless to youth.

The author believes that the modern school is close to the people, that what teachers teach is governed by the needs of the children growing up in the community. The needs of rural children differ from those of their urban friends because home and community backgrounds are not the same; therefore a rural teacher's instructional practice in the modern school varies from the methods employed and content used by her urban colleague. This book is planned as a textbook for courses in elementary school methods for students who are preparing to teach in rural areas. Its emphasis is on the teacher's part in instructing children who live in a small community or town, or in the open country. It will help elementary school teachers who work in one-teacher and two-teacher schools, in graded and ungraded schools of towns and villages, and in consolidated and reorganized school districts.

The book begins by explaining why the teacher who works in rural areas needs an appreciation of the values of farm and village life if she is to enjoy working with rural people. She must be concerned with the environment of the rural child and the community problems which have a marked bearing on child development. To understand the problems of the rural people, the teacher needs a perspective of the changing character of farm and village life. She needs to be a constant student of local traditions, customs, social values, habit patterns, and problems of family and community life. She should know that progress toward the realization of the large goals of education must start where the people are, and she must therefore understand community life and customs which determine the patterns of behavior of the children. The text also indicates that the school of the rural community has certain responsibilities and concerns for community improvement.

The teacher must know not only the rural community and the rural environment but also the children. She needs a knowledge of the techniques of child study and must understand the nature of child growth and development, including the principles of learning. While no attempt is made in the book to furnish a complete treatment of child growth and development or of learning, some principles which are basic to any organization of instruction in elementary education are treated. These basic concepts are essential to the organization of curriculum and method in either rural or urban schools.

In curriculum development in the modern school, the teacher and her educational beliefs are very important. What does she consider the function of the school in a rural democratic society? If it is to help the people to live better lives, she will consider the needs of children and the aspirations of parents for their children. The general educational objectives for all schools are considered in this book, as well as the specific ones for rural areas. The teacher will want to know how educational experiences can best be organized into a program that gives continuous development for children. She should know how to organize and carry out units of work which meet the needs of the children and which utilize available resources to help the children develop the skills, attitudes, appreciations, and understanding required for more effective living. This text aids the teacher in organizing the curriculum to provide appropriate experiences for the children.

Changes in the curriculum are evolutionary rather than revolutionary. The teacher should start with present practices and make changes which furnish experiences designed to lead to better learning. Since most schools are organized on a subject or a broad-area basis, the teacher may begin by improving the program of instruction within the present framework, although more marked changes can sometimes be made. The book discusses curriculum experiences and procedures in teaching in the various subject areas and treats the broader aspects of teaching the language arts, with special attention to speaking and listening, writing, spelling, handwriting, and reading. It suggests experiences and procedures in arithmetic, social studies, science, health, physical education, safety, and the arts. This organization for purposes of discussion does not imply a necessary separation in presentation, but the experiences suggested should lead to the development of a well-balanced program which utilizes the concepts of child development and learning. Specific experiences which utilize the resources of the community are discussed and illustrated in the chapters dealing with subject areas.

An attempt is made to define the responsibilities of the public, the school staff, and the children in the processes of evaluation of the school program. Evaluation by citizens often uncovers changes needed to provide adequate educational facilities. A guide which teachers can use for the study and evaluation of instruction is provided in the Appendix.

Each chapter has a selected list of readings. These references suggest additional source material for college students who are preparing to teach and for those teachers who wish to do further reading. Students who have had recent courses in child development and learning may be satisfied with the summary given at the end of each chapter, but the use of the references will permit an extension of study in areas of interest.

The author wishes to express appreciation to Myrtle B. Archer and to many professional associates for reading various chapters and offering valuable suggestions. For permission to use some of the quotations, the writer is indebted to

Mr. Howard Dawson, Department of Rural Education, National Education Association; Miss Effie Bathurst and Mr. Paul E. Blackwood of the Office of Education, United States Department of Health, Education, and Welfare; Mr. Henry Harup, Division of Surveys and Field Studies of George Peabody College for Teachers; Mr. Nelson B. Henry, Secretary of the National Society for the Study of Education; Mr. John J. DeBoer, editor of *Elementary English;* and Mr. Arthur Adkins, Department of Public Instruction, the State of Wisconsin.

CLIFFORD P. ARCHER

Minneapolis
  January, 1958

CONTENTS

Elementary Education
in
Rural Areas

1

IMPORTANCE AND MEANING
OF RURAL EDUCATION

The farm area and towns and villages with small populations comprise the rural portion of the United States. Despite the enormous populations of the cities, a major segment of America's population is to be found in this vast rural area. Furnishing education for the people of these communities is no easy task. The diffusion of the population and the distinctive problems facing these communities make it necessary to adapt both school plant and pedagogical techniques to the sociological and economic needs of the area. And with a successful adaptation goes the reward of educating a large percentage of America's children, thereby allowing them better to contribute to the welfare of the nation.

Importance of agriculture

Agriculture has often been considered the most fundamental of occupations. The food that man eats and the raw materials from which he houses and clothes himself are products of the soil. More than half of the people of the world work that soil and millions more process or distribute its products. Prosperity for the farmer, therefore, influences not merely farm life but also the occupations and lives of almost everyone else in the nation.

Challenge to the teacher

The rural community offers a challenge to the teacher. This challenge stems from the various qualities which enhance rural life—the neighborliness, fairness, and wholesome personal living which have become by reputation the hallmark of the rural area. It can be shown that many of our most outstanding citizens have come from rural areas. *Rural Education News* has published a summary of responses to a questionnaire distributed to a number of currently prominent citizens. Out of 63 college presidents who answered the questionnaires, 53 are rural born, as were 41 senators out of 58, and 35 of our present governors. It has been estimated that 80 per cent of the ministry, 75–80 per cent of successful business and professional men of our cities, and 85 per cent of those listed in *Who's Who in America* have come from rural communities. All but three of the presidents of the United States were rural born.[1]

The type of school should be no less a challenge to the teacher who is interested in the adaptation of a program to meet the needs of the pupil who has far more opportunity than the city child for direct contacts with nature. The schools themselves are small and have an intimate atmosphere. They range in size from the very small establishments with one, two, or three teachers to the larger graded schools with a staff of from fifteen to forty teachers and administrators. The teacher in establishments of this size has almost limitless possibilities for better acquaintance with the pupil and better understanding of him by participation in and study of his environment.

A study of the home is of prime importance to the understanding of the child at school. The rural teacher usually develops a personal relationship with the families of her

[1] From *Rural Education News,* National Education Association, for September, 1953.

pupils either through participation in community affairs or direct acquaintance. She, therefore, studies the home environment at much closer range than can the urban teacher whose only contact with families is ordinarily a biannual interview with one parent. She can learn to see the rural child as a member of a closer-knit family unit than that of the urban child. And she can learn the place of the rural child in community activities. The child at the family homestead may experience the satisfaction of caring for animals, cultivating himself a small plot of land, or sharing in the work of the family truck garden or the farm, possibly even making some money from the sale of his animals or produce. This same child will participate with neighbors and friends, his own and those of the family, in making a better community for all.

Rural schools

Rural education is the education provided for people who live on farms and in villages and small towns. Formerly, the term *rural school* was applied to schools with one, two, or three teachers, "ungraded schools," as they were called. Many of these schools have become part of larger, reorganized administrative and attendance units, but they still serve the same people.

Today, rural schools include both graded and ungraded schools. They may be graded schools with kindergartens, high schools, junior high schools, junior colleges, or even community colleges. They may have one or two teachers or thirty or more teachers. They may have one teacher for several grades or a teacher for each grade and may have several teachers in special fields of work.

In these rural schools are the children of families in which the father's occupation may be farming, forestry work, mining, business, transportation, or factory work. Some rural fathers are only part-time farmers. Some are transient workers. Some may work part time in factories which are located in their rural area. Thus the children come from homes with widely different interests and ways of living.

Previous to 1950, the United States Census Bureau defined the term *rural* in such a way as to include not only people who live in the open country but also those who live in towns or villages of less than 2,500 population. In 1950, however, the definition was changed to exclude communities located in the suburbs of cities even though the population was less than 2,500. In these suburban areas, the occupations, mores, and sense of values were thought to be more urban than rural in character. All towns with a population of 2,500 or more are called urban; yet some towns of even 10,000 or more are essentially rural community centers. They are primarily farmer trading posts. Children of these towns go to school with the children of the farms in the surrounding country. The families of the town and of the farms go to the same church, attend the same social events, and shop in the same stores. The school in such a community is a *rural school* in the strict sense of the term, but it must adjust to children from both urban and rural families.

Rural population

The population served by rural schools constitutes 36 per cent of the people of the United States. Particularly in the farming areas, however, this proportion is decreasing. Table 1 shows the decrease in the total rural population from 57.2 million in 1940 to 54.2 million in 1950.

There has been a change in the rural school-age population as well as in the total rural population. Table 2 shows that nearly 17 million children of ages 5 to 19 were available for education in 1940 as compared with just over 15 million in 1950.

Rural school enrollment

Not all available youth of school age in rural areas were in school, however, as shown by Table 3.

TABLE 1

RURAL POPULATION OF THE UNITED STATES, 1940 AND 1950[2]

	1940		1950*		1950†	
	Number (millions)	Per cent of Population	Number (Millions)	Per cent of Population	Number (millions)	Per cent of Population
Rural nonfarm	27.0	20.5	38.6	25.7	31.1	20.7
Rural farm	30.2	22.9	23.0	15.3	23.0	15.3
Total	57.2	43.5	61.7	41.0	54.2	36.0
Total U.S.	131.6	100.0	150.6	100.0	150.6	100.0

* Based on old definition of *rural*.
† Based on new definition of *rural*.

TABLE 2

NUMBER OF CHILDREN, 5 TO 19 YEARS OF AGE, IN RURAL POPULATION OF THE UNITED STATES, 1940 AND 1950

Age	1940			1950		
	Rural Farm	Rural Nonfarm	Total Rural	Rural Farm	Rural Nonfarm	Total Rural
5–9	3,154,575	2,216,869	5,371,444	2,561,239	3,103,972	5,665,211
10–14	3,387,598	2,276,308	5,663,906	2,474,958	2,571,869	5,646,827
15–19	3,356,475	2,483,112	5,839,587	2,112,974	2,327,944	4,440,891
Total, 5–19	9,898,648	6,976,289	16,874,937	7,149,171	8,003,785	15,152,929

[2] Figures for Tables 1 and 2 are taken from 1950 United States Census of Population, U.S. Dept. of Commerce, Bureau of the Census, "Characteristics of Population," Vol. II, Part I, U.S. Summary.

TABLE 3

TOTAL UNITED STATES AND RURAL SCHOOL ENROLLMENTS
BY AGE GROUPS, 1950[3]

Age in Years	Total U.S.	Rural Farm	Rural Nonfarm	Total Rural
5–6	2,160,160	382,425	486,065	868,490
7–13	16,077,270	3,330,320	3,744,725	7,075,045
14–15	3,963,575	864,970	887,380	1,752,350
16–17	3,104,265	615,860	649,040	1,264,900
18–19	1,400,700	181,850	238,415	420,265
Total	26,705,970	5,375,425	6,005,625	11,381,050

Actual percentages of the population of 5 to 19 years of age who were in school in 1950 are given in Table 4. Both tables include kindergarten and are based on a 20 per cent sample. It must be remembered, however, that these are not enrollments reported by the schools but are data from the 1950 United States Census. Also, it should be kept in mind that kindergarten enrollment is not so common in rural areas as in urban.

TABLE 4

PERCENTAGES OF AGE GROUPS OF POPULATION ENROLLED IN SCHOOL
IN THE UNITED STATES IN 1950

Age in Years	Total U. S.	Urban	Rural Farm	Rural Nonfarm
5–6	39.3	41.1	37.1	36.9
7–13	95.7	96.1	94.7	95.5
14–15	92.9	94.8	88.1	92.1
16–17	74.4	78.8	67.2	70.2
18–19	32.2	36.5	25.1	25.0

A study of Table 4 shows that the percentages of the various age groups are somewhat lower for the rural farm and nonfarm children than for the urban children, although the differences are less at the elementary school ages of 7 through 13.

[3] Tables 3 and 4 taken from the 1950 United States Census of Population, United States Survey—General Characteristics (Table 42).

Howard Dawson[4] has furnished slightly different figures, indicating that rural schools enroll 11,890,000 pupils (about 39.5 per cent of the national total) and that of these pupils 5,150,000 (17.1 per cent of the national total) are farm children and 6,948,000 (22.4 per cent) live in villages.

Exact figures on school enrollment of rural and urban children are difficult to secure, partly because of the lack of uniformity in school district organization. Sometimes figures for urban districts are given with county figures because all schools of the county are under one administration. Likewise, farm children may attend school in urban districts. The United States Office of Education's Biennial Survey of Education for 1950–52 reported that city school systems enrolled 46.2 per cent of the 20,668,000 pupils enrolled in 1951–52 from kindergarten through eighth grade in all public schools of the nation. Thus the remaining segment of the public school population—mainly rural but including urban centers whose schools are part of a larger unit of administration, such as a county—accounted for an elementary school enrollment of 53.8 per cent.

It appears that while the total urban population is larger than the rural, the *public* school enrollment in kindergarten through eighth grades in the urban areas is appreciably smaller than the comparable enrollment in rural school areas. This reflects the fact that there is a smaller proportion of children in urban areas and a larger proportion of these are in private or parochial schools.[5]

So for 1951–52 about half of the elementary school children in *public* schools were in rural areas, and of this number nearly half of the children lived on farms.

The United States Office of Education figures for 1954–55 show 30,673,300 public school pupils and 35,160,000 pupils in all public, private, and government schools together. It

[4] Howard Dawson, "Rural Education—A Backward and Forward Look," in *Rural Education—A Forward Look,* 1955 Yearbook of the Department of Rural Education of the National Education Association, p. 218.

[5] Lester B. Herlihy, *Statistics of City School Systems: Staff, Pupils, and Finances,* Biennial Survey of Education 1950–52 (Washington, D.C.: Department of Health, Education, and Welfare, Office of Education, 1955), chap. iii.

may be estimated that 12,200,000 of the public school pupils were in rural areas. The Office of Education estimates for 1955–56 show 32,895,000 pupils in public schools only, and it may be assumed that 13,158,000 would be in communities of less than 2,500 population. Projected figures for 1960 and 1965 place the rural school enrollment of children of ages 6 to 17 at 15,125,000 and 16,156,000, respectively.[6]

In rural farm areas the proportion of children who attend school has always been below that of urban areas, but 1950 census figures show that between 1951 and 1954 school enrollment of youth 10 through 15 years of age rose sharply in rural areas, bringing the proportion of available youth in school closer to urban figures. During this period, enrollment of children of 10 through 15 years of age in rural farm areas rose from 94 to 97 per cent, which closely approaches the urban figure of 99 per cent.

Educators who serve in rural areas are working with an increasing enrollment of rural children, with the increase chiefly in towns and villages; but the increase in rural area enrollment has not equaled that of urban sections.

Educators in rural areas

According to Dawson[7] schools in rural areas are staffed by 467,000 teachers, 47 per cent of the nation's total. These areas also have 10,250 local superintendents and supervisory principals, 977 county superintendents, and 2,362 intermediate unit superintendents. Dawson points out that 70 per cent of the 17,000 school administrators of the United States are administrators of schools in rural areas.

Studies of the qualifications of teachers in rural areas show that, on the average, the amount of schooling is less than that required for urban teachers. In a study made by the Research Division of the National Education Association,

---

[6] Calvin Beale, "Population Trends and Distribution in Rural Areas" in *Rural Education—A Forward Look*, 1955 Yearbook of the Department of Rural Education of the National Education Association, p. 300.

[7] Howard Dawson, *op. cit.*, p. 218.

it was found that about 64 per cent of elementary school teachers in rural areas do not have a college degree. The typical rural teacher works in a school system employing only ten teachers besides herself and teaches in a school with an enrollment of 67. The typical elementary school teacher has had 14 years' experience, as contrasted with about 10 years' experience for the rural secondary school teacher.[8]

Rural educational problems

Rural teachers and administrators face educational problems different from those in urban sections of the country. Because of the sparsely settled character of the rural population, there are problems of organizing and financing an adequate educational program. Because of the distribution of the pupils over a wide geographic area, pupils are either assembled for instruction in schools with a low enrollment per teacher, making the cost of instruction per pupil high, or the pupils are transported to centers for instruction, thus adding the cost of transportation to the cost of education.

Where pupils attend small one- or two-teacher schools, there is likely to be less equipment, fewer instructional supplies, fewer special services for handicapped and gifted pupils, and less supervisory help for the teacher. Some small schools have been made a part of larger school administrative units, and their instructional facilities have been increased; some rural sections have organized strong intermediate units of administration and supervision by establishing district or county offices to provide supplementary services which are not otherwise available to small schools; but these arrangements are still too few.

The teachers in rural schools often have had little college preparation; many of these teachers have returned to teaching after a period of absence from the classroom. There is, therefore, a greater need for in-service education of teachers in rural areas than in urban districts, where the preservice

[8] National Education Association, "Rural Teachers in 1951–52," *Research Bulletin No. 1*, XXXI, February, 1953.

preparation period is longer and often immediately precedes the teaching.

Problems of organization of the curriculum offerings differ in rural and urban schools. Not more than half of the children who are born on farms will remain on the farms; the others will find their way to towns and cities. There is therefore, a need for guidance by the school and for development of an understanding of urban life. In addition, the economic problems of rural life reveal an interrelationship between the problems of making a living on the farm and the prices of goods produced in the cities. To understand the problems of farm and village living it is necessary to study the relationships of farm life to urban life.

Economic and social problems of living in rural areas demand the development of cooperation among people. Learning how to attack a problem cooperatively and developing communication skills are very important aspects of education in rural areas.

Just as rural and urban adults differ in habits and customs, so do the children differ in ways of thinking and acting. The rural educator needs to study the children and the community—to understand the traditions, customs, social values, and habit patterns of the family and community life and realize how they differ from those of other areas, even other rural areas. The local needs of the people must be kept in mind, as well as the major goals of education in a democratic society like ours.

Because teachers have not always understood and appreciated rural life, or known how to study the community in which they work, and because they have not realized the impact of community mores on child behavior, education in rural areas has not always served rural people as effectively as it should.

Rural education begins where the people are—with their deep-seated traditions, attitudes, sentiments, desires and ways of doing things. Administrators do not impose a program upon the people but instead, foster the gradual realization of the best potentialities of each rural community and its people. Their aim is to improve the quality of living in the local community.[9]

Summary

Education in rural areas offers a real challenge to the teacher because of the important part which rural communities play in our national life and economy. Life in rural areas is friendly. Children have an opportunity to learn by observation of nature, by the close ties of family life, and by participation in community affairs.

Rural education serves the people who live on farms and in villages and small towns. The schools may be large or small, and they may provide development from the kindergarten through grade 12 and sometimes through grade 14. The fathers of the children may be engaged in agriculture, forestry, mining, business, and other fields common to small towns and country regions. While *rural* communities were once defined as those having a population of less than 2,500 people, many larger communities are now included in this category because they depend upon agriculture for economic and social welfare and because there are many farm children attending the schools in these communities.

The areas served by the rural schools comprise at least 36 per cent of the total population and over 40 per cent of the children of school age. Pupil enrollment in the schools is increasing, chiefly in nonfarm sections.

Education in rural areas is carried on by 47 per cent of the nation's teachers under the supervision of about 70 per cent of the nation's school administrators.

The teachers in rural schools are not so well trained as the teachers in urban schools. This creates the need for in-service education of the teachers if the instruction is to be effective and adequate.

Because of the nature of rural life and the sparsely settled character of much of the population, rural educators face

[9] National Society for the Study of Education, *Education in Rural Communities*, Fifty-first Yearbook, Part II (Chicago: University of Chicago Press, 1952), p. 4.

distinctive problems of school finance, school organization, adequate educational facilities, teacher education, and curriculum adjustments to meet the needs of rural living.

Knowing how to study the community and the children must be a part of the rural teacher's preparation. The aim of the school to improve the lives of the people can best be accomplished by teachers who know and like rural life and are willing to study its needs and problems.

Selected references

AMERICAN ASSOCIATION OF SCHOOL ADMINISTRATORS. *Schools in Small Communities*. Washington, D.C.: The Association, 1939. Chap. ii.

Outlines the advantages inherent in a small school system which offers a challenge to the educator.

BUTTERWORTH, JULIAN E., and DAWSON, HOWARD A. *The Modern Rural School*. New York: McGraw-Hill Book Co., Inc., 1952. Part I.

Gives the extent of rural education today and data in school population, enrollments, and attendance.

LINDSTROM, DAVID EDGAR. *American Rural Life*. New York: The Ronald Press Co., 1948. Chap. iv.

Gives the distribution of the rural population and the changing character of the population.

NATIONAL EDUCATION ASSOCIATION. "Rural Teachers in 1951–52," *Research Bulletin No. 1*, XXXI (February, 1953). Washington, D.C.: The Association.

This is a report of responses to questionnaires made by teachers in rural areas regarding such factors as age, marital status, dependents, professional status—including education and experience—living conditions, nature of teaching position and working conditions, teaching facilities, and teacher income.

————, DEPARTMENT OF RURAL EDUCATION. *Rural Education—A Forward Look*, 1954 Yearbook. Washington, D.C.: The Department, 1955. Part I, chaps. i–iv, vi, viii–xvii; Part II, pp. 209–50, 280–94; Part III, pp. 299–305.

Part I gives an overview of issues and problems of rural education, together with possible solutions reported at the National Conference on Rural Education in 1954, and reviews ten years of progress and challenge to rural educators. The section in Part II outlines a series of papers dealing with the importance of rural education and the problem in that field. The Part III reference shows population trends and distribution of population in rural areas.

NATIONAL SOCIETY FOR THE STUDY OF EDUCATION. *Education in Rural Communities*. Fifty-first Yearbook. Chicago: University of Chicago Press, 1952. Part II, "Rural Education Today."

Discusses the organization of schools in rural areas, number and sizes of schools, status and preparation of teachers, and educational facilities and services.

TAYLOR, CARL C., *et al. Rural Life in the United States*. New York: Alfred A. Knopf, Inc., 1949. Part III.

Describes the rural population, characteristics, and occupational patterns.

2

SOCIAL AND ECONOMIC
PROBLEMS OF RURAL AREAS

Any good educational program is closely related to the problems and activities of community life. The curriculum of the school is built around the problems of the people living in the community—problems which bring stresses and strains for children growing up in the community. Hence, the teacher who is responsible for the curriculum in the rural area needs to understand the social and economic problems of the farm and the village where the economic welfare of the people depends upon the prosperity of the surrounding trade area.

The economic problems of the American farmer are very complex and vary with the type of farming and the region of the country. A study of the changes taking place shows certain trends which have helped create difficulties for the farmer and have affected the social and economic fabric of farm and village life.

Economic trends and problems of the farmer

The Industrial Revolution which brought marked changes in urban life invaded the farming sections also and produced dislocations and maladjustments in agriculture as a means of living. Some of the trends in agriculture and some of the problems which have arisen as a result of these changes are outlined below.

1. Technological advancement in agriculture changed the character of farm operations from the use of human and animal labor to machine operation. Farm tractors and trucks gradually replaced horses and mules. Milking machines, electrically powered cream separators, and mechanical grain operators became standard equipment on the farm. The mechanical corn and cotton pickers and wheat harvesting machinery powered by gasoline engines reduced the number of workers and the hours of labor. Since 1920 the number of hours of labor required to produce 100 bushels of corn has been reduced, by 26 per cent; to produce a bale of cotton, by 32 per cent; and to produce 100 bushels of wheat, by 46 per cent.

2. Better management and better methods have increased farm production.

Research in genetics and chemistry has produced new varieties of seed and livestock and helped control animal diseases. For example, the development of hybrid seed corn has increased the yield of corn per acre. Insecticides now control pests, and vaccines help reduce diseases of farm animals.

Crop rotation and the shift to more productive crops and livestock have increased the productivity of the farm acre.

3. Because production on the farm has increased faster than consumption, surpluses have accumulated.

Better farm management, better farming methods, and the increased use of farm machinery have increased farm production to a point where the supply exceeds the demand. The resulting surplus of farm products cannot be sold on the domestic market without depressing farm prices nor can they be sold on the foreign market without creating international difficulties. Other nations too produce wheat, cotton, and dairy products, and they want to sell on world markets. World markets can be expanded but little because many of the people who need these products do not have the money to purchase them.

Efforts of the government to help maintain the balance between production and consumption have resulted in an accumulation of huge stocks of surpluses.

4. Cost of farming has increased more than income.

Although production has increased, the cost of operating the farm has increased even more. Farm machinery is expensive, and it requires fuel to run it. There are still young farmers who begin operating with an investment of $5,000 besides the cost of the land, but many family-size farms represent a capital investment of $40,000 to $50,000 over and above the cost of the land.

The farmer must buy at retail prices and sell at wholesale prices. This often leaves him at the mercy of the wholesalers.

Farms have been increased in size, due to the use of machinery, but the increased production that has resulted has not always benefited the farmer. Surpluses result in a drop in price. Government subsidies have attempted to maintain farm income at a parity with costs, but this has helped build up the stock of surpluses.

Income can be increased to some extent by farming more land. If prices remained stable, this would help balance expenses and income, but prices are affected by many things.

Farm incomes are also affected by variations in weather and by soil erosion. Efforts to grow crops which yield the largest incomes have often resulted in poor land. Contour farming and other measures used in water-erosion areas and wind-swept regions are being taught by the Agriculture Extension Service and by schools located in some regions, and these measures will in time help the farmer.

Farm life and income are governed in some regions by the water supply. In many regions of the Southwest, the development and preservation of water resources constitutes one of the major farm problems with which rural education must be concerned. Dry farming and irrigation are problems for the school to work out in connection with the people it serves.

One serious effect on farm income has been the fluctuations in both domestic and foreign demands. For example, the per capita decrease in the consumption of potatoes in the United States between 1910 and 1953 was 50 per cent, and the decrease in the consumption of cereals in that same period was 25 per cent. Similarly, the development of synthetic fibers reduced the demand for cotton. American cotton sales abroad declined also as a result of large-scale production of cotton in other parts of the world.

5. Farms have increased in size and, consequently, decreased in number.

In 1940 the average farm size was 174 acres; by 1952 it was 210 acres; and in 1955 it was 242 acres. The number of farms decreased from 6,812,000 in 1935 to 4,782,000 in 1954.

Higher operation costs have made it necessary to farm more land, and the use of machinery has made it possible for one family to handle a larger farm. Many farmers have increased their holdings by buying up the land of neighboring farmers who could not meet the increased cost of farming. The family-size farm which spreads over dispersed homesteads still constitutes by far the most common operation: 78 per cent of rural farm people are engaged full-time in agriculture. Many of these family farms are in the South, but they are not restricted to that region. *The Minneapolis Star* reported in 1955 that 325 family-size farms in southern Minnesota showed a wide gap between the high-income group with large farms and the low-income group with small farms. In 1940 the difference in income between these groups was $3,642; in 1945, it was $6,907; in 1950, $10,418; in 1954, $11,088. A family farm needs to be large enough to support the family economically, but not so large that it requires much labor to operate it.

How large the farm must be to support the family depends upon the type of farming. Chicken and turkey ranches and vegetable farming require only small farms, but the cattle ranches of the West must be large. A farm of 160 acres is no longer large enough for the corn and wheat farmer. Yet the ability of the farmer to shift from a type of farming which requires many acres to an operation requiring fewer acres depends upon the proximity of the farm to the market.

6. Part-time farming is increasing.

The solution of the income problem for many farmers has been to take part-time work at some other occupation. Of the 23,000,000 Americans living on farms, about 30 per cent work part of the time in processing plants, factories, or other establishments in neighboring communities. While there has been a decrease in the number of family-size farms, there has been an increase in the number of small farms run by part-time farmers. About 6 per cent of the 23,000,000 Americans live on farms of over 500 acres; only about 1,250,000 of the approximately 5,000,000 farms are 10 acres or less.

Government subsidies for the inefficient farmer may be a solution of the small-farm problem, but many farmers believe that this is at best only a temporary solution of the matter.

7. The economic prosperity of the farm is dependent upon the development of a more adequate marketing system.

Means must be found to move farm products from the producer to the consumer with a minimum of effort and cost if the farmer is to receive a fair share of the consumer dollar. Even in periods of falling prices, the cost of processing and distributing farm products has continued to increase, thus reducing the farmer's income. The problem of organizing the processing and distribution of farm products should command the attention of both the people and the schools in rural areas.

Social problems of rural life

The revolution in agriculture with the introduction of machinery affected the social structure of rural life. One of the most noticeable changes has been the shift in population from the farms to the cities. Table 1, page 7, shows that the rural population decreased by nearly 7,000,000 between 1940 and 1950, until it constituted only 15.6 per cent of the total population for the nation, or about 23,000,000. During the same period the rural nonfarm population increased about 20 per cent to approximately 32,000,000, and the urban population increased about 20 per cent to approximately 99,000,000.

This migration from the farm to the city accompanied the mechanization of farm life. The number leaving the farm has increased greatly during periods of good employment opportunities in industry. Even with the consistently high birth rate of farm families, relatively half the farm children will leave to work in towns and cities, keeping the farm population from increasing. This emphasizes the need for the schools to provide guidance for these young people and to increase the understanding of urban life.

The farm population shifts also from one region to another. The greatest increases in population have been in the Southwest, the West Coast States, the Middle Atlantic States, and the Northeast. The development of more industry in the South may halt the shift of population to some extent; with numbers leaving, some states have shown no decrease in population because of the numbers coming into the state. Such shifts in population bring conflicts of culture and create further social and educational problems.

The shifts of farm people to urban centers have affected life in the villages and towns which were the former centers of the business and social life of the rural area. Good roads and automobiles have enabled the farm people to travel greater distances to where better trading services are available, and to the theaters and moving picture houses. Many small communities of 200 to 300 people have lost much of their function as trade centers. There has been a disintegration of many older community centers and a widening of community borders. This change has affected local institutions. The rural school has lost many pupils; the rural church has suffered a decline in attendance. Smaller enrollment in the school has meant a higher cost of education per pupil. The demand for a more adequate education to meet the changed conditions has led to the reorganization of many school districts into larger administrative units. Rural schools everywhere are striving to meet the challenge of the changing times and to make a better contribution to the solution of the economic and social problems of the community and the home.

Because of the use of farm machinery, requiring fewer hours of labor than formerly, and because of better transportation between the farm and the town, living standards of the town and the farm have tended to become more alike. In 1920 few farms had telephones, running hot water, bathrooms, kitchen sinks, or electrical appliances. Noticeably since that time over 90 per cent of the farm homes have acquired electricity; many have electrical stoves, washing machines, and other electrical appliances. Radios are common on the farm, and television sets are rapidly increasing in number. While bathrooms and running water are still not as common in the farm homes as in the town homes, the number of farm houses so equipped is increasing.

Health and cultural facilities, such as hospitals, clinics, libraries, and schools, are limited in areas of low farm income. The changing rural society is endangering the continuance of the moral, social, cultural, and religious qualities of the traditional rural mode of life. The preservation of rural social values in our fluctuating economic structure offers a real challenge to the churches and schools of the rural areas.

Rural schools in particular must recognize the complexity of the economic and social problems which confront rural people and try to serve their needs. This means that the schools will recognize the fact that the changing character of rural life creates a need for the continuation of the learning process throughout the lives of the people. Social and economic problems can be solved only under the leadership of an enlightened people. The school should cooperate with the community in helping develop such leadership and in finding satisfactory solutions to the problems.

Summary

Educators in rural areas need to be familiar with the economic and social problems of the people of the community.

The curriculum offerings should be closely related to the life of the region.

Complex problems now face the American farmer as a result of many things: use of machinery to replace animal and hand labor; increase in production; decrease in income; increase in size of farms; inadequate marketing systems.

The economic problems of the farmer are likely to continue because of changes in demand for products, fluctuation of prices, effect of soil erosion, water supply, and increased costs.

The solution for the economic problems of the farmer may be found in an increase in the size of his farm to a point where the income will permit a profit above costs, in a change of the type of farming where the farm is near a good market, or in a shift to a part-time farming operation.

Changes in the social life of farm people are due largely to shifts in population and the increased facilities of transportation. Increased use of electricity has brought many conveniences into farm homes. The schools must be geared to meet these changes. Rural life is now in touch with urban life at many points, but its character and sturdy independence should be retained.

Selected references

BUTTERFIELD, JULIAN E., and DAWSON, HOWARD A. *The Modern Rural School*. New York: McGraw-Hill Book Co., Inc., 1952. Chaps. ii, iii, and iv.

Major trends in rural life shown as related to education. Treatment of social and economic problems as backgrounds for education.

KOLB, J. H., and BRUNER, EDMUND DE S. *A Study of Rural Society*. Boston: Houghton Mifflin Co., 1946. Part I, chaps. ii and iii, and part II.

Describes the rural population and the changing patterns of life and economic problems and their relationships to national and world economy.

KREITLOW, BURTON W. *Rural Education: Community Backgrounds*. New York: Harper & Bros., 1954. Chaps. iii and xvii.

Discusses economic problems of rural areas and the trends in rural life.

LINDSTROM, DAVID EDGAR. *American Rural Life*. New York: The Ronald Press Co., 1948. Chaps. v and vi.

Treats of social and economic changes in rural life and the ways by which conditions can be improved, with some discussion of federal attempts to improve economic conditions.

NATIONAL EDUCATION ASSOCIATION, DEPARTMENT OF RURAL EDUCATION. *Rural Education—A Forward Look*, 1954 Yearbook. Washington, D.C.: The Department, 1955. Part I, chaps. v and vii, part III, pp. 316–26.

Discusses the social and economic changes in rural life and the disadvantages of certain groups in rural areas, with the economic changes in rural areas.

NATIONAL SOCIETY FOR THE STUDY OF EDUCATION. "Education in a Changing Rural Life," *Education in Rural Communities*, Fifty-first Yearbook. Chicago: University of Chicago Press, 1952. Part II, chap. ii.

Gives an overview of trends in the economic life of rural areas.

NELSON, LOWRY. *Rural Sociology*. New York: American Book Co., 1952. Chaps. iii, iv, vii, and xiv.

Shows regional patterns of agricultural life and describes types of farming and problems of land settlement, the relation of social and economic problems to population migration, and the different farming systems.

TAYLOR, CARL C., *et al. Rural Life in the United States*. New York: Alfred A. Knopf, Inc., 1949. Chaps. xvii, xviii, and xxx.

Description of significant trends and changes in the social and economic life of rural areas, and the levels, standards of living, and differences in the social life of rural and urban areas.

3

RURAL COMMUNITY
AND THE SCHOOL

The modern school cannot operate except as a part of the community which it serves. The school owes its existence to the people of the community and derives its functions from their needs. As part of the community, it must be concerned with ways by which community consciousness can be strengthened. The teachers in the school must have some concept of what a good community is and understand the factors which make for community strength; they need to know the role of the school in the community and must understand how to study the community and its people, its institutions and its activities.

The teacher who hopes to provide guidance in learning for rural boys and girls must understand their problems of adjustment to an ever-widening circle of contacts with people, institutions, and organizations as they grow up, and will need to know community life. If school experiences are to have meaning for children, the activities of the school must be closely associated with living. If improved behavior is the goal, learning must deal with problems of living at the child's level of development. Furthermore, a major function of the school should be to help the child grow in understanding of the community institutions, how they may serve him, and how they may be improved. A truly functional school can do much to make education meaningful for children and at the same time improve community life.

Rural community concept

Many efforts have been made to define the rural community and to determine its boundaries. In most rural areas of other nations, the rural community is easy to determine because the farmers live in villages and go out daily to work the land. In the United States, the first farmers settled on dispersed farmsteads which originally meant much isolation of the farm family. The neighborhood, however, often served the social, educational, and religious needs of the farm groups. Recent technological changes in farm life have brought a reorganization of centers of activity for farm groups and a disintegration of many rural community centers.

The community is not just a collection of people living close together, nor is it merely a series of neighborhoods. Political dividing lines, such as those marking a township or a county, are not the boundaries of a community. Neither is a community a group of people who have personal acquaintance: such a group constitutes a neighborhood.

Some rural sociologists have defined the rural community by describing its trade area, yet studies show that a farmer may go to the nearest village for groceries and gasoline but motor to a larger town for clothing and hospital services. Some definitions of *rural community* emphasize the village or town as the center, the social relations of the people of farm and town, and their common interests. In some studies of rural communities in Michigan, the area from which the village high school drew its students seemed to correspond closely with the rural community territory.

We would define a rural community in the following way.

A rural community is an aggregate of farm and village people inhabiting an area limited by ease of transportation, which makes frequent contacts possible, and unified by such bonds as common beliefs, a common language, similarity of purposes, traditions, manners, and customs, common interests, face-to-face relationships, effective leadership, and experience in achieving goals. Such a community has as a center a village or a town in which most of the activities take place.

By this definition, communities exist only in certain degrees, and they vary from those where bonds are so few and so weak that community consciousness is scarcely noticeable to those where community strength is great and group action to achieve goals is both democratic in method and effective in result.

If there is to be solution of common problems, there must be frequency of contacts. Unless there is a common language, there can be no united action. Without effective leadership, common goals cannot be achieved. Experiences in achievement are required if group strength is to be built.

The community which is likely to develop the strongest ties between individuals and families has as a center a town or a village which is large enough to render most of the services needed by the surrounding farming territory and to serve as a center for the religious, educational, and social life of the people. Rural sociologists stress the importance of the center's being small enough to provide frequent contacts among the people.

On the highway entering Sebeka, Minnesota, there is a sign which reads, "Large enough to serve you, small enough to know you." Centers too small to offer services to the surrounding area are not likely to remain community centers for long. Villages with fewer than 500 population usually have two or three grocery or general stores, a garage and gas station, one or two churches, a small school, and a village hall for meetings of a few farmers' organizations. Villages of 500 to 1,200 often have, in addition, hardware stores and drug-

stores, banks, hotels, high schools, lodges, and medical offices. Towns or large villages of 1,200 to 2,500 usually have
clothing stores, furniture stores, a motion picture theater,
and an undertaking establishment. The smaller the village,
the greater likelihood of eventual loss of population, service
facilities, and trade advantages.

A good community center has desirable relationships with
the people of the surrounding country. In the past, such
relationships have not always been good. The high school
of the village admitted the farm children as "nonresidents"
and the farmers did not seem to belong. In many rural areas
this relationship is improving, partly because of greater prosperity on the farm and partly because of efforts of the village
people. Newcomers to town or country are now welcomed to
the community and made to feel that they belong.

A good community is characterized by democratic organizations sufficient in number to meet the needs of the people.
Major social, educational, and economic needs of the people
are being met by organized effort, and the organizations of
the community are open both to people of the village and to
people living on farms. Religious as well as educational institutions are operating to serve the needs of all the people.
Facilities are provided for recreation, medical service, hospitalization, and cultural development. An integrating or
coordinating council will probably be developed to assist
organizations in sponsoring community events and to study
the needs of the community.

The good community develops effective democratic leadership. Its center will not be a one-man town, no matter how
benevolent the one man may be. The leadership of several
good leaders will help the people to organize their efforts to
achieve desired goals for the community as a whole.

The people of a community need to feel that they are part
of a group with common interests. This community consciousness is important to the growth of local institutions.
Common traditions, customs, and activities do much to build
a pride in the "home town."

A good example of the way in which the people of a community can work together to solve a community problem is the action of the people of Perryville, a village of 1,200 located in a farming district fifteen miles from a town of 4,000 people. Perryville is a trade center for farm people living within a radius of ten miles of the village. It has four churches and a good business district. The village school has grades one through twelve, and a few farm boys and girls join the village children in the secondary school grades. Six years ago the people of the town and of 16 one-teacher school districts in the section voted to form a single school district. With the help of some laymen the superintendent of schools and the teaching faculty made a study of the institutions, organizations, and interests of the people in the newly formed district. They discovered that while the farm people did most of their trading in the village and often attended church in Perryville, there was almost no social contact between the people of the village and the people living out in the country. Also, the farmers' organizations which had used some of the one-teacher school buildings for their meetings were concerned about the closing of the one-teacher schools. Where would the local Farmers' Union and Grange be able to meet?

A community council was organized to include representatives of the school, churches, commercial club, farmers' organizations, and other groups. It secured the use of the local theater for the farmers' organizations until the new high school building was completed. Committees were formed to plan and carry out community-wide participation in a centennial celebration of the founding of the town and other social and educational events. With the growth of the new high school, departments of agriculture and home economics were established, and 4-H Clubs and units of Future Farmers of America were formed, with community-wide participation by farm youth. Farmers and townspeople came to parent-teacher meetings at the school, and committees of townspeople and farm dwellers were formed, at the request of the faculty, to help in determining the kind of school program to be offered. The service club of the town invited farmers to become members.

Perryville's doctor had served the community for a long time. He had reached the age when he wished to retire, but efforts to secure a new doctor had been fruitless. Young doctors who came to look over the community refused to move to Perryville because it had no hospital and no clinic. The community council and the service club were determined to remedy this defect. When a businessman offered to donate the land for a hospital, a campaign was organized to raise funds for a building and equipment. A "Sell-Your-Service Day" was organized, and farmers and townspeople agreed to give their wages for a day's work to the hospital fund. The school superintendent worked at a gasoline service station; the banker mowed lawns; a grocer washed windows; a farmer delivered groceries—everyone who could work did so. The necessary funds were raised and a hospital was built. Soon two doctors came to Perryville, and a dentist followed.

In six years Perryville built community strength: traditions were developed through a series of annual events; community use of the school building provided frequent contact between the farm and village people. A program of adult education for all ages gradually emerged, and the people grew in their awareness of ability to do things together.

The farm people who have shared in the work take pride in the town they have helped to build. Much remains to be done, but Perryville has demonstrated how community strength can be developed under leaders with vision and with a willingness on the part of the people to cooperate.

Rural community school

The community school should be intimately related to the life of the community, serving as a center of education both for the children and for the adults. The school building can be used for many educational and social activities of the pupils, their parents, and the young people who are no longer in school. The good community school studies the needs of the people. Evening classes may help parents to keep up to date on matters concerned with their occupations; they may provide instruction in child care or home improvement; they may furnish cultural development through a study of art, a reading club, or work in some handicraft; they may provide lectures to give an understanding of national and world affairs. The size of the school and the availability of instructors will determine the program, of course, but the school should foster the idea of continuing one's education in adult life. This calls for the cooperation of such agencies as farmers' organizations, women's clubs, and youth clubs with the school.

The school is not the only educational institution for the people of a rural community. Close collaboration between the school faculty and the county agent, the home demonstration agent, the county nurse, a social welfare worker, and the staff of the intermediate school unit (which may correspond with the office of county superintendent of schools) will provide many extracurricular features.

Some have pictured the community school as the center of all education with ties to the local community and to society at large. Others have pictured the school as located on an island with bridges to all parts of the community. Certainly the school should assume the major role in the development of the understandings, skills, attitudes, and appreciations needed by the people for better living. It is established primarily to provide education for growing youth, but it should cooperate in helping all the people to continue their education after the school years. This is becoming a necessity in a society which daily grows more complex.

The community school should not be purely local in character. Most problems of living today can be understood only through an examination of national and world situations. For example, if the chief crop of a community is sugar beets, a large crop of sugar cane in Cuba or the Philippines is certain to affect the market for sugar beets. Again, increased production of cotton in Egypt may affect the market for the cotton produced in California or in the South. And consider the grocery store in La Paz, Bolivia, where people buy Minnesota corn shipped in tin cans made from tin mined in Bolivia. Here are people of two countries joined in a single enterprise; the fortunes of each member of the group are related to the fortunes of the other member. A failure to obtain tin from Bolivia could cripple the transaction, just as the failure of the corn crop in Minnesota could affect it, or a revolution in Bolivia stop the shipments.

National security is a matter of concern for all communities. Much of the education in rural communities is unfortunately provincial in character. There is need of world-wide understanding and cooperation among the nations if there is to be peace and prosperity throughout the world. Stronger bonds of friendship with other nations are needed. The school has a duty to perform in making people conscious of the place of their country in world affairs and in developing an understanding of other peoples among the young people of today. Only thus can wise leadership for the nation in the future be provided.

The curriculum of the rural school should be organized about the aspects of living in the community, the place of the community in the nation, and the place of the nation in the world-wide picture. The operation of the school must be democratic, with the children helping to plan and develop the curriculum. The good school community is one in which the child feels that he belongs and in which he has had an active part in the work.

The characteristics of the good community school may be summed up as follows:

1. Its major policies are determined by the people of the community, partly through a representative board of education and several committees.

2. The faculty members live in the community, know the community, and are accepted by the people of the community.

3. The members of the school staff work democratically with the students and the parents, recognize the worth of the individual, and engender in the students a feeling of belonging and sharing.
4. The school maintains a professional staff who are constantly studying ways to improve guidance of the children. The faculty is constantly growing.
5. The teacher is considered to be the guiding individual in the organization of the learning experiences and in determining the curriculum and the procedures.
6. The school recognizes that the specialist has a function to perform in any democratic society.
7. The school provides a well-balanced curriculum which is always in a state of change to meet new life needs and problems and new understandings of child development. The curriculum is built around the needs of the learners in their adjustment to conditions.
8. The people of the community and the children help the faculty to plan the curriculum.
9. The school uses individual standards of achievement rather than grade standards. It prizes high achievement toward well-defined goals for the individual.
10. The school uses community resources to vitalize and facilitate learning, making the community a laboratory for the learning process.
11. The school is conceived as being one of the community educational agencies and cooperates fully with other institutions and organizations to provide a good environment for the people, good facilities for education, and a good community program of activities.
12. The school seeks to improve the quality of living in the community by joining with others to contribute to community welfare.
13. The school keeps the people informed about the school program and its difficulties and accomplishments. It seeks the advice and cooperation of the people, and endeavors to build close home and school relations.
14. The school attempts to strengthen the bonds which unite the people, the organizations, and the institutions to make a community team concerned with the welfare of the individual. It fosters the community council idea.

15. The school teaches pupils and adults to use scientific and democratic methods in attacking problems of community concern, in defining problems, in seeking facts to be studied and discussed, and in making decisions.
16. The school distinguishes between the functions of elected officials and the work of informal committees in organizing for cooperative community action.
17. The school conceives of education as a lifelong process and joins with other agencies in developing educational programs for all, suited to the interests and needs of the people.
18. The school program and the community program are coordinated to foster the development of intelligent democratic leadership and followership.
19. The curriculum reflects the interrelationships of local, state, national, and international problems and tries to build local learning and cooperation to have a wider scope, to consider conditions in other localities and in other nations.
20. The school tries to lead the adults in the community into giving the school pupils an active part in community affairs.
21. The school demonstrates good planning and operation by proper care of the school building, its grounds and gardens, and its farm, if it has one.
22. The school program is continuously evaluated in terms of the behavior of its graduates. Has family life been improved? Are the economic conditions better? Are there better recreational, social, and religious facilities in the community?

Making surveys of the community

If the teachers in a community school are to guide the learning of the children effectively, they must know the community. It is necessary also that the administrators understand the community life, its customs and traditions, and the general character of the available resources. This may best be done by an informal survey of the community. Such a survey may be made part of the orientation program for new teachers.

The community of Perryville has provided an illustration of how an informal survey may be made. The school staff developed a relatively complete program for the induction of new teachers which included social events and a tour of the section. The tour started in the village with visits to business places, the bank, the post office, the churches, and the hospital, and the new teachers were introduced to many of the townspeople. The trip was then extended into the surrounding country, giving the teachers an opportunity to meet some of the farm families and see the types of farming. Dairy and fruit farming, corn growing, and hog raising are the chief types of farming near Perryville. The tour ended with a coffee hour at a farmhouse where several neighbors had come to meet the teachers. The talk at this gathering informed the teachers that most of the people in the community are of Swedish ancestry with strong elements of German and Danish stock.

In addition to this tour, new teachers in Perryville are given a handbook which tells the history of the community and gives the results of a survey that was made of the people and their occupations, the sizes of the farms, the organizations and their functions, and the resources available to the school. In the school the teacher found files which supply lists of the visual and auditory aids owned by the school. There is also a school museum which contains exhibits of many local products. The files and the museum exhibit are increased each year by the students and the faculty as part of their cooperative program of curriculum enrichment.

Some schools may not have all the material supplied at Perryville, but every community can see that the new teacher makes a tour of the community, visits the newspaper office and the library, and has a chance to talk with ministers, businessmen, farmers, and others in the community.

The new teacher should also have a chance to meet the county superintendent of schools in the section, the home demonstration and county agricultural agents, and any others who work with the people of the community in any capacity.

During the school year, teachers and pupils can use survey work as part of the curricular program. In one small rural elementary school, the fifth and sixth grades made a survey of the poultry raising in the community. They first made a list of the things they wanted to know about the work and divided the classes into committees to study the questions they outlined. At a parents' meeting in the school, the children told their plan and secured permission to collect the information. A map of the homes was made and the children divided the sections to be visited among the committees. The data they collected were combined and organized into records on breeds of chickens, turkeys, ducks, and geese, types of feed, egg and meat production, and so on. While the tabulation was being made, the children learned that disease had attacked one of the flocks. They wrote to the Agricultural Extension Division for bulletins on poultry diseases and secured the help of the county agriculture agent. The agent did most of the work in treating the flock, to be sure, but the children helped him and in so doing learned much about the care and treatment of poultry.

Sometimes more extensive surveys are undertaken by the school or by school and community on a cooperative basis. These may be surveys of housing, occupations, opportunities for employment, radio listening habits, or need for library service. Other surveys can cover an equally wide variety of items. Such surveys help the school to become aware of community needs, to learn about community resources, and to find answers to many problems, and they often establish better communication between the school and the community.

Words of caution about community surveys are needed here. Unless the purpose in making the survey is well defined and understood and unless plans are carefully drawn, the results are likely to be of no value. There is little merit in a survey made merely to make a survey. The survey should be carried out because that is the only way to secure the information and because the information is needed for a worthwhile purpose. Before undertaking a survey, those concerned should make sure that the data have not already been collected by some other agency. If the survey suggested is complex and time consuming, the group may lose sight of its purpose and lose interest. Again, it is possible to make wrong interpretations of the data collected unless there is careful planning. Where the sampling technique is used, care must be taken to see that the sample is representative. For instance, a sampling of the attitudes toward the teaching of cooperatives in the school made by questioning the people attending a parent-teacher meeting would not represent the attitudes of all the people in the community. And finally, the information sought must not be of such a personal nature that the people questioned will resent the questioning. It is wise to avoid all such matters as income, how money is spent, religion, or politics.

The steps to be taken in conducting a fairly extensive survey are as follows:

1. Define clearly the purpose of the survey and state the objectives carefully.
2. Find out what data assembled by others exist.
3. List the sources from which data may be obtained.
4. Determine what techniques are to be used in collecting data, such as interviews, questionnaires, and so on.
5. Select the portion of the population to be surveyed, making sure it is a representative sample of all the people.
6. Outline the form to be used in collecting and tabulating the data.
7. Select the persons to collect the data and instruct them regarding the techniques to be used.
8. Combine the data collected by the various persons or groups and interpret them.
9. Discuss the data collected and evaluate the work of the survey.

As already stated, a study should be made of the surveys and reports already completed by others before an attempt is made to collect information from a community. The records of local county and state historical societies, of geological surveys, of the chamber of commerce, and of the newspaper will furnish this information. Surveying material which is already on record is a waste of the children's time and would be resented by them if they discovered the existence of the official record. The survey should serve some useful service in the education of the pupils and should be related to their daily life, if possible. Or it should serve the purpose of strengthening the tie between the school and the community.

Some of the techniques which can be used in collecting data in a systematic survey are listed below:

1. Using questionnaires, enrollment blanks, and the like. Questionnaires may be used if the information sought is quite objective and if the wording of the form is carefully planned to avoid misinterpretation. Enrollment blanks usually have places for recording the father's occupation, the names and ages of the children, and the length of time the family has resided in its present home.

2. Interviewing people. To interview people in a conference or in their homes, the interviewer must be able to make pleasing contacts with them. A check list of the questions to be asked is helpful.

3. Studying records. Much information can often be obtained from the documentary material which exists in census reports, minutes of meetings of organizations, maps and charts, and reports filed in county and state offices.

4. Observing conditions. Such matters as a count of traffic, the attendance at church, and the number of farmers who attend meetings can best be determined by personal observation.

Subjects for studies made should be related to physical, social, or economic influences on the community. Some suggestions for specific topics are these:

1. Physical features: location, accessibility, topography, soil, water supply, climate, amount of rainfall
2. Population: size of age groups, distribution, nationalities, birth rate, death rate, mobility, density
3. Societal factors: economic conditions, store sales
4. Agricultural factors: sizes of farms, crops, stock, poultry, machinery, marketing of products

5. Housing: number and sizes of homes, types of homes, condition of buildings, conveniences, assessed valuation
6. Industries and businesses: wholesale and retail establishments, number of employees
7. Organizations: clubs, Grange, youth organizations, Red Cross, church groups, building and loan association
8. Employment opportunities: seasonal farming, part-time employment in the town, full-time employment in stores, the bank, the library
9. Civic services: police, firemen, traffic control, health clinic, water plant, electric plant, storage facilities, post office, library
10. Transportation: bus service, train service, airplane service, condition of roads
11. Recreational facilities: playgrounds, parks, gymnasium, auditorium, swimming pool, skating rink, movie theater, radio and television programs, athletic events, community social affairs
12. Educational facilities: schools, adult education classes, library, newspaper, special services of some organizations

This list is merely suggestive. The topics to be covered will vary with the communities. A more detailed discussion of community factors is given in later chapters.

If teachers and students want to understand their communities, however, they will need much more than facts or cold statistics. To know that there are certain institutions in the town is not enough; the student who wishes to understand them must study their history, traditions, leadership, services, and problems. It is not sufficient, for example, to know that there are a certain number of people who live on farms; they must know what the life on the farm is. It is not enough to know that there are hospitals, churches, radio stations, hardware stores, and carpenter shops; they must see these in terms of services to the people and assets to the community center.

As a part of their search for understanding, the pupils in their surveys usually cover only one aspect of community life. If the data collected are filed for future reference, gradually much information is assembled to add to the instructional program. Such a plan is not very time consuming at any one period and results in much motivation of learning by linking the learning experiences with the life of the people.

Responsibilities of the school

In 1955, at the National Conference of Elementary School Principals in Chicago, an attempt was made to define the school's responsibility to the community. A classification was made into areas of prime responsibility, areas of shared responsibility, and areas of concern.

Areas of prime responsibility dealt with developing the school program, interpreting that program to the people, furnishing professional leadership in evaluating school plans and programs, opening new channels of communication with the community, relating school to community activities insofar as they affect child development, complying with state statutes regarding education, promoting needed educational legislation, and leading in developing and maintaining ethical practices for the profession.

Areas of shared responsibility included helping to establish and maintain a good environment to promote child growth, developing in children understanding of civic responsibilities and democratic processes, guiding children to know themselves with their strengths and weaknesses, encouraging fundamental spiritual values, promoting accuracy and reliability of school communication channels, helping provide community recreation for children, and aiding in teacher recruitment and adequate staffing of the school.

Areas of concern covered social problems that affect the child, religious and spiritual development, facilities and materials to meet the needs of children, and establishing teaching at a desirable level in community life.

Educators are agreed that the school has certain primary responsibilities to the community. Some of these responsibilities can be shared with other institutions in the community and with service agencies. Some phases of community life may be listed as areas of concern rather than as special responsibilities of the school. But whatever the area, the teachers in a good community school can do much to make the learning vital and meaningful in the lives of the children and to help better the living in rural areas.

Summary

The modern school is an integral part of the community in which it operates. It derives its functions from the needs of the people and should make distinct contributions to community life. Teachers need to understand the concept of a good community and the characteristics of a community school in a rural area.

A good rural community has as a center a town large enough to render many services to the people of the surrounding area but small enough to permit frequent face-to-face contacts among the people. There are good relationships between the people of the town and the people of the countryside, and the people all identify themselves as belonging to the community.

Teachers and other school personnel need to understand that community strength can be built by activities in which all of the people take part. A good school furnishes education for both young and old and cooperates with the people in planning community activities. This planning is often carried out through a community council.

A community school must not be purely local in character. Complete understanding of local life involves a knowledge of the broader community of the state, the nation, and the world.

Students, parents, and faculty should work together constantly to better the education and meet the needs of a changing world. The school is continually shaping the curriculum to meet the life needs of the people. Standards of achievement are high, but they are individual in character. The community is regarded as a laboratory of learning in which efforts are being made constantly to improve the living conditions.

The school seeks to develop leadership and followership in the community. It is continually evaluating its work in terms of local conditions.

Surveys made by the pupils increase the understanding of the community for both the teacher and the pupils. The subject of the survey should be related to the educational program, and the data collected should be filed for use by future classes.

The school's responsibilities to the community fall in three categories: areas of prime responsibility, areas of shared responsibility, and areas of concern.

Selected references

BUTTERWORTH, JULIAN E., and DAWSON, HOWARD A. *The Modern Rural School.* New York: McGraw-Hill Book Co., Inc., 1952. Chaps. v and xvii.

Gives the rural community concept and outlines some guiding principles for education. Discusses the community-centered school and its functions.

COOK, LLOYD ALLEN, and COOK, ELAINE FORSYTH. *A Sociological Approach to Education* (2d ed.). New York: McGraw-Hill Book Co., Inc., 1950. Chaps. iii, iv, ix, xvi, xvii, and xviii.

Discusses the nature of the community, the school and the community as partners in progress, the zones of school action in the community, leadership roles, resolving community conflicts, the teacher's community contacts, and the use of community resources in the schools.

GRINNELL, J. E., and YOUNG, RAYMOND J. *The School and Community.* New York: Harper & Bros., 1954. Chaps. iv, v, viii, x, xi, and xiii–xvi.

Describes the rural community, the neighborhood, the changes in communities, and the role of the school in community life, organizations, and institutions.

LINDSTROM, DAVID E. *American Rural Life.* New York: The Ronald Press Co., 1948. Chaps. ix–xii.

Defines rural community procedures in community organization, gives directions for self-analysis, and describes special-interest groups, farmers' organizations, and the problems of the rural church.

MORGAN, ARTHUR E. *The Small Community.* New York: Harper & Bros., 1942. Part I.

Discusses the significance of the small community, the community concept, the relation of the community to larger social units, and the creation of new communities.

NATIONAL EDUCATION ASSOCIATION, DEPARTMENT OF RURAL EDUCATION. *Developing Community Schools.* Washington, D.C.: The Association, 1954. Pp. 22–28.

A concise treatment of the characteristics of rural communities and the social and economic factors affecting the community.

———. *Rural Education—A Forward Look,* 1954 Yearbook. Washington, D.C.: The Department, 1955. Part I, chap. iii; Part II, pp. 270–80.

Describes the school and the community and their close relationships in operation.

NATIONAL SOCIETY FOR THE STUDY OF EDUCATION. *The Community School,* Fifty-second Yearbook. Chicago: The University of Chicago Press, 1953. Chaps. ii, iii, iv, vi, vii, and xiv.

Defines and explains the community school concept; describes distinctive features of community schools and of how people work together to improve the school programs. Emphasis is on the wider community relationships.

———. "Pilot Program in Rural Education," *Education in Rural Communities,* Fifty-first Yearbook. Chicago: University of Chicago Press, 1952. Chap. v.

Describes specific community schools and the ways in which the community helps the school and how the school program is related to community needs.

NELSON, LOWRY. *Rural Sociology.* New York: American Book Co., 1952. Chap. v.

Defines the rural community and shows the differences which distinguish the community from the neighborhood.

OLSEN, EDWARD G., *et al. The Modern Community School.* New York: Appleton-Century-Crofts, Inc., 1953.

Discusses the community school concept, the development of the community school, and how school and community work together. Describes leadership, community schools, and their operation.

———. *School and Community.* Englewood Cliffs, N.J.: Prentice-Hall, Inc., 1954. Parts II and III.

Outlines understanding the community, planning community experiences, and using resources and surveys.

TAYLOR, CARL C., *et al. Rural Life in the United States.* New York: Alfred A. Knopf, Inc., 1949. Chaps. iv and v.

Discusses rural neighborhoods and communities, trade areas and villages, and the changing character of rural communities.

THELEN, HERBERT A. *Dynamics of Groups at Work.* Chicago: University of Chicago Press, 1954. Chaps. v and xi.

Describes the training of adults for group participation by the laboratory method and the coordination of the efforts of group members toward group goals through good leadership.

4

RURAL ENVIRONMENT

The term *environment* may be used to designate all objects, forces, and conditions which affect the individual through such stimuli as he is able to receive. The difficulty for the educator lies in ascertaining which stimuli the child is able to receive and what effect the child's physical condition and mental and emotional processes have on this ability. The teacher needs to study each child in an effort to understand him. Chapter 5 gives some suggestions on how this can be done and a general description of the internal forces which affect behavior. In this chapter we discuss aspects of the environment: those experiences commonly found in rural areas and the characteristics of rural culture which influence the behavior of the child.

Any good educational program starts with the child's stage of development and helps guide him through experiences to the achievement of skills, understandings, attitudes, and appreciations which make for effective living. To do this, the teacher needs to know what out-of-school experiences the child has had, what influence his home has had on his development, and what learning he has experienced. These have all helped form his judgments and opinions, and these the teacher must know if he wants effectively to guide the child into right thinking and right acting.

Experiences in family living

The beginning of the child's education is in the family. In that social group he gains his first experiences in living, working, and playing with others. The farm boy works with his father and the farm girl works with her mother, learning the skills needed for farm living. The farm boy develops self-reliance and dependability through his work on the farm and in the 4-H Club, and he may develop mechanical skill through use of the farm machinery. The girl is taught how to handle farm animals, how to care for poultry, and how to do the many chores connected with housekeeping. Both children have contacts with farm management, cooperative marketing, conservation practices, soil fertilization, and matters pertaining to the use of better seed and better breeds of livestock. Under the guidance of their parents, they may learn to keep records of milk and egg production and recognize the importance of culling out nonproducing animals. They may also learn methods of controlling insect pests and diseases of crops and animals. They realize the importance of the weather in farm production.

Even the young child soon learns that the milk he drinks comes from cows and the vegetables and meat he eats come from plants and animals on the farm. As he grows older, he is taught to help with the milking, the planting, and the care of the animals. His parents often make him the owner of some livestock or some field crop, thus awakening his pride in ownership. As he matures, he may be allowed to share in the family planning and learn the importance of making sound decisions.

The experiences of the nonfarm child do not parallel those of the farm child, but he may spend some time on the farm with his friends and he often has the opportunity to work on the farm. While the village boy's experiences in farming may be limited, yet he is exposed to discussions about the weather, plant and animal diseases, and conservation because the people of the village are directly concerned with the welfare of the farmer, since their own welfare is in good part related to it. Thus, the nonfarm boy encounters many of the same influences as the farm boy.

The character of the family life is important for both the farm children and the village children. The child's speech and behavior are patterned after those of his parents and associates. Another influence on the child is the size of the family. Farm families have usually been larger than urban families, although this disparity is decreasing. Children in large families are generally more self-reliant, cooperative, and pliable.

The bonds of the rural family are close. Members of the family work and play together. They attend social events together and often belong to the same clubs. In contrast, children in the village families may have different interests from their parents. The ties of the rural family, thus, can give its children a sense of security which the village child often does not have.

Family dissention or disruption, though not very common in rural areas, causes deep emotional disturbances and sometimes antisocial attitudes in children. The teacher should be alert to any of the signs of disturbance in children and do her best to help the child with sympathy and understanding to adjust to existing conditions.

Experiences in community living

While the rural child is growing up in the family, he is gradually introduced to experiences in the neighborhood and in the community. These experiences enlarge his concepts, develop his attitudes and appreciations, and teach him new social skills. The importance of such learning will not be overlooked by the skilful teacher.

The smaller community offers superior advantages in the study of community life and local government. Frequent face-to-face contacts and the neighborly character of small communities make it possible for growing youth to share with adults the responsibilities of group life. Greater simplicity of organization makes it possible for the young people to understand the activities of their parents in promoting the welfare of the people in the community. The farm child is familiar with the Farm Bureau, the Farmers' Union, the Grange, cooperatives, and other organizations concerned with the economic and social welfare of farm people. The 4-H Club, Future Farmers of America, Future Homemakers, and similar groups provide active participation in sharing the social and economic life of the community and stimulate development of individual responsibility and cooperation among their members.

Villages and country towns are small enough for children to understand the functions of their institutions and business concerns. Visits to the grocery, hardware store, garage, bank, clothing store, and newspaper office provide opportunities for learning. Health and library facilities may be limited, but many rural communities have established a hospital with a clinic, and small rural areas are served by bookmobiles. The activities of the local government can easily be studied by the youth, and they can learn at first hand the functions of a mayor, a city council, a health officer, a fireman, and a policeman. The people connected with the mail are often glad to tell young people about the services of the post office department.

While the community does much to educate the child in an informal way, definite educational programs are provided by many community organizations, such as the Red Cross, Boy Scouts, Girl Scouts, YMCA, YWCA, Future Farmers of America, 4-H Clubs, Homemaking Clubs, the Grange, the Farm Bureau, the Farmers' Union, and numerous other organizations for adults, young men and women, and children.

Joseph Hart[1] has described the educative influences of the out-of-school environment. He emphasizes that people are

[1] Joseph Hart in *Social Foundations of Education* by William O. Stanley (New York: The Dryden Press, Inc., 1956), pp. 59–60.

educated by whatever they touch and that while schools play a part in all education, it is not so large as schoolmen like to believe. How influential the school may be in the education of the child is determined by the extent to which school experiences are real life experiences. The school is the chief agency of the community to help the child acquire the tools of learning without which learning outside school would be considerably limited.

Guidance in learning out-of-school experience is affected by the utilization of the resources of the community for learning in the school. Misconceptions developed outside school may be corrected by utilization in the school of more complete experience in the community. How influential the school is in developing tastes, appreciations, and emotional patterns will vary from school to school, from teacher to teacher, and from one experience to another. The meaningfulness of school experience will help determine modification of behavior.

Observation of institutions, people, events, and the like does not always produce understanding, but sometimes a background of history will provide that understanding. The good school will capitalize on the out-of-school experiences of the child, but a perspective of an event in time and place may be required to create true understanding. A comparison of manners and customs and modes of behavior of the local community with those in other regions of the world may be necessary for a true perspective. Learning limited to personal experience in the community may be as fruitless as learning divorced from community life. Prejudices and misunderstandings can occur without the broader experience that comes vicariously. The farmer may know that the price he gets for his hogs is too low to pay the costs of farm operation, but to get a true picture of his problem he needs much reading, discussion, study, and reflection. The farm boy who depends on observation alone for growth in the understanding of farm operation will not likely keep pace with the rapidly developing practices based on recent research. Also, his field of observation is limited and he may get wrong impressions from what he sees in the local neighborhood because other neighborhoods follow different practices. The breadth and depth of the broadly educated man can easily be distinguished from that of the individual whose education has been limited to personal experience in the local community.

Travel is helpful, but money and time are limiting factors. Even travel experiences, to be fruitful, must be tied in with reading, discussion, and reflection. Mere travel does not bring about an understanding of why the people of the Andes use wooden plows or why the exchange rate of money in Bolivia is so high.

Growth in understanding comes through both direct and vicarious experiences. The school provides most of the vicarious experiences, and it can make the happy combination of vicarious and direct community experiences to achieve more complete understanding of life. Whatever people touch does educate them to form either good attitudes or prejudices, to develop the use of skills either correctly or ineffectively, to create understandings which may be correct or erroneous. The school's mission is to give guidance in learning which will lead to broader outlooks, more complete understanding, true appreciations, and emotional attachments which encourage further learning.

Rural cultural and economic influences

The rural school is concerned not only with the informal and planned experiences of the children, which educate them, but also with the rural culture, which dictates acceptable behavior. *Culture* is that aggregate of ideas, manners and customs, folkways, attitudes, prejudices, behavior patterns, and the like which have been developed by the social group over a long period of time and through many experiences in living. The cultural pattern of the rural area differs from that of the urban area and, likewise, from one section of the rural or urban area to the other.

Local customs with regard to food may affect the health of the child, and ways of dressing can be so different from those of the village children that the farm child is embarrassed. Some families have brought customs from their native foreign cultures and refuse to change to more modern ways. However, these handicaps are rapidly disappearing. The farm family now listens to programs on the radio, sees demonstrations on the television set, attends meetings in which habits and customs may be discussed, and reads many books, magazines, and newspapers. In most areas of the United States the people use the services of child-care specialists while the children are young.

The modes of behavior of the people are derived in part from those of the community. For example, in some sections it is considered bad form to make any outward display of affection. Yet the young child needs love and affection if he is not to develop into a shy individual who finds it difficult to join others in activities when he enters school. Older pupils may pose a considerable number of problems for their teachers unless their home background is known and the local customs are understood.

The prejudices of the adults in the family affect the child's attitudes toward others. If the community looks down on some of the people because of their race, their economic status, or their religion, the school has the task of educating the pupils in the concept of the American way of life in which all are equal and have equal rights and opportunities.

Rural communities in the United States differ in their customs partly because of the national origins of the people who inhabit them. Some regions may frown upon card playing, dancing, or brightly colored dress. Others may approve of Saturday night dances but restrict all activity on Sunday to the essentials. Improved transportation and communication have done much to change these conditions. The farmer no longer looks down on the "city slicker," and city people rarely refer to farmers as "hayseeds." But the culture of the two areas still differs in many respects.

The economic conditions have a marked influence on farm life and therefore on the child. Many former activities of the farm—such as soap making, canning fruits and vegetables, making sorghum, butchering farm animals—are now carried on as community enterprises or even relegated to the cities. The farmer now has more leisure time which he utilizes to broaden his outlook and change many of his ideas through cultural activity of one sort or another. The rural teacher, however, should not lose sight of the fact that the child in the rural home, despite the increases in family libraries and radios, often lacks many of the cultural advantages of the child in the city home.

Economic conditions have forced farmers to join organizations to help market their products, finance improvements, and improve their crops and animals. These conditions have forced the acceptance of government advice and control in matters of soil conservation, crop rotation, irrigation, and the like, and, though he may resent government intervention, government officials have become a part of the farmer's life. The teacher should study the local conditions and learn the economic pattern of the community.

The school administration must remember that the farm boy or girl has a real economic value to the farm. On the family-size farms—160 to 240 acres—the boys are frequently kept out of school to work in the fields. When the crops ripen, the girls are often needed to help their mothers put up food for the family's use in winter. An adaptation of the curriculum to the planting and harvest schedule in the farm area is therefore essential.

Migrant labor groups may be another factor of the economic situation. The children of these families may attend the school, but their parents may not be interested in helping with the expenses of educating the youth of the area. This may create a financial burden for the people of the community and may also be a source of contention between the two groups. The school should attempt to ease the situation and help solve the problems that arise.

The economic situation differs with the region and with the type of farming. In some arid regions of the west, where cattle, sugar beets, beans, and potatoes are the principal products, the struggle for an adequate water supply is an essential threat to the farmer's success. In sections where dairy farming and cotton raising are the chief occupations, the pattern of life differs from that in a section given over to the production of wheat or the raising of fruit crops.

The economic condition of the family often influences its attitude toward education. Some farmers question the value of education beyond the eighth grade, others question the value of education altogether. The family's opinion of education, of course, influences the child's attitude toward school. The school must assume the responsibility to change these attitudes by demonstrating the value of education. This can only be done by relating education to the daily life of the people.

The observant teacher will notice all these conditions and endeavor to adapt the teaching to the pupils' needs. Cultural patterns which are good should be preserved. Prejudices which are harmful should be dealt with carefully. Knowledge is the best antidote for prejudice. Where local habits and customs are harmful to progress, it will take tact and care to show the people why their ways should be changed. A knowledge of the customs of other regions and peoples often opens the eyes to the inadequacy of local ways of living.

Summary

In order to understand rural children, the teacher should know the cultural patterns of the community and understand the economic situation. The children who enter school have been conditioned in their homes and in the community to follow certain patterns of behavior, and they may have formed opinions and prejudices like those of their parents.

The rural environment develops the child's knowledge of nature, of farm management, and often of machinery. He may have had an opportunity to learn about the local government, and he is almost certain to know the work of the community institutions. He is usually self-reliant and cooperative. The school's responsibility is to relate his learning activities to his daily life so that he will want to continue his education as far as possible.

Pupils from families new to the region and the children of migrant workers make special problems for the teacher. They are part of the rural background with which the teacher must become familiar.

Selected references

ASSOCIATION FOR SUPERVISION AND CURRICULUM DEVELOPMENT. *Creating a Good Environment for Learning.* Washington, D.C.: The Association, 1954.

Shows the importance of the child's environment to learning.

———. *Growing Up in an Anxious Age,* 1951 Yearbook. Washington, D.C.: The Association, 1952. Chaps. vi, vii, xii, and xiii.

Describes the behavior patterns expected of children and how children learn roles and develop relationships.

COOPER, SHIRLEY. "The Rural Neighborhood School," *Bulletin of the National Elementary School Principals* (April, 1950), pp. 3–6.

A discussion of the rural neighborhood of the rural elementary school.

GREENE, SHIRLEY E. *The Education of Migrant Children.* Washington, D.C.: National Council on Life and Labor and the Department of Rural Education, 1954. Chap. viii.

The educational background and the attitudes of migrant families are discussed.

LINDSTROM, DAVID EDGAR. *American Rural Life.* New York: The Ronald Press Co., 1948. Chaps. iii and vii.

Describes the environment, rural cultural patterns, and family life in rural homes.

MARTIN, WILLIAM E., and STENGLER, CELIA BURNS. *Child Development and the Process of Growing Up in Society.* New York: Harcourt, Brace, & Co., 1953. Part II.

Discusses the meaning of society and culture and describes growing up in the culture of a society.

NATIONAL EDUCATION ASSOCIATION, DEPARTMENT OF RURAL EDUCATION. *Developing Community Schools.* Washington, D.C.: The Department, 1954. Pp. 32–38.

John A. Holden's section "Conserving Values in Rural Community Life" shows the cultural values of rural life.

————. *Rural Education—A Forward Look*, 1954 Yearbook. Washington, D.C.: The Department, 1955. Part I, chaps. iv and vii; Part III, pp. 306–11 and 341–44.

A discussion of the impact of the rural environment on children, and a view of the cultural changes in rural life.

NELSON, LOWRY. *Rural Sociology*. New York: American Book Co., 1952. Chaps. x and xv.

Discusses the culture of various farm groups, the assimilation and acculturation among culture groups, and rural family life.

OLSEN, EDWARD G., *et al. School and Community*. Englewood Cliffs, N.J.: Prentice-Hall, Inc., 1954. Chap. iv.

Discusses the social status of families and its effect on social beliefs and values.

STANLEY, WILLIAM O. *et al. Social Foundations of Education*. New York: The Dryden Press, Inc., 1956. Chap. ii and pp. 102–14.

Culture which develops the individual, relation of education to culture and cultural change, how the community educates; discussion of family life includes comparison of rural and urban families.

TAYLOR, CARL C., *et al. Rural Life in the United States*. New York: Alfred A. Knopf, Inc., 1949. Chaps. iii, vii, viii, x, xix, xx–xxviii.

Treats of the rural home and family, rural church, rural local government and welfare, rural culture with characteristic differences in culture and rural life in cotton, corn, wheat, range-livestock, dairy, and other farming areas and farm people's attitudes and opinions.

5

THE RURAL ELEMENTARY
SCHOOL CHILD

In the educational program of the modern school, the central figure is the child and his problems of growing up in the community. Before coming to school, the child has been learning from experiences in the home and the community and has made some kind of adaptation to the culture of the family and the neighborhood. This interaction between the child and his environment has not always been satisfactory to him, and his adjustment to what is expected of him is not always complete. It therefore becomes the mission of the school to help the child to continue the learning process and to satisfy those needs which are basic in all human beings. Many of his social needs may not have been met because of failure to resolve the conflicts between his individual wants and acceptable behavior as determined by the culture into which he was born.

The ability of teachers to fulfil the mission of the school in the life of the child is determined by their knowledge of the nature of child growth and the learning process, and by their understanding of the nature of human needs which must be met if the child is to be well adjusted to living with his fellows. Since children coming to school are so different in their inherited potential for education in their previous experiences, and in their adaptation to cultural demands, teachers need to know how to study individual children and to understand child growth, and learning, and the common needs of children.

How the child grows

Understanding the nature of the growth process will help the teacher to realize why children at a given age level are not equally ready for school activities. It will help her, also, to recognize the reasons for changing interests and variations in achievement and understand as well that emotional reactions, social adjustments, mental development, and physical growth are interrelated.

A full treatment of the nature of child growth would require a complete volume, but some basic facts about child growth, necessary to the development of a good school program, can be summarized.

1. Each child inherits certain potentialities for growth. Within the limits of those potentialities and with a good environment, good health, good food, and a friendly, stimulating atmosphere, the child will continue to grow. Arguments about the greater influence of nature or of nurture have been going on for many years, with considerable research to support either viewpoint. They seem to add up to the conclusion that circumstances in the environment can prevent a child from realizing his growth potential and that two children, given the same advantages, do differ with respect to physical and mental development. Malnutrition, disease, or injury may retard both physical and mental growth, while good health and a wholesome environment facilitate growth. Such influences may also affect the emotional and social development.

2. Each child has his own individual pattern of growth, with variations in rate of growth and time for the maturing;

yet his growth is continuous and follows an orderly sequence. Some patterns show gradual physical growth, while others show temporary retardation followed by periods of more rapid development. From early infancy, physical growth occurs according to the child's individual pattern. At first the movement of arms and legs are random and uncoordinated, but eventually the child develops control and learns to pick up objects. Later he learns to walk and run about, but many kindergarten and first-grade children are just developing the ability to cut paper and hold pencils. From the beginning, the circulatory system grows to keep pace with body growth, but growth of the heart does not match growth of the rest of the body until pre-adolescence or possibly not until adolescence itself. Consequently, strenuous physical contests for elementary-school children are often considered undesirable.

The rate of child growth is no evidence of the eventual size or capabilities of the individual. Children who walk early or talk early are not necessarily brighter or more agile than those who show such ability later. The child cannot be judged as inferior or superior simply because of late or early maturing of functions.

Boys and girls do not mature at the same rate. Boys are usually taller and heavier than girls except between the ages of 10 and 15. On the average, girls reach puberty a year earlier than boys. Some children (usually girls) of the sixth grade of the elementary school have reached the pubertal or pre-adolescent period, while others do not make the physical changes characteristic of sex before reaching the senior high school. Changes in interests and the development of physical characteristics are expected to be earlier for girls than for boys. Group behavior reflects these earlier changes on the part of girls.

3. The infancy and early childhood period are important in establishing normal emotional and personality development. For young children, love and affection and a sense of belonging to the family develop a feeling of security. With continued physical and mental development, the child begins to show a measure of independence. Tasks attempted which

are in keeping with his maturity provide opportunity to experience the success so essential to normal growth. Out of the experiences of infancy and early childhood emerge personality characteristics, such as aggressiveness, friendliness, sympathy, good sense of humor, and the like.

4. As boys and girls develop from the dependency of infancy and early childhood, they turn away from adults to friends of the same sex. This period of greater independence, usually found among pupils of the intermediate grades, is accompanied by antagonism toward the opposite sex, more marked on the part of boys than girls. Boys form gangs of boys, and girls form cliques with other girls. At this time the boy or girl is more influenced by the behavior and dress of his gang or clique than by the standards of his parents. He is less concerned about neatness, and his speech follows that of his age group. His allegiance to his crowd is of great significance to him.

The boy's interest shifts during this period from the fanciful to the factual. He is interested in science and mechanics and he wants to know how things are made and how they work. School work and books pertaining to automobiles, trains, and airplanes have a great attraction for him. He likes to make things with his hands and is interested in shop work at school or at home. He makes a shack or a boat for his own satisfaction but often loses interest in the project when it is completed. His standards of performance are his own.

Adults need to respect the child's desire for secrecy at this period and must realize that the ways of the gang are his standard. This is the period when club work under wise and understanding leadership will have great appeal for the child. It is also a period when the study of a second language will interest him, as nothing pleases him more than to be able to use a language which he and his classmates understand but which may not be known by the adults.

5. The child develops as a whole organism. Physical growth is accompanied by mental development and emotional maturing, and there are constant interactions between the child and other persons and objects in the environment. Basic

emotional reactions accompany his physical and mental activity, and the culture patterns of his environment affect his emotional life, helping to form attitudes, appreciations, and habit patterns.

6. Each child is normally active and directs his energies toward goals. He selects from his environment those things which attract him and actively provide experiences for him. Parents and teachers should expect the child to "fidget" when forced to sit still. Inhibition of impulses has to be learned. The young child follows his impulses and remains active during waking hours. If he appears sleepy and uninterested in things, parents and teachers should be concerned, as he is likely to be ill. The normal child is active and curious about his environment. He will ask questions and develop interests.

7. Associations with objects and events develop language concepts and give meaning to words and objects, and events in the child's life help him to see cause and effect relationships. Since judgments are made on the basis of experience, thinking and reasoning at any age can be effective only if the problem to be solved comes within the realm of related previous experience. The child builds up his own background of understanding of his environment. If his experience has been rich enough, he will reason well; but he must have a fund of concepts with which to reason. For young children these concepts are based on limited or single experiences, so the reasoning may be faulty if the problem is beyond the stage of their development.

8. Each child is unique at every age level. There are differences in height, weight, color of hair and eyes, and all other physical characteristics. Likewise, there are differences in mental, emotional, and social development. These differences are due in part to heredity and in part to environmental experience. No two children get the same experience out of a single event in which special interests develop, likes and dislikes appear, and aggressiveness or reticence for the activity is manifested. Health and sanitation and learning experiences play a part in widening differences among children. The older children grow, the wider the differences in

traits, abilities, and interests become. Teachers of the modern school recognize the need to broaden the school program, helping the child continue to grow by beginning with his current level of development, helping him to meet his special needs, and appealing to his interests. Differences in maturity account for many differences in interests.

Growing up requires time. Attempts to get the child to walk before he is ready, use finer muscles too early, to talk before his time, or try to learn to read before he has sufficient maturity are likely to yield poor results and may even be harmful.

How the child learns

The school facilitates the growth of children by expanding the learning of the out-of-school environment. Understanding how children learn is therefore fundamental to organization of school experiences in keeping with the growth process.

Learning is change or adaptation of behavior as a result of experience. In the process of learning, behavior patterns may be altered or new patterns established. Learning may be distinguished from maturation—that portion of growth due largely to natural causes—but maturation is important in planning learning experiences for children, to make sure that the physical growth and general maturing of the organism have progressed to a point where the child is ready for the learning experience.

Many psychologists have distinguished between learning and mere repetition or drill. They maintain that repetition only fixes a behavior pattern already learned and is not learning at all. Yet there can be almost no pure repetition of behavior. Even in such a simple function as learning that $2 + 4 = 6$, the various practices given are accompanied by the establishment of new associations. In planning the mastery of such number combinations, efforts are made to build associations to give meaning to and develop favorable emotional attachments.

A comprehensive treatment of the meaning of learning would involve discussion of the various theories regarding its operation, such as *connectionism, field theory,* and *conditioning.* The various systems of learning have made contributions to an understanding of the learning processes. However, in this brief discussion of learning only some general principles of learning are extracted from the various theories—principles needed to explain the organization of instruction as discussed in other chapters of this volume and needed by the rural teacher in the organization and execution of experiences for children.

1. Learning begins with life and proceeds continuously throughout life. Some psychologists believe that learning may begin even before birth. It certainly takes place immediately after birth as the child is developing associations with the feeding process, with persons, and with objects. From birth onward the ever-active child is responding to stimuli and exploring his environment. He gets deeper and deeper meanings from his experiences as he grows and develops and perfects his skills.

2. The child learns with his whole organism. He learns by the use of his muscles, eyes, ears, and fingers and through his sense of taste and of smell. For example, a young child looks at an object new to him, picks it up, and handles it to get a feeling of roughness or smoothness, of hardness or softness, or of heaviness or lightness. His judgment is based on his past experiences. He may put the object into his mouth to taste it or put it to his nose to see if it gives off an odor. He may put it to his ear to see if it has sound. If an object is bright and shiny and yellow in color, the older child will wonder whether it is tin or silver or gold. Only past experience will help him to tell.

In teaching children to learn to spell new words, teachers use auditory, visual, and kinesthetic sensations to facilitate learning. Combined sensory experiences are found to be most conducive to learning. In a single experience, the child learns many things through the use of his whole body. He develops skills and understanding and, at the same time, experiences satisfactions and often physical activity.

3. Each experience utilizes past experiences and consists of a process of reorganization and expansion of previous learning. For a child to learn from a given school activity, the new experience must be related to his past experience. Consequently, when a new topic or learning unit is introduced, the teacher uses pictures, stories, and a discussion of previous experiences to make sure that the children have a background for understanding it. However, for learning to take place, the new experience must add to or reorganize the earlier concepts of the children. A good curriculum is a design of experiences so planned in sequence as to bring relatedness of the old to the new and thus help the child to grow in understanding and skill by gradual changes.

4. Learning begins with a broad, complete experience. It proceeds from the whole to the parts rather than from the parts to the whole. When new skills are to be learned, they should be introduced in the complete situation in which they are used. For example, teachers begin the teaching of spelling and handwriting by letting the children dictate and then write letters to real people. The skills have meaning for the children because of the real writing situations. Again, if the parent or teacher wants the child to understand the meaning of money, he takes the child to the grocery store where the child learns that people must have money to buy things. But the child does not yet know the value of commodities in terms of money; that will take additional experiences in buying. The child must make a purchase or do some work for which he is paid, in order to develop the meaning of money further. The learning in these various experiences is affected by many factors present at the time of each experience. In the visit to the grocery store, for example, the child is affected by the grocer and his behavior, by the presence of other customers, by the cart used to haul purchases, and by many other elements present at the time. All these elements are important in giving meaning to the child's experience.

Having learned the meaning of money through complete experiences, the child learns how change is made and he may practice making change at school. The important thing to remember is that the whole experience of seeing money used to purchase articles came *before* the activity of learning to make change. Likewise, drills on number combinations should come *after* experiences which call for a use of number combinations. When the skill to be mastered first appears in a complete experience, drills which follow have meaning and purpose. When children memorize poetry, they are most successful if the whole poem is studied first as a unit. Experimentation has demonstrated the superiority of whole learning over part learning.

5. Skills or understandings learned in one experience are utilized in a variety of others to expand the learning. This principle is illustrated in the case of a child who first sees that money is needed to make purchases in the stores, then learns how to make change, and perhaps then makes purchases of his own in a real store or in a play store at school. Another illustration is the case of a fifth-grade class which was studying a unit on the weather. The children found it necessary to learn how to use the encyclopedia and how to keep records of the weather. Later, in a study of seed germination, the class found further use for these skills, merely changing the system of record keeping to fit the new topic. Practicing functions already learned in one situation fixes the learning in the mind.

6. Learning takes place by association. Words have meaning for people because of the character of associations in experience. To the urban child, *milk* brings a picture of a bottle; to the rural child, it means a cow. To most Americans the word *billy* means a club carried by a policeman, but to the Australian *billy* means a small pail in which the workman brews his tea.

Not only words but events have acquired meaning because of associations. Because of past experiences, Christmas for some children means candy, gifts, a Christmas tree, and Santa Claus; for others it has a religious significance. Teachers build meaning by the process of association through experience.

7. The process of learning is from the specific to the general, from the concrete to the abstract. For example, if a rule in spelling is to be taught, children are led to examine a large number of specific words. If the rule says to "double the final consonant preceded by a vowel when adding a suffix beginning with a vowel," then the children examine such words as *resist* and *resisting, occur* and *occurred,* and *counsel* and *counseling.* By a study of such words they may conclude that the rule is not quite complete, since it applies only to words accented on the last syllable and since it says nothing about retaining the vowel sound of the base word. Contrast this procedure with that of giving the children a rule to be memorized. Learning does not begin with generalizations but with the concrete, and it ends with generalizations and applications.

8. Learning occurs best when there is a goal or an incentive. The more real and vital the goal, the greater the effort children will make to learn what is needed for achieving their purposes. For instance, when boys want to build a baseball diamond, they will work hard for long hours to complete the task. When children are genuinely concerned about a problem in the classroom, they will cheerfully work hard to overcome any difficulties which stand in the way of a solution.

Purposes not only create drives in learning but also determine the nature of what is learned from a given activity. In a fourth-grade unit on dairying, the children discussed what they already knew and then listed questions which they wanted answered. In the search for answers, some were interested in the types of cattle which produce the richest milk while others were interested in butter making or in the production of cheese. What the children learned varied with their interests. A further illustration may be found in reading; children sometimes read a story just to enjoy the story while at other times they read to understand how the author expresses himself. Goals create drives in learning and determine the nature of the learning which takes place.

9. Children learn to do by doing if the doing helps to realize goals, meets some need in the learner, or brings a satisfying outcome. They learn best if the experience includes a problem which they know is important in their own lives. They want to study butter making by making butter and by watching others make butter rather than simply by reading about the process.

10. People learn both through direct and vicarious experiences. In the study of dairying, for instance, children visit dairy farms, creameries, and cheese factories and they also read about butter making, dairy farming, and the like. Learning which is acquired purely through personal experience is likely to be limited, and that which is confined to books may be abstract and erroneous. True understanding is most likely to result when book learning or oral information is combined with observation and personal experience.

11. Most learning includes some trial and error. The learner makes many responses in an effort to hit upon one which satisfies him. But he must know whether the response which he finally accepts is the best one. An example of trial-and-error learning is that of the sixth-grade child who was trying to use a typewriter. She used her past observational experience to punch out letters, and she made several trials to learn how the carriage worked. Each time that it did not work, she was annoyed, but she tried again and again until she hit upon the correct way to do it. She was able to pick out letters to make words and finally developed a series of typing habits. She succeeded in typing a letter to her friend and was satisfied with the result. However, she had not developed a good system of typing; she had established habits that were not good ones. Learning by trial and error involves having a goal, making trials, evaluating the results of those trials, and knowing when they are right. Much of the guidance of learning in school involves frequent evaluation of progress and diagnosis of errors.

12. Learning depends upon readiness to learn. The ability to learn depends upon the mental, physical, social, and educational maturity of the learner. Many teachers do not realize that some children have trouble with speech because of immaturity, or that handwriting is difficult for some because the finer muscles have not been well developed.

13. Learning often involves problem solving. Teaching children to solve problems involves locating and defining the problem, determining what information is needed, looking for the facts bearing on the problem, filtering these facts in the light of predictable outcomes, and generalizing from those facts to a decision. The school program should include a series of problem-solving situations appropriate to the developmental level of the children. Step-by-step experiences in problem solving will enable children to grow in ability to use the procedures needed in any learning situation.

14. Transfer of learning from one situation to another varies with the similarity of the situations. Teachers expect the transfer of identical elements from one situation to another, as when the child who has learned to read one road map can read another. Can he read the maps used at school, however? This depends on their similarity to the road maps. The child who learns to spell *walk* has little difficulty with *walks, walking,* and *walked,* but after learning to spell *try* and *trying* he may have difficulty with *tried.*

Transfer of general principles also can occur, as when the child observes from reading books and seeing the writing of his teacher that each sentence begins with a capital letter and transfers this generalization to his own writing.

Educators try to organize and direct the school program so that behavior which is learned in school will transfer to life outside the school. How well the school learning will transfer depends on how similar school life is to community life—on how much school experiences are like those of the community.

15. Ability to recall and use previous learning depends upon the intensity and recency of the previous learning, upon the amount of practice or use, upon the associations

accompanying that learning, and upon the satisfaction attached to the learning. Experiences which are vital and meaningful are likely to be recalled, as well as those which have been satisfying. Recent experiences can also be remembered. The ability to recall learning is not governed purely by the lapse of time, however, but also by intervening experiences which interfere. For example, the child learns to spell *their* as in "I went to their house." Subsequently, he learns to spell *there* as in "I went there yesterday." The intervening learning interferes with a later recall of the correct spelling of *their*. Some children who made a trip to a flour mill learned much about the use of wheat in the making of flour. They subsequently made a trip to a factory where cereals were produced, and later they gave evidence of confusion about the process of flour making.

In studying functions which it is important to remember, teachers should give frequent reviews of skills or functions previously learned. For example, children who had learned to read graphs and maps in one experience unit are subsequently given further practice of the same skills in another unit.

16. Best rewards for learning come in the form of satisfaction with achievement. Finding answers to questions or solving problems, with adventure or discovery through experimentation or from a recognition of newly acquired prestige in a group is a satisfying accomplishment. These are intrinsic rewards derived from the activity itself, and such rewards build confidence and an interest in further exploration. In the schools of today, teachers have not yet succeeded in getting away from extrinsic rewards such as grades or prizes or special favors, but the trend is toward better methods of recording progress. In every case, there should not be fear of punishment for failure to obtain a certain standard of performance; such fear is more likely to produce emotional maladjustment than progress in mental and social development. True success in learning, with the accompanying satisfactions, strengthens the learning and stimulates further growth.

Needs of the rural child

Learning experiences organized by the school to help the child with the growing-up process must help him meet certain needs basic to the welfare of all human beings. These needs may be classified as (1) physical needs, (2) social needs, and (3) achievement.

All children need a large amount of physical activity during the growing period. Teachers notice that when children have been sitting still for a long period of time, restlessness develops. Mental work that requires sitting still should be broken up at times by periods when there is freedom to move about or to engage in active games.

Children need sufficient rest, good health, and comfortable bodies. Young children tire easily and must have regular periods of rest, and all children need good health if they are to be happy and well adjusted in their relations with one another. When children show evidence of poor progress in learning, parents and teachers sometimes find poor health to be the explanation. And while children may be able to work even with uncomfortable bodies, such things as classroom temperatures and regularity of elimination do affect the health and happiness of the children and their readiness to cooperate in group activities.

Social needs of the child include a feeling of belonging and of status in his group. He needs to know that he is accepted and wanted by others. If the child feels that he is not one of the group, emotional depression may be very intense and he will need the help of the teacher in learning how to win the respect of his classmates.

There are many reasons why some children are popular, some ignored, and some rejected. In a study of social acceptability, Bedoian[1] gave 743 pupils in 22 classes three choices of answers for each of these four questions: (1) If you were changed from this class to another class, which

[1] Vagharsh H. Bedoian, "Social Acceptability and Social Rejection of the Underage, At-Age and Overage Pupils in the Sixth Grade," *Journal of Educational Research*, XLVII (March, 1954), pp. 513–20.

boy or girl from this class would you choose to go with you? (2) Which boy or girl from this class would you choose as a team captain for a game of sports? (3) Which boy or girl from this class would you choose as president of your class? (4) Which boy or girl from this class would you choose to help you if you needed help to do your school work? He found that underage children were more often accepted by their group than either at-age or overage children, and that at-age children are more likely to be popular than overage children. Bedoian concluded that age determines social acceptance to a considerable degree, and that "If overage children are placed together, they enjoy a higher degree of status than overage children who do not make up a large share of the class." His evidence showed that the overage child not only was less likely to be accepted in the group but also was most often disliked or rejected.

Margaret Buswell[2] examined critically the social acceptability of children in relation to school achievement. She based her study on results obtained with 321 children in the late fifth and early sixth grades and 286 children as they progressed from late kindergarten into the first grade. In an effort to discover factors associated with social acceptance, she used measures of intelligence and achievement, the Sim's score card for determining socioeconomic status, the sociogram, and the Ohio social-acceptance scale. From her findings one may conclude that children at these grade levels who are succeeding in their school work are also succeeding in their social relationships with their peers. There seems to be some basis for the conclusion that, for these groups, achievement precedes rather than follows acceptability, although both may be true. Children in the kindergarten did not show any distinction in achievement in choices of friends; but upon entrance to the first grade, where achievement of a different kind became evident, those who were successful in achievement were also the most acceptable to

[2] Margaret M. Buswell, "The Relationship Between the Social Structure of the Classroom and the Academic Success of Pupils," unpublished Ph.D. Thesis, University of Minnesota, 1950.

their classmates. If social acceptability were responsible for the achievement, children who were most popular in the kindergarten would have shown up as the high achievers in the first grade; but in reading readiness, used as the measure of achievement, this was not the case. While evidence is not complete enough to permit generalization, it seems possible that teachers may help children to grow in social acceptance by helping them to achieve in school work and to contribute to group welfare.

Each child has a need for status in his social group—to feel that he is respected and admired. Status in a group is affected by the child's achievement in sports or other school activities and by the family status in the community. Studies of rural and urban groups show that differences in emotional stability depend chiefly upon the socioeconomic status of the family in the community. Emotional instability tends to come from lack of status in the social group. Teachers can often help the child achieve status by giving him an opportunity to carry responsibilities in activities in which he can excel.

The child needs to be loved and to have someone who is interested in his welfare and has confidence in him. Parents and teachers as well as classmates can help supply this need.

In order to have self-respect as well as the respect of his fellows, the child needs to experience success in his activities. Where he is asked to engage in activities for which he is not sufficiently mature, he may develop a feeling of failure. When he is properly motivated and attempts tasks in keeping with his ability, he will be likely to experience achievement and, with achievement, self-respect, the admiration of his fellows, and confidence in attempting new tasks.

Collecting information about the rural child

While the basic needs of all children, rural or urban, are the same, the environment in which the rural child lives is different from that of the urban child and affects his development. His learning will be different, even if the process of learning is the same. His growth pattern will vary from that of his playmates in the same way that growth patterns of urban children vary. Yet since his learning and growth are so much affected by local culture and local experience, much information about the child must be collected by the teachers if they are to organize curriculum experiences in such a way as to meet the individual needs of the pupils.

With the beginning of the school year in the small town, the village, or the open country, the teacher faces a new group of children. These children vary in height, weight, color of hair and eyes, body build, manner of dress, social adaptation, and freedom of expression. The teacher soon learns that there are marked variations in readiness to begin work, in reaction to experience proposed, in attitudes toward the teacher and the school, in sense of values, in confidence with which tasks are undertaken, in persistence toward completion of work, and in ability to solve problems. The good teacher knows that each child is in a process of growth and that his education must begin with the level of development to which he has attained. The teacher needs to know about his family and its culture, about his home experiences and educational progress, his adjustment to social groups, and his special interests and abilities. Such information may be collected over a period of time and recorded for use in the study of any difficulties the child may have in developing.

One of the best sources of information for the teacher is a good set of cumulative records. Such a set of records, passed along from grade to grade and from teacher to teacher or filed in the principal's office, can provide a storehouse of valuable information about each child's scholastic success or failure, chronic diseases, school attendance, age, height, weight, occupation of parents, home conditions, special talents, special achievements, and personal development. The accuracy of these data should be recognized as important.

Anecdotal records of the achievements and problems of the children can be very helpful. These reports should be written as soon as possible after an observation of behavior. In making such records, the teacher should avoid prejudgment regarding the *cause* of any questionable behavior.

Writing the records requires practice in making objective observations and recording what the child says and does, without making any interpretation before several observations have been made. An interpretation of every event is usually impossible; such interpretation can be made only after a series of records reveals trends or patterns of behavior. Judgments made about the child from one observation would reveal bias rather than an explanation of the child's behavior. When writing the record, therefore, it is important to give the social settings in which the observations are made.

A major source of information for the teacher is observation of the child in the classroom and on the playground. Teachers are more likely to be attracted to the behavior of the child who disturbs the social group or the child with unusual talents or extreme retardation in learning than to notice the child who conforms to the group or who just does not participate in group activities. Some teachers find it helpful to make a special study of one child at a time, observing and making records of his behavior.

On the playground the teacher can learn much about the social acceptance of a child by his peers, and can readily recognize the leadership qualities and the interests of the individual children. Classroom activities as well can reveal much about children to the observant teacher. Some teachers have a free story hour when the children talk about books they like to read and other interests. Classroom discussions often reveal information about hobbies or out-of-school activities and help in understanding the sense of values of children. Creative writing, which is possible only under a free, relaxed atmosphere, reveals much about desires, ambitions, and inhibitions. Sometimes children write autobiographies as a part of their writing experiences. These have been very helpful in understanding children. Observing habits of work, persistence, problem-solving ability, enjoyment, and readiness to participate will add to understanding.

Some teachers make it a practice to record evidences of special achievements or special behavior problems at the end of every school day. These accumulated descriptive records can be studied later to see what trends or common factors are evident.

Information about the children can be secured from such professional people as the school nurse, the social worker, or a school doctor, where these specialists are available. Sometimes a former teacher can answer many questions about the children.

Contacts with parents represent another source of information. Parents who attend parent-teacher meetings and school visiting days usually want to talk about their children, and informal conversations of this type are often helpful. In some schools regularly scheduled interviews with the parents have become common practice, and teachers find parents most helpful in adding to their information about children. Home visitations will obviously be helpful, but because of the pressure of time, this source of information is not used as extensively as desirable. Where it has become standard practice and where diplomacy is observed, such visitation has been of great value.

Informal interviews with the children represent another source of data. Some data can be secured from the child without embarrassment if he can be engaged in informal conversation. The teacher should avoid direct personal questions or the appearance of being merely inquisitive, but she should keep in mind what information is needed and strive for the answers. A record of the interview may be made later. How much a child will reveal voluntarily depends largely on the kind of comradeship established between the teacher and the child.

Some teachers make use of check lists and published inventories, such as the Haggerty-Olson-Wickman Behavior Rating Schedule (World Book Company), the Mental Health Analysis (California Testing Bureau), and the Rogers Test of Personality Adjustment (Association Press). These forms have places for additional data to supplement observational and interview procedures. Many school systems also make use of some test of mental maturity and use tests of school achievement.

Sociograms have been found very useful in helping teachers study the social acceptance or rejection of individuals and understand individual relationships. To avoid embarrassment, the teacher may use an occasion when committees of chil-

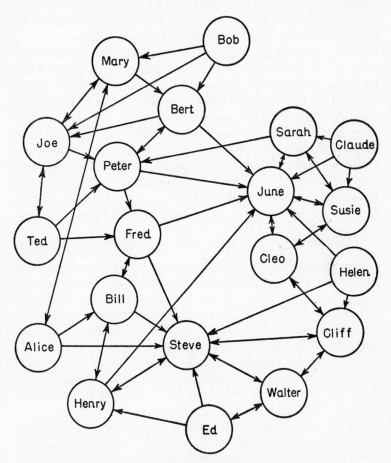

Sixth-Grade Sociogram.[3]

[3] Instructions for constructing a sociogram will be found in references at the end of this chapter.

dren are to be selected to prepare for an event or other activity. Each child is asked to write his name at the top of a slip of paper and to put below his name the names of two or three persons whom he would like to have work with him on the committees to be made up the next day. The slips are then used to tabulate choices for each person and a sociogram is drawn. It is thus possible to pick out the most popular pupils who are the accepted leaders, to note the cliques whose members choose only each other, to see the chums or pairs of mutual choices, and to identify the isolates who are not chosen by anyone. The sociogram on page 75 was made for a sixth-grade class in which each member selected three other children with whom he would like to serve on a committee for a Christmas party. It will be noted that there were two leaders, June and Steve, that there were 16 pairs of mutual choices in the group, and that Bob, Claude, and Helen were not chosen by anyone. The teacher thus sees that these three children need help in adjusting to the group and in winning friends. If the selections were being made for team mates in some sport, the selections would probably vary.

Summary

The program of the modern rural school is organized about the child and his problems of growing up in the community. In the growing-up process there are basic needs which must either be met through out-of-school experiences or through the activities of the school if the child is to be a well-adjusted individual. To facilitate the continued growth of the child by the organization of suitable learning experiences, teachers must understand the growth and learning processes of children, the nature of basic human needs, and the techniques of child study.

Problems of learning and adjustment occur if children are faced with activities before being ready for them. Teachers recognize that understanding the behavior of Fred or Alice is possible if enough can be known about their backgrounds of experience and the nature of their growth patterns. There are common developmental tasks for children who often need the guidance of the teacher to help them secure rich experiences to facilitate growth.

Physical, emotional, mental, and social growth all take place at the same time. Each child is unique in his physical, emotional, mental, and social characteristics, and no two children get the same results from an experience.

Learning is a complex process. There are many factors in child growth operating interdependently to affect learning: previous experience, permanent mental sets or attitudes, temporary emotional reactions, motives or goals, the nature of the task, methods of work, physical condition, expectation of reward or punishment, culture patterns of the group, and many others. Learning may be called a change in behavior which results from experience. Teachers try to bring about changes in behavior in school in such a way as to bring corresponding changes in life outside the school.

The study of the social relationships of the child in his group, together with information about home and community behavior and conditions, health and physical fitness, and educational history, is very helpful to the teacher in planning educational experiences to meet the needs of the child and providing guidance for the pupils who do not adjust to the group. The use of records of the teacher's observations, anecdotal records, interviews with parents and children, consultation with other professional people, and sociograms for some class activities are helpful in understanding the interaction between the child and his environment. The successful teacher understands these techniques and makes use of them.

Selected references

ANDERSON, JOHN E. *The Psychology of Development and Personal Adjustment.* New York: Henry Holt & Co., 1951. Chaps. iii, v, vi, vii, viii, xi, xii, xiv.

Physical, mental, emotional, and social development and learning skills, problem solving, and emotional control are discussed.

BECK, ROBERT H., COOK, WALTER W., and KEARNEY, NOLAN C. *Curriculum in the Modern Elementary School.* Englewood Cliffs, N.J.: Prentice-Hall, Inc., 1953. Chaps. ii, iii, and ix.

Individual differences, motivation, child needs, and principles of learning are outlined.

BUHLER, CHARLOTTE, *et al. Childhood Problems and the Teacher.* New York: Henry Holt & Co., 1952. Chaps. viii, ix, and xii.
Studying and working with individual children and working with parents.

BURTON, WILLIAM H. *The Guidance of Learning Activities* (2d ed.). New York: Appleton-Century-Crofts, Inc., 1952. Parts I and II.
Good explanation of learning as experiencing, group and individual learning, backgrounds of learning, and goals and outcomes.

CRONBACH, LEE J. *Educational Psychology.* New York: Harcourt, Brace & Co., 1954. Chaps. iv, ix–xiv.
Development and satisfaction of needs, learning concepts and principles, transfer of learning, developing attitudes and skills, retention of learning, and nature of goals.

ENGLISH, HORACE B. *Child Psychology.* New York: Henry Holt & Co., 1951. Chaps. ii, xiv, xv, and xvi especially.
The study of children, their social behavior and growth of personality.

GESELL, ARNOLD, and ILG, FRANCES L. *The Child from Five to Ten.* New York: Harper & Bros., 1946. Chaps. vi–x especially.
Behavior of the child from ages 6 to 10 and his maturity traits.

HERRICK, VIRGIL E., *et al. The Elementary School.* Englewood Cliffs, N.J.: Prentice-Hall, Inc., 1956. Chap. v.
Meaning and nature of child growth, development, and learning.

HILDRETH, GERTRUDE. *Child Growth Through Education.* New York: The Ronald Press Co., 1948. Chaps. iii and iv.
Trend toward unified learning and psychological foundations of unified learning.

JERSILD, ARTHUR T. *Child Psychology* (4th ed.). Englewood Cliffs, N.J.: Prentice-Hall, Inc., 1954. Chaps. iii, v–xiv, xvi.
Characteristics of development and learning—motor, social, emotional, and mental; children's interests.

MARTIN, WILLIAM E., and STENDLER, CELIA BURNS. *Child Development and the Process of Growing Up in Society.* New York: Harcourt, Brace & Co., 1953. Chaps. ii–iv, especially.
Principles of child growth and development and individual differences in children.

MILLARD, CECIL V. *Child Growth and Development in the Elementary School.* Boston: D. C. Heath & Co., 1951. Part II and chap. xv.

Growth, learning, and mental hygiene.

NATIONAL SOCIETY FOR THE STUDY OF EDUCATION. *Learning and Instruction,* Forty-ninth Yearbook. Chicago: University of Chicago Press, 1950. Part I, chaps. iii–viii.

How children learn information, concepts, generalizations, personal and social adjustment, and problem solving.

OLSON, WILLARD C. *Child Development.* Boston: D. C. Heath & Co., 1949. Chap. viii.

Human relations in the classroom, including use of sociometric techniques.

SMITH, HENRY P. *Psychology in Teaching.* Englewood Cliffs, N.J.: Prentice-Hall, Inc., 1954. Parts I and II.

Growth and development and learning of human beings.

THOMAS, R. MURRAY. *Ways of Teaching in Elementary Schools.* New York: Longmans, Green & Co., Inc., 1955. Chap. iv.

Human needs and motivation.

TORGERSON, THEODORE L. *Studying Children, Diagnostic and Remedial Procedures in Teaching.* New York: The Dryden Press, Inc., 1947. Chaps. ii–v.

Studying children, writing anecdotal records; interviewing; and observation methods.

WEBER, JULIA. *My Country School Diary.* New York: Harper & Bros., 1946. Chaps. i and ii.

Learning to know rural children and how they grow, written in diary form.

6

RURAL SCHOOL CURRICULUM

The curriculum of the modern school is an organization of educational experiences designed to supplement and reinforce the learning of the home and the community, to facilitate the continued growth of the children, and to help the people achieve better living. Because rural life is ever changing, the curriculum of the school must always be in a process of revision. New social and economic problems of the community provide new tensions and new learning for children, and these require changes in goals and in curriculum procedures.

To build a curriculum to meet the needs of children growing up in a changing community, teachers should have: (1) an intimate knowledge of the social and economic problems of the people and of community life; (2) an understanding of children, of their environment, and of how they learn; (3) a good working philosophy or beliefs about education; (4) a clear conception of the goals of education in the community; and (5) a knowledge of how to proceed to improve curriculum practices. Preceding chapters contain discussions of social and economic problems, community life, the rural environment of the child, and child growth and learning.

This chapter (1) provides some discussion of the effect of teacher beliefs upon curriculum procedures, (2) outlines some goals of education in rural areas, and (3) offers suggestions for improvement and organization of the curriculum for schools of rural areas.

How teacher beliefs affect the curriculum

What the teachers of a school believe about the education of children determines more than anything else what the nature of the curriculum will be. Modern teachers believe that children are in a process of growth and that it is the mission of the school to provide stimulating experiences which will continue that growth toward goals determined by the people and based upon the needs of individual children. Most teachers believe that the school is concerned with all of the growth needs of children—physical, mental, social, and emotional; that the school is a part of community life and that community problems are also school problems; and that the school can help improve the quality of life in the community.

But what teachers believe is not always reflected in what they do. Many teachers believe that schools should provide the guidance needed by children in the process of development, that the school should be a part of community living, and that the school should educate for democratic life, yet the way they work with children may not show instructional adaptation to the needs, abilities, and interests of individual children. They may organize educational tasks with little relation to the problems of the local area, and they may not provide real experiences in the classroom to help children learn the respective roles of leaders and followers in a democratic society. The mere verbal acceptance of a set of principles as an expression of the educational philosophy of the school does not provide a true working philosophy for the teacher. Only the teacher's behavior in the classroom, in faculty activities, and in the community can reflect her true philosophy of education. Some teachers could profit from a comparison of their stated beliefs with their behavior in the school and in the community.

Real changes in the curriculum can occur only as there are changes in the true working philosophy of the teachers. Revisions of courses of study which may be made by school administrators and supervisors and handed to the teacher will not bring the changes expected if those changes are at variance with the true beliefs of the teacher. Hence it is important that the teachers participate with the school officials and parents in planning the curriculum and in selecting the learning experiences. Such a selection and organization will be a reflection of the educational philosophy of the teachers, their associates, and the school patrons who help determine the nature of the goals and the procedures for the school. If the teacher has had a share in the planning, she is in a good position to carry out the plans in accordance with accepted beliefs as to what education should do for children. Also, if the teacher truly understands and accepts the child-development point of view, she will want to organize the curriculum to provide continuous growth and to meet the needs of the children. If her belief in democracy is genuine, she will practice democracy and lead the children to work together democratically. If she fully accepts the view that the school is part of the community life and responsible for improvement of the living of the people, she will make the educational experiences in the classroom real to the children. If she believes that parents have a stake in the school, she will be concerned with the goals of education which the people think are important.

Goals of education in rural areas

Teachers of one- and two-teacher schools in an area usually work together on a county or intermediate-unit basis and meet with school patrons to study the goals of education which are in keeping with local beliefs. In larger consolidated or reorganized school districts, the studies of the local community and of the needs of the people are often made within the school district. Certain of the goals of education in rural areas are the same as those of urban sections, but they often require different approaches to achievement in different environments.

The objectives of education for all schools have been stated many times and in many forms. The Educational Policies Commission of the National Education Association has provided a list of objectives stated in terms of the behavior expected of children. The White House Conference on Education,[1] composed of nearly 2,000 laymen and educators from all states and territories, was held in Washington in 1955 and formulated the following list of competencies which the schools should continue to develop:

1. The fundamental skills of communication—reading, writing, spelling as well as other elements of effective oral and written expression; the arithmetical and mathematical skills, including problem solving. While schools are doing the best job in their history in teaching these skills, continuous improvement is desirable and necessary.
2. Appreciation for our democratic heritage.
3. Civic rights and responsibilities and knowledge of American institutions.
4. Respect and appreciation for human values and for the beliefs of others.
5. Ability to think and evaluate constructively and creatively.
6. Effective work habits and self-discipline.
7. Social competency as a contributing member of his family and community.
8. Ethical behavior based on a sense of moral and spiritual values.
9. Intellectual curiosity and eagerness for life-long learning.
10. Esthetic appreciation and self-expression in the arts.
11. Physical and mental health.
12. Wise use of time, including constructive leisure pursuits.
13. Understanding of the physical world and man's relation to it as represented through basic knowledge of the sciences.
14. An awareness of our relationships with the world community.

[1] See Report of the White House Conference on Education, Washington, D.C., November 28–December 1, 1955, pp. 1 and 2.

Schools in rural areas have special goals or adaptations of goals for education. While studies of the local needs should be made in each area, it is helpful to examine some results of surveys of what rural people of the United States think about their schools and what rural leaders believe to be important goals of education.

In a survey[2] based on 321 replies from members of the Grange, the American Farm Bureau, Cooperative Councils, and the Farmers' Union, selected by the United States Department of Agriculture as representative of rural America, county farm leaders reported that they believe the schools should do better work in preparing their pupils in (1) conservation of natural resources, (2) individual and community health, (3) home and family life, (4) farmers' cooperatives, (5) community recreation, (6) political issues, and (7) sex education. Forty-six per cent of the leaders in agriculture believed that schools in small towns tend to overemphasize preparation for city life. They believe that rural youth needs a high school education as much as city youth does, and they have some opinions about what that high school education should be. Leaders in agriculture believe that the quality of teaching now is better than when they went to schools but that present-day teachers are not adequately prepared for the specific job in rural areas and that they do not take enough responsibility in community life, do not use community resources enough in teaching, and do not serve the rural community needs effectively. Seventy per cent of the leaders believe that the services of rural teachers should be utilized 12 months of the year, and 88 per cent believe that teachers should have the same right to express themselves on political and economic matters as other citizens in the community do.

Recommendations regarding the kind of education that leaders of rural life want were made in a series of conferences in eight regions, namely, the Northwest, South Atlantic, Midsouth, Great Lakes, North Atlantic, New England, Midwest,

[2] National Education Association, American Institute of Cooperation and Department of Rural Education, *Farm Leaders and Teachers Plan Together* (Washington, D.C.: The Association, 1947).

and Western and Rocky Mountain States. The recommendations as given in *Farm Leaders and Teachers Plan Together* contained statements from which we have derived the following list of goals:

1. *Understanding and practicing democracy and the American way of life* includes understanding in historical prospective the present functioning of farmers' movements for better social and economic welfare, cooperative enterprise, interdependence of labor, industry, and agriculture, and learning to live with minorities.

2. *Understanding the American economic system* covers problems of agriculture, business and labor, cooperatives, distribution of goods and services, and understanding of labor organizations and the farmer's relation to the industrial worker.

3. *Comprehension of interdependence of community, state, national, and international welfare* involves social, economic, and personal development, and security for all peoples.

4. *Improvement of agricultural production, processing, and marketing of farm products*

5. *Development of dignity of labor* involves giving work experience and teaching the idea that people cannot get something for nothing.

6. *Understanding and practicing the science and ethics in human relations* includes problems of understanding of and cooperation among special-interest groups; local, state, national, and international, training for membership in general farm organizations, cooperatives, and rural youth groups, and preparation for community living with closer relationships between village and country people.

7. *Development of human resources* includes development of talents, leadership, and cooperation.

8. *Conservation of natural resources*

9. *Development of basic skills* includes such skills as reading, speaking, writing, and arithmetic.

10. *Preparation for home and family life* includes sex education, home improvement, and parent-child relations and child care.

11. *Promotion of individual and community health* covers physical and mental health, safety, and sanitation.

12. *Improvement of community recreation* is for the development of skills and enjoyment through participation, and for the improvement of facilities for games, handicraft, reading, and similar activities.

13. *Provision of guidance for youth: vocational, educational and personal*

14. *Development of moral and spiritual values conducive to a higher type of citizenship*

15. *Enjoyment of fine arts and appreciation of cultural values of rural life*

Recommendations regarding the implementation of the above goals of rural education as given by representative village and farm leaders revealed much of value to those who would build the school program to meet the needs of rural people. These recommendations may be summarized as follows:[3]

1. Education is a continuous process throughout life; the home, the church, the school, and community organizations should cooperate to the fullest extent to continue education of youth beyond the school period and also make education available to all adults. All education cannot be crowded into the early years of the individual's life. Changing conditions require constant learning and relearning.

2. More work in schools should be devoted to the real problems of living, as is done in such organizations as 4-H Clubs and Future Farmers of America. More functional teaching of arithmetic, English, and the social studies comes from using the local environment.

3. Teachers and pupils should discuss controversial issues such as watershed control, operation of state and local governments, financing of schools, taxation, and political, national, and international problems.

4. Teachers in rural areas should be well paid, have adequate living conditions, be employed on a year-round basis, and have a thorough understanding of farm organizations, of work done on the farm and in farm homes, and of resources of the rural community available for teaching. Teachers should be judged by the same social standards as

[3] Adapted from *Farm Leaders and Teachers Plan Together,* National Education Association.

other people and be participating members of organizations.

5. Either through representative leaders or individually, farmers and village people should work closely with educators in making school curriculums and in determining school policies.

6. Rural school buildings should be available for meetings of community organizations and recreational activities. Their library services and other educational, social, and cultural activities centered at the school establishment should be made available to the public.

7. Closer relationships between farm and town children should be developed. Farm children should have equal opportunity with town children to participate in all school activities.

8. The rural people should be kept informed of the progress of the school through such channels as assemblies of people, the press, and the radio.

9. More research should be undertaken in determining the goals of the schools and how to implement them through better organization of the curriculum and better teaching methods.

10. The rural school curriculum should be designed to meet the needs both of those who remain on the farm and those who will work in cities.

11. The rural school should foster a high standard of living in the community. This involves helping the people secure an income adequate to their needs and developing a sense of values regarding the use of the income. Consumer education should be a part of the program.

12. Educational experiences should bring an expansion of vocational education, particularly in agriculture and homemaking and in the basic skills and understandings used in industry and business.

13. All education should be directed toward the preparation of the children for living, working, and playing together.

14. Education must be a proper blending of earning a living and living a life. Vocational, cultural, and social values and skills are learned through school and home activities. Understandings, appreciations, and skills should be developed.

15. Children should be taught to be self-sufficient and to recognize that labor is honorable. They must not think that the world owes them a living. They must realize that one's own freedom is a part of freedom for all, and that responsibility goes with rights and privileges.

16. The primary aim of rural education should be the development of good citizens. This involves a philosophy of living and a sense of values that lead to better social understanding and a keener sense of social responsibility. Education is not learning *what* to think but *how* to think.

17. Children should compete with their own best records rather than against each other. The main motivating force should be the goals of the group.

18. The school should give serious attention to assisting young people in becoming farm owners. Costs of farm operations are high and much study and planning is required in beginning farming operations.

19. Better state and federal aid to local education, reorganization of school districts to permit developing a more comprehensive school program, and tax reforms are means of implementing the rural educational program.

Teachers and laymen should study local needs for education and develop goals for their schools. The professional staff should then determine how they can proceed to organize experiences to achieve goals of education which they have helped formulate.

Curriculum changes

Most curriculum changes in American schools have been evolutionary rather than revolutionary. Many schools retain the subject organization while changing the content and procedures of the subjects, although some have combined subjects into broad fields, and some have developed an entirely new pattern. In spite of efforts by nearly all states to develop other patterns of organization, however, the prevailing pattern in schools appears to be subjects taught in isolation. Some elementary schools have developed broader subject areas through combining geography and history into social studies, and combining speaking, writing, reading, and listening into language arts. Some schools include new areas, such as conservation, in their programs. But the majority reflect the pattern of the subject organization.

In a process of curriculum revision, teachers usually start with the program as it is and study curriculum practices in the light of goals developed from an analysis of community life and of society at large. They utilize the results of research in child development to organize educational experiences which will be meaningful to the children. They study the needs of individual children and make adaptations in the program to meet these needs. They may change the framework of subjects but little at first while the approach and the content are being reorganized. They may find that greater flexibility in curriculum improvement can be achieved by using a longer class period organization and by feeling no compulsion about the retention of subject-matter lines. Eventually they may be teaching some subjects, such as reading, arithmetic, spelling, and handwriting, and organizing the rest of the program into experience units with purposes well defined. The pattern of the experience units provides the learning formerly covered as social studies, science, health, art, and possibly language. Or they may retain these subjects but introduce a flexible period into the school day with experience units covering a part of the learning found in the various subjects. The following is an example of a daily class schedule of a sixth-grade class where the teacher and pupils have followed the gradual approach to curriculum improvement.

9.00– 9.30	Reading
9.30–10.00	Arithmetic
10.00–10.15	Rest and recreation
10.15–12.00	Experience curriculum units
12.00– 1.00	Lunch
1.00– 1.30	Language laboratory
1.30– 2.00	Handwriting and spelling laboratory
2.00– 2.30	Fine arts and crafts
2.30– 2.45	Rest and recreation
2.45– 3.30	Committee work, story hour two days

Here the content material of history, geography, science, and health was organized under experience units so planned and balanced as to provide experience in all areas. A systematic reading program was being carried on to ensure controlled development of reading skills. Time for practice of the skills of arithmetic was provided in the program, but the experience units also included much arithmetic. In the experience units, activities involving speaking and writing were pursued by individuals and small groups and by the whole grade. The language laboratory was really a period for individual and small-group instruction, with instruction growing out of difficulties encountered in the units. Sometimes the language period and the story hour were devoted to creative writing. The spelling and handwriting laboratory period was closely related to the need for improvement of skills used in the experience units. Words encountered in the experience units were studied in the spelling period, development of handwriting and spelling being a single process much of the time.

Such a program of gradual change need not be haphazard if the program of experience units is well planned to give the important experiences needed by the children in development toward definite goals. Time devoted to broader experiences may be divided in such a way as to give opportunity for the children to have the experiences they need. But gradual changes may eventually lead to quite a different pattern of curriculum organization.

Patterns of curriculum organization

Patterns of organization of learning experiences may be classified as (1) subject curriculums, (2) broad-fields curriculums, (3) core curriculums, and (4) experience curriculums. What teachers and children do when working under the respective patterns may not always be greatly different. Under any of these patterns, children's differences in abilities and interests are considered; teacher-pupil planning is possible; and either subject-matter units or experience units are possible.

The *subject curriculum* is the most common type of organization, but it has been modified considerably from the practices of the past. Subject-matter headings are retained, but efforts are made to relate the instruction closely to the life of the students. Some of the subjects may even include experience units which do not stay within subject lines if information is needed from other sources. Generally this trend in instruction gradually changes in part to the use of broad fields which permit of greater flexibility.

A *broad-fields curriculum* attempts to fuse subjects or to integrate subjects, and sometimes the attempt has been confusing because of a lack of goals about which integration could be made. A broad-fields program can be as abstract and meaningless to children as the older subject curriculum was, or it can include an internal organization geared to specific goals. In both subject curriculums and broad-fields curriculums, attempts have been made to correlate the teaching of subjects or fields. Some years ago the teachers in a community in Iowa tried to correlate the subjects about corn. In science, the pupils studied how corn was grown and went to the cornfields to select seed corn. On the same days, the reading class read bulletins on corn; the language class wrote stories about corn; the history class studied corn history; the geography class studied regions where corn was produced, and the music lesson was a corn song. The experiment seemed to prove that this type of instructional organization is unnatural and impossible to carry on effectively.

The *core curriculum* is an attempt to organize educational experiences about common elements which make up good living in the community. Other terms for this curriculum are *common learnings, social living, basic living,* or *problems of living.* The form of organization of material into a core does not in itself guarantee real life learning. In the past, organization has been made about themes or principles as contrasted with subjects. In this respect, the curriculum differed little from that organized around broad fields or subjects as topics for learning. Some cores are organized about centers of interest and some are merely groups of subjects designed to provide learning needed by all people. Harup summarizes a core curriculum as follows:

1. The core consists of the common elements which make up good living in a democracy.
2. The core is the basic education of all children and youth. A large block of time is devoted daily to this phase of total school life.
3. The core is made up of a sequence of units of work selected with reference to the major areas of living, such as home life, economic life, citizenship, and the like.
4. The unit of work is a large ongoing experience having a purpose which pupils have accepted as their own.
5. The pupils have a part in deciding what they shall learn and in planning their work. Therefore, step by step, they are aware of the progress they are making toward achievement of the goal which they have set up.
6. The pupils have a wide variety of active, lifelike, and creative experiences. They have many outlets for self-expression and for the development of their special talents.
7. The pupils work together in groups and gather from time to time to share their findings with the rest of the class. All the pupils have an opportunity for leadership in large and small groups.
8. Information is drawn from all the conventional subjects as the need for it arises. The pupils have access to a variety of sources such as books, pamphlets, periodicals, informed persons, field trips, and films.
9. The pupils live in a cheerful and stimulating learning environment that is abundantly stocked with materials for active and lifelike learning.[4]

The term *experience curriculum* is applied by its exponents to an organization of the curriculum about the needs and interests of the pupils. It attempts to ensure learning that starts with the needs and interests of the learner and leads to solution of social problems and the development of social

[4] Used by permission from *Social Living in the Curriculum* by Henry Harup, p. 6. Copyright, 1952, by George Peabody College for Teachers, Nashville, Tenn.

values. Some exponents of this program would have decisions made in the classroom regarding the needs and interests of the learner. Yet such a proposal prevents advance planning by the teacher and makes it possible to omit significant aspects of development. The child sometimes has to be led by the teacher to discover his own *needs;* and *interests* may be developed by the skilful teacher through school activities.

The name of the curriculum organization does not in itself guarantee a better education. Curriculum improvement is reflected in changes in teacher-pupil relations and in the philosophy of education of the teaching force. Yet careful planning is needed, regardless of the pattern used, or teachers and pupils are likely to lose sight of goals to be achieved and mere activity becomes a substitute for purposeful learning.

Steps in curriculum planning

Many procedures have been used by local school faculties in studying and reorganizing the school curriculum. The following is a suggested procedure:

1. Study the community, its people, and its problems.
2. Define the goals of education with the cooperation of lay committees.
3. Develop a frame of reference for the staff, embodying a philosophy of education.
4. List the areas of living under which experience units are to be built.
5. Determine the sequence of experiences.
6. Develop a plan of procedure which may provide a gradual revision of the curriculum with only parts changed at any given time.
7. Plan experience units to be replanned with students.
8. Experiment with some of the experience units and evaluate the results.

Chapter 3 offers suggestions for the study of the community and the needs of the people for education. Goals of education may be prepared by committees of laymen and teachers and submitted to larger groups for study and discussion. The following frame of reference, developed by one local school faculty in a rural school, offers an illustration of what may be needed to arrive at common understandings as to the philosophy of education and modes of operation.

1. The school is the institution of the people, established by them for the education of youth. Since schools belong to the people, the school program cannot be far ahead of the wishes of the people, who must participate in defining the school purposes.

2. Education is rooted in the culture of the people and derives its purposes from that culture. A program destined for urban districts does not suit the rural community.

3. We accept the child-development approach to education. Each child is in process of development, and it is our mission to help him grow in understandings, attitudes, skills, and appreciations which in turn serve as a foundation for continued development.

4. Education should be provided for all children of all the people of the community.

5. We accept democracy as a way of life among people and realize that if it is to be learned, it must be practiced in the classroom, in all school affairs, and in the community.

6. The school is one of the educational institutions of the community. Cooperation with the home and other community institutions and organizations is essential to effective guidance of child development.

7. Life is constantly changing and the school curriculum should reflect those changes. To this end a continuous study of the community and of the curriculum must take place.

8. The child develops as a whole organism, and all aspects of his living should be the concern of the school.

9. Children differ in needs, interests, ability, and backgrounds of learning. Any good program of the school will help them meet those needs. The school will help correct deficiencies in out-of-school learning of the child.

10. The school curriculum is a series of educational experiences so organized and conducted as to provide continuous growth for each child in skills, understandings, attitudes, and appreciations required to solve his life problems and to develop social competence.

11. Curriculum development is a cooperative enterprise in which teachers, parents, and children should share responsibilities.

12. Continuous evaluation of outcomes of educational experiences should be involved in all aspects of the curriculum.

Differences of opinion exist regarding the organization of curriculum areas for lower, intermediate, and upper grades. Some would devote experiences in the lower grades to exploration of the immediate environment; in the intermediate grades, to the wider area such as state or nation; and in the upper grades, to world-wide relationships. Others believe that there are elements in the local environment which are complex and need study and in the wider world affairs which are simple enough for primary children to understand. Hanna, Potter, and Hagaman suggest that experience units be developed within a framework of basic functions of life to make certain that a year's work will provide a balance of experience in the various functions of living. They believe that almost all of the needs of individuals in our culture can be included under these headings:

1. Conserving human and natural resources
2. Producing, distributing, and consuming goods and services
3. Cooperating in social and civic action
4. Communicating
5. Transporting persons and commodities
6. Expressing and satisfying esthetic and spiritual impulses
7. Enjoying recreation
8. Earning and spending a living
9. Living in the home
10. Securing an education and extending knowledge[5]

These broad areas of living illustrate how a faculty may set up a framework and then develop a program of work units for each year so as to provide a well-balanced program. With proper planning, teachers need not neglect important learning areas.

[5] By permission from *Unit Teaching in the Elementary School* by Lavone Hanna, Gladys Potter, and Neva Hagaman, p. 77. Copyright, 1955, by Rinehart & Co., Inc., New York.

Some faculties have planned one series of units for the primary grades, a second series for grades 4, 5, and 6, and a third series for grades 7 and 8. The same unit may be developed in a simple fashion in the primary grades and used for more complex learning in the higher grades. For example, primary-grade children in one school studied housing with emphasis on homes for people and for animals. The intermediate-grade children worked on the materials used in building houses and the effect of climate on the type of house. At higher grade levels, deeper meanings were secured by a study of the costs of building the various types. In another primary grade the children studied "how we clothe ourselves," with emphasis on clothes for summer and for winter and styles of clothing used here and in other lands. Intermediate grades studied "how clothes keep us warm," which involved a study of such materials as wool and cotton, selection of clothing for the individual, and how to judge a good piece of cloth. Upper grades studied the shift from hand looms to factory production of clothing and world trade in clothing materials. Such gradation of experiences may be made on the basis of difficulty of comprehension.

Defining areas to be covered to reach objectives helps to give balance to the program, and an analysis of the difficulty of experiences in terms of the maturity of pupils provides a guide to sequence. Sequence is affected also by current needs of the learner. Much gradation that has been done is not based on research which reveals inherent difficulties in learning. If a child needs to use a word in writing in the fourth grade, he should learn how to spell that word in the fourth grade, even though his spelling book lists the word for the sixth grade. But the maturity of the children must always be considered. Attempts to teach children to write and spell before muscles and mental ability have developed may result in frustration; attempts to get children to solve problems before they have sufficient background can result in confusion. Work units of some kind should be organized in such a way as to give balance to the program within the defined curriculum areas and should be directed toward the goals of education graded to suit the backgrounds, interests, and needs of the children.

Developing units of work

Having defined the areas of the curriculum needed to achieve goals of learning, teachers become involved in planning units of work for the more specific divisions of the curriculum. Many teachers believe that not all instruction can or should be confined to work units. As illustrated in the class schedule on page 89, the class may have time for some reading which is not related to the work unit but is designed to bring a gradual growth in reading skills. However, there may also be reading as a part of the unit of work. Likewise, the class may have time for work in arithmetic and spelling which are not always a part of the unit of work, but the need for these separate activities to develop special skills grows out of the more complete work unit.

Work units are often organized either as subject matter units or as experience units. The subject matter unit is an organization based on relatedness of content while the experience unit includes an organization of such material as is needed to help children achieve purposes which are real to them.

In the experience unit, children are led to define their purposes, to list the questions they would like to have answered, and to seek the answers wherever they may be found, crossing subject-matter lines if necessary. There should be no crossing of subject-matter lines simply to drag in other content but only to achieve well-defined purposes. There is no merit in correlation or fusion of subject matter just for the sake of correlation or fusion; but there *is* merit in giving children a complete, unified experience which may sometimes require source material from several subjects in order to realize the purposes of the learner. The name of the unit does not always signify whether organization has been made about purposes which are real to the children or about similarity of subject matter. The difference is partly one of approach and procedure. In the experience unit, the procedure and content are governed by purposes.

Purposes of children in an experience unit may grow out of other learning situations. Any good learning situation stimulates children in many ways and offers other fields to be explored. However, the interest in exploration may not come from previous experiences. The teacher must then set the stage for learning through the approach she makes to the subject.

In planning a unit, purposes should be defined by the children under guidance of the teacher. A part of the plan includes a list of what the children already know and a list of information they would like to secure. This defines the area of work and helps to keep the work moving toward a realization of goals. Every interest awakened during the progress of the unit cannot be explored. Groups have to learn to stick to the subject. By-paths of interest can serve as avenues for individual exploration or group work at another time. For example, in a fifth-grade unit on homes, the children wanted to know about materials used in some home construction in the area and studied different kinds of lumber. This led to an interest in trees—an area which could not be explored without deviating from the plan developed by the teacher and pupils—and this interest helped set up some real purposes for the next unit, forestry.

Steps in developing an experience unit may be the following:

1. Selection of the unit. Selecting a unit will be in line with a pattern of experiences planned for the whole school under a design which has been agreed upon—a design based on achievement of goals for the school, with each level of experiences leading toward those remote goals. This design is based also on maturity levels common for the grade and known interests of the grade level. Children contribute toward this selection by expressing their interests, but the teacher must keep both current interests and eventual goals in mind in selecting and carrying forward the unit.

2. Pre-planning. Teachers need to anticipate the operation of the unit and plan carefully or the experience will not produce desired outcomes. This plan of the teacher should be in the form which best serves the needs. Many outlines as to what the plan should include have been made. Here is a suggested list:

   a. Definition of area and overview
   b. Objectives of the teacher—contribution to long-term goals
   c. Expected outcomes—skills, understandings, appreciations, and attitudes
   d. Anticipated purposes of the children
   e. Approach—how the unit will be introduced
   f. Anticipated questions and outline of content
   g. Sources—books, magazines, encyclopedias, visual and auditory aids, community resources in things and persons
   h. Necessary activities to complete the experience—field trips, committee work, individual research, help with reading to answer questions, outlining and preparing a report, discussions
   i. Provisions for continuous evaluation—checking progress against goals
   j. Culminating activities—summary, generalizations, applications, creative work, dramatization, and the like

3. Introducing the proposal to the children and planning with the children. The introduction should be developed to arouse interest and stimulate thinking. The approach may be in the form of a motion picture, a story, pictures in books, a child's account of a trip he has taken, or a discussion of a previous unit. Many adjustments may have to be made in the teacher's plan as children reveal what they want to know and where information may be found. Planning the activities with the children includes assignment of responsibilities to individuals or committees who may secure information and report it in class. Assignments should not always be made on the basis of who can best do the work; more often they should be based on the need of the individual for learning which is involved in the assignment. Of course any task the pupil undertakes must be within his range of ability, and he

may need help with it. The motivation of sharing in group planning will do much to help the individual in learning.

4. Execution of the work. Frequently pupils will need to get together to assess their progress, to revive their interest, and to keep their work within previously defined channels. The ability to work independently or in groups will obviously vary with individuals. The teacher must always keep in mind the purposes of the children and the ultimate goals of the learning.

5. Culminating activities. How the work is concluded will be affected by the learning which is expected to result from what is done and by the time likely to be consumed in the activity. Some units may stimulate children to prepare bulletins or exhibits or to write stories or letters. If learning is to be most effective, variety in the activities used to terminate the unit experiences is highly desirable. Summaries, generalizations, and applications of the knowledge acquired are included in all unit work. Sometimes new words have been learned and time is taken to review them and use them.

Experience units give practice in cooperative planning, problem solving, and a variety of individual skills. They may awaken new interests, and they can be so operated as to meet many of the social needs of the children. Because of a high degree of motivation, much learning can take place.

Desirable characteristics of an experience unit are as follows:

1. The unit must be of interest and socially significant to the children and important to them in their lives in the community. Mere passing fancy is not interest. The good unit presents a problem which is a challenge.

2. The unit should not only satisfy the needs of the learner but also contribute to the development of the learner toward achievement of many of the ultimate goals of education.

3. The nature of the unit must be appropriate to the maturity of the learner. Since the units considered are for

group action, not all children are equally ready for the experience, nor will all learnings be the same. However, a series of units should help all to grow toward the realization of ultimate goals. Background materials should be supplied for those pupils who are not equipped to derive full benefit from the experience.

4. The children should share in the planning, selection, execution, and evaluation of the unit.

5. A good experience unit provides practice of a multitude of individual and social skills in a natural setting. Individual skills, such as those involving the use of books and other resources, skimming to find answers, interviewing, outlining, and preparing reports, are involved. Learning to work together in groups involves defining a problem, using discussion techniques, and making decisons. The experience involves withholding decisions until research is completed and valid conclusions can be drawn.

6. The unit study requires thinking on the part of the students. It is not a mere physical activity. It is hard work which children are eager to do because the work is necessary to achieve their purposes. Clear thinking can bring correct learning.

7. Good units of experience bring out the relatedness of local, national, and international life and the fact that all aspects of local life are affected by national and international affairs.

8. Source materials should be determined by the purposes of the learner, by their suitability as to the level of understanding of the learner, and by their cost and the time required in using them. Textbooks, library and museum materials, community features and persons, and visual and auditory materials can be used as needed to answer questions involved in problem solving. Field trips may be required to get answers to some questions, but the field trip considered may require going a great distance, and the time and the cost will have to be weighed against the contributions to learning which can be secured as compared with the learning values found in a motion picture covering the same topic.

9. The teacher's objectives are those skills, attitudes, appreciations, and understandings which the community and the school are trying to get the children to achieve; pupil purposes are the things the children want to do. The teacher's objectives are not achieved by one experience, but the pupils' goals usually are. As children become more mature and approach adulthood, their purposes are likely to become similar to those of the teacher, but they will never be the same. Young children do not often realize that the object of a unit is to increase their ability to use individual skills or to develop social competence.

10. Good experience units result in generalizations which can be applied in other situations. Children will have no doubt about the facts they have learned, although they may not realize all of the changes which have taken place in themselves.

Resources for unit planning

Planning units of experience requires much time and effort, and the busy teacher will need the help of others in finding materials suited to the interests and maturity levels of the children. Many teachers plan a few such units each year and make adaptations from time to time for each group. Some teachers find resource units available for their use.

Resource units are collections of suggested instructional materials and activities or sources of material and activities organized about such topics as water and soil conservation, family life, and health. Resource units have been built by teachers, librarians, state departments of education, and colleges and universities. Librarians frequently help the teachers by assembling lists of books, pamphlets, visual aids, and community resources suitable for given units. Community surveys will reveal much of value, and for some experiences local people can serve as sources of information. Teachers in small school districts should make use of county libraries, county historical societies, and county officials.

Many resources for education can be found in the school itself. One resource unit which dealt with improving the classroom gave the pupils an opportunity for planning and working cooperatively as well as a chance to do creative work in art. Another unit in a one-teacher school dealt with the landscaping of the school grounds and used materials brought from the woods of the farm homes. A unit on nutrition and school lunches included using the resources in the homes, and the grocery stores, and having the help of the home demonstrator of the Agricultural Extension Service. The school garden offers a fine stimulation for study and the use of the resources of the community for learning. In one small school where older children were helping care for younger ones, it was suggested that the older pupils study child care, including health, feeding, games, and stories to tell.

Teachers can find many resources for education available in the community. A teacher tells the story[6] of how the pupils in a one-teacher school discovered that many of them were using different kinds of paper and ink and wanted a store that could supply paper and ink of uniform character. Since the school was located in an area served by four cooperative associations, they asked if they could establish a store of their own. Committees were selected to interview officials of the Rural Electrification Association, Farmers' Cooperative Creamery, Farmers' Telephone Company, and the Cooperative Oil Company. The findings were discussed and the principles of cooperatives listed. From the encyclopedia the children learned that cooperatives were first established in Norway, Sweden, Finland, Denmark, and Great Britain. They adopted the principles of the Rochdale pioneers of England as their guide and set up secondary principles of a cooperative store. They secured information about laws and regulations governing cooperative businesses; drew up articles of incorporation; selected a name and a place for the store; decided on period of operation, capital stock, number of shareholders, and par

[6] Leone Davison, "Consumers Cooperative of Centerville" in *Progressive Education*, XVIX (April, 1942).

value of each share; and secured signers for shares of stock. A board of directors was chosen and decisions were made regarding the duties, salaries, and qualifications of a clerk and a manager. The Board of Directors met with the manager and made out the first order for goods: tablets, pencils, erasers, crayolas, note paper, notebooks, pens, paper towels, soap, and cough drops. Display shelves and counters were arranged and account books were set up. The children learned how to keep accounts, check invoices, and make out sales slips and price labels to be fastened on goods. It was the children's store, but after the grand opening the store drew customers not only from their own school but also from neighboring schools. The store operated for eight months and made a profit of $22.00. After paying three per cent interest on shares, the children set aside $4.00 to begin next year's store and $6.00 for an educational fund and distributed $12.00 to customers as dividends. The educational fund was used for an excursion. The store served as a stimulus for compositions in language, furnished problems for arithmetic, and added to the group skill of working together.

In one community a survey was undertaken to learn what resources were available regarding health, homes, people, farms, factories, art, music, recreation, religion, safety, organizations, agriculture, transportation, and community events. The data secured were classified and used in a handbook for teachers and students to aid them in finding sources for learning.

The experiences in the school camp can often be used to give the pupils a better understanding of many of the subjects studied in the classroom.

Summary

The curriculum of the school in rural areas is an organization of educational experiences designed to supplement the learning of the home and the community, to facilitate the continued growth of the children, and to help the pupils achieve better living.

The ultimate goals of elementary and secondary education are the same. Educational experiences at both levels are designed to meet the immediate needs of children at their various age levels and to continue development toward the ultimate goals of education. The goals define the scope of education, but teachers need to organize learning activities in sequence from simple to complex, placing at each grade level those experiences which are in keeping with the maturity and special immediate needs of the learner. For many teachers, the organization of these experiences presents a difficult problem, and they are sometimes uncertain as to how to affect changes.

Most changes made in the school curriculums have come about through revision over a period of time. The new patterns developed are classified as subject curriculums, broad-fields curriculums, core curriculums, and experience curriculums. Units developed within the curriculums are organized about the purposes of education and the goal of the unit.

In order to build a curriculum, teachers should have a knowledge of the social and economic problems of the people, an understanding of children and how they learn, a good philosophy of education, and a clear conception of the goals of education.

Resources for learning are to be found in abundance in the school, in the homes, and in the community. Books, magazines, newspapers, pamphlets, and other publications furnish documentary material. Many uses can be made of visual and auditory aids to learning in such forms as motion pictures, slides, film strips, records, transcriptions, charts, maps, globes, radio and television programs, still pictures, museum specimens, and objects brought to the classrooms. People can be invited to the school to give information on agriculture, science, business, and local history. Committees or individuals can go into the community to get information through interviews and well-organized field trips, and school camping experiences can be used to help children gain better understanding of the problems studied in school.

Selected references

AMERICAN ASSOCIATION OF SCHOOL ADMINISTRATORS. *American School Curriculum.* Washington, D.C.: The Association, 1953. Chaps. iii, v, and vii.

Organizing the curriculum, approaches to curriculum improvement and aids to instruction.

ASSOCIATION FOR SUPERVISION AND CURRICULUM DEVELOPMENT. Washington, D.C.: The Association, 1951. Chap. iii.

Ways of initiating curriculum changes, cooperation of parents, pupils and teachers in planning.

BATHURST, EFFIE G. "Where Children Live Affects the Curriculum." *Bulletin No. 7,* Office of Education, Federal Security Agency. Washington, D.C.: United States Government Printing Office, 1950.

Story of how the curriculum is built to meet the needs of rural communities.

BATHURST, EFFIE G., and FRANSETH, JANE. "Modern Ways in One and Two-Teacher Schools." *Bulletin No. 18,* Office of Education, Federal Security Agency. Washington, D.C.: United States Government Printing Office, 1951.

Organizing the school program, group planning, deciding what to teach and teacher-pupil planning.

BECK, ROBERT H., COOK, WALTER W., and KEARNEY, NOLAN C. *Curriculum in the Elementary School.* Englewood Cliffs, N.J.: Prentice-Hall, Inc., 1953. Chap. xiii.

The use of units of work in teaching; suggestive units and criteria of units.

BURTON, WILLIAM H. *The Guidance of Learning Activities* (2d ed.). New York: Appleton-Century-Crofts, Inc., 1952. Chaps. ix, xii, xiii.

Emphasis on purposes in learning and planning and developing units of work.

CLAPP, ELSIE RIPLEY. *The Use of Resources in Education.* New York: Harper & Bros., 1952.

The story of discovery and use of community resources in two rural schools, one in Kentucky and one in West Virginia.

DAWSON, HOWARD A., and BUTTERWORTH, JULIAN E. *The Modern Rural School.* New York: McGraw-Hill Book Co., Inc., 1952. Chap. vi.

Defining, classifying, and cataloging resources.

HANNA, LAVONE A., POTTER, GLADYS L., and HAGAMAN, NEVA. *Unit Teaching in the Elementary School.* New York: Rinehart & Co., 1955. Parts I, II, and III.

Framework for unit selection; developing units of work; resource units; and developing research skills.

HARUP, HENRY. *Social Living in the Curriculum.* Nashville: Division of Surveys and Field Services, George Peabody College for Teachers, 1952. Chaps. i–ix.

Descriptions and illustrations of unit and core program.

KEARNEY, NOLAN C. *Elementary School Objectives.* New York: Russell Sage Foundation, 1953.

Recommended goals of achievement for primary, intermediate and upper grade periods.

MACOMBER, FREEMAN GLENN. *Principles of Teaching in the Elementary School.* New York: American Book Co., 1954. Chaps. iii–vi.

Concept of experience unit; selecting and planning experience units.

OLSEN, EDGAR, *et al. School and Community* (2d ed.). Englewood Cliffs, N.J.: Prentice-Hall, Inc., 1954. Pp. 34–42, chaps. vi, vii, and xiii.

Principles of using community resources; materials and people as resources; and cataloging community resources.

RAGAN, WILLIAM. *Modern Elementary Curriculum.* New York: The Dryden Press, Inc., 1953. Chaps. iv and v.

Educational objectives and organization of the curriculum.

RICHMOND, LUCILLE McGRAW, and BATHURST, EFFIE G. "Colloden Improves Its Curriculum," *Bulletin No. 2,* Office of Education, Federal Security Agency. Washington, D.C.: United States Government Printing Office, 1951.

The process by which one school improves the curriculum.

SANDS, LESTER B. *Audio-Visual Procedures in Teaching.* New York: The Ronald Press Co., 1956.

Resources to use in curriculum development and teaching.

STRATEMEYER, FLORENCE, *et al. Developing a Curriculum for Modern Living.* New York: Teachers College, Columbia University, 1947. Chaps. vi, vii, viii.

How groups of children, the whole school, and the community can work together for curriculum improvement.

7

DEVELOPING LANGUAGE ABILITIES

Changes in farm and village life have produced conditions which reflect a great need for proficiency in listening, speaking, reading, and writing on the part of boys and girls growing up in rural areas. The need for rural people to take an active part in our economic, social, and political affairs is apparent to all. The economic welfare of people outside the large cities is now closely related to the nation's political life. The interdependence of urban and city people necessitates the preparation of all groups to work together in the solution of problems of living. These problems are world-wide in scope, and the use of democratic techniques in the study and solution of them requires proficiency in reading and fluency in communication. Farm and village people who were quite self-sufficient under the horse-and-buggy economy are sometimes confused by the complexity of today's social and economic conditions and fail to recognize the interrelationships which exist between the income of farmers, the income of urban workers, and world market conditions. The solution of complex economic and social problems involves reading, studying, sharing viewpoints, and attacking problems unitedly to achieve the common welfare of both rural and urban people.

Intelligent and effective leadership in rural areas, so much needed today, tends to emerge through the group activities made possible by a truly functional language program. The 4-H Clubs and similar groups recognize the value of language facility by providing training in public speaking as part of their program. Proficiency in the use of language is needed by rural boys and girls in their frequent contacts with urban youth.

The need to have the people of the local community function as a democratic unit underscores the importance of language development in the school. The goals set up for group achievement can be reached only if individuals have freedom of expression and facility in making their views known to other members of the group. Citizens of a democracy are loyal to the processes of free discussion, free criticism, and group decision making. They want freedom of speech and press. They respect the opinions of others and defend the right of all to express themselves. The good citizen believes in the worth of his fellow men and the part which each can play in the group process; he believes in seeking the truth and learning scientific methods of finding the best solutions to problems. The skills used in group processes are not inherited nor do they develop effectively by accident; they must be learned.

Language skills are needed also to permit full development of personality and to insure good mental health. Personality develops in the child along with his ability to share his thoughts with others and to form friendships with other children. Facility in expressing his ideas enables the child to win the approval of his associates, and such approval is essential to good mental health. Only the child who feels that he is wanted by his social group can be a truly happy and well-adjusted individual. Development of freedom of expression changes shyness to active participation, reticence to confidence, and aloofness to social competence.

There is some evidence that boys and girls on the farm have not been as well prepared to play an active role in local, state, and national affairs as their urban counterparts. Farm youth often have not had the opportunities of urban youth to develop their vocabularies or general language abilities. Studies which included the use of intelligence tests containing vocabulary items brought lower scores for farm children than for village and urban boys and girls.[1] On achievement tests involving skill in the use of language, farm youth generally gave evidence that their language experiences had not been as numerous as the language activities of children of nonfarm areas. Farm children who attended consolidated schools, where there are wider social contacts, were found to be superior to children in one-teacher schools on intelligence test scores. Kreitlow[2] found that farm children who attended graded schools excelled farm children in ungraded schools in an experiment involving letter writing. This seems to indicate that differences between urban and rural children are due more to language development than to natural intelligence. More group contacts outside the homes and the formation of larger school districts are improving the opportunities for language development of farm youth.

In developing the language program, teachers need to understand the nature of the early experiences of the children in their homes and in the community and to know the growth potentials of the individual pupils. They need to realize that language development is deeply rooted in the early experiences of infancy and childhood and that family and community speech patterns determine the children's modes of expression. A good language program begins with the child at his level of development and helps him grow in the ability to use speech and listening skills more effectively and ac-

[1] See "Rural Education III, Elementary Schools," Walter S. Monroe (ed.), *Encyclopedia of Educational Research* (New York: The Macmillan Co., 1950), pp. 1042–43.

[2] Burton W. Kreitlow, "A Study of the Teaching of Letter Writing in the Sixth Grade of Graded and Ungraded Rural Schools," unpublished Ph.D. Thesis, University of Minnesota, 1949.

quire the skills needed for effective reading and writing. Teachers also need to know the characteristics of a good language program and how the various language arts are inter-related and reinforce each other. It is necessary to recognize that some children, such as those who are bilingual, present special problems and need help, because for many of them the language program involves acquiring a new language.

Home influence on language

Language development for each child begins in the home where the child first expresses his needs and acquires his vocabulary and modes of expression as a part of family culture. The need for expression is deeply rooted in the biological structure of the human organism; the coos and cries of the infant are a part of his organic and social development.

In early infancy the child is developing control over the voice mechanism while the senses of touch, sight, and hearing are continuing to mature. As he continues his growth, he repeats the sounds he hears. He uses his cries to express himself, and he may invent a vocabulary of his own to make his wants known. He repeats the vocal symbols and words he hears, but they have no meaning for him until associations are established. If his mother holds up a doll and says *doll,* the child says *doll.* If the experience is repeated several times, he learns to associate the word *doll* with the object. The word has no meaning for the child until the correct association with the object is established.

Studies[3] have shown that the average child acquires a vocabulary of three words at one year of age, of 272 words at two years, of 896 words at three years, of 1,540 words at four years, of 2,072 words at five years, and of 2,562 words at six years. Seashore's research on vocabularies,[4] however, revealed that the first-grade child sometimes has a vocabulary of 24,000

[3] See *Encyclopedia of Educational Research,* "Child Development VIII, Language," pp. 165–71.

[4] R. H. Seashore, "How Many Words Do Children Know," *The Packet,* II (November, 1947), pp. 3–17.

words. These findings have been questioned by Dolch[5] and others, but it seems certain that the vocabulary of the six-year-old may be considerably more than 2,500 words. Some authorities even give the six-year-old child a vocabulary of about 7,000 words.

An understanding of how the young child acquires facility in the use of language through experience is especially important to the teacher who must provide the school experiences in the language work. The process of language learning of the pre-school years is continued in the school years: vocabularies and sentence structure are increased through experience in living. This gives meaning to words and establishes habits of expression.

Experience in the home provides the medium for language development, and the character of the language is determined by the culture pattern of the family. Whether the vocal symbols are in English or another language does not matter so long as they serve the child's purpose in making his wants known. The culture pattern of the family includes modes of expression as well as words. This pattern of communication, established in the developing process of the child, however, may not be the pattern accepted by his teacher or his classmates, the greater the difference of his early speech pattern from that of his larger environment, the greater the adjustment the child has to make to conform to his new social relationships when he enters school. The child of Mexican parents in an English-speaking community often has difficulty in adjustment. The child of parents who came from certain rural areas of the Deep South acquires modes of expression which are unlike those of the rural areas of Michigan.

The home provides the influences which bring vocabulary development and determine the early speech pattern of the children, and it may also provide the social atmosphere and experience in which language facility can increase. Children listen to their parent's directions, their answers to questions,

[5] See E. W. Dolch, "Implications of the Seashore Vocabulary Report," *Elementary English*, XXVI (November, 1949), pp. 407–10.

and their stories. Parents who spend much time in work and play with their children and encourage free conversation in a warm, friendly atmosphere contribute much to the language development of their children.

Since emotions play such an important part in language use, the emotional tone of the home is very important. Parents of stuttering children are often found to be perfectionists or worriers or people of a tense nature. Children from homes where there is little contact between parents and children are likely to show handicaps in language development. In studies of intermediate-grade children, the children in the highest third of the class in language achievement were found to come from homes where there was affection, security, and a good family atmosphere, while those from the lowest third of the class came from homes where the children were accustomed to being ordered about and were often prohibited from doing the things they wanted to do.

Community influence on language

The gangs and the adults of the community have significant influence on the language development of the child. The socioeconomic status of the family in the community has an important bearing on how the child is received by his peers and by older people. This acceptance or rejection has a strong influence on the child's emotional life, and emotional development and language development are closely related.

Families and communities differ with respect to cultural advantages for children. Children who grow up in highly cultured communities score higher on language tests than those from communities where reading and other cultural activities are more limited.

Mass media provide important influences in language development and other learning.[6] Parents have reported that listening to radio programs and watching TV programs gave children new ideas, helped them with their speech, gave

[6] Muriel Crosby, "Community Influences on Language Growth," *Elementary English*, XXX (January, 1953), pp. 34–41.

them something to talk about, provided a substitute for the mother's storytelling, improved the children's diction, increased their vocabularies, and helped the children with their spelling. However, more studies are needed to determine the total influence of radio and television programs on child development and to measure the real advantage from such programs. Some parents believe that televiewing interferes with reading, but some librarians report that television influences the character of the reading rather than the quantity. Programs on science or aviation are likely to bring an increase in demand for books dealing with those topics.

The extent to which the child has a share in community events will determine the impact of community functions on his language development. The good school fosters those relationships which provide significant opportunities for the use of language as well as providing opportunities for other important learnings.

Teacher influence on language

The teacher and the atmosphere of the school provide important influences on language development. The speech of the teacher is recognized as conditioning the language of the child. The child tends to be influenced by his age group, but the teacher's enunciation, articulation, sentence structure, and modes of expression can be very influential, especially with younger children. The teacher also plays a major role by setting the emotional tone of the school. A free, relaxed atmosphere is conducive to freedom of expression. The teacher influences the attitudes of children toward one another by her attitude toward them. Encouraging the efforts of children to speak or write causes them to work more promptly and effectively than verbal hurrying.

The classroom seating arrangement can facilitate socialization and language development. A seating arrangement which groups children so that they face one another will contribute to free discussion; the isolation of individuals interferes with group activity which involves the use of language.

Spaces for committee work, workrooms, or shops also contribute to the social process through which language development occurs.

Readiness for the language arts

All educational experiences involve the use of the language arts. The readiness for these activities depends on the maturation and learning of the child in the pre-school and kindergarten periods. The child who grew up in a home where parents play and work with him and talk with him has a great advantage over other children. If the members of the family take trips together and engage in many activities as a social unit, the child will reflect these experiences in the greater language facility so essential in developing a readiness for future language arts. Without that well-developed background, failure in early language experiences in school may result. Success in the initial stages of reading, speaking, and writing serves as a stimulus to continued development of the skills of communication. Parents should be helped to realize the value of building a background to ensure the child's early achievement.

Children are fortunate if their community has a kindergarten where guided learning and the correction of any inadequacies of their out-of-school experiences can take place. If there is no kindergarten, the teacher of the first grade will need more time to prepare children for the pre-primer program and for listening, speaking, and writing activities.

Ethyl Vandeberg[7] has given a fine description of kindergarten activities useful in preparing children for further learning in the language arts. The teacher builds up favorable attitudes toward reading and listening by reading interesting stories to the children. She may also invite the pupils from last year's kindergarten class to visit and read to the pupils from this year's class. Reading skills are not yet taught, but the desire to read is stimulated.

[7] Ethyl Vandeberg, "Readiness for Language Arts Begins in the Kindergarten," *Elementary English Journal,* LIII (April, 1953), pp. 447–53.

There are many good experiences which can be used to stimulate children's speech and build their vocabularies while enlarging and extending their concepts. Such experiences can include visiting museums, parks, farms, and stores; planting seeds and watching them grow; caring for birds and squirrels; experimenting with magnets and prisms; studying trees, leaves, and flowers; and collecting stones of different colors. Such activities develop group skills which will be used later in such school activities as cooperative planning, determining goals, discussing to clarify understanding, using dramatic play, and such creative work as dictating stories and poems.

Conceptual learning is facilitated by classifying objects into such categories as animals, food, and furniture. Spontaneity in speech is developed if the children are encouraged to utilize their experiences and their imagination in telling stories. Sentence sense is developed when the children are given a chance to complete sentences which the teacher begins. Playing games which involve listening to sounds develops auditory discrimination. Handling toys and kindergarten materials helps develop visual and tactual discrimination. Muscular skill and hand-eye coordination are developed through painting, drawing, modeling, paper cutting, and the like. This coordination is an essential factor of handwriting, just as the auditory and visual discrimination are essential to later activities in speaking and reading.

Language development program

The characteristics of a good language program presented here are applicable to all the language arts. Additional discussion is given in later chapters which deal with listening and speaking, spelling, handwriting, and reading.

1. The activities of life furnish the content of the language development program. Language has no content of its own. It is not a series of exercises in speaking, writing, or reading; one must speak, write, or read about something. As in the pre-school period, language growth takes place in the proc-

esses of living, and the whole school program provides the experience which stimulates communication. Science, health, and social studies can cover a multitude of real-life experiences which give occasion for the use of reading, discussing, reporting, writing, listening, and the like. This does not mean that English is to be taught incidentally. There should be periods of the day devoted to the improvement of the skills of reading, spelling, handwriting, and using language, but school activities provide the experiences about which children talk and write.

Studies have shown that too much of the language instruction has been a matter of doing exercises found in a workbook instead of using vital experiences so gripping that the child must express himself. Following the class session or activity when the pupil has a chance to talk or write, there should be time for evaluation and for treatment of his difficulties; but the practice which develops habits should occur in stimulating natural settings.

2. The program provides a balance of types of communication most frequently needed by children in everyday life. There are party situations calling for conversation and problem-solving activities which require cooperative planning, research, organizing and preparing reports, discussion and decision-making, and evaluation. The program includes letter writing, telephoning, writing for the newspaper, and other situations which provide full development of all language functions. Language is a social instrument and calls for learning in its natural setting—the situation appropriate to the type of expression.

3. Efforts are made to meet the needs of the children for personal and social adjustment. Children do not grow in communication ability without some changes in themselves. In planning work units, an effort should be made to appeal to the interests of the shy child, to help him make a contribution to group welfare, and to replace reticence with confidence. Needs of individual children for the practice of neglected skills should be included in program planning.

4. Potentialities and limitations of children are considered

in the program. Teachers must discover and develop the talents of the children for leadership, for creative writing, and the like. They can find something in which each child can meet with some measure of success.

Teachers should recognize unequal stages in maturation of the children and in their readiness for learning. When the group engages in an experience, all members will not reach the same level of achievement, but each child will increase usable skills and other learnings toward ultimate goals of development.

5. Teachers should think of the child as being in a process of development and attempt to provide the experiences which will improve his thinking, perfect his skills, and develop good attitudes and appreciations. The Commission on the English Curriculum of the National Council of Teachers of English has emphasized two basic principles of the language arts program: (1) development of language power as an integral part of the total pattern of the child's growth and (2) the need to develop language in the social situation in which it is used.

6. The language program should help develop social values. Through their activities the children develop an allegiance to friends, home, church, school, and community; they learn when it is appropriate to speak and when to listen; they develop a regard for the feelings of others; they learn the value of honesty and fair play.

7. Curiosity should be aroused and new interests developed which can be satisfied through reading, travel, radio listening, televiewing, motion pictures, and other channels. Learning should not be confined to the school nor cease with the formal school period of life.

8. Language arts should develop the skills and habits needed for effective study. Children learn to analyze a problem and to use source material to find answers. They learn to use the table of contents and the index of a book in the search for answers to questions. They learn to find information in encyclopedias and dictionaries. They secure practice

in reading factual material and in interpreting and organizing what they have read.

9. An understanding of self and of others should come from social interaction. The child should become sensitive to the feelings of others and know what is appropriate in the way of expression. Classroom experiences provide opportunities for individual choices in reading and for group sharing of the fruits of individual study. By this process the child gains a conception of his own worth and an appreciation of the worth of others.

10. Planning is needed to secure continuity of experiences in listening, speaking, reading, and writing. Vocabulary development is a continuous process, and skills learned will be used again and again in new situations. Letter writing is not learned through practice at any one time but through continued use during the school years, with gradual improvement in richness of expression, in sentence structure, and in expression of personality. Reading improves through a continuous program that builds up a reading vocabulary, more effective interpretation of what is read, and better skill in reading.

11. Correct usage is taught as needed to improve speaking and writing, but not in isolation from real speaking and writing situations. Studies of the teaching of grammar have revealed that grammar rules can be learned, yet composition ability fails to improve. Many believe that grammar instruction should not be given in the elementary school or, at least, given only to the brighter students. However, as children evaluate their speech and writing, they want to improve these skills and will try to develop generalizations to guide them. In such circumstances, grammar generalizations may be developed from concrete situations and can then be applied to other situations. However, modes of expression are habit patterns which are changed through listening to others, reading, and conscious effort. Habit patterns of speech are established through using language when the child has something to say or to write; they are not established by isolated drill on usage for six weeks. Grammar can be made

to function only if it is a definite part of the effort to improve one's speaking and writing. Teachers should realize that freedom of expression must be encouraged, not destroyed by constant efforts to correct the child's grammar. Children must really want to change before efforts to help them can be fruitful.

Teachers should realize that our language is constantly changing. Expressions which were formerly considered incorrect have become acceptable through current usage. In an article on changes in our language, Knode[8] explains that *propaganda* at one time meant "missionary work of a religious faith," that *clumsy* formerly meant "fingers numb with cold," and *clown* originally meant "peasant." He shows how *nice* has changed its former meaning of "silly" and *deck* no longer means "covering" or "ceiling." Even slang expressions sometimes become acceptable usage through popular use. The teacher should be concerned only with the major illiteracies and should not try to change local ways of expression unless they are grammatically wrong. A good dictionary will tell whether a word or a phrase is a colloquialism or slang.

Even the grammar rules cannot always be followed rigidly. The children may be told that inanimate objects do not *lie,* but they find they can say, "The book is lying on the table" and be correct. The grammar rule may say that inanimate objects do not possess, yet such phrases as *the sun's rays* and *the car's top* are heard frequently. The best plan for the teacher is to see that the children hear and use correct language and form habits of correct speech, without too much attention to rules which have many exceptions.

12. Language textbooks and workbooks are tools to aid the child in improvement of expression, but they should be only a part of the language program. They are sources of reference for the child to use when he wants to know the form of a written letter, how to improve his sentence structure, how to make an outline, and so on. Selected pages of

[8] William P. Knode, "There's No Freeze on Language," *Elementary English,* XXVIII (October, 1951), pp. 336–38 and 346.

the workbook can be used when the pupil makes errors and needs drill to establish better habits. The real program is the plan of balanced experiences in conversation, discussion, reporting, telephoning, and other activities used in the affairs of life. A basal series of readers is needed to insure continuous development of vocabulary and skills, but much additional reading should be provided in the unified school experiences.

Interrelationships of the language arts

Many language skills reinforce each other. A good speaking vocabulary is part of the necessary equipment of the child learning to read, although readiness for reading depends on other factors too. These are discussed later. The child's reading ability depends largely on his ability to organize ideas and express them. The child learns to interpret what he sees and hears, to relate new impressions to past experiences, to reorganize his conceptual thinking, and to react to the new experience. Reading merely substitutes meaningful printed symbols for the spoken symbols in the thought process.

Speaking, writing, reading, and listening have common elements, such as vocabulary, sentence structure, interpretations, and organization of thinking. There is a close relationship among these language arts and it takes many of the same functions to succeed in all of them. For example, spelling and handwriting are involved in written communication, so achievement in one affects the achievement in the other. However, each language function includes skills not used in other functions, so that proficiency in one function is no guarantee of success in another. Some children may write well but speak poorly, and again, some may be good readers but poor writers.

Specific instruction is needed in all situations where language is used. The pupils may learn to spell the words encountered in their reading but be unable to use the words correctly in sentences. They may improve their handwriting skills through letter writing, but it is necessary to stress the quality of their expression. Some children may get the meaning of a story by reading it silently but fail to listen carefully when a story is read aloud. Each language function should have much practice in natural settings to ensure maximum development.

Problem of bilingual children

Bilingualism in an individual is his use of two languages. In many rural areas of the United States, some children learn English outside the home while using another language with his parents and their friends at home. These children create problems for the teacher when they enter school, since their use of English is often deficient for their age group.

The problem seems to vary with the individual, with the manner in which the two languages have been acquired, with the social status of the child's family in the community, and with the child's acceptance by his peers. Simultaneous development of facility in two languages usually results in better readiness for the school experiences. Learning one language in the home and using English only rarely outside the home may cause emotional disturbance when the child enters school. The child does not have enough proficiency in English to communicate easily with his classmates, and his social acceptance may be endangered. The teacher will have to exercise patience and tact in handling such children and helping them develop their use of English. The older the child before he learns his second language, the harder it is for him to master the second language and the more difficult the teacher's task. Special extracurricular instruction may be the remedy.

Authorities differ as to the advantage or disadvantage to the child of his pre-school knowledge of two languages, but there is no real proof for either claim. Bilingual children and monolingual children have achieved the same results on nonverbal test items on intelligence tests. Tests which are relatively free of cultural and linguistic bias, such as the new

Cooperative Inter-American Tests, may yield better measurements of intelligence. The separation of children for testing purposes into those who have learned two languages simultaneously and those who have learned a foreign language first and studied English later may give a better understanding of the relative values of each.

It seems to be certain that learning another language through experience without having any stigma attached to the language already used develops no emotional or mental strain in the children. In Istanbul twenty children seven years of age who spoke fifteen different languages attended a school in which only English was used. No formal method of English instruction was employed during the nine-month experiment. Simple English was used in the classroom, during lunch periods, and on the playground. At the end of the nine months the children were speaking English well at school and using their native tongue at home, but they gave no sign of any mental strain.[9]

Bilingual children in the intermediate grades can do as good work in the language arts as monolingual pupils. The background of the home has a great influence on the child's adjustment to the school experience. Children in families of Mexican ancestry or of poor means may not be fully accepted in the community and be handicapped in their development of the use of English. The teacher should endeavor to know the home background and learn whether the child speaks only one language at home and another outside the home or has had the advantage of hearing and using two languages in the home. Social acceptance may be encouraged by having the class study the history and customs of the nations from which the families have come. In some cases the parents can be encouraged to come to the school to show pictures, costumes of their native land, or art objects brought from their native country. The mothers may be invited to supply native dishes for a school party. The

[9] Paul Christopherson, "Bilingualism," An Inaugural Lecture (London: Metheun and Co., Ltd., 1948), p. 8.

children may be asked to demonstrate native dances or sing songs in the language. No child should be made to feel that his knowledge of another language besides English is anything but an asset. The more the other pupils can be shown about the culture of other peoples, the more tolerant will be their attitude toward any foreigners among them.

Much has been learned from research and teaching experience about the needs of the bilingual child and how he should be taught. Good teachers recognize that the child with a foreign cultural background is not inferior to others but is just different. He displays not only differences in language but also in interests and appreciations and in many cultural factors. Differences in customs and economic conditions of the family should be taken into consideration in working with the child. The needs of the bilingual child are the same as those of other children, and he wants to learn the same skills and understandings, but the manner of presentation may need to be different. The child with a two-language ability may make a substantial contribution to the learning of other children as a sharing of cultures takes place. An effort should be made by the teacher to help the child to gain social acceptance by his peers. A happy, wholesome classroom atmosphere in which the child can make use of experiences to facilitate language growth is important. The use of experience units of work allows flexibility in assignments and permits the child to work according to his interests and ability. Like any other children, bilinguists must experience progress to be happy, and to make progress they must be interested in the activities. Vocabulary growth should be stressed and expression encouraged in the use of English, but no stress should be given to grammar. Even the mastery of 500 most frequently used words will enable the child to start work in English without a serious handicap.

Teachers should recognize the importance of having the child feel that his native language is not inferior to English and that the school is merely trying to help him acquire proficiency in English. The sharing of some of his language skills with other children will sometimes develop his pride and gain the appreciation of his associates.

Some reports of language growth on the part of bilinguists show the value of the playground for language development during a period of active participation with other children in games and other activities.

The alert teacher will keep an eye on any bilingual children in her classes and watch their development carefully. Any report she may be able to make concerning their progress in English may·be valuable to educators.

Learning a second language in school

We are becoming conscious of the need of English-speaking people to extend their range of communication beyond the use of their own language. The ability to communicate with others in the community depends on the use of a common language which permits the people to share their thinking about social and economic problems. The ability to communicate with others in other countries requires the use of another language.

Some educators advocate teaching a second language as early in life as possible. Many schools now teach a foreign language to elementary school children, and in some places the instruction is begun as early as the kindergarten. Much of the instruction is at first incidental to learning about the manners and customs of the people of another country, and it is often included with a study of the history or the geography of a country. More systematic instruction is introduced gradually through experiences. Facility in speaking the language is developed, without the use of grammar or formal vocabulary lists. This follows the method we use in learning our own language.

The study of a foreign language enriches the study of all other subjects and contributes to better understanding of other peoples. Where foreign languages are to be taught will vary with the availability of language teachers and of adults in the community who speak other languages and are willing to help. Some schools are unable to include foreign languages in their courses because of lack of instructors, but this situation is being gradually improved.

European schools have taught several languages for many years. This has been necessary largely because of their proximity to neighbors of different nationalities. With modern transportation and communication, American people are now closer to Europe than Europeans were to one another a few decades ago. Moreover, the present position of the United States in world affairs demands that our citizens understand the peoples of other countries. Thousands from other countries visit this country each year, and increasing thousands of Americans travel and work in other countries. The extension of the means of communication with others has increasing importance today.

Some educators oppose the teaching of a second language in the elementary grades on the ground that all children do not have the same ability to acquire a foreign language; but that is true also of all other subjects. If the second language is taught through experiences similar to those through which the first language is learned, the work is no more difficult than the child's learning to speak English. Some teachers believe that the child's mind is like a sponge and can hold only so much learning, but we know that the human organism is capable of unlimited learning. With better methods of instruction, better understanding of how children learn, and better knowledge of the home and community background on the part of the teachers, pupils are now acquiring more skills and information than they did fifty years ago.

Most curriculums now have a place for the teaching of one or more foreign languages. The choice of the language to be learned may be the pupil's unless the school is limited in its ability to provide instruction in more than one other language. The methods formerly employed in teaching a foreign language are no longer used: the use of word lists with their English equivalents and rules of grammar to be learned. Instead, facility in the use of the second language develops spontaneously in the process of group living.

Summary

Rural people need facility in the use of English more now than at any previous time because of the closer contacts among people and the social and economic interdependence of all in the nation. The influences of the home and the community are important in determining early speech patterns. Experience units can be used in school to develop the use of English and broaden the vocabulary.

Teachers in the kindergarten and the first grade can help prepare the child for his later work in the language arts. The language program should be so organized that it gives the children practice in all social situations. There should be provision for both sequence and scope to ensure educational experiences which will develop all language-arts skills.

Bilingual children sometimes provide problems for the teacher. Some children develop use of two languages simultaneously in the home; some speak one language in the home and learn a little English outside the home. Still other children know only one foreign language before they enter school. Each child will need the special attention of the teacher in adjusting to the school and his classmates.

A second language is sometimes taught as part of the curriculum. The method of instruction should follow the process by which one learns his mother tongue.

The people of the United States are becoming increasingly aware of the importance of correct speech and the ability to talk and write well. World relations are making the ability to understand other languages a necessity.

Selected references

DAWSON, MILDRED A. *Teaching Language in the Grades.* Yonkers, N.Y.: World Book Co., 1951. Chaps. i–iv.

Emphasis on general function of language, sequence of development, and organization of the language arts program.

HATCHETT, ETHEL L., and HUGHES, DONALD H. *Teaching Language Arts in Elementary Schools.* New York: The Ronald Press Co., 1956. Chaps. i–iv, xiv, and xvi.

Treats nature and function of language learning, curriculum problems, teacher-pupil planning, and interrelationships of the various language arts.

HERRICK, VIRGIL E., and JACOBS, LELAND B. (eds.). *Children and the Language Arts.* Englewood Cliffs, N.J.: Prentice-Hall, Inc., 1955. Part I.

Gives the role of language in the elementary school, including trends, functions, growth, and development and learning.

NATIONAL COUNCIL OF TEACHERS OF ENGLISH, COMMISSION ON THE ENGLISH CURRICULUM. *Language Arts for Today's Children.* New York: Appleton-Century-Crofts, Inc., 1952. Chaps. i, ii, iii, xi, and xii.

Provides treatment of language needs of children, language development in children, a good language program, and cooperation of home and school.

NATIONAL COUNCIL OF TEACHERS OF ENGLISH, COMMISSION ON THE ENGLISH CURRICULUM. *The English Language Arts.* New York: Appleton-Century-Crofts, Inc., 1952. Chaps. i–v, viii, ix.

Deals with the purpose of teaching language arts, child growth in language, goals and experiences and curriculum.

ROJAS, PAULINE. "Reading Materials for Bilingual Children," *The Elementary School Journal*, XLVII (December, 1946), pp. 204–11.

A study of the vocabulary content of preprimers and primers in three standard series which are designed for English-speaking children, containing a vocabulary load too difficult for Spanish-speaking children, resulting in retardation of the children who are learning to become bilingual. Study of value to teachers of bilinguals and of English-speaking children learning a second language.

STRICKLAND, RUTH C. *The Language Arts in the Elementary School.* Boston: D. C. Heath & Co., 1951. Chaps. i–v and viii.

Discusses the function of language in behavior and thinking, relationship to other factors of growth, and language for exceptional children.

TIDYMAN, WILLARD F., and BUTTERFIELD, MARGUERITE. *Teaching the Language Arts.* New York: McGraw-Hill Book Co., Inc., 1951. Chaps. i–vi.

Discusses language programs, the functions, abilities, and skills needed, grading and sequence, planning a program with a class, units of work, and the place of language in the integrated program.

8

DEVELOPING LISTENING
AND SPEAKING ABILITIES

Improvement in the quality of living is facilitated by improvement of the skills used in communicating with people. Children learn these skills by direct observation and through their speaking, listening, and reading. Deficiency in any of these language skills places a definite limitation on the development of the individual. The sharing of life experiences through vocal and printed symbols has always been necessary to the progress of the human race.

Listening and speaking are two aspects of the same process: sharing the interpretations of events. People listen, and they react by speaking or using other means of communication. Few people talk to themselves, and when they do they are really carrying on a conversation with some imaginary person.

The listener must show some response to the speaker. This response may be only a change in facial expression or in posture. If the speech is to be a success, however, there are mutual responsibilities for both the speaker and the listener.

The speaker must present his material in an interesting manner and must use words which are within the comprehension of the listener. The listener, on his part, must give careful attention to what is being said and show his appreciation by unspoken reactions which stimulate the speaker.

The many activities of the school provide abundant opportunities for children to set up standards for speaker-audience situations in which the respective responsibilities of speaker and listener are clearly outlined. In the experience-unit type of work organization, children define their purposes and list questions which they would like to have answered; then individuals or committees seek the answers and report back to the group. Reporting calls for a speaker-audience situation. In the storytelling period, children read or tell interesting stories to each other, and again there is a speaker-audience situation. In oral reading the child reads something of interest to the audience and again there is an opportunity to emphasize the responsibilities of the listener as well as those of the reader. Conversations, discussions, excursions, club work, and giving directions, as for a game, all provide practice in development of the two-way process of speaking and listening. Radio broadcasting and telephoning are also used extensively in schools to develop these skills. But teachers must remember that an activity does not provide maximum learning unless there is planning in advance and evaluation afterward, at which time the children consider acceptable behavior on the part of both the speaker and the listener.

Learning to listen

In spite of the fact that people spend approximately 45 per cent of their time in listening and about 30 per cent in speaking, learning to listen is often a neglected area in the instructional program of the school. Of course, the amount of time which should be spent in learning a skill is not necessarily directly related to frequency of use of the skill, and abilities may develop without formal instruction. However, much more attention should be given to the function of listening than teachers have accorded it in the past.

Children listen a major part of the school day, and often teachers do not realize how much they themselves monopolize communication in the school. Wilt[1] reported a study in which 1,452 teachers in 42 states indicated how much of the time they believed the children listened during the school day. They gave an average of 74.3 minutes; but a check made by visiting 19 classrooms showed that children actually listened an average of 158 minutes per day, or 57.5 per cent of the time. Of the 1,452 teachers, 61.8 per cent believe that reading is more important than listening or speaking. If teachers talk much of the time, the children do get practice in hearing, but teachers who talk excessively are really developing bad listening habits in the children, since the pupils hear but do not listen because they have learned to expect the teacher to repeat many times.

Hearing is not listening, any more than saying words is reading. Both require that words recall the past experience of the listener. If the child hears familiar words, the listening process becomes a vicarious experience for him, altering his previous concepts and giving new meaning to his generalizations. Each child uses his past experience, mental set, and manner of thinking in listening and interpreting what he hears. The spoken symbols call for mental pictures and interpretation of those pictures in the light of past experience.

In certain respects, reading and listening are alike, but they are not identical. In reading, the child gets mental pictures from printed symbols. These mental pictures or ideas must then be organized and related to past experience to give meaning. In listening, the vocal symbols also recall mental pictures or ideas which must be related to past experience to give meaning. In reading a story, however, if a child misses an idea, he can turn back a page or two to get

<hr>

[1] Miriam Wilt, "A Study of Teacher Awareness of Listening as a Factor in Elementary Education," *Journal of Educational Research*, XLII (April, 1950), pp. 626–36.

the meaning; but in listening to a story being told, he cannot go back and thus may miss the meaning of the whole story. In both reading and listening, children think critically about what they read or hear and they can be taught to separate truth from falsehood and facts from propaganda. Both processes require careful concentration in order to get the main idea and related information.

The listening ability of primary children excels their reading ability. At the seventh-grade level and above, reading ability exceeds listening ability. This may be due in part to failure to teach children to listen as well as to read. Children can learn to improve their comprehension in listening just as they can in reading. Experiments with adults as well as with children reveal marked gains in comprehension from instruction in how to listen.

Instruction in listening must take into account the fact that there are many different life situations in which people listen and that each situation uses different skills and different degrees of voluntary effort. Some listening may be considered involuntary, as when one hears a bell ring or a book drop on the floor. This may even be distracting to other activities. Semiconscious listening or passive listening occurs when a person listens to music while reading a book. Such listening requires little effort. But there is more complete participation when the entire attention is given to the music or the book. The individual then shows evidence of more active emotional response or of enjoyment and appreciation. A still greater degree of participation on the part of the listener occurs in the socal situation in which he listens while engaged in conversation with someone. This is a function which needs to be emphasized as a courtesy and a necessary part of learning social behavior. Effort is sometimes required to eliminate distractions which interfere with desirable listening habits.

In voluntary listening, several factors help determine the degree of participation of the listener, so essential in the learning process. These factors include the following: (1) degree of motivation of the listener, how important what is being said may be to him; (2) distracting elements in the environment, such as other sounds, physical discomfort, or preoccupation with other tasks; (3) the nature of the habit patterns; (4) the difficulty of comprehension of what is being said; (5) the fluency, clearness, and rhythm of the speaker; (6) the listener's ability to hear; and (7) the maturity of the listener. When children are listening to directions on how to play a game or how to make a rabbit pen, they listen intently if they are really interested, other factors being equal. A teacher who gives directions to children about seeing the school nurse, on the other hand, can expect that some children will *hear* but not *listen*, especially if they are excited over the coming Christmas party or the unusual presence of a father or a mother. Some children have established habits of stopping current tasks to listen when the teacher speaks or when someone engages them in conversation; other children continue their activities without really listening to what is being said to them.

In listening, the willingness of the child to listen and his ability to comprehend depends upon his vocabulary and the vocabulary of the speaker. The words used should be within the child's realm of comprehension and the speech should have rhythm, clearness of enunciation, organized character, vividness of expression, and other like attributes.

Hearing ability is as important to listening as eyesight is to reading. Audiometer tests and more complete physical examinations may be needed to determine whether poor comprehension is due to hearing loss. Some evidence indicates that more than half of the so-called deafness in children is merely lack of attention.

Ability to listen varies with the maturity of the learner. Younger children have not established habit patterns of inhibiting impulses to respond to distracting elements, as is the case with more mature boys and girls. There is always competition for the attention of any individual, and younger children are more likely to respond to other stimuli or bodily distractions. With nursery school and kindergarten children, the length of attention is greatest in those activities which are originated by the children or which develop sponta-neously, as contrasted with those proposed by the teacher.

Studies of the relation of intelligence to listening ability show brighter children to have very slight advantages in listening ability, but correlations between scores on listening tests and intelligence quotients are found to be lower than between reading and intelligence. This may be due to em-phasis on reading and neglect of instruction in listening. Be-cause of the difficulty which some children have with read-ing, listening may be a better source of learning for average and slow children than reading is.[2]

Instruction to improve the listening ability and habits of children should include practice in the various life situations in which listening is used. The activities should include listening to music, drama, conversation, discussions, short talks, storytelling, and the like. Work-type listening requires careful listening in terms of purposes previously determined. If questions have been listed, the children listen to find an-swers to those questions. Some teachers make use of record-ings or transcriptions to develop listening skills and also to test listening ability.

In the kindergarten and the primary grades, there are many situations in which children listen to directions, stories, reports, music, and dramatic play. In fact, the major source of learning for such children is through listening. As children advance through the elementary school, the many activities of the school day afford opportunities for education in listen-ing. In addition to setting up standards for other activities, such as for oral reading, storytelling, or conversations, teachers and children should set up standards for listening and the children should be encouraged to make an effort to achieve those standards.

In elementary school classrooms, the children can play a game like the following to test their listening ability. Several children are selected to leave the room. The teacher tells the children remaining in the room a short story. Then one of the

[2] See James I. Brown, "The Measurement of Listening Ability," *School and Society*, LXXI (February, 1950), p. 70.

pupils outside, say George, is called back into the classroom, and Henry, who remained in the room, tells him the story. George then calls Alice, who is still outside, to come back in and he tells her the story. Alice calls in another child and repeats the story, and so on until all the children have returned and been told the story. The class then notes how much change has taken place in the story in the retellings.

In teaching children to listen, as in all language activities, the classroom atmosphere or "climate" is important. A free, relaxed atmosphere with the children at ease with one another and the teacher, freedom from distracting noises, comfortable, healthy bodies, and a comfortable classroom temperature are all essential to good listening and other aspects of communication.

As pointed out in Chapter 5, a purpose or goal is an aid to all learning, and that applies to listening comprehension. If the children are studying a unit on forestry and become interested in the uses of wood, a story with pictures on the making of plywood will hold their attention because they have a purpose in listening to it.

Radio and television programs

Instruction in listening should not be confined to the development of skills used in listening to reports, lectures, stories, and discussions but should include listening to radio and television programs. Much time is spent by both children and adults in watching television or listening to the radio. Radios have had extensive use in rural areas for many years, and recent evidence points to the growing popularity of television in farm homes. The United States Department of Commerce recently completed a census of TV sets in farm homes. Out of 4,782,395 farms counted, 1,699,162 had TV sets. Most of these farms were in the northern part of the country, where nearly 47 per cent of the farms had sets, whereas only 38 per cent of the farms in the West and 25 per cent in the South were so equipped. New Jersey, with 82.9 per cent of farms equipped with television sets, led all states, while only 7.6 per cent of Wyoming farms had sets. Special programs of concern to people in rural areas are being developed and broadcast over both radio and television. Some of the programs deal with the marketing of products, homemaking, and national and international aspects of rural life. These programs are very helpful to the pupils in their social studies, science, and other activities, and they can be used in the teaching of good listening habits.

Listening skills are needed if the pupils are to develop critical thinking about what they hear on the radio and television programs. Children need to be made aware of the influence of such mass media upon their tastes in music, drama, and humor. Criteria for evaluation of radio and television programs should be developed by the children under teacher guidance. Experience units on mass media are sometimes developed for study in school. Such units often include visits to radio and television stations and a study of how programs are produced. The pupils learn about the work of station managers, program directors, announcers, actors, and script-writers. Their own programs are sometimes developed by the children as a part of the unit. The chief measure of the value of such study is determined by the changes in the quality of the programs to which the children listen during their free time.

Broderick[3] has emphasized that the teacher must do more than interrupt a class to listen to a broadcast. The educational effectiveness of a radio program is determined by the preparation for the program and by what happens afterward. She suggests a number of activities which may be used in preparation for the broadcast:

1. Having students summarize what they know about the topic
2. Listing things the class wants to know about the topic
3. Looking at maps, specimens, models, or articles relating to the topic
4. Studying the broadcast manual and attempting to carry out its suggestions

[3] Gertrude G. Broderick, "Radio and Recording as Aids to Teaching," *School Life*, XXXIV (April, 1952).

Broderick suggests that the teacher note the pupils' reactions and any evidence of a need to clarify portions of the program. As follow-up activities, there may be discussions, visits to places suggested in the broadcast, supplemental reading, story writing, script writing, dramatic interpretation, and the organization of a broadcast or an assembly program.

In an account of a work unit on radio listening and appreciation,[4] the teacher's purposes are given as helping the children to understand, absorb, and react to programs, to keep in mind what is said, to grasp the main idea, to express in their own words what they have learned, and to be thoughtful, critical, and objective about the program. It was expected that the unit would stimulate wider reading, discover new interests, enable children to secure information, and serve as an incentive to the sharing of enjoyment. After a survey of favorite radio programs, five programs most popular with the children were scrutinized, discussed, and evaluated. A news reporter from the local station came to the classroom and talked to the children about broadcasting. Homework for the children included listening to a new program and giving an evaluation of it. The unit activities included reports on phases of radio study, such as Marconi's contribution, sound effects, radio terminology, and the like. The culminating activity of the unit was the construction of a radio program in which the children utilized the skills and information developed in the unit. The study brought a close integration of home activities in listening and awakened interest in critical evaluation of programs. It gave practice in language skills by the sharing of experience through discussion and letter writing, reading for information, reporting, and writing creatively in planning the program.

Some teachers have extended radio and television study to include such activities as evaluating music, drama, variety shows, quiz programs, and international broadcasts and writ-

4 See Muriel G. Jacobs, "Are You Listening?" *Elementary English*, XXVII (January, 1950), pp. 19–22.

ing a commercial, a commentary on a music concert, or a spot announcement. Differences in acting on the stage, in a movie, in television, and on radio programs may be studied, along with the functions of announcers. Some pupils have organized mock quiz programs; others have found special interests in the study of radio mechanics.

Radio and television programs undoubtedly do affect the vocabularies of children. The child who develops a large general vocabulary is likely to have the largest special vocabulary, such as that related to sports, movies, or radio. This probably enhances the child's status with his companions. While a large vocabulary is not the only factor in a child's popularity, it does affect his personality and is one of the factors associated with social competence.

Witty[5] reported a series of six annual studies of televiewing habits of children, parents, and teachers. In the six-year period he found a marked increase in the availability and use of television facilities. In 1955 elementary school children spent an average of 23.7 hours per week with television, as compared with an average of 17 hours for high-school students, 21.2 hours for parents, and 12.5 hours for teachers. For the average student it was not found that time spent in televiewing had any relation to intelligence or scholarship, except in the cases of excessive viewing of TV where scholarship seemed to be somewhat lowered. There were individual cases in which televiewing seemed to interfere with school work and others where the effect seemed to be that of a stimulus for children to do better work in school.

Teachers and parents are not well satisfied with the programs usually provided for children. Further studies need to be made of the extent to which television interferes with other worthwhile activities and its influence on child behavior. Considering the amount of time spent in televiewing, it is evident that schools need to include activities designed to develop critical evaluation. Teachers, school administra-

---

[5] Paul Witty, "Children and TV—A Sixth Report," *Elementary English*, XXXII (November, 1955), pp. 469–76.

tors, and parents should be concerned with attempts to induce producers and sponsors to improve the quality of television broadcasts.

Remedial treatment of difficulties

Some children have difficulty in listening, as in reading, and the teacher needs to diagnose the difficulties and provide remedial treatment. Few standard tests exist for use in the elementary school to determine the ability to listen and understand. The Brown-Carlson Listening Comprehension Test (World Book Company) is for use in grades nine through twelve. The teacher should be able to construct her own tests of listening comprehension. The test items may be based on a selection which the teacher reads to the children. This will measure the comprehension but it will not be a complete diagnosis of the difficulty, in all probability. In some schools there are fifteen-minute talks on which the pupils are tested for comprehension. Another device is to test the listening vocabulary with word lists. A detailed study of the child and his social acceptance in the group, as described in Chapter 5, may give further information for diagnosis and treatment.

Teachers as well as children can profit from a study of their own listening habits. A knowledge of how to improve her own listening and comprehension will prepare the teacher to help children listen well and comprehend what they hear.

Speech of the teacher

The effort to improve the speech of children may well begin with an examination of the speech of the teacher. The teacher may not know whether her voice is pleasant or unpleasant, loud or soft; but other people know. Does the teacher speak clearly and distinctly? Do children have to strain to hear? Does she pronounce words correctly and use good sentence structure? Is she cultivating the use of a rich vocabulary which stimulates the imagination of the children? Is she using a vocabulary which the children can understand?

Teachers use speech in all school activities to give information to the children, to lead discussions, to suggest procedures, to explain, to question, to answer questions, to summarize, to make assignments, to tell stories, and in many other teaching situations. Teachers reflect their thinking and their emotions through their words, tones of voice, bodily movements, facial expressions, and gestures. A good teacher tries to improve her own speech while guiding children through experiences designed to improve their speaking. Some very fine scholars are poor teachers because they have not learned the fine art of expression.

A teacher's leadership in community affairs is determined to a large extent by her speaking ability. In the community, the teacher should take a part in the activities of the people by planning and executing plans, studying community needs and problems, and organizing community events. Instruction in the school, which is close to the people, is related to improvement of the living conditions of the people. Working with people becomes increasingly effective as the teacher learns to share her thinking with others.

The teacher's ability to work with other members of the immediate school staff and in the teaching profession is largely determined by her acquisition of the skills used in discussing, reporting, and the like. Modern curriculum practices require much cooperative work among teachers, but this is difficult to achieve unless teachers free themselves of any emotional blockings to freedom in speech and practice the skills used in different speaking situations.

Sorrensen[6] gives valuable suggestions for the teacher in the improvement of posture and gesture as valuable means of communication of emotions and ideas. A study of his aids to voice and diction improvement and to oral reading will be helpful to the teacher.

[6] Fred S. Sorrensen, *Speech for the Teacher* (New York: The Ronald Press Co., 1952).

Speech program

Teachers who have developed good speaking voices will be in a good position to help children continue their development of speech in school. Beginning in the kindergarten, at the child's own level of development, teachers provide the activities through which development may continue through the grades to bring ease, enjoyment, and fluency in speaking.

While teachers use all of the activities of the school as motivation for speaking, they need to plan the speech program to provide practice in all speaking situations of life. A classification of situations in which children and adults use speech might be made under these headings:

A. Small group or individual face-to-face situations
    1. Conversation with family or friends
    2. Telephoning
    3. Giving directions to strangers or acquaintances
    4. Doing business, such as buying and selling, taking subscriptions, or collecting
    5. Answering the doorbell

B. Social group activities
    1. Conversation, as at parties or at the lunch table
    2. Introducing people to each other
    3. Receiving visitors at school or at home

C. Group work-type situations
    1. Cooperative planning
    2. Problem solving
    3. Discussions
    4. Reporting
    5. Giving short talks
    6. Explanations
    7. Giving directions for procedures
    8. Interviewing

D. Play and recreation
    1. Games—giving directions
    2. Dramatic play, puppetry
    3. Creative dramatics
    4. Telling stories, jokes, anecdotes
    5. Reading poetry

     6. Choral speaking
     7. Radio and television speaking

E. Assemblies and club meetings
     1. Introducing a speaker
     2. Presenting a gift
     3. Making a formal speech
     4. Extemporaneous speaking
     5. Conducting a discussion
     6. Using parliamentary procedure

F. Evaluation, diagnosis, and treatment of speech difficulties

It is obvious that such a list does not include all speaking situations and that circumstances determine the skills and values to be learned for each occasion; but the teacher needs to develop a plan to use the activities of the school and the community to give children practice in many situations. While there may be transfer of skills from one situation to another, the climate of the situation may differ in each case and there are special skills peculiar to conversations, to group discussions, to short talks, and the like. It will be recognized, too, that while beginnings are made by children in different types of situations in the kindergarten, there are some which are more appropriate for the intermediate and upper grades.

Giving practice in all speaking situations is important, but practice does not always lead to improvement. Usually the practice should be preceded by encouraging the children to set up standards of performance, and the practice should be followed by evaluation in terms of standards previously established.

Conversational English

From the standpoint of frequency of use, conversational English ranks highest among the speaking situations of life, and learning to converse involves more than understanding words. Courtesy, modesty, sincerity, and interest in other people are included. Children need to know when to talk, what it is appropriate to say, how to interrupt if necessary, how to shift the topic of conversation, and how to share viewpoints.

Activities of the school day often lead to situations which can be used to provide practice in conversational English. For example, in a sixth-grade classroom, the children had just completed an experience unit on the study of turkey production and held an exhibit of bulletins and charts showing the effect of types of feed on meat production and of other material which it was believed would be of interest to other children. As the unit was completed just before Thanksgiving, it was decided to have a Thanksgiving party and to invite the fifth-grade pupils to be their guests. At the party the exhibit would be discussed. Preparation for the party included making plans for entertainment and conversation. After some discussion, standards for a good conversation were set up by teacher and children as follows:

1. Talk about something of interest to the other person rather than of interest to ourselves.
2. Listen carefully and courteously to what the other person says. Avoid asking him to repeat.
3. Do not interrupt when the other person is speaking unless necessary and then apologize for the interruption.
4. Be tactful and kind. Shift conversation if it is likely to offend someone.
5. Avoid saying things that would be harmful to another's character or reputation.
6. Use good language.
7. Speak clearly and distinctly.
8. Try to make the other person feel at ease.
9. Avoid whispering in the presence of others.
10. Do not monopolize the conversation.
11. Include everyone in the group in the conversation by giving all a chance to talk.
12. Be courteous in disagreeing with others, and avoid arguments which cannot be kept on a pleasant level.

The children discussed what to do when two people begin talking at the same time, how and when to interrupt a conversation, and how to disagree with another person's statement. They emphasized that the good listener gives full attention to what is being said and shows interest by asking intelligent questions.

The fifth-grade teacher also worked with her class to prepare the children for the party. The two teachers had as objectives for the experience the development of skills used in conversation, including the value of having things to talk about, being enthusiastic in conversation, developing a pleasing vocabulary, talking without use of mannerisms, observing courtesies in conversation, knowing when to talk, being good listeners, and improving general speech. During the party, the teachers participated fully in the conversation and made mental notes of need for improvement but left the responsibility for refreshments and other activities to committees of children.

After the party each grade evaluated the experience by checking on standards previously developed. Each child wrote down some mistakes which he and others had made. In the discussion, Alice said, "When I talked to Mary, she kept pulling her hair." This led to a discussion of mannerisms which interfere with good conversation. The children reported that they had talked about games, pets, movies, books of common interest, and the activities of their grades. George said, "Henry certainly knows lots about automobiles, and he has pictures of all of the latest cars." The children discussed their pleasure in finding out about the interests of other children and mentioned several who spoke well and were interested in many things. Several new words which came up in conversations were written on the blackboard and studied.

Dora V. Smith gives the following guide to evaluating a conversation:

1. Was the conversation interesting to the listeners? to the conversers?
2. Were the conversers well informed?
3. Did they have worthwhile things to say?
4. Were the speakers courteous to one another?
5. Did each person in the group contribute something?
6. Did the pupils have words to express their ideas well?

7. Were the sentences clear-cut and forceful?
8. Did the audience listen attentively?[7]

Occasions on which the parents are invited to the school can give the children practice in conversation. The teacher should prepare the pupils for their roles as hosts. Some of the outcomes which have been emphasized as desirable are the following:

1. Respect for other's ideas and opinions
2. Consideration of others in the "give and take" of conversation
3. Importance of a pleasant speaking voice
4. Evaluation of the worth of ideas
5. Sense of responsibility for participation

Using the telephone

Communication by telephone is a frequent occurrence in the lives of children today. Recognizing that there are courtesies to be observed and correct methods of using the telephone, children often study telephoning as part of their study of communication.

One group of fifth-grade children decided they used the telephone so often that they needed to learn more about it. They started out by making a survey of the number of homes in the community that had telephones. After some instruction in the correct way to talk over the telephone, they were allowed to take turns in answering the telephone in the principal's office. The school made arrangements to have calls come in so that all the pupils had a chance to answer the telephone calls. Bathurst describes the study they made as follows:

The group discussed telephone courtesy and made a set of rules for themselves. Ordinarily, guidance in the use of the telephone would be provided for children younger than these fifth graders, but for this, their first experience in developing a project together, the pupils were encouraged in making the activity broad and varied.

[7] By permission from "Diagnosis of Difficulties in English" by Dora V. Smith, in *Educational Diagnosis*, Thirty-fourth Yearbook of the National Society for the Study of Education, p. 245. Copyright, 1935, Public School Publishing Company, Bloomington, Ill.

The community aspect of the children's experience came next. Several copies of the Cambridge telephone directory were brought to school and the sections of the book were studied—the classified section in the yellow pages, the main directory on white paper with names listed alphabetically, and the emergency numbers in the front of the book that every user should know without looking up. One girl explained the kind of long-distance calls provided; another explained the classes of service, such as private line, party line, business phone, and long-distance service. Telephone rules for users were mentioned.

Two of the pupils volunteered to visit the telephone company's offices with their parents who went to pay bills. In class the next day they reported what they had seen and answered questions.

One of the boys has become fascinated with the mechanism of the telephone. He has made a hobby of the collection of telephone parts. He brought to school and explained to the class a number of the telephone parts he had collected. One day the principal took him to the telephone office where he remained nearly half a day asking questions and sketching. His report in class the next day was especially interesting. The other pupils arranged to visit the telephone company's offices in three separate groups as the offices were too small to accommodate a visit from the entire class at once.

Following the visits to the offices, the class composed an invitation to the manager asking him to send a representative to the school to answer further questions. This visit was considered one of the high points of the study and the children wrote invitations asking their parents to come and hear the visitor, Robert F. Kah. As Mr. Kah answered questions, some of the ways in which a telephone helps a community were brought out. He showed a film on courtesies to be observed in business conversation. The group invited the sixth, seventh, and eighth grades to look at the film.

Throughout the study were opportunities for the children to learn facts about the history of the telephone. Mr. Kah added to what the boys and girls read about the history of the telephone and made interesting statements about the wide extent of telephone service in the world today.

Four of the children dramatized a play suggested to them by their textbook in English and elaborated on by the boys and girls. In this one pupil played the part of Rip Van Winkle visiting Cambridge today and asking about the new inventions, including the telephone as one of the most useful.

The telephone project afforded the children new experiences in reading. The teacher took care to guide individuals and small groups in locating books she knew they would like and be able to read. As they studied about the invention, development, and improvement of the telephone, the children made comparisons with the invention of other conveniences for better living, and with other events of importance. A boy reported that before Alexander Graham Bell's first crude telephone was patented in 1876, the United States had purchased the Louisiana Territory and the Territory of Alaska, and the war between the North and the South had occurred; that since the invention of the telephone, history has seen extension of its lines across the ocean, and the airplane, radio, and television have entered American life.

The invitations and letters that had to be written in the project made it necessary for the children to consult English books for punctuation and dictionaries for spelling. The costs of local, long-distance, and party-line telephone service were compared.[8]

Giving short talks and reports and telling stories

Success in giving short talks and reports depends upon (1) a high degree of motivation in the speaker, (2) an audience genuinely interested in what the speaker has to say, and (3) the speaker's ability to organize and deliver the speech in a pleasing and effective manner. The teacher will need to set the stage for a high degree of motivation unless she is able to capitalize on a situation already existing. If the motivation comes from within the group itself, the speaker is likely to have the highest degree of motivation.

In much of the cooperative planning now carried on in schools, children express a need for certain information. When individuals accept an assignment to get information for the group, the drive to get the data desired and to present them to the group in a clear and interesting fashion is very great.

Sometimes in adult clubs or societies, a speaker is invited to appear and address the club. The club has not defined its purposes, and the members may have no other plan than to provide social activities and are not seriously concerned about what the speaker has to say. Such academic interest is not likely to lead to any action on the part of the social group. Likewise, in school, teachers sometimes set up artificial situations for children and say, "We are going to have short talks for a few days. You may choose your own topics."

[8] Effie Bathurst, *How Children Use the Community for Learning* (Washington, D.C.: United States Department of Health, Education and Welfare, 1953), pp. 27–29.

Many children are not pleased with the prospect of appearing before the group and there is no real need or interest on the part of the children for the information which the speaker can furnish.

The experience-unit type of organization of learning activities can make children conscious of a need for information. Of course, interest can be aroused in talks which are not a part of an experience unit; but the stage often needs to be set for children to want to know about hobbies, for instance, or hear interesting stories from real life, or read certain books. Children are interested in those things which are close to their daily lives in school and outside the school and also in aspects of activities in which their curiosity has been aroused. Modern classroom activities give evidence of the interest of children in pets, family, people, games, transportation, nutrition, conservation, dress, and the like. The likes and dislikes of children, too, are influenced by the emotional aspects of past experience. Children of rural areas are interested in exploring both their immediate environment and the world beyond.

Children should work with the teacher to set up their own standards for reports, short talks, and stories. A group of children in one fifth-grade class set up these standards for their reports:

1. Make an outline of the topic.
2. Talk about one subtopic at a time. Tell all you know about that topic before going to the next.
3. In thinking about the report, try to make the beginning and the end especially interesting.
4. Use good sentences.
5. Speak clearly and distinctly and loud enough for all to hear.
6. Explain carefully so that all may understand. Act out parts if needed.
7. Know the information you want to give so well that few or no notes are needed.
8. Use maps and charts if needed.
9. Look at the audience when speaking.
10. Speak with enthusiasm and be alive all over.

Storytelling is one of the best ways to teach children to speak directly to an audience. Pupils always enjoy telling and hearing stories from direct personal experiences or from books which are rich in adventure and discovery. They learn by evaluating interesting stories which they hear and by noticing that a good story begins with something which gets the attention of the audience from the start and that the story flows along easily and builds up to a climax. In storytelling, details do not have to be exact in every respect. The child gives his own interpretation of the story, and he may even leave out unimportant details or substitute some of his own.

Elementary school children usually love hero stories, fables, Indian life stories, and those about animals. Children should be encouraged to read widely and to select from their reading newer modes of expression for the purposes of good retelling. Practice in storytelling can easily follow free reading activities if children have access to a rich variety of interesting stories.

Play acting and creative dramatics

Children love to act out character parts in the stories they read and in the experiences they have. In the home, children frequently play school, and at school or at home they love to play the parts of members of the family. They like to act out the parts of government officials, some serving as policemen, others as firemen, and others as the mayor and councilmen. Play acting has always been a part of child life, and the school can capitalize on this enjoyment by permitting children to relive parts of an excursion or to act out the characters in a story. This affords an opportunity for the child who is shy to imagine he is someone else and to act out the role of the character as interpreted by him. Such activities provide good emotional outlets for children, give the teacher a better opportunity to understand the children, and contribute much to freedom of expression by enriching vocabularies, improving sentence structure, and introducing naturalness and directness into speech.

For most of the dramatic activities, the parts should be portrayed impromptu and not memorized. Attempting to memorize the parts tends to destroy much of the value to be derived from dramatic play. The child who forgets what he has tried to memorize is embarrassed; furthermore, he needs the experience of standing and expressing his own thoughts. Imagination furnishes the only stage property for most dramatic play, which is usually carried on in the regular classroom with the teacher and fellow students as audience. Sometimes upper-grade children will not be satisfied without some costumes, but equipment and costumes should be reduced to a minimum consistent with the satisfaction of the group.

Attempts to improve the grammar of the children should not be made during the acting process. In the evaluation process after the acting is over, the teacher can refer to notes made during the play presentation and help the children improve their grammar, voice, and articulation.

Every child in the class must be given an opportunity to act in some dramatic experiences. The child who most needs help may be neglected and in fact is often better satisfied with a spectator role. If he is satisfied to remain on the sidelines, it is certain that he needs the experience of acting; parts should be found for him, even if these are nonspeaking parts at first.

Dramatization stimulates interest in reading and may lead to creative playwriting at higher grade levels. Simple stories such as Aesop's fables and "Little Red Riding Hood" can be used at lower grade levels. Besides the numerous stories available, there are many events in small communities which can be used for creative dramatic work. In Brookville, for instance, the people celebrated the one hundredth anniversary of the founding of the town. Children in the school helped by doing research on the history of the community and writing stories based on the history. This suggested some work in creative dramatics, with the children throughout the school portraying events in local history.

Puppetry is one form of expression of dramatic play or creative dramatics which children enjoy and which provides almost unlimited opportunities for speech development. It will often succeed in helping the self-conscious child when other techniques fail. Cooperative planning should precede the acting, with children and teacher making a list of the scenes and the character parts. The children will then be able to select the parts they wish to play. Stage crews and announcers should be chosen. Either hand puppets or marionettes controlled by strings may be used. Marionette heads can easily be made from modeling clay, and hand puppets can be constructed from paper bags, mittens, socks, or other material. Dividing the story into scenes and having new actors play the characters in each scene will give opportunity for all in the class to take part in the play. Sometimes the shows can be given before larger audiences in an assembly program, or it is sometimes a good plan to invite another class to the room to see a performance. Appearing before larger audiences helps develop the pupil's confidence. If marionettes are used, the fact that the children are out of sight of their audience often helps them overcome any stage fright which might develop in other forms of dramatic play.

Two other methods of dramatic interpretation are pantomime and shadow acting. In shadow acting, the children play their parts behind a translucent sheet or screen upon which their shadows are cast by a light placed behind the actors. Pantomime is well known to children, and they will need little instruction in the methods to be used.

These forms of dramatic interpretation help the child to focus attention on what he is saying rather than on himself. They help him speak as the character would speak, a phase of development which should be of assistance to the child in storytelling and other speaking activities. They lead to the use of natural gestures and facial expression as important aspects of the communication process. Children will work hard to achieve clear and distinct expression in order to play the character parts. Imagination and creative ability are stimulated by the various modes of dramatic interpretation, and these will be used more effectively in both speaking and writing situations as a result of practice in playing the roles of various characters. A greater appreciation of a good voice, careful articulation, clear enunciation, and a rich vocabulary is developed in children through listening to others and through their own acting.

Choral speaking

Teachers are making good use of choral speaking to help children with their articulation and tone quality, and their appreciation of good poetry. If the activity is properly handled, children will use their own ideas of interpretation and their enjoyment of poetry will be enhanced. Breaking up the verse into parts destroys the continuity of the poem, and the mere repetition of memorized poems can be very harmful.

Outcomes of choral speaking experiences for children are reported to be loss of self-consciousness, greater freedom of expression, improved enunciation, increased range and greater flexibility and control of voice, greater power of imagination, better sense of rhythm, better interpretation, and increased interest in poetry.

The librarian of either the school library or the town library can help the teacher find books and articles on methods of using choral speaking, with poems suitable for this activity.

Speech in work-type situations

The school program provides numerous opportunities for children to attack and solve problems. Skills needed for cooperative planning in a group are not the same as those used in other speaking situations. Each child presents his ideas and they are pooled with those of others in defining the problems and in outlining procedures. At times, finding the information requires an interview in which children use language as a means of getting the information needed. When material is brought back to the group, it needs to be sifted and discussed in an effort to weed out unimportant details.

Sometimes the discussion gives opportunities to share personal experiences, and at times an individual is forced to defend his point of view.

For teachers who want to know whether children are improving in group techniques, Blackwood gives the following characteristics of good group thinking:

1. The problem is clarified so that most of the children understand what is being discussed.

2. There is wide participation of children and their contributions are relevant to the understanding and solution of the problem. They stick to the point. The group does not depend upon just one or a few persons for all ideas.

3. New ideas and new problems are sifted out and put aside for discussion at another time if they don't relate to the question being considered.

4. Children insist on getting sufficient and accurate facts to use in thinking through a problem. They realize that many sound facts gained through first-hand experiences help in reaching sound conclusions.

5. The group draws on a variety of sources of information as a basis for thinking. This is important because some children may gain information and experience more readily from one kind of activity than from another type.

6. The members of the group are increasingly more conscious of checking on "cause and effect" relationships. They question "loose" explanations. It is an evidence of good thinking when children correctly foresee connections between things—when they can predict accurately.

7. There is willingness to explore a problem thoroughly before coming to a conclusion. The group does not rush to a conclusion nor does it permit its members to do so. The group is willing to suspend judgment.

8. Prejudices, superstitions, and personal biases do not unduly influence decisions. Children recognize the presence of such factors and take them into account as part of the "data" to be considered in reaching conclusions.

9. The decisions, conclusions, and suggestions arrived at by an individual or a group prove to be all right when carried out, applied, or tested in real life situations.

10. The children begin to generalize the principles of good thinking. There is evidence that basic patterns of good

thinking are present in a variety of situations, not just in classroom group discussion under the direction of a teacher.

11. Children evaluate their thinking processes. They check on whether they are applying the principles of good thinking to their individual and group problems. They are objective and honestly critical of how they have worked on a problem. They improve their thinking by taking into account the weaknesses they have observed.[9]

Since discussion techniques are used so frequently in the school and community and since they are such an integral part of the democratic process, teachers must be concerned with evaluation of the growth of children in this group process. Sherwood furnishes a list of questions which will be helpful to the classroom teacher in judging the growth of children in later elementary grades toward more effective discussion:

1. Does the discussion help to organize the thinking of the group upon the basis of a particular purpose?
2. Does the discussion encourage members of the group to participate freely?
3. Does the discussion help to stimulate group thinking through questions and comments made by different children in the group?
4. Does the discussion help to improve the children's ability to ask questions which stimulate the thinking of others in the group?
5. Does the discussion provide many opportunities to use various sources of information as children make individual contributions to the discussion?
6. Does the discussion thrive in an atmosphere in which children are permitted to make choices by examining alternatives in the light of the evidence which supports them and in the light of their probable consequences to the individual and to the group?
7. Does the discussion imply the wise use of written authorities as one basis for the children's thinking?

[9] Paul E. Blackwood, *How Children Learn to Think* (Washington, D.C.: 1953), United States Department of Health, Education and Welfare, pp. 16–17.

8. Does the discussion . . . become somewhat dependent upon a satisfactory physical setting?

9. Does the discussion use the technique of summarization at appropriate points which may facilitate further progress?

10. Does the discussion provide an invaluable situation in which the children's feelings can be directly related to behavior by serving as one technique in understanding the growth pattern of the child?

11. Does the discussion foster a feeling of security for children through participation in the group experience?

12. Does the discussion eventuate in growth in critical thinking for the children in the discussion group?

13. Does the discussion aid children in developing more effective personalities through their increased control over ideas?

14. Does the discussion provide opportunities for children to develop increasing insight into problems which have real meaning for them within their environment?

15. Does the discussion contribute to increasing the social sensitivity of the group?

16. Does the discussion help children in learning to give thoughtful attention to viewpoints other than one's own?

17. Does the discussion involve individual contributions to group judgments?

18. Does the discussion promote the critical individual self-evaluation and group evaluation of processes and results?

19. Does the discussion encourage improvements in speech habits so that contributions of the children can be clearly understood and are meaningful to the other members of the group?

20. Does discussion serve as an impetus in helping children to become more aware of quoting accurately from reference material?

21. Does the discussion help to satisfy children's needs for achievement?

22. Does the discussion utilize the significant role of the teacher to aid in the learning process?[10]

[10] By permission from "Guides to Discussion in the Middle Years," by Gladys Sherwood in *Elementary English*, XXIX (April, 1952), pp. 207–10.

Conducting meetings

School clubs, student councils, and other organizations frequently exist in elementary schools. These activities should be used to the maximum for teaching speech skills which are important in daily life and which cannot be developed in other situations. The roles of leader and members have to be learned in such real-life experiences, and meetings provide excellent opportunities for individuals to learn the skills needed by a group in arriving at decisions and getting business done.

If a speaker is brought in from outside to address a meeting, the students learn the technique of introducing a speaker to a group. When committees give reports, formal action is required to accept the report or to table it or to refer it back to the committee. *Robert's Rules of Order* is the standard guide for the correct procedure in conducting meetings, and a copy of the book should be made available to the pupils. Merely bringing the children together is not enough. Autocratic leadership, confusion, and frustration can result unless the children know what is expected of them and of the teacher, and what the correct procedure is.

There is probably no group in our society which suffers more from a lack of good democratic leadership and an ignorance of the niceties of parliamentary procedure than the people in rural areas. There is great need for development of the group skills and understanding needed in farm organizations and community affairs. At a meeting of the school board of a small community, one member said, after hours of sitting and some discussion, "I make a motion we hire Mr. James as superintendent." The chairman, who had observed his predecessor at work and had learned only a part of what to do, said, "All in favor say the same as I." He did not open the question for discussion nor put the question to a vote!

Not all decisions of a social group are made through strict use of parliamentary procedure, of course, but enough of the rules should be learned to expedite action. Strictly speaking, a main motion must be made and seconded before there is discussion of the question. That would apply in a formal business meeting. A modified procedure would include some discussion of the issue in an effort to get an expression of opinion as to the wishes of the group before the motion is made. Then a member says, "Mr. Chairman, I move that. . . ." This is the main motion, and it must be seconded before the question is open for discussion. After the motion has been seconded, the chairman says, "It has been moved and seconded that. . . ." and then says "The question is open for discussion." After discussion, the chairman may say, "Are you ready for the question?" and then state the question and call for the vote: "It has been moved and seconded that. . . . All in favor of the motion signify by saying *aye*. Contrary, *no*." The chairman then announces, "Motion carried," or "Motion lost," as the case may be. If he is undecided how the majority voted, he may call for a rising vote, in which the *ayes* and *noes* stand in turn and are counted. Written ballots are rarely used in school meetings.

The simple outline given below explains some of the procedures in a business meeting.

A. Opening business. The first order of business, after the opening of the meeting, is the reading of the minutes of the last meeting, after which the chairman says, "Are there any corrections to the minutes as read?" If there are no corrections, he says, "If not, they stand approved as read."

B. Main motions. Main motions must be seconded. Only one main motion can be before the house (the group) at any one time. Main motions are made for the following purposes:

   1. To introduce new business.

   2. To take a motion from the table. The speaker may be interrupted for this.

   3. To reconsider a motion. The speaker may be interrupted.

   4. To rescind a motion. This requires a two-thirds vote.

C. Subsidiary motions. Subsidiary motions take precedence over main motions. They are made

   1. To amend a motion. This is handled as a main motion. If passed, the main motion as amended is stated by the chairman and becomes the business before the group.

    2. To lay a motion on the table. This is not debatable.

    3. To refer a motion to a committee. This may have limited debate.

    4. To postpone consideration of a motion for a definite time. This may have limited debate.

    5. To postpone a motion indefinitely.

D. Incidental motions. Incidental motions take precedence over main and subsidiary motions and are not debatable. They are made

    1. To withdraw a motion. No second is required.

    2. To raise a point of order or to make inquiry regarding parliamentary procedure. The speaker may be interrupted for this. No second is required.

E. Privileged motions. Privileged motions take precedence over all others. They are made

    1. To adjourn. There may be limited debate.

    2. To take a recess. There may be limited debate.

If other procedures are needed, *Robert's Rules of Order* should be consulted. Children should always practice using the correct procedure. They may try dramatizing the procedures before a meeting is held. This should be followed by evaluation of the activity afterwards, to make sure the children understand the steps in the procedure.

Children in the third and fourth grades can be taught the simple rules for addressing the chair, making a motion, and seconding a motion. Use of these rules can be gradually expanded until pupils in the ninth grade practice all the rules of procedure.

In connection with all club work and school meetings, the children should learn how to write minutes of meetings and how to keep the treasurer's books. These are skills that are needed in all community organizations. Adults who do not know the procedure for meetings or the ways to keep records of meetings and finances are definitely handicapped in community activities; yet many schools have not yet provided practice in these matters.

Vocabulary development

In holding meetings, conversing, telephoning, acting, giving short talks and reports, telling stories, discussing, and the like, children learn many new words and use them in different situations. In fact, throughout the school day children have numerous opportunities to come in contact with new words. When field trips are taken as a part of a unit of study, the children may encounter many terms not used previously. Upon their return to the classroom, the teacher writes the new words on the blackboard and the children are urged to use these words in their discussion of the trip. Words used many times in speaking and in writing become a part of the meaningful vocabulary of the children. Likewise, new words met in reading and used by children in speaking and writing enrich the expression.

Meanings of words are better learned through experience than through isolated drill out of context. Words have multiple meanings and shades of meaning which can best be understood by using the words in different situations. Children describe, explain, and give directions, using new words they have acquired; they use dictionaries and encyclopedias to secure information about words. Frequently in a study of speech or writing improvement, children use the dictionary to find *synonyms* and *antonyms*. In efforts to improve a story to be told or written, teachers have helped children with vocabulary development by having them make lists of *compound words*, such as *rattlesnake*, and of words that suggest sounds, such as *buzz*, *clang*, and *boom* and of words that suggest taste, such as *delicious*, and so on. For their storytelling, children are asked to think up words to describe a cat, such as *soft*, *cozy*, and *warm*. Sometimes children keep lists of new words used in class by visitors who come to give them information needed in units of study. Playing word games, such as giving synonyms or antonyms for words, often helps children enrich their vocabularies.

Many studies have been made of the size of children's vocabularies at various age levels, but the teachers' chief concern is to get each child to develop as rich a vocabulary as possible without regard for standards. Throughout the activities of science, social studies, and the like, the alert teacher will find abundant opportunity to add to the vocabulary equipment of the children.

Common speech errors

The school tries to improve the pupil's use of English. As has been pointed out, good speech is acquired in an environment in which people speak correct English. Some children, however, are exposed to speech patterns in the home which are not used by the larger social group of the community, and they are often embarrassed by their incorrect use of English when they enter school.

The most common errors in children's use of English are in the use of verbs. Children use *seen* for *saw, done* for *did,* and so on. They do not use pronouns that agree with their antecedents in person and number. They use phrases which are not complete sentences. Correction of such errors is best made after the child has completed his talk or his telling of a story. To call his attention to the errors by interrupting his talk disturbs the flow of thought and the coordination of thinking and speaking which are the major goals of free expression.

If children are to improve their speech, they must want to improve. The school needs to be alert to the possibilities of any situations in which the pupils see the advantage of correct speech. A grammar or workbook can then be used to correct errors, but the best remedy is repeated practice in using the correct forms in speaking situations.

Speech difficulties

Some children have difficulty with the pronunciation of words. If this is due merely to carelessness or to having heard the incorrect pronunciation at home, the teacher can remedy the difficulty by having the children practice the correct pronunciations. Common errors are such mistakes in pronunciation as the following, according to Chase.[11]

1. Use of wrong vowels—"git" for *get*, "wuz" for *was*.
2. Consonant errors—"wat" for *what*.
3. Adding sounds—"athalete" for *athlete;* "fil-um" for *film*.
4. Misplacing the accent—"re'search" for *research'*.
5. Sounding silent letters—"oft-en" for *of(t)en*.
6. Omitting sounds—"famly" for *family*.
7. Improper order of sounds—"lar-nyx" for *larynx*.

Children sometimes have difficulty in learning voice control. Some children do not speak loudly enough to be heard while others shout in the classroom as though they were on the playground. They should be taught to speak loudly enough to be heard by all in the room when they are talking to the class, but to moderate their voices when they are talking in a group so that they do not disturb other groups in the class. A controlled and melodious voice can be gained through practice. The children can also learn that changes in the tone of the voice can indicate different emotions.

Speech disorders

Some speech difficulties of children are due to physical deformities, such as malformation of the jaw or teeth. The teacher has the responsibility of calling the attention of the parents and the school authorities to such difficulties and helping find what remedies are possible. Often the family doctor or dentist will know what can be done.

Children who have breaks in the rhythm of their speech are called stutterers. The causes of stuttering are a moot question with many authorities, but it seems certain that strain in the home is one cause. The child who stutters develops mental and emotional disturbances and should have the help of a speech pathologist where possible. The classroom teacher has the major responsibility of avoiding situations

[11] Naomi Chase, "Speech in the Elementary School," *Elementary English,* XXX (March, 1953), p. 140.

which emphasize the child's difficulty. If the stuttering is not serious, however, the child will often improve if he is given the chance to talk at his own pace and without interruption. The teacher can help the parents realize that a pleasant atmosphere and good health conditions with plenty of rest will aid the child. There should be no urging of the child to talk in class and no expression of irritation at his slow speech. Using patience and avoiding emotional strain or excitement will help, but the aid of a speech therapist is important.

Lisping often exists among young children who have heard "baby talk" at home, but it may also be due to malformation of the mouth or teeth. Here again the teacher will do well to consult the doctor and the dentist to discover the cause of the lisping. In the classroom her role is to exercise patience and determination in endeavoring to correct the child's speech.

More serious disorders may exist among the pupils, such as a split palate, or aphasia, which is usually due to injury to the brain or disease in the central nervous system. Such disorders as these need the attention of a speech therapist. The teacher can learn to recognize such disorders and see that they receive proper attention.

Many educators say that the classroom teacher should not attempt to help the child with serious speech disorders because it is the work of a speech therapist. However, many small schools do not have such specialists, and even if they do, the children are under the guidance of the classroom teacher much of the time. Thoughtless treatment of the handicapped in class can do more harm than the therapist can do good. Teachers must learn to identify children with speech difficulties and provide a good environment for improvement.

Summary

Children living in small communities need much help in improving their ability to listen and to speak well. Such skills are of paramount importance in the development of democratic leadership and followership and in communication with our fellow men.

The skills of listening and speaking are learned in the activities of all school subjects. There should be well-balanced practice in all situations in which language is used in daily life, such as conversing, discussing, reporting, cooperative planning, storytelling, telephoning, and holding meetings.

The social stimulus of the group situation provides motivation for correction of errors and speech difficulties.

Serious speech disorders among the children should have the help of a speech therapist, if one is available. The teacher can also consult the local doctor and dentist for remedial practices.

Selected references

DAWSON, MILDRED A. *Teaching Language in the Grades.* Yonkers, N.Y.: World Book Co., 1951. Chaps. vi–x.

Discusses the skills of speaking and listening, vocabulary growth, and oral communication.

FURNESS, EDNA LUE. "A Remedial and Developmental Program in Listening," *Elementary English,* XXXII (December, 1955), pp. 525–532.

Presents the objectives of listening instruction, relationship to reading, analysis and causes of disabilities, and teaching procedures which may be used to remove disabilities.

HATCHETT, ETHEL L., and HUGHES, DONALD H. *Teaching Language Arts in Elementary Schools.* New York: The Ronald Press Co., 1956. Chaps. v, vi, vii, ix.

Listening and speaking experiences; vocabulary growth and English usage; growth in speech; speech difficulties; and speaking situations.

HERRICK, VIRGIL E., and JACOBS, LELAND B. *Children and the Language Arts.* Englewood Cliffs, N.J.: Prentice-Hall, Inc., 1955. Chaps. vi, vii, xiv, xv, xvi.

Experiences in speaking, listening, dramatics, vocabulary development, and mass media of communication.

NATIONAL COUNCIL OF TEACHERS OF ENGLISH, COMMISSION ON THE ENGLISH CURRICULUM. *Language Arts for Today's Children.* New York: Appleton-Century-Crofts, Inc., 1954. Chaps. iv and v.

Nature and kinds of listening, and experiences needed to develop listening ability.

NAU, ELIZABETH SCHIEFERSTEIN. "Making Marionettes for the Classroom," *Elementary English*, XXIX (January, 1952), pp. 19–25.

Directions for making and using marionettes.

PRATT, EDWARD. "Experimental Evaluation of a Program for the Improving of Listening," *The Elementary School Journal*, LVI (March, 1956), pp. 315–20.

Report of a study in evaluation of the effects of a program designed to develop specific skills in the listening process.

RASMUSSEN, CARRIE. *Speech Methods in the Elementary School*. New York: The Ronald Press Co., 1949. Chaps. vi–x.

Discussion of listening, speech defects, storytelling, talks, conversation, discussion, creative dramatics, and the making and use of puppets in dramatics.

SORRENSON, FRED S. *Speech for the Teacher*. New York: The Ronald Press Co., 1952. Chaps. i, iii–viii especially.

Help for the teacher in improving her own speech.

STRICKLAND, RUTH G. *The Language Arts in the Elementary Grades*. Boston: D. C. Heath & Co., 1951. Chaps. vi, vii, xiv.

Speaking and listening program in primary and intermediate grades; essential skills; English usage; use in other school subjects.

TIDYMAN, WILLARD F., and BUTTERFIELD, MARGUERITE. *Teaching the Language Arts*. New York: McGraw-Hill Book Co., Inc., 1951. Chaps. vii, ix, xvi.

Oral communication, dramatization, choral speaking, speech, and speech correction.

TREANOR, JOHN. "Listening Before Writing," *Elementary English*, XXX (April, 1953), pp. 207–9.

Suggestions for listening activities to stimulate children to write.

WARD, WINNIFRED. *Playmaking with Children from Kindergarten to High School*. New York: Appleton-Century-Crofts, Inc., 1947. Chaps. ii–vii, ix, and x.

Discusses the function of dramatic play, rhythms, and pantomimes; gives directions and illustrations for handling dramatic play, stories, and play writing, and shows how playmaking is a means of releasing emotional tension, overcoming timidity and other problems of personal adjustment.

9

DEVELOPING WRITING ABILITIES

Teachers in rural schools report difficulty in getting children to write well and to enjoy writing experiences. Too often the writing lessons have their bases in artificial situations and include too many workbook exercises, so that it is not difficult to understand the lack of interest on the part of the children.

Writing is a complex process which requires the development of special muscles and the transference of speech patterns to written symbols on the page.

Three aspects of the writing program

The writing program has three major aspects: The first aspect is developmental in character and includes the process of helping the children acquire and perfect the skills of handwriting and spelling, expand their concepts of sentence structure and paragraphing, and develop the use of correct punctuation, capitalization, and other skills used in writing.

The second aspect of the writing program is to provide motivation for writing and real-life situations in which children see the need for writing.

The third aspect is that of helping children develop personal responsibility for the quality of their writing and a knowledge of how to improve it. This is very difficult unless the transition from speaking to writing has been accomplished successfully and the first experiences in writing have been satisfying to the children.

Transition from spoken to written English

Learning to express ideas through the use of written symbols is an expansion of the mode of expression through spoken symbols. In the pre-school, kindergarten, and first-grade experiences, children have learned gradually to organize their speech. Learning to write involves putting speech in visible form through the use of a new mechanism. In oral expression the child uses well-established habit patterns which enable him to speak without thinking about the manipulation of the voice, the tongue, and the lips because his speech has become an automatic response to his thinking. In learning to write, however, the child has to establish another complex set of habit patterns. The skills of handwriting, spelling, and punctuation and capitalization are new and must be developed gradually until they become habitual. Only then can the child approach freedom of expression in his writing. It takes time and much practice to establish these habit patterns, and if the transition is not made gradually and through realistic situations, many children develop mental blocks to their progress in written expression of their thoughts.

Developmental experiences

The language activities of the kindergarten and early primary grades are directed toward: (1) building fundamental motor skills to be used in handwriting, (2) developing a consciousness of the need for writing, (3) providing group and individual practice in oral composition followed by dictation of compositions to be written by the teacher and copied by the children, and (4) beginning the development of handwriting and spelling skills.

In the many activities of the kindergarten and early primary grades, children draw and paint pictures and use scissors to cut paper, all of which help develop the finer motor skills necessary in handwriting. Children of the first grade print their names on notebooks and other property and write the names of the school, the teacher, and the village. These are first steps in manuscript writing and spelling, and they are motivated by the needs of the occasion. When parents are to be invited to the school, the children wish to issue invitations. The first invitation may be only a short sentence or two which the teacher writes on the board at the children's dictation and the children copy. The teacher uses a capital letter to begin a sentence or a name and places a period at the end of the sentence, and the children do likewise, thus getting their first realization of the use of capitals and punctuation marks.

In the kindergarten, the children have been telling stories, thus using oral composition in which they have learned to use complete sentences and to put them in sequence. In the first grade, the children make up longer stories, which may be accounts of trips or of parties, and so on. Sometimes the children dictate the story and the teacher writes it on the blackboard. Again the children observe the use of capital letters and punctuation marks and see that each sentence makes a complete statement or asks a question and that the sentences follow a certain sequence. When their skill in their manuscript writing has developed sufficiently, the children may copy the story in their notebooks. Unconsciously they follow the teacher's ways of writing and spelling the words.

Through a continuation of their experiences of composing stories, the children form habits of using good sentence structure and simple punctuation, and they also learn the purpose of capital letters, periods, and question marks. They learn to stick to the point in telling a story and to organize their sentences.

During this early developmental period, occasions may arise for the children to write personal letters to relatives or friends. The letters are at first dictated to the teacher or parent. Where a close working relationship exists between parents and teachers, mothers and fathers have been very helpful at this stage of development.

As soon as the children have made sufficient progress in handwriting and spelling, they take over the responsibilities of writing their letters and stories without previous dictation. Needs for writing are further developed as occasions arise to prepare notices, to make lists of things to bring to school, to record facts observed, and to keep records of such things as changes in the weather.

From the simple letters and stories and records of the first two grades, children are led to write compositions in paragraph form. In the third grade of one school, the children studied nutrition and spent much time discussing different kinds of food. They classified foods in various ways, as "foods we cook," "foods to be eaten without cooking," "meats," "fruits," and "vegetables." This was preparation for writing a cooperative report. In the report, the children were taught to stick to one topic in each paragraph. Writing should not be confined to such cooperative procedures however; independence in style and composition is to be encouraged. Except for the initial stages of writing, children should be encouraged to express their own thoughts individually and in their own words.

As children proceed in the primary grades, growth should take place in length and complexity of sentence structure and in richness of vocabularies. Increased understanding of the nature of a complete sentence and the purposes served by the various marks of punctuation, should be developed gradually. The children should recognize the use of the different types of sentences, such as statements, questions, commands, and exclamations, and learn to organize their ideas and present them in paragraph form.

Throughout the activities of the primary and middle grades, the children continue to improve their habit patterns in writing and perfect their skill in using correct capitalization, punctuation, and sentence form. An attempt is made to carry over into writing the creativeness of oral composition, which is continued along with written composition.

Different kinds of writing

The activities of the school provide the real-life occasions for using the different kinds of writing used throughout life. A work unit on soil erosion, for example, gives an occasion for writing business letters to get material, for writing research reports, and for preparing bibliographies; absent friends provide occasions for writing friendly letters; parties call for invitations and acceptances; the school newspaper provides opportunities for reporting news and writing advertisements; club meetings require the writing of minutes of meetings. The occasions for writing should all be real to the children. Considerable ingenuity may be needed by the teacher to provide real motivation for the practice of the kinds of writing needed in life.

Some teachers may say, "Is it necessary to practice all kinds of writing? Are not the skills of one situation transferable to another?" They assume that if the child can write good business letters, he can write good personal letters; or if he can write a good story, he can write a good news item for the school paper. It is true that there are some skills which are common to the different kinds of writing, but there are also skills peculiar to each type, and each kind of writing has a different purpose.

The character and form of each kind of writing vary with the purpose of the writer. Some writing, such as news reporting, follows one pattern of composition, while the writing of summaries of research takes another form and demands more exactness of detail. Personal letters are informal and conversational, while business letters are formal and brief. Minutes of meetings follow a standard form of recording the proceedings of the club. Writing stories and poetry allows the imagination free rein, but this would not be acceptable practice in a summary of research findings. Creative writing gives free rein to thoughts and emotions, unhampered by much attention to grammar and punctuation, at least at the time of writing, and the child can express his prejudices, anger, fear, love, and good humor in this kind of writing; but such writing is not suitable in news reporting, business letters, and minutes of meetings.

Children of one school learned what kind of writing is suitable for reporting research findings when they wrote up the results of a community survey they had made. They reported details on population characteristics, occupations, and types of farming. They also wrote a community history which called for checking and verification of facts, care in English usage, proper punctuation, and paragraphing. As contrasted with such factual writing, creative writing or personal writing is done for one's enjoyment and for the enjoyment of others, and is not confined to facts.

The purpose of the writing determines the form to be used. Hence, it is important that the teacher utilize real-life occasions in the school to give children an opportunity to practice the various kinds of writing. They will thus learn the different skills needed and gain an understanding of the kind of writing suitable for different occasions.

Should the different kinds of writing have equal practice? Four factors are often considered in determining the amount of emphasis which should be given to learning a function: (1) frequency of use, (2) importance, (3) difficulty of learning, and (4) interest. From the standpoint of frequency of use, writing personal letters would receive most emphasis. Writing minutes of meetings may not occur often, but knowing how to write them is important in the life of most individuals. Difficulty of learning varies with the individual's background of experience, general language development, and maturity. The teacher should not expect equal progress for all children and should recognize that some children need more practice in certain skills than others. Interests of children vary with their experiences inside and outside school, but teachers can do much deliberately to build the interests of children through the activities of the school. The wise teacher will consider all factors in determining the emphasis to be given to each kind of writing. Some kinds of writing are neglected by adults because they do not know how to write or have not experienced enjoyment in writing.

Writing letters

The most common use of writing is in communicating with absent friends and relatives by means of letters. Instruction in letter writing does not consist merely of teaching the proper form for a letter. It should be emphasized that a friendly letter is a written conversation and that it has a real audience—the person to whom the letter is written. The form of the letter is less important than what is said and how it is said. The friendly letter should reflect the personality of the writer and consider the interest of the recipient.

Letter writing begins with children in the primary grades and continues throughout their school careers. Many occasions offer opportunities for children to write personal letters, as when they write to friends who are ill or are away from the community. Some teachers make contacts with schools in other districts of the region or in other parts of the country and secure "pen pals" for members of the class. Correspondence is often carried on with children of the same age in other English-speaking countries, and photographs as well as letters are exchanged. Children in other lands like to send and receive letters, and correspondence with children of other countries helps children to practice letter writing and stimulates the study of geography and history. Such correspondence has often continued after the school years, bringing a sharing of culture and interests and building better understanding among peoples.

In one school where the members of a fifth-grade class all had pen pals, the children shared their letters, reading them aloud to the class. Many of the letters were very interesting and well written, and the children discussed what made them interesting. This led to a discussion of the characteristics of a good letter, a consideration of richness of vocabulary through the use of expressive words and phrases, a study of how the transposition of phrases can clarify the meaning, and an appreciation of the value of paragraphing.

Improvement in letter writing requires much practice in writing real letters to real people and frequent periods of appraisal by each child of his own letter-writing ability. Children are led to think about what the recipient of the letter may want to know and how to arrange sentences to make the letter easier to read. Through real experience they learn to appreciate the importance of good spelling and neat, legible handwriting and what courtesies should be observed in correspondence. If children realize that their letters need improvement, they may voluntarily rewrite some of the letters; but for the teacher to make a routine requirement of correction and rewriting will likely destroy the desire to write.

Frequent practice in letter writing brings steady improvement in this communication skill as children advance from grade to grade, with greater progress usually shown by the more intelligent children. Swenson and Caldwell's study of letters written by children from grades four through twelve showed an average increase from grade to grade in the number of topics discussed and in the length of the discussion of each topic, a broadening interest in people, and a growing interest in the wider community at succeeding levels of development. Younger children tended to discuss the immediate past or present most frequently when there was complete freedom to write, but the older children showed more tendency to write about the future. There was a tendency to use narration more frequently than description, to discuss topics realistically rather than imaginatively, and to write seriously rather than humorously.[1]

In the case of business letters, the pupils should be taught that form is very important. Often the person to whom the business letter is written is unknown to the writer. The ap-

[1] See Esther J. Swenson and Charles G. Caldwell, "The Process of Communication in Children's Letters" and "The Content of Children's Letters," *The Elementary School Journal*, XLIX (October and November, 1948), pp. 79–88 and 149–59.

pearance and form of the letter impress the recipient with the writer's knowledge or his lack of knowledge, according to whether the letter is correct in form or contains errors and is untidy. Many situations in school provide motivation for the writing of business letters. Experience units of work may call for letters requesting bulletins or samples of products or other material. When an excursion is planned, it is necessary to write for permission to visit the farm or factory or museum, and a courteous letter of thanks afterwards is desirable.

Business letters should be brief and should state specifically what is wanted. They should always be courteous, even when it is necessary to make a complaint, as when goods ordered have not been received or are not what was ordered. Many of these letters can be worked out cooperatively by the class and then written by a pupil selected for his good penmanship or his ability to use the typewriter. Good textbooks can be used to study the correct form and arrangement of a business letter.

The rural child does not have so many uses for invitations, either formal or informal, or letters of sympathy or acceptances or regrets as the urban child, but in today's greater mobility of population he may need to know how to write these notes in his adult life. The teacher in the rural school has to be governed largely by the needs of her pupils. However, many of these pupils may not always remain in the local vicinity; they move to the city or marry and settle in other parts of the country. A knowledge of the correct forms is often a social asset.

Writing stories and poems

The child's chief motivation in writing a story or a poem is the activity itself. The child writes for the fun of it or because he has experienced some emotion which he wishes to share. The mood or the inspiration does not come from an assignment by the teacher to "write a story;" such compulsion can lead to a dislike for all creative writing.

Creative writing can begin in the early grades. The teacher may tell a story which arouses the children's interest and suggest another story to them. Or the teacher may tell all except the ending of a story and ask the children to finish it. This work is oral at first, of course, but it can be continued in the written work as soon as the children have learned to write.

Stimulating children to do creative work is so largely a part of the personality of the teacher and her relationships with the children that it is difficult to outline a method. Almost no research has been done to point the way to motivating children to write. However, reports provided by teachers who have been successful in stimulating children to do creative writing may be helpful. Some of the characteristic situations and practices of successful teachers of creative writing are summarized here.

1. Creative writing requires a quiet, friendly atmosphere in which children have a strong feeling of security. Informal story hours in which imagination and interests are developed often help to establish the proper atmosphere.

2. Children who attempt to write should have developed some mastery of the skills of spelling, handwriting, sentence structure, and other mechanics of written expression. This development may not be complete, but it should have established some habit patterns. Children who want to write words which they cannot spell should feel free to ask the teacher, who may write the words on the blackboard for them to copy. If there are many difficulties with the mechanics of writing, however, the creative urge will be lost.

3. Creative writing, as well as creative speaking, is achieved best by children with a rich background of experiences and a rich vocabulary. Children cannot create in a vacuum; they must have something to say. Many speaking, reading, and listening experiences enhance the possibilities of doing creative writing.

4. Children who have had many opportunities to do creative work in speaking seem to be most successful in creative writing. At least for most children, oral storytelling, frequent

discussions, and much listening have proved helpful. Extensive reading is also an invaluable aid to writing; there cannot be much "output" without "intake." Listening and reading not only stimulate imagination and provide background experience but also help children to understand style in writing, to enrich their vocabularies, and to increase their control over the mechanics of expression.

5. Stimulation at the time of writing is necessary to get the children in a mood to write. Some teachers accomplish this through a word, a picture, movies, a story, or an event. If poetry is to be written, teachers need to create situations that evoke poetic responses. For example, one teacher and her class looked at a tree and thought of words to describe the tree and talked about the green, fluffy leaves, the yellow buds bursting open, and the birds and squirrels in the tree. Soon it was evident that many of the children were ready to write a story or a poem about the tree. Other teachers accomplish the stimulation by the study of a picture or the reading of a story or a poem to the children. A third-grade teacher used the technique of telling an unfinished story, giving all but the conclusion. The children were asked to write how they would finish the story. She reported good results, with some children giving a comic ending and others a sad ending. Teachers need not wait for stimulating situations to appear but can create a variety of situations which will bring a response from most of the children. For the purposes of creating a stimulating situation, she must be interested in the world about her, and she must be alert to capitalize on an emotion or experience of the children.

6. Obstructions to creative writing must be removed. When the child is in the mood to write, he must be given a chance to do so and should not be interrupted. He must not be criticized by the teacher or others for his style or mechanics. He must feel free to express his emotions in his own way.

7. The child needs to feel that what he writes is important. It is a great help to him to know that the teacher thinks his product is important, too. If he has done the best he can, he

is entitled to encouragement. He should be given an opportunity to read his own work to the class if he wishes to do so.

8. Children are helped by identifying themselves as writers or poets. As such they are stimulated to study how real authors and poets do their writing and to seek better ways of doing their own creative work.

9. We cannot expect all children to be equally stimulated to write by any one occasion or to do the same type of writing. They will differ in backgrounds, interests, and skills, and they cannot be forced to write. Children's writing is spasmodic. The desire to write comes and goes, and we must allow the child to write when the desire comes and not be impatient for it to come.

A parallel program of writing might be carried on wherein those children who are not stimulated to do creative writing may do the more factual kind, such as may be needed in connection with other activities of the school program. Some educators insist that all children can be stimulated to do creative writing, but boys and girls may not all be ready at the same time, and teachers report varying degrees of success with stimulation. Children who do not find creative expression in writing poetry or stories may find it in dramatics or in painting. To meet the needs of all the children, there should be variety of opportunities for expression.

10. In free creative writing there is no requirement as to form. The child starts and stops the story any way he wishes. Some stories may not even be finished. There are no corrections or copying except when a child edits his story for publication. After much experience in writing creatively and sharing stories, some children want to correct their stories and copy them. Eventually, proofreading should be taught as a part of the process of writing, but the teacher does not do the correcting nor does she require that stories be copied over and over until correct. If there is to be any profit to the child in polishing up his writing, it must come through his own volition.

Much of the learning about better ways to start a story and build up to a climax comes at times separate from the creative act. Children study the writing of others and learn from models. As children become more experienced in creative work, some teachers have found it helpful to form a writing club where each child may read his story and ask for help in improvement. Improvement in the mechanics of writing comes largely through other types of writing.

11. Teachers and supervisors report that a child's interest in further writing is encouraged by exchanging stories with other children, mounting his story with the stories of others in a scrapbook to be added to the library, keeping a scrapbook of his stories which he exchanges with other pupils, contributing his best story to a book of "Best Stories of the Class," reading samples of creative writing by former students in the grade, and becoming acquainted with some children's magazines.

12. Teachers find creative writing to be an excellent medium for understanding children. In a free expression of their emotions, children often reveal their loneliness, insecurity, and prejudices. Sometimes teachers have found that children enjoy writing autobiographies. One teacher wrote her autobiography and read it to the children, who were stimulated to write theirs. When children write, they express their interests and their problems. Stories studied by the teacher may give a better understanding of the child and show how to help him with his adjustments.

13. Creative writing, like other creative work, affords an outlet for the emotions of children and thus has therapeutic value. A shy youngster can be bold in his writing, and the child who lacks social acceptability may have his emotional stress reduced through creative expression. Children write about things that bother them at school and at home. Teachers report that children reduce their fears through their writing and thus enjoy better mental health.

Writing for the newspaper

The school and community newspapers provide excellent motivation for writing of a different kind from that used in writing letters and stories. Where these are not available, classes have sometimes published their own newspapers in mimeographed form and distributed them to their parents and other classes. Such a project affords an opportunity to develop an interest in newspaper reading and in the work of preparing and publishing a newspaper.

In one sixth-grade class, the children made a survey of the newspapers which were taken in their homes and prepared a list of the daily, weekly, and Sunday papers distributed in the community. They studied and discussed the content of a newspaper, including types of news, headlines, editorials, cartoons, comic strips, special features, and advertising. They learned how news is gathered, edited, and printed. They learned the roles of reporters, editors, and printers by visiting a newspaper office and by discussing the work done there. They placed samples of newspapers on the bulletin board with clippings of special interest. The children then decided to produce a newspaper of their own and selected editors and reporters and an advertising and a distributing manager. They chose a name for the paper and made a list of possible sources of news. The paper included news of local school and community events, social affairs, and sports events; farm market quotations; and brief reviews of agriculture bulletins. Editorials dealt with keeping the lunchroom and the classroom neat, using the library, and conducting oneself correctly in the hall and on the school bus. Feature articles dealt with hobbies and included a quiz on current events. Each child accepted some responsibility for the writing of the paper, although some worked in pairs or with committees while others worked alone. When articles were completed, they were read and edited by the editors. The paper was typed by a clerk in the principal's office, enough copies being made for distribution to the members of the class and their parents.

These children learned that news writing requires a different style from other written work. The news story, for example, is told three times: in the headline, in the leading paragraph, and in the body of the article. They learned that news must be new. They studied the leads of articles clipped from newspapers and learned that they told *who, what, when,* and *where.* They interviewed people to get news and collected facts which they organized into readable articles. They learned that news stories do not include the personal opinions of the reporter and that they are written clearly in short paragraphs. By studying the makeup of newspapers and by preparing a dummy to indicate the placement of the articles, they achieved balance on the front page of their paper. The largest headlines were placed at the top of page one and consisted of two or three lines each. By allowing a liberal margin and space between news items, they made the paper attractive.

This newspaper experience led to a study of the history of printing and to an appreciation of the role of newspapers in the lives of a democratic people. Many new words, such as *linotype, dummy, issue, classified,* and *feature,* were added to their vocabularies. The children gained practice in taking notes to be used in writing. They wrote business letters to get information needed for their study. Their interest in current events was increased, and they learned to make more use of newspapers and news broadcasts.

Only two editions of this newspaper were published, but the work greatly increased the pupils' appreciation of news, their understanding of journalism, and their motivation for writing. Many of the pupils who had disliked writing developed a real interest and enjoyment in the work and tried to improve their grammar, punctuation, and expression in order to make their stories more readable.

Developing responsibility for correct English usage

Many teachers complain about the work of correcting the pupils' papers that is involved in teaching children to write. These teachers assume that it is necessary to mark every error with a red pencil and have the children rewrite the papers. They fail to realize that they are depriving the children of the opportunity to develop personal responsibility for improvement of their own writing. In addition to the development of the free flow of expression in response to thinking, children need to learn to be responsible for what they write. They need to be conscious of the importance of polishing their writing to increase its interest and clarity. They need to be made sensitive to the purpose of good sentence structure, paragraphing, and punctuation in making their writing more readable.

In their effort to make pupils conscious of the need of correct expression, some teachers go to the extreme of collecting all papers, marking every error, and requiring the pupil to copy the paper again and again until all errors have been corrected. Other teachers, who realize that this practice destroys all spontaneity and freedom of expression, go to the other extreme, however, when they stimulate the children to write freely and accept the child's creative effort for what it is. These teachers would no more think of correcting the child or asking him to correct his own writing than they would think of asking him to repaint a picture according to adult standards. Some authorities agree with the latter group of teachers and point out that children learn sentence structure and punctuation through the developmental activities previously described in this chapter. Yet, teachers discover that children are not equally ready for those developmental experiences, and some children continue to need help with the skills of expression. Some authorities would utilize only practical writing or cooperative writing situations to help children improve their English usage and would leave personal writing, such as story writing and letter writing alone. While the latter position of teaching improvement solely through developmental and practical writing seems much more tenable than that of teacher correction of all written work for fear of perpetuation of errors, do we not also need to lead children toward self-evaluation and improvement of their own work? Can children learn to write freely while in the mood to write—dashing off what they want to say, depending on automatic habit patterns for mode of expression —and then polishing the writing after the product is completed? Can children of the intermediate and upper grades be led to develop this responsibility? Responsibility is not developed by requirements!

Studying models of good writing taken from books and examining the best writing of some of the children help develop a consciousness of the factors which make a story interesting, clear, and readable. But a consciousness of what constitutes good writing will not necessarily lead to a consciousness of responsibility for improvement. Here is where the most delicate art of teaching is required. How can the teacher lead individuals to want to improve? Praise for good phrases, sentences, and paragraphs helps stimulate the child to better efforts. Working to eliminate one error at a time has proved helpful. Helping the children think of themselves as authors and study the writing of good authors has been of assistance. Forming a writing club has sometimes provided the channel through which young writers have been encouraged by their classmates.

Children need to develop responsibility for their own work and for seeking help when it is needed to improve their writing. This takes time and the practice of using every occasion when the children share their work in writing and feel the need for improvement. Learning takes place through practice only if the practice is made with a definite purpose in mind. The child must be made to want to improve before he will accept responsibility for his own improvement.

Most teachers accept the idea that improvement in English usage is important, but many of them do not know how to accomplish this improvement except through isolated drill. They soon discover that such drill has little effect on the written work of the pupils. Research does not help much in this matter except to reveal that study of isolated rules of grammar does not improve expression. Some teachers have recorded the procedures through which they have obtained good results, however, and it is possible to make certain generalizations from a study of their successful practices.

Salisbury[2] describes one procedure which teachers have

[2] Ethel I. Salisbury, "Children Can Learn to Edit," *Elementary English,* XXX (November, 1953), pp. 434–36.

found to be helpful. After a rich experience, the children do some writing which is carried on as free expression of emotions and thought. They depend largely upon habit patterns to operate in the process of writing, knowing that they will have an opportunity later to polish the writing. The teacher takes the papers and reads them to find ways of encouraging the authors. Then she reads the papers again to secure examples of effective phrasing or good sentence structure, making notes. She looks over the papers a third time to discover one type of language error which occurs so often that clarification and drill are indicated as needed by most of the children. The teacher writes on the board a sentence or a short paragraph which contains an example of this error. She has the children analyze and discuss the error and decide how to correct it. In addition, she gives the pupils a list of the words that were misspelled on their papers and has them copy the words into their notebooks for study before the next spelling lesson. With the permission of the children, the teacher reads aloud some of the compositions which have particular merit and praises them. All papers are then returned to the pupils for examination for the error that has been studied and for misspelling of any of the words in the list the teacher gave the pupils. If drill is needed to develop the correct form or the correct spelling, it is given.

Under this procedure the children work to eliminate only one error of usage at a time. When more papers are written, the free-writing period is followed by an editing period during which the children look for the type of error they have discussed and watch for misspelling of any of the words on their list. The children are given time to study their handwriting, also, and to judge it for legibility, correct form of letters, slant, spacing, and strokes. A good diagnostic handwriting chart will help in this process.

According to LaBrant,[3] some teachers devote the language period to workbook drill on usage because the children do not like to write and the teacher has no time to correct pa-

[3] Lou LaBrant, "Writing Is Learned by Writing," *Elementary English,* XXX (November, 1953), pp. 417–20.

pers. Good teachers disagree over the merits of marking papers for errors. A good plan is for the teacher to check papers for only the one error on which the class is working at that time. A still better plan is for the teacher merely to read the papers without marking them but taking notes on the errors to find the most common error. The children are then asked to read their papers to find this error and correct it. Gradually the children are taught responsibility for proof-reading their own work and improving the phrasing and sentence structure and correcting the errors.

LaBrant makes several suggestions which can save time for the busy teacher and which also give much better promise of improved writing than isolated drill can ever accomplish. Exercises in punctuation accomplish little, for punctuation can best be taught in the "body of the paper." Ninety per cent of the punctuation required consists of ending the sentence with a period. All children know that a sentence ends with a period, but they do not always know where one sentence ends and the next one begins. Time may be saved by omitting exercises and getting directly to papers.

Learning punctuation is a gradual process which takes place in writing activities. Eventually the child needs to learn the common uses of the comma, such as separating words in a series; the use of the apostrophe to indicate possession; and the use of quotation marks to enclose words spoken. None of these is taught through separate drills but rather as a part of the process of writing and improving one's own writing.

Children can learn to improve their sentences and paragraphs with some help during the group work previously described. As LaBrant says, "Much of the correcting we do teaches nothing but copying."

Time spent on identifying the parts of speech will help children to distinguish nouns from pronouns, adjectives from adverbs, and so on, but this will not improve their speaking and writing in most cases. In a discussion of correct writing, a few terms like *subject* and *predicate* can be introduced during the evaluation of their work by the children. The names of the parts of speech can be learned gradually through experience, just as other new words are learned. Time spent on mere drill on the parts of a sentence and the parts of speech is time wasted insofar as improvement of expression is concerned.

There has been much discussion of the teaching of grammar in the schools. College teachers have complained that their students were not taught grammar in high school, and secondary school teachers blame the lower school for the poor writing of their pupils. Formal grammar has been included in language textbooks, then taken out, and then put back in again without any apparent reason except to meet the waves of criticism. Investigations show that children who do not know the rules of grammar seem to do as well in speaking and writing as those who are familiar with the rules. When people speak or write, they are using habit patterns established through extensive expression over a long period of time. The beginning of those patterns and the modification of them are influenced by the practice of persons with whom the individuals have been associated or are the result of modes of expression found in their reading. The chief function of grammar, aside from enabling the pupil to pass grammar tests, is to help the individual evaluate his own speaking or writing—to know how to judge the correctness of his expression—and thus lead to an effort to modify his habit patterns. Rules of grammar are a series of generalizations about the construction of the language; and if generalizations are to be learned and used, they must be developed inductively from concrete situations and then applied to other situations. In the process of correcting their own writing, suppose children consider a common error found by the teacher: the pronoun does not agree with the antecedent in number. The children are led to examine models in books and are made to realize that the pronoun must agree with the antecedent if the meaning is to be clear. They then write a few sentences which illustrate this principle. That is the only grammar studied that day, and it is used only to help the children with editing their own writing or improving their speech. Before the rule can be effective, changes in speech and writing patterns must be well established through use. The study of grammar from workbooks or textbooks is deadening to an interest in improving one's expression.

Pooley[4] indicates that the present trend is to postpone the teaching of grammar to approximately the seventh grade, with the emphasis in prior grades on correct and fluent speech and correct usage in composition. Trends are a doubtful justification for practices. There have been trends toward teaching grammar and trends toward discontinuing it. When should children learn grammar, and does it help to improve their speaking and writing? It is known that children can learn to generalize and that many will do so without help from anyone. More research is needed to determine whether grammar helps the children to improve their language usage; but more important than *when* or *whether* grammar is taught is *how* it is taught. Children of the fifth and sixth grades can generalize and apply their generalizations if they are properly taught. Knowledge of child development and of the process of learning lead to these conclusions: the teaching of grammar is not desirable in the primary grades; when it is taught, only one or two concepts should be taught at a time; grammar should be a part of the process of improvement of speech and writing only in specific situations where it is needed to explain correct construction; and generalizations should be developed from a study of model forms of construction. Since brighter children show greater ability to generalize and apply the generalizations than slow children, it may be expected that they will profit more from the instruction. Some research seems to indicate that this is true. In any case, grammar instruction must not replace emphasis on the formation of correct habits of expression and on the improvement of those habits.

The child who faces the problem of improvement in his usage of English should learn to attack one error at a time. Having all children work on the same error at the same time

[4] Robert C. Pooley, "Grammar in the Schools of Today," *Elementary English*, XXX (May, 1954), pp. 268–72.

is not always so helpful as getting each child to work independently to improve his own work, although there may be several children making the same error.

The habits which most seriously interfere with understanding should be attacked first. Studies of frequency of errors in writing lead us to anticipate the errors which children are likely to make, and studies of frequency of use of punctuation marks serve as guides to the relative importance of the rules of punctuation. Studies of the most frequently used punctuation marks show the following to be most common: period at the end of the sentence; apostrophe to show possession; quotation marks to set off direct conversation and to call attention to a word or a phrase used with some special meaning; dashes to set off a parenthetical expression; and commas to set off inserted or added elements in a sentence, to separate words or numbers in a series, and to separate the independent clauses of a compound sentence.

The most common errors made by children in letters are in punctuation (40 per cent of the total number), sentence structure, capitals, paragraphing, and use of homonyms, adjectives, adverbs, and verbs. Other common errors are run-on sentences, omission of periods and question marks, incomplete sentences, and use of capitals. Errors in the use of verbs are most common, with punctuation and pronouns having a high frequency of incorrect usage. The most common errors in oral expression have been found to be incorrect sentence structure, wrong pronunciation, nonagreement of subject and predicate, and use of loose and unnecessary connectives.

While these are the errors which teachers may expect children to make most often, the specific errors made by John and Alice will be the ones with which to be concerned. Drill on the most common errors does not produce improvement in expression equivalent to that obtained by getting each child to develop responsibility for improvement of his own compositions. The child should be led to identify his most serious mistakes and drill himself on the correct forms in order to rebuild his habits of speaking and writing.

Summary

In learning to write, children need to develop writing habit patterns that are as nearly automatic as possible. While habit patterns of spelling and handwriting are being established, composition ability is being developed through speaking situations. An effort is made to carry over creative oral expression into writing as soon as the mechanics of expression have become fairly well established as responses to thinking.

The program of teaching writing includes activities which are developmental in character and are designed to help children acquire skills of writing to be used as a new mode of expression and use oral composition ability in written composition and highly motivated real-life occasions for writing. There is an attempt to develop individual consciousness of good writing and responsibility for individual improvement.

Activities of the early school period cover the following: (1) building the fundamental motor skills to be used in writing; (2) developing a consciousness of a need for writing; (3) providing practice first in oral composition, then in dictated composition, and finally in written composition; and (4) developing the handwriting and spelling skills.

Children are not equally ready for writing experiences because of differences in backgrounds of language development and in motivation and ease of learning; hence, progress will be unequal among the children in any class. Effort is made to get the children to develop responsibility for their own improvement. Correct English usage is learned in the process of speaking and writing, not through isolated drill.

The total school program provides the motivation and the occasions for different kinds of writing. The purpose determines the type of writing, but the different kinds will not have equal appeal for all children. The aim is to have each child grow in skill and enjoyment of written communication, to discover and develop special talents, and to use the expressive arts as emotional outlets.

Selected references

APPLEGATE, MAUREE. *Helping Children Write*. Scranton, Pa.: International Textbook Co., 1949. Entire volume.

Much emphasis on writing stories and poetry and vocabulary development.

DAWSON, MILDRED. *Teaching Language in the Grades*. Yonkers, N.Y.: World Book Co., 1951. Chaps. xi, xii, xiii, and xiv.

Written communication, creative expression, and correct usage and grammar.

FEREBEE, JUNE, *et al. They All Want to Write*. New York: The Bobbs-Merrill Co., Inc., 1939. Entire volume.

Beginning experiences and further development; creative writing stressed.

HATCHETT, ETHEL L., and HUGHES, DONALD H. *Teaching Language Arts in Elementary Schools*. New York: The Ronald Press Co., 1956. Chaps. x, xii, and xiii.

Writing letters and reports; making a class dictionary; and creative writing.

HERRICK, VIRGIL E., and JACOBS, LELAND B. (eds.). *Children and the Language Arts*. Englewood Cliffs, N.J.: Prentice-Hall, Inc., 1955. Chaps. x and xiii.

Children's experiences in writing and usage and functional grammar.

NATIONAL COUNCIL OF TEACHERS OF ENGLISH, COMMISSION ON THE ENGLISH CURRICULUM. *Language Arts for Today's Children*. New York: Appleton-Century-Crofts, Inc., 1954. Chap. vii.

Child writing needs; personal and creative writing; goals of all writing; and suitability in writing.

NATIONAL COUNCIL OF TEACHERS OF ENGLISH, COMMISSION ON THE ENGLISH CURRICULUM. *The English Language Arts*. New York: Appleton-Century-Crofts, Inc., 1952. Chap. xii.

Modern view of grammar and linguistics; excellent treatment of the changing character of the language.

POOLEY, ROBERT C. *Teaching English Usage*. New York: Appleton-Century-Crofts, Inc., 1946. Chaps. iii, v, vi, vii, and viii.

Levels of English usage; sources of usage information; problems of grammar, syntax, and word choice; modern view of usage and grammar.

STRICKLAND, RUTH G. *The Language Arts in the Elementary School.* Boston: D. C. Heath & Co., 1951. Chaps. x, xi, and xii.

Usage and grammar; dictation goals; creative writing; and steps in growth.

TIDYMAN, WILLARD, and BUTTERFIELD, MARGUERITE. *Teaching the Language Arts.* New York: McGraw-Hill Book Co., Inc., 1951. Chaps. viii, xv, and xvii.

Written communication; usage and grammar; and remedial instruction.

10

INCREASING SKILL IN SPELLING

Life today in rural areas requires more writing ability than it did in the past. Continual changes in the character of our social and economic life create new problems, and in the process of working together to solve those problems there is much need for effective writing ability. The free flow of communication is impossible unless spelling and handwriting skills have been developed.

Some children learn easily to spell and enjoy writing; others, who may be equally intelligent, are handicapped by their inability to spell correctly and seem unable to make progress in this line.

Despite extensive research on the teaching of spelling, there is much confusion as to procedure in organizing a developmental program. Many word lists have been prepared, based on analyses of child and adult vocabularies, and new methods of teaching have been tried, yet children still have difficulty with their spelling. The practice of holding "spelling bees" has been used, discarded, then revived, but the only merit of this practice is to raise the esteem of the successful spellers.

Much of the confusion on the subject of how to teach spelling is the result of failure to understand the complex nature of the problem and to realize that not all children have equal mastery of the same skills because of variability in their developmental patterns. Furthermore, many teachers do not seem to realize that spelling is an intregal part of the total language program. Teachers should know how to develop readiness for spelling, have a clear understanding of the objectives of the program, understand how to motivate learning, and realize what procedures are likely to bring greatest progress.

Readiness for spelling

Some of the difficulties of learning to spell are the result of attempts to teach children to spell before they have reached the level in development where they are ready for the next step in their language growth. Lack of preparation for spelling may lead to failure, and failure in the early stages of learning can lead to a disposition toward continued failure. On the other hand, most children who have sufficient maturity and who have developed the necessary manual skills for writing are likely to be successful with spelling from the beginning.

The mental and social maturity of children who are being taught to spell is an important factor. While studies of the effect of intelligence upon ability to spell do not agree completely, it is known that the attention span and the ability to concentrate and to do abstract thinking are related to spelling ability. Also, the extent of the social development is an important part of the readiness for spelling.

Development of speaking, listening, and reading vocabularies is an important part of the foundation for learning to spell. All studies show that knowledge of the meanings of words is necessary to correct spelling. Experiences in the home, the kindergarten, and the primary grades which develop meaningful vocabularies for children do much to prepare the children for spelling.

The spelling of words should not be taught until the words have been encountered in reading. This is especially true in the primary grades, where the children are learning to associate mental pictures or meanings with word symbols as a part of the process of learning to read. In reading, children learn to recognize words as a whole—as a configuration—and to recall meaning from the general appearance of the word. If the first experience children have with a word requires them to notice the letters in the word—as is required in learning to spell the word—interference with reading development will result. Furthermore, since the meanings of words and their use is an aid to spelling, it is important that the words to be learned in spelling *first* become a part of the reading and speaking vocabularies.

Physical handicaps can affect success in spelling. Hearing loss, defective vision, and even poor health in general have been found to impede learning to spell. Malnutrition, glandular disturbances, and diseases of the nasal cavities may be of importance, since all physical defects tend to lower physical efficiency. The child with defective hearing or eyesight will certainly have difficulty with spelling, which requires visual discrimination in the study of printed words and auditory discrimination in their pronunciation.

Experiences in the kindergarten and primary grades can be used to develop visual and auditory discrimination and prepare the children for spelling. Games in which children learn to identify sounds and to judge the sizes and shapes of objects are also helpful. Puzzles, picture dictionaries, and similar devices all help develop visual discrimination.

Readiness for spelling includes also the ability to make all the elementary vocal sounds and to distinguish between them. This development has not always been reached by the first grade. Bradford[1] constructed a test of ability to distinguish the phonemes in spelling words of the first and second

[1] Henry Franklin Bradford, "Oral-Aural Differentiation Among Speech Sounds as a Factor in Spelling Readiness," *The Elementary School Journal,* LIV (February, 1954), pp. 354–58.

grades and found that the ability was not general. This shows a deficiency in the activities which precede spelling instruction.

Some authorities emphasize instruction in phonics as an aid to learning to spell, but there is disagreement as to the value of such help. Knowledge of phonics seems to help children with those words which are spelled phonetically but to be a handicap with nonphonetic words. Children who depend on phonetics spell *thread* as "thred" and *colonel* as "kernel" and *ride* as "rid." Hanna and Moore state that four-fifths of the 3,000 most commonly used words represent regular spelling, that three-fourths of vowel phonemes are spelled with regular letter representation 57 to 99 per cent of the time, and that single consonant phonemes are represented by their regular spellings 90 per cent of the time. Thus phonic instruction intended to develop independence in word mastery in reading helps with the spelling of a high percentage of words.[2] However, teachers should be cautioned against emphasizing phonic rules for spelling and against permitting phonic study to become a substitute for the actual study of the words.

Since handwriting and spelling are taught together to a great extent, the development of eye-hand coordination in the kindergarten contributes much to success in spelling. Many errors in spelling are simply errors in handwriting, so handwriting skill aids spelling skill.

A major part of the development of readiness for spelling is the many experiences which help create a desire to learn to write and spell. Letter writing and story writing from dictation become motivating forces. In the primary grades the children are sometimes led to keep a list of "Words We Use." Skinner[3] suggests placing these words on a chart which the children can consult when writing letters or stories. The list

2 See Paul A. Hanna and James T. Moore, Jr., "Spelling—From Spoken Word to Written Symbol," *The Elementary School Journal*, LIII (February, 1953), pp. 329–37.

3 Blanche Skinner, "Spelling—A Part of the Language Arts Program," *Elementary English*, XXXI (February, 1954), pp. 79–81.

can be expanded and typed for insertion in a booklet as it grows.

The program of learning to spell actually begins before there is any attempt to spell words. It is part of the total program of development in the language arts. Procedures are affected by the knowledge the children possess at each age level and the recognition of the fact that the language development and readiness for further work is not the same for all children.

Objectives of spelling instruction

The organization of a program for teaching spelling and the selection of procedures require a clear knowledge of the objectives of the program. These objectives may be stated as follows:

1. To teach children to spell correctly the words which they need to use in writing
2. To help children to learn how to study and master words
3. To develop independence in word mastery, that is, to know how to find the correct spelling of words not already known
4. To develop an awareness of when words are spelled correctly
5. To help children acquire a desire to spell correctly and have pride in good spelling
6. To improve pronunciation of words
7. To contribute to vocabulary enrichment
8. To teach complete understanding and meanings of words and their correct usage

Formerly, children learned to spell hundreds of words which they did not understand or use. Spelling should not be rote learning but learning to spell words which are clear in meaning and needed in writing. Without help, children do not use the most effective methods of study, and they do not know how to use the dictionary to get information about words. In addition to learning how to spell words, many schools help children learn something about the structure of words by some emphasis on roots, prefixes, and suffixes. Pupils do not memorize lists of affixes and roots, but they learn to analyze them, a practice which is helpful in learning new words. Children are taught to proofread their own written work, to develop a spelling conscience, and to be aware of any misspellings.

Selection and gradation of spelling words

While children learn to spell many words incidentally as a part of their experiences, there are many words which must be studied to achieve mastery of them. Children learn to spell many words through experiences in the home and the community and in the activities of the school. Words used in reading are spelled correctly without special study, and sometimes children can spell words because of transfer of learning from other words. This incidental learning is not sufficient to give children the mastery of all words they need to use, however, and some selection of words for specific study must be made.

How should the words for study be selected? Are the spelling needs of children in urban and rural areas the same? Are the spelling needs of all children in a rural district the same? Is there a common core of words which all children need to know?

There are several schools of thought on the method of selecting words for spelling instruction. One group advocates selecting the words from the daily writing needs of the children. Using his letters, stories, and other writing, each child makes a list of the words he needs to know. The teacher checks the words on a good frequency-of-occurrence list to determine whether they are used often enough to justify the time required for mastery. If the words are used frequently, they can constitute the study list for the child. In this plan, each child builds his own spelling ladder.

A spelling list should certainly grow out of the children's need for expression rather than be a list prepared by some educator. Using a prepared list may make the pupils do relatively well on a spelling test and yet fail miserably in their spelling on a report. There is considerable difference between the words children need to use in their daily school work and the words on most spelling lists in textbooks. Gunderson[4] analyzed the free writing of second graders and found 1,741 words used by 21 children. She compared these words with those found in nine commonly used spellers and reported great disagreement between the spelling lists and the words the children in the group used. Wilson[5] reported a study of three groups of third-grade children in which a list was compiled of the words the children asked to have spelled when writing compositions. An "errors list" was also made from words misspelled in the compositions. She compared these lists with those found in three third-grade spellers, studied the overlapping of the lists with the lists in the spellers, and reported that no one spelling textbook was adequate to fulfil the spelling requirements of the children's written composition. Other teachers have made similar comparisons of words used in the children's compositions and the words in prepared lists and found that about half of the words in the prepared lists were not used at all by the children.

The educators who believe that the study list for children should be composed of the words used in daily written work point out that as children enlarge their vocabularies through reading and listening, the words used in spelling become more complex in character and children are less likely to forget the words they have learned because of use in writing. But Deacon[6] reported an experiment with children in the second, third, and fourth grades in which comparisons were made between the effectiveness of studying a prepared word list and studying words which children needed to learn to spell when writing. He found significantly greater gains from

[4] Agnes G. Gunderson, "Writing Vocabularies of Seven-Year-Olds," *The Elementary School Journal*, LXIII (June, 1943), pp. 590–600.

[5] Lois Ada Wilson, "Children's Spelling Needs and Their Implications," *The Elementary School Journal*, XLVII (October, 1946), pp. 98–102.

[6] Lawrence Deacon, "The Teaching of Spelling Can Become Too Individualized," *Education*, LXXVI (January, 1956), pp. 300–02.

the prepared list as measured by spelling tests, reading tests, and an analysis of children's writing of experience stories. However, the children who studied the words used in their writing had had their writing interrupted to learn the words, and such study bars concentrated effort either in writing or in learning to spell and might be expected to be less fruitful of learning. Deacon questions the value of a list of words based only on needs in daily writing as limiting the number of words to be used. Vocabulary development may not take place with such a practice. On the other hand, experiences in reading, speaking, and listening enlarge the children's vocabularies and add words continually to the spelling list if words are selected on the basis of need to use them.

One group of educators would select the words to be studied by children either from an analysis of adult writing vocabularies or from a prepared list of words based on children's writing vocabularies. Two lists of commonly used words were prepared by Horn and by Rinsland. Horn's list[7] is the result of extensive investigations which included the tabulation of words used by adults in personal and business correspondence and in other forms of writing. A total of over 5,000,000 running words were tabulated to get a list of 36,373 different words after excluding proper names. From this list Horn selected the 10,000 words most commonly used and reported this list with the frequency of occurrence for each word. Rinsland[8] furnished a list of 14,571 words selected from 25,632 different words used by elementary school children in their writing. The words selected were those which were used three or more times in his tabulation of over 6,000,000 running words. Additional lists of words have been provided by Fitzgerald[9] and others, but those furnished

[7] Ernest Horn, *A Basic Writing Vocabulary, 10,000 Words Commonly Used in Writing*, University of Iowa Monographs, First Series, No. 4 (Iowa City: University of Iowa, 1926).

[8] Henry D. Rinsland, *A Basic Vocabulary of Elementary School Children* (New York: The Macmillan Co., 1945).

[9] James A. Fitzgerald, *A Basic Life Spelling Vocabulary* (Milwaukee: Bruce Publishing Co., 1951).

by Rinsland and Horn are the results of the most extensive investigations of writing vocabularies. Such lists are useful to the teacher in checking frequency of use of words.

While Horn's words were taken from adult writing and Rinsland's from the writing of children, most of the words of high frequency on the Horn list are also on the Rinsland list. Fitzgerald found that 72 out of the 100 words most commonly used by adults were found in the writing vocabulary of children of intermediate grades. He also found that 320 of the 500 most useful words for children were also used by adults and that there was an overlapping of 4,927 words on the adults' writing list of 10,000 words and the children's writing list of 7,587 words.[10]

Because of this overlapping in word lists, there have been attempts to develop a common core of words likely to be used by all. Such a common core of 501 spelling words is furnished by Kyte and Neel,[11] and similar and larger lists by Rinsland, Fitzgerald, Dolch,[12] and others are available. Such a list of core words will not be very extensive. Three words make up 10 per cent of the total running words used; ten words make up 25 per cent; 100 words, about 59 per cent; 500 words, over 80 per cent; 1,000 words, about 90 per cent; and 2,800 words, about 95 per cent. Fitzgerald has provided a list of 350 most useful spelling words and 450 useful and crucial words; these 800 words make up 90 per cent of the running words which children use.

Another group of educators would not make the spelling list for children from just the words used by children in their daily writing, nor solely from prepared lists such as previously described, but from a combination of the two sources. Since children can be expected to master the spelling of 3,500 to 4,500 words in the elementary school, a core of not

[10] See James A. Fitzgerald, "The Selection of Vocabulary for Basic Spelling Instruction," *Education*, LIIVI (January, 1956), pp. 286–90.

[11] George C. Kyte and Virginia M. Neel, "A Core Vocabulary of Spelling Words," *The Elementary School Journal*, LIV (September, 1954), pp. 29–34.

[12] Edward William Dolch, *Better Spelling* (Champaign, Ill.: Garrard Press, 1942).

more than 1,500 to 2,000 most frequently used words could be selected from a prepared list, such as that furnished by Rinsland or Horn, and to this list would be added words needed by children in their daily writing at each grade level. This proposal is based on the known fact that while there is a limited list of words used by all children, there are also great differences among children with reference to words needed for writing. After the first 2,000 words commonly used by children, the vocabulary becomes greatly diversified. It is also known that while spelling textbooks usually contain from 3,500 to 4,500 different words, many of these words are not commonly needed by children. Also, the lists in the commonly used spelling textbooks are not in agreement. Betts found that 17 spelling books had 8,645 different words with an average of 3,763 words per book.[13] In a later study of eight spellers, he found 8,652 different words with an average vocabulary of 3,719 words.[14] In the first study, the books agreed on 543 words; in the second study, they agreed on 483 words. It would appear, then, that teachers would do well to consider as the child's study list a small core of words selected on the basis of frequency of use as determined by scientific investigations and to add to this list words needed by the children in their daily work. On such a list there will appear some words which are peculiar to the environment. On the list for a sixth-grade farm child, for example, there may appear such words as *fertilizer* and *fencing*—words of very low frequency on the Horn list and not among the words of a spelling book which includes no more than 5,000 most frequently used words. The farm child's list might also include *contour* and *ration*—words not found among the first 10,000 words on the Horn list. Both the environment and the topics about which they write have an influence on the words the children use in writing.

[13] Emmett A. Betts, *Spelling Vocabulary Study* (New York: American Book Co., 1940).
[14] Emmett A. Betts, *Second Spelling Vocabulary Study* (New York: American Book Co., 1949).

If a common core of words is to be selected as part of the words to be taught, how can the busy teacher make the selection? Some teachers will use a list of most frequently used words or a core vocabulary; others will simply use some words taken from a good spelling textbook, with word selection based on careful investigation, and will add to this list words which the children have difficulty in writing. Salisbury[15] would use an alphabetical list of 5,000 words with each child making his own selection of the words he needs to use and can master in a given week.

The teacher who uses the small core of words as a part of the spelling list needs to know at what grade level the words should be taught. A common criterion for gradation of their words is their difficulty; but difficulty is usually determined by frequency of error at a given grade level. Yet it is known that what makes a word persistently difficult is its nonphonetic character or peculiar construction which makes the spelling different from most words commonly used. The so-called "spelling demons" include words which are not spelled phonetically and words which involve doubling the final consonant or dropping final *e* when a suffix is added. For example, a child taught to spell *canoe* and *canoeing* may have trouble with *having*. Some find that longer words are more difficult for children than shorter words, but this may be due partly to the fact that words of several syllables are more likely to include "hard spots" than short words. Some children have difficulty not only with long words but with double vowels, double consonants, hyphens, and apostrophes.

Words are graded on the basis of difficulty and also on their importance, frequency of use, and need in writing. Some words which are not used often are important to know, but, other things being equal, the words of highest frequency of use should be taught first. Hence we can make this statement: *The chief criterion for determining the grade level at which a word should be taught is the child's need to use the word in his writing.*

[15] Ethel Salisbury, "The Weekly Spelling List," *The Elementary School Journal,* XXV (April, 1948), pp. 208–11.

It should be possible for the child to ask the teacher for help when he cannot spell a word he wants to use in his writing. The teacher should write the word on the blackboard for the child to copy. If the word is one frequently used by the children, it should be added to the spelling list.

Lists of words for study, then, may include a small core of words commonly used by all children, to which are added words which individual children need to use. A part of such a list is individual in character, and some organization of class procedure is required to permit each child to master his individual list. Some teachers handle this program by testing the children on words needed by *all* the children and by having children work in pairs to test each other on mastery of words needed by individuals.

Procedures in teaching spelling

Having determined what words children should learn to spell, the teacher becomes concerned with organization of the instructional program to help children master the words needed for writing. She knows that the children must be highly motivated to want to learn to spell, that time must be provided for instruction and study, that children must learn a good procedure for word mastery, that words are not fully mastered unless spelled correctly in written expression, and that responsibility for proofreading written work includes being aware of any misspelled words, knowing how to find the correct spelling, and taking pride in correct written work.

Motivation of children to learn to spell is a part of the motivation to write, as discussed in the preceding chapter. The desire to write real letters to real people and to write stories and news items for the paper provides the natural motivation for learning to spell. When the words used in the spelling lesson include, at least in part, those words causing difficulty in his writing, the child will have a genuine reason for learning to spell, and the words have real meaning for him, too, because they are part of his vocabulary. Motivation is increased also by success. The child who makes an easy, gradual transition from speaking to writing and who learns a good technique of word study will be motivated toward further mastery because his previous efforts have been fruitful.

If words are to be mastered, time must be provided on the school program for teaching and study. Words for study can be selected from the writing activities of children, but word mastery should not be carried on during the writing process. Such a practice is likely to interfere with free expression and to result in insufficient attention to spelling. Although the amount of time devoted specifically to spelling varies with circumstances, most schools allow 60 to 75 minutes a week for specific instruction. How much time can be profitably spent depends upon the maturity of the children and the variety of activities included in the period. If some time is devoted to word analysis and to the use of the words in writing, more time might well be allotted to spelling. Some teachers devote 60 minutes a week to specific study of words and take time for vocabulary development as part of the follow-up of a unified experience in science or the social studies.

The spelling period can be organized to permit testing, teaching, study, and review. Most research seems to support the view that children profit from a pre-test of the words to be mastered, although some teachers insist on having children study the words before being tested on them. A good procedure used by many teachers is the following:

First Day. The teacher pronounces words twice carefully, emphasizing syllables. She then asks the children to pronounce the words carefully. The teacher also makes certain that the children know the meanings of the words. Then the teacher pronounces each word carefully and uses the word in a sentence. The children write the words, after which each child checks the spelling of his words on a list of words to be mastered during the week. This procedure applies to words to be studied by all children. Additional words for individual study may be handled by having children test each other.

Second Day. Attention is given to words causing most difficulty. The teacher has glanced at the papers and noted common errors, and often the teacher is able to note whether the difficulty is due to mispronunciation, to poor handwriting, or to difficulties inherent in the language. Pronunciation, meaning, and some word analysis may be given before children start to study. Also, there may be a review of procedure for word mastery at intervals of time.

Third Day. Further attention is given to words causing difficulty, and the children are retested on the entire list.

Fourth Day. Attention is given to difficult words and to individual and group difficulties, after which time is spent on study of words misspelled on the third day.

Fifth Day. There is a retest on words for the week, plus a review test of words studied two weeks ago. Testing may be followed by the study of any words still causing difficulty.

How many words children should attempt to master each week will vary with their maturity and ability. Younger children may attempt to master seven words a week, and children of the middle grades may attempt 15 a week. Of course, there are some who can be tested on more words if the children are divided into groups according to ability.

Division of the class into groups may be made by administering a spelling test of two or three words taken from each weekly list of the year. Since children are not equal in language ability, the teacher must group them so that the better spellers have a chance to work at a maximum level of achievement. Grouping permits each child to achieve mastery of approximately 100 per cent of the words he attempts. It is not the number of words which a child studies that is important, but rather the number he learns.

There should be reviews to test the children on the words studied during a period of two weeks or, if the teacher prefers, during the past month. The test should cover all words of persistent difficulty, and it should be followed by study of words misspelled. Investigations show that such reviews are of much help in securing permanent word mastery. Many of these reviews, as well as the regular lessons, should be accompanied by the use of the words in writing. Words are not fully mastered until the child is able to use them in writing so that they become a part of his writing vocabulary. If most of the words which he studies have come from his need to spell them in writing and if he uses them again in writing after mastering the words, gains are likely to be permanent.

An important part of word mastery is correct pronunciation. An analysis of spelling errors of children reveals that many errors are due to faulty pronunciation. In the spelling lesson, the teacher pronounces the word, then pronounces it again, emphasizing each syllable. The child likewise pronounces the word and emphasizes the syllables while also looking at the word.

Meaning also is important in word mastery. As indicated in Chapter 5, children learn with greater ease those things which have meaning for them rather than what may be only a series of abstract symbols. Furthermore, the only need for spelling is its use in writing. Words which have come from their writing needs are likely to have meaning for children, but words taken from a prepared list may not.

Research findings reveal not only that correct pronunciation and meaning are important factors in learning to spell but also that good spellers have good auditory and visual discrimination. Specific training in auditory and visual discrimination helps children improve their spelling ability. In teaching children to master words, attention is focused on both auditory and visual perception of details of the word. As previously pointed out, spelling by sound seems to help with words of regular phonetic spelling, but the child who depends upon phonics to guide him will have trouble with nonphonetic words and those are the words which are of persistent difficulty. Consequently, much attention must be given to the letters of the words. In this respect, teaching the child to spell is in conflict with teaching him to read. In reading, he does not give attention to the parts of the word but to the whole word to which he is attaching meaning; in spelling, he must note the specific letters and the sequence of those letters in the word, so that he can reproduce the word.

Some teachers emphasize the careful study of syllables which make up the word. Evidence regarding the desirability of teaching children to spell by syllables is conflicting, but good spellers are known to be conscious of the syllables in a word. Although primary children would be confused by word analysis, older children seem to profit from the practice, which helps them to identify, pronounce, and spell the syllables of words, especially the common roots, prefixes, and suffixes. Osburn[16] has provided an inventory of syllables of words found on the Rinsland list and has furnished frequency of occurrence of those syllables. He warns teachers to give special attention to unaccented syllables, such as the median syllable consisting of a single vowel, as in *animal*, which the child may spell "anamal," "anemal," "anomal," "anumal," "anymal," or "animal." Osburn found 724 words on the Rinsland list with a single vowel as a median syllable and 899 words having a median syllable of a vowel preceded by a consonant—such words as *appetite, hospital, cereal,* and *period*, which cause confusion in spelling. Children need to be taught to watch for the unaccented syllables in words.

In the intermediate and upper grades, teachers find that many children are aided in spelling by learning to identify syllables and by being familiar with the pronunciation and the correct spelling of roots, prefixes, and suffixes of words. Learning such parts of words tends to transfer to other words having similar syllables and construction. A child who learns to spell *received* correctly will be able to spell *deceived* because he has learned the median syllable. But negative transfer can occur, also, as when a child who has learned to spell *receive* spells *believe* as "beleive" or transfers his knowledge of the way to spell *furnish* to his spelling of *refer* as "refur."

The transfer of general principles similarly from one word to another sometimes facilitates learning but at other times confuses the child and causes him to make mistakes. For instance, a child who has been taught to double the final letter of *refer* in *referred* has trouble when he comes to such words as *limited* and *plastered*. If he has learned to drop the final *e* of *deceive* in *deceiving*, he will expect *hoe* to become

[16] Worth J. Osburn, "Teaching Spelling by Teaching Syllables and Root Words," *The Elementary School Journal*, LV (September, 1955), pp. 32–41.

"hoing." How to use transfer to advantage and how to help the child avoid incorrect transfer is a problem. Normal children and bright children tend to generalize from word constructions they learn and transfer these generalizations to new words. The best course seems to be to give guidance to the generalizing process in the case of words to which the rule does apply generally and to avoid generalizing in other cases.

Many rules of spelling have been used to aid children in learning but most of these rules should not be taught because they help with so few words and because there are so many words to which the rules cannot be applied. There are only a few with sufficient applicability to justify teaching them even in the higher grades. Four rules may be worth teaching to children of the fifth grade and above because of applicability to many words. These rules are as follows:

1. Words of one or more syllables which end in a final consonant preceded by a single vowel usually double the final consonant when adding a suffix beginning with a vowel, provided that the root word is accented on the last syllable.
   Examples: sit, sitting; refer, referring
   It is not applicable to benefited or benefiting.
2. Words which end in silent *e* usually drop the final *e* when a suffix beginning with a vowel is added. If the suffix begins with a consonant the final *e* is usually retained.
   Examples: believe, believing; sure, surely
   It is not applicable in such words as hoeing and canoeing.
3. Words ending in *y* preceded by a consonant usually change the *y* to *i* when adding suffixes unless the suffix begins with *i*. If the final *y* is preceded by a vowel, the *y* does not change to *i* when a suffix is added.
   Examples: carry, carrying, carried; pray, praying, prayed
4. In English words the letter *q* is nearly always followed by *u*.
   Examples: quack, queer, quit

Experiments have shown that the rules should not be taught until the generalizations have been developed inductively. Merely asking children to memorize a rule is contrary to learning procedures. There should be examination of many words, noting their construction, and the formation of a generalization which apparently applies to most of the words. In any case, the mere learning of rules is not the key to good spelling. Words must be studied, and there must be careful auditory and visual perception of the words as a whole and of the parts of which the words are constructed.

Children need to develop a system of word study to aid them in learning words on a spelling list and to help them become independent in word mastery. A good system involves imagery, recall, and repeated writing of the word with careful checking for accuracy. Several types of imagery are used at the same time: auditory, visual, and kinesthetic. The child pronounces the word, carefully emphasizing each syllable, and at the same time looks at the word and notes each syllable. He tries to visualize the word and recall its appearance without looking at the list. He then writes the word and checks to see if he has written it correctly. This process is repeated until he is sure that he can write the word correctly without looking at the list. How many times the child will have to write a word to master the spelling will vary with the ability of the individual child to concentrate and visualize. The sound, meaning, visual image, and feel of the word in writing all seem to help children in mastering the word.

A word is never fully mastered until the child is able to use it in writing. Many teachers provide writing experiences in which words recently learned are used. They also follow many writing activities with the checking of spelling. This becomes a part of the program of developing responsibility for proofreading of written material, discussed in the preceding chapter. When writing news items, business letters, and minutes of meetings, children are led not only to improve composition and usage but also to give attention to spelling and handwriting. They must learn to know when a word is spelled correctly and to take pride in correct spelling.

To assist children in checking their spelling, alphabetical word lists readily available to children will be helpful. Children should form the habit of using the dictionary to look up the spelling of words, but many children find difficulty in looking up a word they cannot spell. Training in word analysis, and for many words a knowledge of phonics, will help the child to get the spelling of the first part of the word. Words like *pneumonia* will be impossible for him unless he knows how the word starts, but for most words he can at least start the word because of a knowledge of other words, and with this help he can find the word in the dictionary.

Independence in word mastery can gradually be developed by helping the child acquire pride in correct spelling, by helping him learn the correct spelling of words, by teaching him a system to be used in word mastery, and by making available sources to which he may go to check his spelling.

Disabilities in spelling

There are sometimes a few children in a class who have difficulty in learning to spell. Their difficulty may be inherent in the language or in their early environment, but sometimes it is due to such disabilities as emotional tensions, visual or auditory defects, lack of good motor control, frequent absence from school, frequent change of schools, nervousness, or hypersensitiveness.

Findings bearing on special disabilities in learning to spell reveal that much is yet to be learned about the causes of difficulty for some children. An analysis of the children's misspellings and observation of how the children work to master words, however, will give the teacher many clues. Children who misspell words which are nonphonetic in character are making normal errors, but children who continually reverse syllables or who have continued difficulty with words that can be spelled phonetically show an abnormal linguistic functioning.

Betts[17] lists the following causes of poor spelling: limited

[17] *Op. cit.*

reading ability, hearing impairment, visual defects, faulty listening skills, poor handwriting, overemphasis on phonics, poor study habits, inability to judge spelling accurately, and inability to visualize words. The physical handicaps should be treated by appropriate professional people, but the other disabilities need the special attention of the teacher. Individual instruction in remedial classes seems the best solution to most of the problems. It is to be hoped that more research on the matter will eventually produce methods of procedure to help the teacher.

Summary

People of rural areas have increasing need for written communication, which involves spelling. Teachers are still confused on how to teach spelling, however, and what words to teach. Readiness for spelling is developed through experiences in the pre-school period and in the kindergarten and early grades. Physical handicaps affect the ability to learn to spell, just as they affect all learning.

The objectives of spelling instruction include the following: (1) teaching children to spell correctly the words they use in writing, (2) helping them learn how to study and master words, (3) developing independence in word mastery, (4) developing an awareness of correct spelling, (5) inculcating a desire to spell correctly and a pride in correct spelling, (6) improving pronunciation of words, (7) enriching the vocabulary, and (8) teaching the meaning and use of words.

Words for spelling lists should be selected from those the children use in their daily writing and from lists of words which have a high frequency of use. Some words which give special difficulty and other words peculiar to the environment may be added to the children's individual lists.

Organization of the spelling program and the procedures to be followed are directed toward a high degree of motivation, correct methods of study, time for testing and analysis of words, reviews, and the development of pride in correct spelling and usage of words.

Some children are helped by generalizations and phonics, and a few simple rules may be taught. More research is needed to determine the causes of some spelling difficulties. Physical disabilities should have the attention of the proper professionals.

Selected references

BETTS, EMMETT A. "What About Spelling?" *Education* LXXVI (January, 1956), pp. 310–25.

Characteristics of poor spellers, determining level of spelling achievement; grouping of pupils; and how to improve spelling ability.

BRUECKNER, LEO J., and BOND, GUY L. *The Diagnosis and Treatment of Learning Difficulties.* New York: Appleton-Century-Crofts, Inc., 1955. Chap. xi.

Diagnosis and treatment of spelling difficulties.

DOLCH, EDWARD W. *Modern Teaching of Spelling.* Champaign, Ill.: Garrard Press, 1950. Entire volume.

Word selection; organizing the program; and methods of teaching.

FITZGERALD, JAMES A. "The Selection of Vocabulary for Basic Spelling Instruction," *Education,* LXXVII (January, 1956), pp. 286–90.

Discussion of research bearing on selection of words to teach.

——. *The Teaching of Spelling.* Milwaukee: The Bruce Publishing Co., 1951. Entire volume.

Selection of useful and crucial words; list of 350 most useful and 450 very useful words; methods of teaching; spelling rules; methods of study; and diagnosis and remedial instruction.

GATES, ARTHUR I. "Developing the Basic Spelling Techniques in the Language Arts," *Education,* LXXVI (January, 1956), pp. 275–79.

Spelling taught as a part of the total language program.

GATES, ARTHUR I., and RUSSELL, DAVID H. *Diagnostic and Remedial Spelling Manual, A Handbook for Teachers* (rev. ed.). New York: Teachers College, Columbia University, 1940. Entire volume.

A handbook for teachers to assist in diagnosis and remedy of spelling difficulties.

HILDRETH, GERTRUDE. *Teaching Spelling.* New York: Henry Holt & Co., 1955. Chaps. i–ix and appendix.

Gives principles of learning applied to spelling; methods of teaching in primary and upper elementary school grades; selection and grade placement of words; and techniques of word study. See the appendix for word lists of 350 most common words for grade two, 500 for grade three, and 700 for grades four through six to be used for study, reviews, or construction of achievement tests.

HORN, ERNEST. *Teaching Spelling, What Research Says to the Teacher.* Washington, D.C.: Department of Classroom Teachers and American Educational Research Association, National Education Association, 1954.

Brief treatment of teaching of spelling, including procedure and word selection.

SPACHE, GEORGE D. "What's Wrong with Our Teaching of Spelling," *Education,* LXXVI (January, 1956), pp. 296–99.

Discusses the selection and gradation of words; and newer practices in teaching.

11

DEVELOPING SKILL
IN HANDWRITING

Handwriting skill is an essential part of the process of written communication and the recording of ideas which are needed by people. Handwriting functions not as an end in itself but as one set of complex skills used in written expression. The process of writing is the process of translating thoughts into symbols in order that these symbols may again be translated into thought by the reader. In this total process, thinking must be organized into composition form to give it meaning, and the skills of spelling and handwriting are required to record that composition. This complex process requires adequate manual skill to produce symbols automatically in response to thought. It also requires accurate visual imagery and a drive that comes from having something to say. Consequently, handwriting skill should not be taught as an isolated subject but rather as a part of the whole process of learning to write, because from writing letters and stories handwriting derives its purpose.

In spite of much study and experimentation, teachers have much difficulty in getting children to develop legible handwriting, and they find that many children dislike handwriting. This dislike and failure to acquire skill causes many children to be blocked in the whole process of learning to express their thoughts in writing. Use of commercial systems of teaching handwriting often results in a program of teaching which is unrelated to the rest of the school program, yet without such a system many teachers do not know how to organize a handwriting program. Why do some children show drive and facility in handwriting from the beginning while others show poor motor skill and lack of interest? What are the objectives of teaching handwriting? If legibility is the chief goal, what factors are involved in legibility? What trends and principles should be followed in organizing and teaching the program? Should both manuscript and cursive handwriting be taught? If so, how should they be taught and how should the transition be made from manuscript to cursive handwriting? What should be done about the left-handed child? How can children learn to develop a desire for good handwriting and how can handwriting be made to function in the total school program? These and similar questions are asked by teachers who are concerned with getting children ready to write and with the development of a program designed to perfect writing skills.

Readiness for handwriting

As pointed out in Chapter 5, the child does not suddenly begin to learn new skills at a given time; he is always in a process of development and develops at his own rate. All children of any grade group are not equally ready for handwriting at any one time. Poor eyesight, low mentality, and lack of motor control have a tendency to delay readiness for handwriting. If vision is poor or not fully developed, the child is handicapped in learning to write. If there is not good motor control of the body, firm control of arm and hand muscles, and proper eye-muscle coordination, the child is not ready for handwriting.

Activities of the kindergarten and primary grades can do much to facilitate muscular development and control and eye-hand coordination. The children should have ample opportunities to use large body muscles in games, rhythms, and physical activity. They can learn to use tools and materials, draw pictures, and paint. Hammers, saws, scissors, blocks, finger paints, clay, and puppets are helpful tools in the development of muscular control and eye-hand coordination. Children use chalk at the blackboard and crayons on large sheets of unruled paper; they scribble, draw, and paint; and they cut paper. Through manipulation of these materials and through games, dramatic play, and the like, children observe similarities and differences in objects and pictures. Early reading activities before any writing begins introduce the child to symbols and the meaning of symbols.

Pre-handwriting development also includes the development of a desire to write. Practice in storytelling and other oral composition help the children develop a desire to express themselves in writing. Oral expression, listening to stories, and early reading experiences of the first grade help to develop attitudes and appreciations for what has been written. The use of dictated stories, as described in Chapter 9, will do much to develop a desire to write on the part of the children themselves. Also, they want to write their names on their property and write notes and invitations to relatives and friends.

If children have developed a strong desire to write, made progress in acquiring muscular control and coordination of eyes and muscles, and removed much of the tension connected with the use of crayons and pencils for drawing, they have developed readiness for writing. The teacher will then be concerned with gradually introducing them to practice in making symbols to be read and with a continuous program of experiences designed to develop handwriting skill in a meaningful fashion.

Objectives of handwriting instruction

The objectives of handwriting instruction are given in the outline which follows:

1. To teach children to write legibly with ease and with sufficient speed for practical purposes
2. To awaken in children a consciousness of the importance of good handwriting and a desire to extend to readers the courtesy of readable written expression
3. To help children perfect skill in handwriting so well that writing becomes automatically a response to thought
4. To teach children to adjust speed of writing to suit their purposes. For example, personal notes may be written with considerable speed, but letters and other material to be read by others should be written no faster than the maintenance of legibility will permit.
5. To teach children to proofread their own written work, to watch legibility, and to correct deficiencies which interfere with the readability of what is written

Children should learn not only to write legibly but without mental and physical strain. This means that the style will be adapted to the motor and emotional characteristics of the writer.

Factors in legibility

The chief goal of the child and his teacher is to write symbols in such a way as to make them easy to read. Hence, it is important to know what aspects of handwriting contribute most to legibility. The following characteristics have been listed as determining the quality of handwriting: (1) letter formation, (2) spacing, (3) alignment, (4) slant, and (5) quality of line. Quant[1] made an objective study of the eye movements of readers of several paragraphs of handwritten material, each paragraph differing from the others in some characteristic, such as alignment, letter form, and weight of lines. Photographic records of eye movements of each subject who read the sample paragraphs were made; in addition, each student was tested on comprehension of material read. On the basis of these data, Quant was able to

[1] Leslie Quant, "Factors Affecting Legibility of Handwriting," *The Journal of Experimental Education*, XIV (June, 1946), pp. 297–316.

determine that letter formation was the most significant factor in legibility. Readers frequently paused in the reading process and regressed to get the meaning when letter formation was not good. Compactness of letters and regularity of slant were also important factors in the readability of the samples of handwriting.

No one characteristic of handwriting operates independently of the others; all are interrelated. Letter formation is closely related to slant, alignment, spacing, and weight of lines. Irregular slanting of letters affects letter formation, as do alignment and spacing. So the teacher should be concerned with slant, alignment, spacing, and weight of lines not as ends in themselves but as aspects of the handwriting which contribute to good letter formation. Medium or narrow spacing of letters is usually most conducive to good letter formation. While alignment in itself does not seem to affect readability, uneven alignment is likely to result from poor letter formation. Handwriting of good quality comes from rhythmic movements, and even alignment is likely to result from such movements.

Trends and principles in the teaching of handwriting

Several surveys of current practices in teaching handwriting and research directed toward discovery of best procedures have served as a basis for the following summary of trends and principles to guide the teacher in helping children to develop legibility and ease in writing.

1. Surveys of practices in schools made by Freeman[2] and Polkinghorne[3] indicate that handwriting instruction is most commonly begun in the first grade, although in some schools the practice is delayed until the last half of the first grade. Polkinghorne found that 93.1 per cent of the schools teach handwriting in the first grade.

---

[2] Frank N. Freeman, "Survey of Manuscript Writing in the Public Schools," *The Elementary School Journal*, XLVI (March, 1946), pp. 375–80.

[3] Ada R. Polkinghorne, "Current Practices in Teaching Handwriting," *The Elementary School Journal*, XLVII (December, 1946), pp. 218–24.

2. Manuscript writing is commonly used for beginners, with a change to cursive writing taking place in grade three or above.

3. Children are commonly taught to write large letters at first and gradually to decrease the size.

4. A commercially prepared system of handwriting is used by nearly two-thirds of the schools; but unless care is exercised by the teacher, the result may be to divorce handwriting instruction from the writing activities of the school day.

5. About 15 to 20 minutes a day are commonly devoted to handwriting instruction. This seems to indicate that in most schools such instruction is confined to a single period of the day, yet such practice will not give meaning or purpose to learning. A single period may be used best as a laboratory period during which children try to remedy the defects in legibility which were observed in writing throughout the school day. Some attention to the problem should be given at other times than during a separate period.

6. Skill in handwriting is considered a tool for expression and not an end in itself. Instruction should grow out of situations where children have a need to express their thoughts in writing and should continually be considered as a part of learning expression through writing.

7. Handwriting is still necessary in spite of the use of the typewriter, and it must be specifically taught. Emphasis on its use in functional situations does not imply that handwriting is to be taught incidentally. Specific instruction is required to perfect skills in handwriting.

8. Individual differences in coordination, rate, position, and writing needs are considered in helping children improve legibility of writing. Children are not equally ready for writing at any given time, and much individual instruction is required to help them with their problems. Left-handed children require special consideration.

9. Tools and materials used by children in handwriting practice seem to be based partly on custom rather than on research findings. It is a common practice to use large pencils and wide-ruled or unruled paper in the primary grades

on the assumption that such materials are conducive to making the larger letters which are easier for young children. However, Miles conducted an experiment with 833 first graders in which pencils of various diameters were used and paper had rulings of various widths. In this controlled experiment, physical reactions of children and their achievements were checked and there seemed to be no advantage in the use of large pencils or wide-ruled paper. Miles states, "In the light of these findings, plus the knowledge of principles of habit formation, there seems little justification for allowing beginners to employ handwriting tools other than those already standardized and recommended for use throughout life."[4]

In the middle and upper grades it is a common practice to have children begin to use ink, but Otto[5] found that in only 3 out of 69 school systems studied were there any definite attempts made to teach children to use fountain pens. Over half of the schools still required the use of steel pen points and pen staffs. In some school systems, the fountain pen was permitted at early grade levels only. In other schools, use of fountain pens throughout the grades was neither prohibited nor specifically recommended. Yet in view of the current practice in society, it would seem reasonable to teach the use of pencils, fountain pens, and ball-point pens. If some other type of pen is needed for children which is different from those used by adults, research findings do not reveal the fact. The use of steel pen points and pen staffs cannot be justified by any known research findings nor by custom in life outside the school.

10. No attempt is made to teach children to learn one exact pattern of handwriting but to develop legibility in all individual writing. This is in contrast to the practice in some

4 Marion E. Miles, "Effect of Different Sizes of Tools in the Handwriting of Beginners," *The Elementary School Journal*, XLIII (March, 1943), pp. 412–14.

5 Henry J. Otto, "The Use of Ink and Fountain Pens in Elementary Schools," *The Elementary School Journal*, XLVIII (March, 1948), pp. 379–84.

schools of trying to get all children to write like the form in the commercial system provided. However, it must be pointed out that this effort is never achieved.

11. In teaching children to write, no attempt is made to secure the use of arm movement exclusively. Even when such an attempt is made, children combine finger movement with arm movement. Each child should learn a method of writing which results in legibility and ease of writing.

12. No attempt should be made to achieve speed in writing, especially in the lower grades. Even in the upper grades, emphasis on speed may lead to the sacrifice of legibility. Each child should learn to adapt his speed to his own ability and to the purpose for which he is writing.

13. A good program of development in handwriting skills begins with a pre-writing period in which children achieve readiness for handwriting. The children are gradually led to use simple manuscript writing in functional situations combined with efforts to improve legibility. They then make the transition gradually to cursive writing over a period of time and continue to emphasize improvement in all writing of the school day. Handwriting periods are motivated by the problems of legibility arising in the writing situations.

Teaching manuscript writing

Most educators seem to agree that beginnings in writing should be in manuscript form because the manuscript writing of young children is usually more legible than any cursive writing they can do and because manuscript writing is more like printing and thus facilitates reading. Furthermore, such writing is easier for children since it consists of simple curves and straight lines and the letters are not connected. Also, manuscript writing tends to make for greater accuracy in spelling since children are reproducing the form most like the printed words. Some authors indicate that manuscript writing at the early stage contributes to more power and satisfaction in written composition because the form is easier to make. Some educators say that manuscript writing tends to build good posture because it employs vertical rather than slanting form.[6]

In the various systems of teaching manuscript writing, considerable variation exists in the form of letters to be taught. Some authorities refer to manuscript writing as printing, while others point out how it differs from printing. The small letters *a* and *g* are good illustrations of the variation from printing as found in many books. Lewry studied the forms used in handwriting systems and, after finding marked differences, recommended the form used in telephone directories, namely, the Bell-Gothic or its equivalent, the Spartan type, which provides maximum visibility for quick recognition and which will probably be used more and more in primary grade readers in time.[7] Parke and Bristow also suggest a form similar to the Bell-Gothic because of its legibility.[8]

Teaching children to write begins with the pre-writing period during which readiness for writing is developed. Children are anxious to write their names, and the teacher can provide models of letter forms needed. Then short invitations or letters dictated to the teacher and written by her on the blackboard may be copied by the children. The teacher gives help on how to sit at the desk, how to hold the pencil, how to hold the paper parallel with the edge of the desk, and how to form letters. Learning to form the letters which make up the word is accompanied by learning the names of the letters and the order of the letters in the word, that is, learning to spell the word. Sometimes messages to go to parents are copied and children print the word *mother* at the top. One group of first-grade children played store and printed sale signs for *dolls, kites, boats, balls, bells,*

[6] See Mary T. Sullivan, "A Functional Handwriting Program," *Elementary English*, XXX (February, 1953), pp. 85–90.

[7] For illustration of form and further discussion, see Marion E. Lewry, "Improved Manuscript Writing in Primary Grades," *The Elementary School Journal*, XLVII (May, 1947), pp. 508–15.

[8] Margaret B. Parke and William H. Bristow, *Practices and Problems in Handwriting* (New York: Board of Education of City of New York, September, 1947), pp. 30–2.

wagons, and *boxes.* Throughout the first and second grades, children use their experiences to acquire skill in shaping letters as a part of using words in meaningful situations. If they have difficulty thinking about what they want to say at the same time that they are thinking about the form of the letters, they may want to dictate it for the teacher to write on the board. They can then give attention to copying the words and forming the letters. Later, models of letter forms may be furnished by posting a chart or by using forms furnished in a commercially prepared system. Children can use these models to improve their letter formation.

After learning how to form the letters, the children require much practice until they can write words without having to think about the form of the letters. And because children at any age level differ in eye-hand coordination, some will need to give more attention to improvement of form than others. To assist the children, the teacher may emphasize a few fundamental techniques, such as these:

1. Begin all letters at the top of the letter.
2. Make letters with straight lines and circles.
3. Move from left to right in writing. For example, in making B, make the straight line first, then the round parts.
4. Make all capitals and tall letters two spaces high, and make small letters one space high.
5. Place round letters close together, round letters and vertical letters farther apart, and vertical letters farthest apart.
6. Space words four letters apart for blackboard writing, two letters apart for newsprint, and one finger width apart for first attempts on ruled paper. When the size of writing is reduced, space words the width of an *O* apart.

Improvement in manuscript writing is directed chiefly toward securing good letter formation, better spacing, and uniform proportion and alignment. The letters *a, e, r, g, m, y, q,* and *z* are difficult for most children. They may be taught by making round forms first. Roundness and straightness of strokes are emphasized. Children can learn that round letters look best when spaced closely together and that straight letters need space between them. Children next learn to reduce the size of writing and still retain the proper proportions in sizes of letters. From models, they learn that good alignment makes for neatness and ease of reading. Some teachers have found it helpful to use standard handwriting scales to help children evaluate their own work and find the defects which interfere with legibility.

While educators generally agree that manuscript writing is more suitable for younger children, there is not complete agreement that such writing should be completely substituted for cursive. Most authorities favor changing the form of writing between the last half of the second grade and the end of the fourth grade, or when the child is ready for the change. Nulton[9] suggests that the child is ready for the change when he has sufficient control of the finer muscles to direct a pencil, chalk, or crayon in forming recognizable lines other than a straight line or a circle, when he shows some evidence of rhythm in writing rather than jerks and stops, when he is able to make coordinated movements without extreme muscle tension or emotional disturbance, when he shows satisfaction with accomplishment of control, and when he is able and willing to make large letters rather than small cramped ones. The child should also show the ability to write all letters of the alphabet from memory and to read simple passages in cursive writing. The change from manuscript writing to cursive should not be made until the child has developed some facility in manuscript writing, as too early a change may not permit him to gain satisfaction from the use of skills in expressing ideas. He should have learned about the relative sizes of letters and parts of letters and to write from left to right and have given some evidence of wanting to do "real writing" before the change is made.

Teaching cursive writing

Teaching children to do cursive writing in a gradual transition from manuscript to cursive involves a program of de-

[9] Lucy Nulton, "Readiness to Change from Manuscript to Cursive," *Elementary English*, XXXII (October, 1955), pp. 382–83.

velopment with numerous opportunities to write and many experiences in learning when difficulties are diagnosed and defects are remedied.

Children will often voluntarily make connecting lines between letters during the transition, but they have to be led to join all letters and slant the letters toward the right. They need to learn to hold the paper on the desk at an angle, to watch spaces between letters and words, to lift the pencil at the end of a word rather than after each letter, and to dot the i and the j and cross the t after the whole word has been written. With charts of both manuscript and cursive writing available, children can see how the letters b, e, f, k, r, s, and z require changes from manuscript form to permit joining the letters in a word.

The transition from manuscript to cursive writing should be carried on usually during the third year of schooling. Some children may revert to manuscript writing because they can still use those skills more effectively. This need not alarm the teacher, for as the changes in form become a part of the writing habits, children will gradually use the form which they know to be used more commonly by adults. If the transition is properly made, no difficulty is likely to occur.

As the change to cursive writing is completed, continuing improvement should bring better coordination and increased skill. Much attention is given to handwriting throughout the school day, the special writing period being a laboratory period during which attention is given to individual needs for improvement and to securing automatic responses in the form of writing. Studies of errors in form which most frequently interfere with legibility show the following difficulties to be prevalent:

1. Looping of non-loop letters such as t and i
2. Failure to loop such letters as e and l
3. Using straight strokes where rounded are needed, as in a and o
4. Failure to close such letters as a and o

Nearly half of the illegibilities occur in the four letters *a, e, r,* and *t,* and illegibilities in numbers are most frequent in 5, 6, and 7. Teachers should help children proofread their own work, analyze their difficulties, and learn methods of correction. While most of the difficulties in handwriting are due to poor letter formation, some children have difficulty in securing a uniform slant. This is often due to poor posture while writing or to incorrect position of paper or pencil. Also, children have difficulty with uniform spacing. Some teachers say that the space between two letters should be about equal to an *n* and the space between two words to an *m.* In any case, the spacing should be such as to facilitate reading. While Quant's study of legibility did not reveal alignment or line quality to be of significance, other samples might bring different results in reading comprehension. Good alignment contributes to neatness, and doubtless extreme deviations in alignment might interfere with reading. Likewise, when lines are too thick, they are likely to run together, and when lines are too thin, the writing tends to become faint and difficult to read.

As children advance through the elementary school, their handwriting tends to decrease in size. How soon the decrease takes place depends upon muscular coordination and eyesight. In decreasing the size of handwriting, right proportions in the sizes of letters should be maintained.

Some teachers emphasize speed of writing. A fair amount of speed is desirable, but that will usually develop as more writing is done in response to thinking. If speed is to receive consideration in the instruction program, teachers must recognize that the speed which each child can achieve and still retain legibility is an individual matter. There should not be one standard for all. More important than speed is rhythm which is of assistance to good writing and to ease of writing. Easy swinging strokes followed by short pauses seem to contribute most to ease of writing and to good letter formation.

Many teachers find the use of handwriting scales of value in helping to develop independence on the part of children to appraise the quality of their own handwriting and to diagnose difficulties. The best known of these scales, provided by Ayres,[10] is helpful in determining general quality. More diagnostic scales are furnished by Freeman,[11] West,[12] and Pressey.[13] Some authorities believe that when children achieve a score of 60 on the Ayres scale, the handwriting is legible enough for easy reading.

Children with special writing problems

Some children need special attention in writing instruction because of physiological or psychological differences from other children. Some of these children may give evidence of physical strain when writing; this is often due to the violent contraction of the muscles controlling the fingers and the arm. An effort should be made to secure freedom in arm movement and the development of a steady rhythmic movement.

Some children have difficulty in writing because of left-hand dominance. Left-handedness is a natural and probably inherited trait in a small proportion of people. There seems to be some connection between the brain center that controls the preferred hand and the speech center; hence, efforts to force a child with definite left-hand preference to use his right hand has sometimes resulted in a disturbance of speech and a retardation in handwriting progress. Some teachers test the children by such activities as throwing a ball, cutting paper, or putting blocks in a box to determine if there is a real preference for the use of the left hand. If such a preference exists, the child is taught to tilt his paper toward the right instead of the left, as right-handed children do,

[10] Leonard P. Ayres, *A Scale for Measuring the Quality of Handwriting of Children* (New York: Russell Sage Foundation, 1917).

[11] Frank N. Freeman, *The Freeman Chart for Diagnosing Faults in Handwriting* (Boston: Houghton Mifflin Co., 1937).

[12] P. V. West, *The West Chart for Diagnosing Elements of Handwriting* (Bloomington, Ill.: Public School Publishing Co., 1926).

[13] S. L. Pressey and L. C. Pressey, *The Pressey Chart for Diagnosis of Illegibilities in Handwriting* (Bloomington, Ill.: Public School Publishing Co., 1928).

when writing. He then can move his forearm about the elbow as a center, thus avoiding the awkward position often seen in left-handed children. The child may slant the top of his paper toward the right so that the diagonal of the paper points toward the center of his body, and use his right hand to hold the paper. The bottom of the paper will thus be at approximately a right angle to the arm of the child. Some teachers emphasize the "pull method" of writing, which brings the down strokes toward the body. If left-handed children find it easier to use vertical or backhand writing, they should be permitted to do so, as legibility and not exactness of style is desired.

Some authorities on handwriting believe it desirable to encourage the left-handed child to change to use of his right hand, but speech pathologists are opposed to the practice, and all agree that the left-handed child should not be *required* to change.

Some children make reversal errors in writing. These may be due to failure to develop auditory or visual discrimination, to poor memory as to order of letters, to poor perception, to writing unfamiliar and meaningless words, or to poor reading ability. If reversals occur in certain letters, words containing those letters may be isolated for special attention. Children may be helped by writing from a copy rather than from memory. Attention is called to the proper order of the letters in the word and an effort is made to develop skill in observation.

Some children require special attention because of lack of interest in learning to write. This may be due to immaturity, to emotional disturbances, to antagonism toward classmates or the teacher, or to a failure to see the value of practice or the purpose in learning to write. Such children may have met failure and frustration in the early stages because of lack of readiness when handwriting instruction was begun.

Each child must experience some measure of success if he is to be encouraged to learn further. Helping the child diagnose his difficulties may help him achieve progress. Saving samples of his handwriting and comparing them from time to time may bring encouragement if real progress has been made. The emphasis on handwriting in meaningful situations throughout the school day may help the child see some real purpose in learning to write.

Making handwriting functional

As previously emphasized, the making of signs and labels and the copying of dictated letters and stories help younger children realize the purpose in learning to write. But this functional approach must be continued if purpose and meaning in writing are to be recognized. Manuscript writing is easily mastered, and young children quickly learn to express their ideas on paper. In the middle and upper grades the activities continue to provide real purposes for improvement in handwriting. Children of the intermediate grades have occasion to write personal and business letters, copy directions, make poster captions, write items for the newspaper, keep minutes of meetings, record entries in a diary, write original stories and poems, or take notes.

Some teachers combine spelling and handwriting instruction in a single laboratory period but motivate the instruction in both by taking words to be studied from the writing activities of the school day. Children give attention to learning to spell the words they need to use and to diagnosing their difficulties in handwriting at the same time.

Success in teaching handwriting requires the use of the functional approach rather than isolated drill on letter forms without reference to use in writing activities. Children must be made to realize the value of practice in order to develop writing skill and correct habits.

Summary

Handwriting is an essential part of language development. It consists of the development of a complex set of habit patterns to a point where writing becomes an automatic response to thought.

The objectives of handwriting instruction are to teach children to write legibly and with ease, to recognize the importance of good handwriting, to want to write well, to adjust their speed of writing to their ability and purpose, to develop responsibility for proofreading their own work, and to know how to diagnose and correct their difficulties.

Readiness for handwriting is developed through activities in the kindergarten and first grade which are designed to achieve eye-hand coordination, to teach the meaning of symbols used to express ideas, to develop the ability to compose stories and poems, and to arouse a desire to write so as to express ideas in written form.

The most important factors in legibility of handwriting are letter formation, spacing, and regularity of slant, all closely related.

Surveys reveal that instruction in handwriting in most schools begins in the first grade with manuscript writing and changes to cursive writing at about the third-grade level. Some commercially prepared systems of teaching handwriting are commonly used.

It is necessary to *teach* handwriting, but it is best *learned* in functional situations which give purpose and meaning to the work.

Trends in handwriting show a shift from exclusive emphasis on arm movement to a combination of arm and finger movement and toward more emphasis upon legibility and less upon speed of writing.

Instruction in writing requires special attention to children who have difficulty in learning to write. Children who show physical strain in writing, left-handed children, and children with reversal tendencies or a lack of interest in learning to write all need special treatment.

Any good program of handwriting instruction will provide for gradual development in skill, will take into account individual differences in ability and progress, and will attempt to establish habit patterns which result in writing legibly and easily.

Selected references

BRUECKNER, LEO J., and BOND, GUY L. *The Diagnosis and Treatment of Learning Difficulties.* New York: Appleton-Century-Crofts, Inc., 1955. Chap. xii.

Objectives and principles of teaching handwriting; manuscript and cursive writing; hand preference; general diagnosis of difficulties; handwriting scales and other techniques; self-diagnosis; causes of difficulties; and corrective procedures.

FREEMAN, FRANK N. *Teaching Handwriting, What Research Says to the Teacher.* Washington, D.C.: National Education Association, 1954. Entire volume.

Aims and standards; motivation; role of meaning; effect of child growth and development; important features; posture and position; individual differences; diagnosis of difficulties; and right and left handedness.

FURNESS, EDNA LUE. "Diagnosis and Remediation of Handwriting Defects," *Elementary English,* XXXII (April, 1955), pp. 224–28.

Outline of defects, possible causes, and appropriate remedial measures.

HERRICK, VIRGIL and JACOBS, LELAND B. *Children and the Language Arts.* Englewood Cliffs, N.J.: Prentice-Hall, Inc., 1955. Chap. xii.

Brief discussion of evaluation of handwriting, manuscript and cursive; transition from manuscript to cursive; major factors to consider; and writing instruments.

LEWRY, MARION E. "Improving Manuscript Writing in Primary Grades," *The Elementary School Journal,* XLVII (May, 1947), pp. 508–15.

Report of study to discover best form for manuscript handwriting; discussion of Bell-Gothic and Spartan type, giving illustration of form to be used.

NATIONAL EDUCATION ASSOCIATION, DEPARTMENT OF ELEMENTARY SCHOOL PRINCIPALS. *Language Arts in the Elementary School,* Twentieth Yearbook. Washington, D.C.: The Department, 1941. Pp. 439–73.

Systems used in schools; procedures in primary and intermediate grades; attacking difficulties; special methods.

PARKE, MARGARET B., and BRISTOW, WILLIAM H. "Practices and Problems in Handwriting," *Educational Research Bulletin.* New York: Board of Education of City of New York, September, 1947. Entire volume.

Facts about handwriting; what to teach; manuscript and cursive writing; children with special problems; and the role of parents in the program.

QUANT, LESLIE. "Factors Affecting Legibility of Handwriting," *The Journal of Experimental Education*, XIV (June, 1946), pp. 297–316.

Excellent report of a study of readability of samples of handwriting to determine factors in legibility.

THOMPSON, STANLEY I. "Integration of Fifth Grade Spelling and Handwriting," *The Elementary School Journal*, XLII (January, 1942), pp. 347–57.

Report of an experiment in integration of spelling and handwriting instruction.

12

INCREASING SKILL AND
USE OF READING

The complex problems of modern living call for study and research in which reading plays a major role. If farm and village people are to solve their social and economic problems, they need to keep abreast of new developments and to know how people live in other sections of their country and in other parts of the world.

Newspapers, magazines, books, and bulletins are sources of information for rural youth and adults. To get the real meaning of what they read, however, people need to know how to read for information and how to apply what they read. To read for recreation they need to learn the enjoyment of leisure reading and where to find the types of reading they enjoy. Extensive reading can enrich the cultural life of the people and increase their enjoyment in living.

Surveys have revealed that many farm homes have fewer books, newspapers, and magazines than most urban homes, and that the library facilities of rural communities are often limited. Many families have their reading restricted to a weekly newspaper and a monthly farm journal. Cooperative efforts of many people have brought library facilities to rural sections through bookmobiles, and some county library associations work with the school administrators to supply reading material for farm people. In Haskell County in Oklahoma, for example, when a local library was forced to close for lack of financial support, the cooperative efforts of the home demonstration agent, the extension service, and the state library extension division, with the help of volunteer library aids, made possible the opening of eleven community libraries in the homes of home demonstration club members. Such accomplishments point the way to improvement of library facilities in rural areas and to help for the teacher who is concerned with the development of reading skill and the establishment of the habit of extensive reading.

In spite of extensive research on the teaching of reading, there are still many children who have trouble in learning to read and never do learn to like to read. Reading disability is often reported as the chief cause of failure in school and of dislike of school. Teachers need to know what can be done to help these children and what they should expect to accomplish in the reading program. They want help in planning the reading program to bring continued growth in reading skills and development of enjoyment in reading.

Reading readiness

Probably the most important factor in learning to read is the development of general mental, emotional, physical, and educational preparedness for reading. This includes making an easy and gradual transition from listening to spoken symbols to seeing printed symbols as representing ideas. Some authorities object to calling the pre-reading program a "reading readiness" program because they say it is all a part of learning to read. It is true that the development of skills eventually used in reading is so gradual that teachers can scarcely say just when the real reading program begins and preparation ends, and that preparation for reading does not end with the beginning of the use of printed symbols to express ideas—that is, with the reading process. But for convenience in the discussion of the sequence of reading development, the stages or steps must be mentioned even though there are no real lines of demarcation between them.

Both teachers and parents can play major roles in getting the child ready for reading. Where schools have kindergartens, teachers have a better opportunity to carry on a pre-reading program; but with or without kindergartens, teachers who get the intelligent cooperation of parents will be able to make progress in the development of readiness for reading.

Both parents and teachers recognize the fact that getting ready to read involves having good vision, good hearing, motor coordination, and general good health. Vision and hearing should be tested at the earliest possible time because undetected lack of acuity of vision or hearing can result in early failure, and with failure come serious emotional problems. Motor coordination which was emphasized in Chapter 11 as important in handwriting, can be important in reading, too, since deficiencies may lead to emotional disturbances. Good general health is important; the child who lacks sufficient rest and sleep or who is undernourished will show evidence of fatigue and lack of interest. Early physical examinations, with any necessary corrective measures, are a part of the process of getting the child ready for reading.

Good emotional adjustment is important in reading. Emotional maladjustment may come from experiences in the home, school, or community. The child who has learned how to make friends easily, who has experienced love and affection, who has many interests and hobbies, and who gets along well with his playmates is likely to be well prepared emotionally for reading. But the child who brings to early reading experiences extreme shyness or serious emotional problems is facing serious handicaps to learning to read and to sharing his reading experiences.

Research seems to indicate that most children do better in reading if the child has reached a mental age of six and one-half years. However, the age at which children may learn to read is affected by teaching methods, teaching skill, teaching materials, size of class, and the like. If classes are small enough and if a large variety of materials is available, it is possible for the skilful teacher to adjust her instruction to help each child make an easy transition from the use of spoken symbols to the use of printed ones. In all beginning reading classes, all children do not arrive at the mental age of six years and six months at the same time. Hence, flexible grouping and individual instruction may be needed.

The reading readiness stage of the program should be designed to do these things:

1. Develop a good experience background
2. Continue the development of a good speaking vocabulary and freedom of expression
3. Help children with auditory and visual discrimination
4. Give children practice in interpretation of pictures
5. Develop good listening habits
6. Help children learn to arrange ideas in sequence, as in making a story
7. Teach children to follow directions given by parents or teachers
8. Guide children in learning to handle such equipment as books, crayons, and pencils
9. Help children learn how to work together in groups
10. Develop orientation toward the printed page, that is, to read from left to right and from top to bottom
11. Give children a desire to read
12. Teach children to recognize the meaning of a few words at sight

In other words, the purpose of pre-reading experiences is to develop certain skills basic to reading, to develop an interest in reading, and to make children aware of what reading is like.

To develop reading readiness, teachers provide a wide variety of activities, some of which are designed to develop a rich background of experience. In getting these experiences, children also enrich their vocabularies, increase their ability to express ideas, develop good listening habits, and increase their auditory and visual discrimination ability.

Many teachers use a series of pictures to stimulate the telling of an imaginative story. Children give their own interpretations of the pictures and learn to arrange the pictures in sequence to tell the story. Many teachers encourage children to recognize one-word signs, such as those posted in the school, on the playground, or along the highway. The children thus learn that words have meaning, and they soon learn to recognize many words at sight. Reading stories to children helps to develop their desire to read. Children look at the pictures in the book and retell the story which has been read to them. In addition to the use of rich personal experiences to help children get ready for reading, many teachers use picture story books,[1] reading readiness books, and pre-primers to help develop basic skills and an interest in reading. These are often included in a basic reading series.

A part of the pre-reading program should include opportunities to increase visual and auditory discrimination and to remedy physical handicaps. The child needs to see well and to have visual discrimination to tell the difference between such letters as *m* and *n*, *c* and *e*, *n* and *u*, and between such words as *want* and *went*, *boy* and *bay*, *hot* and *hog*, and the like. He needs to be able to distinguish between the sounds of *then* and *them*, *big* and *dig*, and so on. The child who has poor vision and defective hearing is handicapped in learning visual and auditory discrimination. Speech defects can also handicap reading ability, for while silent reading is possible even with serious speech defects, oral reading is not, and even silent reading may be retarded because of the emotional disturbance which accompanies the defect.

How can teachers know when children are ready to begin the reading process? There are good reading readiness tests which help secure data on the extent of development, such as the following:

Gates Reading Readiness Tests, by Arthur I. Gates. New York: Teachers College, Columbia University, 1939. Consists of "Picture

---

[1] A selected list of picture story books, together with factors to be used in selection, is furnished by Janet L. Miller in "Some Picture Story Books," *Elementary English*, XXXIII (April, 1956), pp. 210–16.

Directions," "Word Matching," "Word-Card Matching," "Rhyming," and an individual test on the use of capital letters and small letters.

Metropolitan Readiness Tests, by Gertrude E. Hildreth and Nellie L. Griffiths. Yonkers, N.Y.: World Book Company, 1950. Consists of "Sentences," "Numbers," and "Information."

Tests prepared by teachers and their observation of the children can help also in determining readiness for reading.[2] The teacher will need to answer the following questions about each child:

1. Is he physically prepared for reading?
2. Is he emotionally and socially well adjusted?
3. Has he learned to work as a group member?
4. Does he have a good experience background?
5. How effectively does he express himself? Does he take part in class discussions? Does he have a good speaking vocabulary? How does he respond to stories?
6. Can the child follow directions?
7. Does he interpret pictures well? What does he say about pictures he has drawn or about those others have drawn? Does he look at pictures to get information? Can he identify a story by the pictures?
8. Is he interested in the sound of words? How does he respond to rhymes? Does he notice odd-sounding words? Can he discriminate between sounds of words?
9. Can he make gross discriminations in word forms? Does he recognize his own name or signs? Does he recognize words which start like his own name? Does he notice when a word is used more than once? Is he interested in how the teacher writes words? Can he note differences in single letters of separate words?
10. Does he show an interest in wanting to read? Does he bring books from home? Does he enjoy hearing stories read to him? Does he seek books on a library table and look at pictures?
11. Does he have the habit of working from left to right and from top to bottom of a page? In coloring pictures in a book, does he follow that procedure?

[2] A good summary of research on reading readiness has been furnished by Nila Banton Smith in "Reading Readiness," *Elementary English,* XXVII (February, 1950), p. 91.

Objectives of reading instruction

Reading is the process of securing meaning from printed symbols—the meaning the writer intends to convey, interpretation of what is read in terms of the reader's background of experience, and the ability to recall what is read. It is a process which calls for thinking, interpreting, and reacting. Printed symbols which have meaning start the thought process. Teaching children to read must include teaching skills used in the reading process and, in addition, using reading for purposes which are important to development. Since reading is such an important tool in all learning and is a means of communication, the use of reading in the school and community needs to be emphasized.

The objectives of reading instruction may be outlined as follows:

1. To help the child acquire the skills of reading effectively by developing an ever increasing word-recognition vocabulary, learning to read smoothly by word groups, developing independence in word mastery, adjusting speed of reading to purposes and difficulty of materials, and acquiring habits of careful interpretation, organization, and remembrance
2. To teach the child to use reading to enrich life, expand understanding, and broaden culture—to know and love good literature
3. To teach the child to use reading to help solve problems and seek the truth
4. To develop permanent interests in reading for recreation and enjoyment
5. To extend the child's range of communication with other regions of the world
6. To improve the child's social life through his sharing of books and reading
7. To facilitate group living
8. To promote a growing appreciation of the finer aspects of life in the community, the nation, and the world
9. To help the child develop a sense of values regarding books and a knowledge of sources of reading materials

10. To reinforce and extend the child's learning in all aspects of school and community life

The teacher who is helping children realize these goals in reading will find them growing in skill in the use of symbols, in understanding what they read, in adjustment of reading techniques to purposes, and in knowledge of when and how to turn to books for help. They will also be growing in ability to evaluate critically what they read, in ability to interpret for others, in independence of interest in books, and in a desire to read.

Trends and principles in the teaching of reading

Current trends and the principles applied in the teaching of reading in the schools today may be summarized as follows:

1. The program for reading development should begin with the child's level of development and provide experiences which will bring increased proficiency and enjoyment in reading.

2. The reading program should be developed to provide a sequence of growth in reading skills. From the pre-reading period of learning, the program should lead gradually toward an increase in the sight vocabulary, reading by word groups, accuracy in interpretation, independence in word mastery, use of the table of contents and the index of a book, use of the dictionary and the encyclopedia, and use of reading to help solve problems.

3. Most authorities agree that a basal reading series of textbooks is needed to ensure a continuous sequence in development of reading skills. This means a complete set of readers extending from the kindergarten through the elementary school. A good basal reader series is carefully constructed to bring a gradual growth in vocabulary, adequate repetition in use of words, and a gradual increase in complexity of concepts. Even easy words known to children can be used in sentences which express ideas too complex for young children to understand, so careful construction is needed. Research findings reveal that "simplification of the

vocabulary has less effect on comprehension than does simplification of language structure and the relative difficulty of the concepts involved."[3]

A good basal reader series will also have a rich variety of stories to appeal to varied interests of children and to broaden their experience. There will be stories to read for fun and sections which require careful reading to get information.

It would be highly effective if a series could include several readers for each age level, with the same stories appearing in each book but with different vocabulary content. This would help provide for varying degrees of development of children at the same grade level. However, a series of this type has not yet been produced. Many authors have provided the teacher with workbooks to accompany their series and these give opportunities to develop additional skill. An outline for judging a reading series is furnished by Charlotte E. Patterson in *Reading for Today's Children,* the Thirty-fourth Yearbook of the Department of Elementary School Principals, published in 1955.

4. The basal reader series should be considered as a step-by-step series rather than a grade-by-grade series. Thus, not all children of a given class will always be reading the same books because the children are not equally ready for each step in development at the same time.

5. A basal reader series should be supplemented by the reading of many other books. These supplementary books should use about the same vocabulary at each grade level as that used in the basal readers. Children need much practice with material which is easy to read if the easy flow of reading is to develop and if interest in reading is to remain high. Much reading outside the basal series should be given as a part of experience units developed throughout the school day. Units of work in science and social studies will provide enriched reading experiences.

[3] Mary C. Serra, "Amplifying and Simplifying Instructional Materials: Effect on Comprehension," *The Elementary School Journal,* LV (October, 1954), pp. 77–81.

6. The teacher should "set the stage" for a reading experience by awakening interest in the story to be read. The pictures in the readers are often of assistance to the teacher in accomplishing this.

7. Children are divided into flexible groups for reading, and the needs of individual children are met by special help and by providing materials of varied reading difficulty. Each child should be given the help that he needs, as not all children are equally ready for a reading experience. Groups of children may be formed not only on the basis of ability and need for help but also on the basis of interests. At times, children who wish to read and discuss what they read should be grouped to share reading experiences of common interest.[4]

8. The classroom environment plays an important part in the reading development program. An attractive classroom with plants, animals, pictures, museum specimens, bulletin boards, and the like can help awaken interest in adventure through reading. A library corner in the classroom will be an encouragement to further reading for pleasure and for problem solving.

9. Reading experiences should be pleasant, stimulating, and free from pressure. When interest is great and purposes real to children, they will want to read. When the results of reading are used in dramatic play or in discussion or similar situations, reading becomes a stimulating and worthwhile experience.

10. Teachers should build favorable attitudes toward reading and encourage children to use their initiative in finding reading materials of interest to them.

11. Many authorities agree that speed in reading has sometimes been overemphasized by teachers who attempt to speed up the process by artificial devices. When emphasis is placed on meaning, acquiring a good sight vocabulary, reading by word groups, and reading extensively, children will increase the speed of reading in line with their development. Increased speed of reading is important, but it should not be

[4] For further help in grouping, see E. W. Dolch, "Groups in Reading," *Elementary English*, XXXI (December, 1954), pp. 477–81.

given emphasis in the lower grades, and at no time can there be one standard speed for all children. Speed will vary with the child, with the types of material to be read, and with the purpose which the child has in mind. When children read stories, they may read rapidly to find out how the story ends; but when they read to get facts, they will need to read carefully, which takes more time. Reading speed will vary also with the difficulty of the words and concepts in the material.[5]

12. Children should know their progress in reading. Scores on annual reading tests and a glance at books used in reading the year before will help children to see their progress. Parents can lend encouragement to children by praising their progress in reading.

13. More and more, good teachers are giving increased attention to the relationships which exist between reading and the other communication areas. Reading, writing, speaking, and listening supplement and reinforce each other in child development. Reading activities sometimes serve as a pivot around which speaking, listening, and writing experiences occur. At other times, the experience in securing material for writing or speaking involves much reading. Before there is expression, there must be impression. Before there can be expression, the child must secure something to express either through his reading or through personal experience. Successful reading depends on the ability to organize ideas and to express them. Reading is not just a process of finding meaning in printed symbols; comprehending, organizing, and using ideas are also included. The skills of reading, writing, speaking, and listening are developed concurrently. Using the information obtained from reading for speaking situations helps strengthen and reinforce reading as well as give purpose to reading.

Oral and written expression are improved by making children aware of sentence structure, good usage, and the use of

[5] See Guy L. Bond and Eva Bond Wagner, *Teaching Children to Read* (rev. ed.; New York: The Macmillan Co., 1950), pp. 322–25; and Paul Witty, "Evaluating Methods and Devices to Improve Reading Rate and Comprehension," *Elementary English*, XXXI (May, 1954), pp. 260–67.

punctuation marks as they read. Punctuation marks are used to help the reader get the author's meaning. Likewise, the child who writes uses punctuation to help make his meaning clear.

14. Attention is being given to the gifted reader as well as to those who are handicapped in ability. The gifted child should have a rich variety of reading material suited to his reading needs and commensurate with his accelerated ability. His superior ability should be put to good use in helping solve problems and in enriching his life through extended reading.

15. Children need practice in doing the different kinds of reading required. Even though the vocabulary is the same, different skills are used in work-type reading from those used in reading for mere enjoyment. Also, oral reading uses skills not included in silent reading. The reading program should provide practice in the different kinds of reading.

16. Reading instruction may follow any one of several methods, but the trend seems to be in the direction of using a composite of several methods. For some teachers, reading instruction seems to mean teaching children to recognize isolated words either by learning the words by letter or by sounding out the letters or by drilling on the words. The disadvantage of the first two procedures will be recognized. Also, if the word-drill method is used alone, children are likely to become overconscious of isolated words and read word-by-word. Some teachers use oral reading as a means of instruction on the supposition that it permits the teacher to check on the pupil's performance; but this is a slow process and it may lead to the development of slow readers. Other teachers use the silent reading method only, presenting symbols in association with objects or actions and thus attaching meaning to them. This procedure seems to get good results, but when used alone it makes some teaching difficult. Many teachers are now using a combination of several methods which include the use of real-life activities about which to center the thought-getting process. An experience chart may be used, as well as motivated lessons taken from the basal

reader series. The teacher is not confined to silent or oral methods of reading but introduces words through experience. Various techniques (discussed later) are used to secure independence in word recognition and to help children overcome difficulties in reading.[6]

17. The developmental reading program includes the following stages: (1) a strong program to develop reading readiness and, during early reading stages, to develop certain basic skills and good attitudes toward reading; (2) the beginning stage in learning to read; (3) the stage of wide reading to increase power and excellence in reading; and (4) the stage of refinement of reading skills, interests, and tastes through extensive personal reading. There are no fine lines of demarcation between the stages; as a matter of fact, the stages overlap in the developmental process.

18. A major trend in the reading instruction program is to enlist the help of parents. Many school systems publish manuals or guidebooks for the use of parents. Fathers and mothers can do much to help get the child ready for reading by equipping him physically, emotionally, socially, and educationally. Parents who read stories to children and get children to learn to listen and to tell stories of their own from pictures will do much to aid the child's reading development. Parents can also help later by providing suitable reading material at the child's level of interest and difficulty and by encouraging him to read outside school. Rural people need to be educated to an understanding of the role which parents can play in the educational development of the child.

Instruction in beginning reading

The teacher of the first grade should make an assessment of the extent of development of each child before actual reading begins. Some children may not have had the benefit of a pre-reading program in the kindergarten, and some may have experienced excellent development in the home envi-

[6] For a more complete treatment of different methods, consult Guy L. Bond and Eva Bond Wagner, *op. cit.*, and William S. Gray, *On Their Own in Reading* (New York: Scott, Foresman & Co., 1948), chap. i.

ronment. It is certain that all the children in any first grade will not be equally ready for each new experience in learning to read. For many children the reading readiness program has not been completed when the children enter the first grade. In any case, an easy gradual approach must be made to the process of using symbols to get meaning. Symbols have no meaning except as meaning is attached through associations in experience. Repeatedly attaching associations through pictures, objects, or direct experience gives meaning to single words, phrases, and sentences. Some word symbols take on meaning in context by association with known words. In the pre-reading period the child has learned to read stories by pictures, going from left to right and from top to bottom of the page, and has learned that words have meaning. In fact, he has already attached meaning to many words and can easily attach meaning to words in groups if short sentences are introduced.

Authorities and classroom teachers vary in recommendations regarding the early organization of the reading program. Some teachers handle the class as one group at the beginning of the first grade, but others find that best results are secured by grouping children on the basis of readiness tests or other reading readiness evidence mentioned earlier in this chapter. Group I may include those children who still need considerable help with the pre-reading program; Group II, those mature enough to proceed with the next steps; and Group III, those who already recognize many words by sight and can go forward rapidly. Group I may use reading readiness books for a time, while Groups II and III proceed with the primer. The range of talent may even determine that there should be four or five groups.[7]

Some teachers will start the reading program with an experience story which the children cooperatively compose and dictate to the teacher. The children then learn to read the story. Because it is their own story written in words familiar

[7] See Guy L. Bond and Eva Bond Wagner, *op. cit.*, and Lillian Gray and Dora Reese, *Teaching Children to Read* (2d ed.; New York: The Ronald Press Co., 1957).

to them, it is easy for them to associate meanings with the word symbols. Manuals which accompany the basal reader series give help to the teacher and often suggest experiences which may be used in introducing the stories in the primer. The difficulty with dependence solely on experience charts is the fact that there may be little vocabulary control or little repetition in the use of words. Also, the words used may not be the ones which are used in the basal reader. Regardless of whether an experience chart or a primer is used in the beginning, the teacher must provide real experiences to give meaning to the words. Some authorities suggest the use of the experience chart as a supplemental device, with the teacher using only words which the children have learned to recognize in the basal reader.[8]

Vocabulary development

When the children have had considerable reading experience and have acquired a fairly large reading vocabulary, the teacher begins to develop independence in word mastery and to secure a continuous growth in a meaningful vocabulary through the use of the basal readers, experience units, and supplemental reading materials. Efforts are made to introduce new words through experience, but the child will need to learn techniques of word mastery, partly because the meanings of words vary with the context and partly because he will encounter words which have not yet appeared in his reading experience. Most reading textbooks are built for urban children, however, so the children in rural areas may need a variety of procedures to help them determine the meanings of words. Among the word mastery techniques which children can use are the following: (1) context clues, (2) word similarities, (3) visual appearance of words, (4) word structure analysis, and (5) phonetic analysis. As children

[8] Additional help with beginners will be found in Lillian Gray and Dora Reese, *op. cit.*; Margaret McKim, *Guiding Growth in Reading* (New York: The Macmillan Co., 1955), chap. v; Paul McKee, *The Teaching of Reading in the Elementary School* (Boston: Houghton Mifflin Co., 1948), chap. viii and ix; and Guy L. Bond and Eva Bond Wagner, *op. cit.*, chap. viii.

grow in experience in reading, they will learn to expect certain ideas to appear in the stories they read and, thus, will have some clue as to what new words mean. This can be used by asking the children to tell what they think the author is going to relate in his story, using the pictures in the book to suggest ideas. Completion exercises are also helpful. The teacher may give a sentence like the following: "George went to the mailbox to get the ———." She then asks the children to tell what word should be used to complete the sentence. The children will know a few words like *mail* and *letters* which will make sense. If they later find a sentence reading, "John went to the mailbox to get the package," they know that the word *package* is the written symbol for something which comes by mail.

The similarity of a new word to words the children already know often helps them get the meaning of it. For example, the word *barnyard* is made up of the familiar words *barn* and *yard*. Again, if they know the words *turn* and *go*, they are not likely to have trouble with *turning* and *going*. A new word like *monkey* may have the visual appearance of some word already known, such as *donkey*. In the sentence, "Henry went to the henhouse to gather the eggs," the children know *hen* and *house* and can also associate the familiar word *eggs* with the compound word *henhouse*. Since any farm child knows that the eggs must be collected, the meaning of the new word *gather* becomes clear to them.

When easier procedures fail, children have been enabled to learn the meanings of words by dividing the words into syllables. Phonetic analysis also will help with new words, but it does not always solve the problem because letters have more than one sound. However, a knowledge of the most frequent sounds is often helpful. The words used for practice should be those with which the children are already familiar, and the phonetic elements taught should be those which occur most frequently. The primary object is to develop a general eye-ear sensitivity, not to drill a number of phonograms into the children's heads. The trend is to give more emphasis to phonics in the second and third grades than in the first grade. In any event, it must be remembered that the techniques of word study should be taught as part of the reading process and not through drill with isolated words.[9]

As progress is made in reading, the children should be taught to use the dictionary to find the meanings of words and to know how to pronounce new words. This requires teaching the children alphabetical order of words. They must then be shown how the words in the dictionary are listed in the order of sequence of letters in the words. They should learn the use of the guide words on the dictionary pages and the need to read all the definitions given for a word in order to select the definition which applies in the sentence they are considering. The study of phonics will help them master the way the pronunciation of a word is indicated in parentheses after the word, and their attention should be called to the help which the pictures and diagrams give to making meanings clear.

The major avenue for vocabulary development, of course, is extensive reading and many personal experiences in the school and the community. Words learned in their reading can be made a part of the children's speaking and writing vocabularies if they are used in daily activities. A good plan is to encourage the children to keep vocabulary notebooks in which they write the new words they encounter in their reading and record how often they use these words in class discussions.

Recreational reading

Children should be led to explore new books both to enrich their vocabularies and give practice in reading and to experience pure enjoyment. Many maladjusted children have been helped by reading appropriate books. Books represent

[9] Help with phonetic analysis and other techniques to develop independence in word mastery may be found in W. S. Gray, *op. cit.*, chaps. v–viii; Lillian Gray and Dora Reese, *op. cit.*; and Paul Witty, "Phonic Study and Word Analysis—I," *Elementary English*, XXX (May, 1953), pp. 296–305.

a storehouse of enjoyment and culture. An adequate reading program emphasizes the use of reading as a recreation.

To carry forward successfully a good recreational reading program, the teacher must know the children—how well they can use their reading skills and what their interests and problems of social and personal adjustment are. Suggestions for the study of children were made in Chapter 5. Some children will show the need for the emotional security they have not found in the home or among playmates, and every child has a need for achievement. This is not to suggest that books should be used as a means to escape facing emotional problems in real life but rather that they be used to understand how such problems have been solved by others. Books provide outlets for suppressed emotions and for frustrations in early life. As such outlets they contribute to mental health. Books also help to increase the teacher's understanding of children as she observes the appeal of different types of stories for individuals.

The teacher must know children's books and be familiar with good book lists. Books of varying degrees of difficulty as well as books to appeal to a wide variety of interests should be available. Children like adventure stories, stories about animals, fanciful tales and myths, biography and history, and mystery stories. Studies of children's interests reveal differences in preferences of boys and girls, especially at the intermediate grade level and above. Boys like adventure stories, while girls show greater interest in romantic fiction. Mystery stories appeal to both sexes. In choosing books for children, not only the interest factor but also the literary merit and artistic quality of the book should be considered. Good books are well written and appeal to the imagination of the reader. They have "a plot that is full of realistic action, danger, and suspense; a vivid vocabulary, rich in imagery; a mood and tone that harmonize with the content; and a style that is clear, direct, and appropriate to the thought."[10] Good lists of children's books are frequently published in issues of

[10] Helen Huus, "Experiences in Literature," *Children Learn to Read* (Chicago: National Council of Teachers of English, 1949), p. 27.

Elementary English, Childhood Education, The Horn Book, Story Parade, and the *Wilson Library Bulletin.* The references at the end of this chapter give other sources to which the teacher may refer for book lists published at various times.

Children should have available for recreational and informative reading much current reading material. Magazines such as *Child Life, Play Mate, Jack and Jill,* and *Junior Language and Arts* appeal to children as they contain many stories, games, poems, and other interesting features. *Young America, Junior Scholastic, Current Events,* and *My Weekly Reader* contain news of interest to children.

To carry forward a successful program of recreational reading, the teacher must know the children, have available reading materials, and furnish guidance in use of the materials. Some teachers have story hours or free reading periods at which time the teacher reads stories to the children. The children are encouraged to read and to share their interest in reading by telling others about the books they have read and by reading portions of the story to them. Group members can be enlisted to develop standards for book selection. Some teachers find that interest in reading is stimulated by the organization of a book club or by having the children keep lists of the books they read and ranking them on the basis of their likes and dislikes.

Many parents want to provide magazines and books for their children but do not know which ones are most suitable. The school can do a service by helping the parents know what magazines and books are appropriate for their children and see the value of encouraging their children to read outside the school. Extensive reading at home helps the child achieve a permanent interest in reading.

Factual reading

While the reading materials children use merely for enjoyment are often informative or factual in character, it must be recognized that a program which includes the use of reading only for recreational purposes is not a well-rounded program. There must be provision for the development of habits of using printed matter to solve problems.

A good school program in rural areas is closely related to the problems of the living of the people. Many of the work units in social studies or science and agriculture deal with problems peculiar to rural communities. Soil erosion, cooperative marketing, diseases of farm animals, poultry raising, cattle feeding, and the like have real meaning in the lives of farm children. And while the general reading skills needed for careful reading and research are the same for rural and urban children, the reading materials are different and the vocabularies used in factual reading are not identical. Some children of the middle and upper grades have progressed sufficiently in reading skill to permit the use of federal and state government bulletins and farm journals, and some children's books and magazines contain factual material which will help the children in dealing with problems peculiar to the rural community.

Learning to use the skills of research is a closely integrated part of the whole school program. Children learn to outline their problems and make a list of possible source material. They need to learn how to use a card catalogue, a readers' guide to periodical literature, encyclopedias, bulletins, books, and magazines. Reading to get the information desired calls for skimming through paragraphs and pages to find answers to questions. Children must learn to be careful in finding answers—to develop a respect for accuracy; be able to read maps, charts, and graphs; learn to select and evaluate findings; organize information; and follow directions. Teachers will need to help children learn the meaning of unique words, practice the kind of careful reading required, and master the study skills as needed.

Oral reading

Recreational reading and factual reading may involve individual or group activity in which oral reading is needed to report findings to the group or to outline a story read for the benefit of the others. Oral reading for diagnostic purposes is recommended as part of the early reading development program by some authorities.

Oral reading uses the same skills as silent reading to get the meaning of the material, but in addition it requires the skills of the speaker to make his understanding of the meaning clear to his listeners. This is done by the inflections of his voice, the pauses he makes for emphasis, and the changes in reading pace he uses.

Throughout the grades, opportunities to use oral reading may be provided as a part of the unified language arts program. Children who have difficulty in giving short talks may learn to improve through oral reading, developing better poise, posture, voice control, voice quality, and articulation. Stories from books which children read may be used for dramatic interpretation, with the parts read by the children rather than spoken from memory.

Some teachers find that oral reading is improved by having the children cooperate in setting up standards. One fourth-grade class listed the following characteristics of the good oral reader:

1. He knows his story well, understands the words, and pronounces them correctly.
2. He enjoys the story and makes us enjoy it, too.
3. He reads a part as the characters would speak it.
4. He uses a good voice and has a good standing position.
5. He makes us excited and interested.
6. He makes us want to read the story.

Materials for oral reading will often be those which children find in their individual recreational reading and want to share with others. American folk literature makes good oral readings, and most teachers use much poetry because poetry can best be enjoyed by sharing it with others; in fact, it can never be fully enjoyed unless read orally. Reading poetry should be given more emphasis in the school program than is commonly the case. From early childhood children enjoy poetry. They listen to Mother Goose rhymes before they come to school; the primary teacher permits them to make up poems and recite them; and the teacher reads poetry to the children. This interest in poetry can be continued throughout the elementary school if selections are used which are appropriate to the level of development of the children and if they are used in social situations in which poetry can be enjoyed. There are many fine approaches to poetry, such as rhythm exercises, free reading, choral reading, group writing of free verse, paintings, and music. In a variety of ways, teachers can introduce poetry for the enjoyment of the children. References to anthologies and other materials for oral reading are given at the end of this chapter.

Situations in school often give occasion for oral reading. Some occur frequently and others less often. They include the following: (1) reading a poem or a story to classmates; (2) reporting to the class on a favorite book and reading a portion of it; (3) reading from an article to prove a point in a discussion; (4) reading information needed in an activity and not available in the library; (5) reading announcements, reports, original papers, or minutes of meetings; (6) reading aloud to oneself to test one's speech or to appreciate some literary selection; and (7) choral reading.

Children with special reading problems

Even with a good program in reading development, some children may have trouble with their reading progress. They may show faulty word recognition; they may fail to associate words with the correct meanings; they may read word by word and fail to get the meaning of the sentence. Bond and Brueckner have classified these individuals as cases of "simple retardation," cases of "specific disability," and cases of "complex disability."[11]

The simple retardation cases include those children who have a good reading pattern but lack experience in reading,

[11] Guy L. Bond and Leo J. Brueckner, *The Diagnosis and Treatment of Learning Difficulties* (New York: Appleton-Century-Crofts, Inc., 1955), pp. 119–20.

especially in certain types of reading, and who have failed to keep pace with the others in the grade in the development of reading skills. Progress will usually be made if attention is given the child in applying the regular techniques which have been found helpful in bringing about more rapid development and securing greater interest in reading.

The special disability cases have such difficulties as interfering habits, faulty word-recognition techniques, excessive articulation, and so on.

The limited number of complex disability cases are the more seriously retarded children, three-fourths of whom are likely to be boys. They may show considerable emotional disturbance, which may be a cause or a result of their reading difficulty, or possibly both.

Standardized tests of reading ability and teacher-made objective tests and the results of the teacher's observation can be used to determine the extent of the pupil's retardation. Good reading achievement tests are the *Iowa Every Pupil Silent Reading Test* (Houghton Mifflin Company), the *Coordinated Scales of Attainment* (Minneapolis Educational Test Bureau), and the *Gates Reading Survey* (Teachers College, Columbia University). Diagnostic tests can be used to make more complete analysis of the difficulties and especially of the more serious cases of reading disability. (See references at end of chapter.) Data of value to the teacher can be secured from such tests if the teacher understands the limitations of these instruments.

Diagnosis should proceed only as far as necessary to locate difficulties which children are having with reading, and the remedial instruction should be closely integrated with the diagnosis. If the child shows that he has an inadequate sight vocabulary, the teacher can use real experiences to give meaning to symbols and build a good vocabulary. Most reading difficulties respond to a straight educational approach.

Studies of children with reading disabilities show that many of them are the result of inadequate techniques in the school or in the home. Hence the major effort of the classroom teacher should be directed toward the development of an adequate program which recognizes that children do not develop at the same rate and that individual needs must be met as they become evident if the child is to avoid frustration and more serious maladjustment.

Summary

There is a great need for teachers in rural schools to develop a program which will lead to proficiency in and enjoyment of reading.

Preparation for reading begins early in life, and growth in experiences, in vocabulary, and in mental maturity is gradual. Parents should be made to see the importance of good eyesight, good hearing, and good general health to the child.

In school the pre-reading program builds a rich experience background, extends the speaking vocabulary, helps the social adjustment, and develops good listening habits. The children learn to follow directions, to tell stories from pictures, and to recognize some words as symbols of ideas.

Reading instruction starts when the children are ready for it. The program helps the child acquire skill in reading and word mastery, use his reading to broaden his vocabulary and secure information, and enjoy good literature.

The use of a basal reader series is necessary, but there should be much supplementary reading available to the children and they should be encouraged to read both for pleasure and information.

Speed of reading should not be emphasized at the expense of comprehension. Each child has his own rate of speed, and the rate will vary with material read for pleasure and material read for facts. In other words, the purpose of the reading should determine the rate of reading.

As one of the language arts reading is closely integrated with speaking, writing, and listening. The method to be used in teaching reading is often a combination of methods: recognizing easy words, reading groups of words, organizing words into sentences and paragraphs, and recalling material read. Children learn to use context clues, visual appearance, word analysis, and phonetics to understand new words. They are taught how to use the dictionary and how to find information in the library.

The stages in reading development are not well defined but overlap.

A major part of the reading program is the development of a desire to read. The teacher makes use of her knowledge of the children's interests to encourage recreational reading, and she often employs such techniques as dramatic interpretation of a story or choral reading of a poem. Oral reading plays an important part in giving the child poise, voice control, and a larger vocabulary. The children may also learn the value of oral reading at home to increase their appreciation of a poem or a selection or to test the sound of a story or a report they are to read to the class the next day.

Some pupils are slow in developing reading ability and some have more serious reading disabilities. Standard reading tests and diagnostic tests will help the teacher determine the extent of the difficulty and decide how to treat it.

Selected references

BOND, GUY L., and WAGNER, EVA BOND. *Teaching the Child to Read* (rev. ed.). New York: The Macmillan Co., 1950. Entire volume.

Gives considerable emphasis to reading readiness, primary grade work, word recognition, reading in content fields, developing reading interest, and to appraisal of reading abilities.

BOND, GUY L., and TINKER, MILES A. *Reading Difficulties, Their Diagnosis and Correction.* New York: Appleton-Century-Crofts, Inc., 1957. Parts II, III, and IV.

Discussion of the nature, causes, diagnosis, and remedial treatment of reading difficulties.

BRUECKNER, LEO J., and BOND, GUY L. *The Diagnosis and Treatment of Learning Difficulties.* New York: Appleton-Century-Crofts, Inc., 1955. Chaps. vi and vii.

Treatment of diagnosis of reading difficulties.

DURRELL, DONALD D. *Improving Reading Instruction.* Yonkers, N.Y.: World Book Co., 1956. Chaps. ii–xiii.

Discusses instructional materials, reading readiness, grouping pupils, word analysis, and study skills.

GRAY, LILLIAN, and REESE, DORA. *Teaching Children to Read* (2d ed.). New York: The Ronald Press Co., 1957.

Deals with reading at all levels including preprimer, lesson plans for teaching, structural and phonetic analysis, developing study habits, securing good oral reading, and reading in content fields.

GRAY, WILLIAM S. *On Their Own in Reading*. Chicago: Scott, Foresman & Co., 1949. Chap. ix especially.

Teaching children to find words in the dictionary. The entire book deals with development of independence in word mastery.

HARBAGE, MARY. "Using Poetry with Children," *Elementary English*, XXVI (November, 1949), pp. 385–90.

Suggestions for teaching children to enjoy poetry. List of twenty-two anthologies from which teachers may select poetry for children.

McCONNELL, GAITHER. "Achievement Factors in Juvenile Biographies," *Elementary English*, XXXII (April, 1955), pp. 240–44.

Content analysis of twenty-four biographies for children; showing emphasis on personal factors and environmental influences.

McKIM, MARGARET G. *Guiding Growth in Reading*. New York: The Macmillan Co., 1955. Chap. v, Parts III and IV.

Describes the reading program for primary and intermediate grades, emphasizing informational and recreational reading, oral reading, and word mastery techniques.

NATIONAL COUNCIL OF TEACHERS OF ENGLISH, *Children Learn to Read*. Chicago: The Council, 1949. Chaps. iii and iv.

Very helpful to the teacher in furnishing information as to sources of book lists for children and current reading materials. List of inexpensive books, reference material, and dictionaries for children. Suggestions for use of reading materials.

NATIONAL EDUCATION ASSOCIATION, DEPARTMENT OF ELEMENTARY SCHOOL PRINCIPALS. *Reading for Today's Children*, Thirty-fourth Yearbook. Washington, D.C.: The Department, 1955. Chaps. ii–vii.

Tells how to use reading in the whole school program and gives aids in book selection, in using the library, and in choosing a basal reader series. Footnotes provide good sources of books and magazines for children.

NATIONAL SOCIETY FOR THE STUDY OF EDUCATION. *Reading in the Elementary School*, Forty-eighth Yearbook. Chicago: University of Chicago Press, 1949. Part II, chaps. iii–vi and x especially.

Gives criteria of a good reading program, tells how to appraise pupil needs, and helps with the selection of literature for personal reading. Has good book lists for children (page 211).

PARKE, MARGARET B. "Picture Dictionaries," *Elementary English,* XXXII (December, 1955), pp. 519–24.

Discussion of the use of picture dictionaries. List of fifteen picture dictionaries for young children.

WITTY, PAUL. *Reading in Modern Education.* Boston: D. C. Heath & Co., 1949. Chap. v, Appendices A and B.

Gives good discussion of book selection and stimulating interest in reading. Appendix contains lists of books and current periodicals for children.

YOAKAM, GERALD A. *Basal Reading Instruction.* New York: McGraw-Hill Book Co., Inc., 1955. Part II.

Emphasizes beginning reading, choosing reading materials and a step by step program of reading development. Has list of sources of children's books.

13

SOCIAL STUDIES
FOR RURAL SCHOOLS

Of all of the areas of the curriculum, the social studies are often the most confusing to the classroom teacher. There is uncertainty regarding objectives, content, organization, and procedures. There is confusion regarding the meaning and scope of the term *social studies*. Some programs give major emphasis to local community life while others represent studies of regions of the world or of epochs of history.

Several factors seem to be responsible for the confusion which exists. Society is constantly changing, and the philosophy of education changes accordingly. Changing world conditions give importance to aspects of life hitherto of little concern. The spread of Fascism or Communism or some other ideology brings increased demands for emphasis on democracy, American history, and citizenship. Statistics regarding juvenile delinquency cause people to insist that the schools do something to improve behavior. Increased knowledge regarding the interdependence of people and a recognition of the new American leadership role in world affairs make necessary better understanding of and cooperation with the people of other nations. Pressure groups are formed to support this cause or that, and teachers who are rather uncertain about their objectives and program have little defense against such groups.

State education leaders have not entirely saved the teacher from confusion on how to proceed. Published state courses of study or guides usually leave the teacher much freedom in determining the content and plan of organization of a subject. Courses now emphasize the importance of the local community but leave to the teacher the responsibility of determining the needs of the people. So the teacher in a rural area is concerned about how a program can be developed to help the people achieve happy and useful lives.

Rural life needs

The social and economic problems of rural people, as indicated in Chapter 2, are very complex and must be the concern of rural educators who consider that the school must help the people solve the problems of life. Agriculture is the chief interest of the people outside the town or village, and the people of the rural center are also concerned about farm life.

Rural people have some very definite ideas about what they need in the way of education in social studies. Farmers want to know how they can increase their income and reduce the cost of production and marketing. They want to know how farm prices are affected by national and world conditions. They are interested in taxes, insurance, soil, forestry and conservation, and in good health for themselves and their families, friends, and neighbors. They are concerned with government, politics, war, peace, education, and culture. They love freedom and believe in the democratic way of life. They want their children to be good citizens who will assume their responsibilities in political and social affairs, respect the dignity of labor, and grow in understanding of the American economic system. They need happy family life and recreation for themselves and their children.

They desire closer contacts and better cooperation with the people of the cities. The migration of youth from the farms to the cities has created a need to prepare farm youth for both rural and urban life. Those who move to the city need to be prepared for urban living, while those who remain in farming areas need to understand the interrelationships in welfare of the rural and the urban population.

Because of their common social, economic, and religious interests, the people of the small town and those of the surrounding farm area need to build better understanding and develop machinery for the achievement of common goals. The community center is the focal point of religious life, recreation, cultural pursuits, and education for both children and adults. How to secure better services for all the people in the area is the concern of the community and educational leaders.

All people have personal, social, civic, and occupational needs, but each area may have needs peculiar to the region. Some people live in arid regions, others in regions with an oversupply of water. Some people live on farms too small to make operation economically profitable; others, on large farms of thousands of acres. Some people live in villages of decreasing use as trade centers; others, in rural cities of rapid growth. Some regions produce cotton; others, wheat or dairy products. Some people are concerned with forestry and others with mining. The particular needs of the people of a region can be determined only by a careful survey of the area and consultation with the people.

Schools are established to bring a better life to people, and it is chiefly through an adequate program of social studies that children can secure experiences which will enable them to achieve their aspirations and the hopes of their parents. Teachers need help in clarifying the goals to meet the needs of rural people, in determining the meaning of social studies, in planning the procedures and content of the social studies, and in understanding the way in which social education can be carried on in the school.

Social studies defined and identified

Social studies is a term used to designate a broad field of the curriculum. The course was formerly covered in part by such subjects as history, civics, and geography, but to these three subjects there has been added some economics, anthropology, sociology, and social psychology. In efforts to give more meaning to educational experiences and to influence behavior, educators have found the narrow subject divisions too restrictive, as pointed out in Chapter 6. Social studies as an area of the curriculum now include more than history, civics, and geography because the content of those subjects is used in new relationships. History is no longer studied as an accumulation of facts used to trace the development of civilization; it now includes a background of information needed to understand present-day institutions and practices. Civics was once a study of the structure of governments; now it is broadened to give understanding of the functions of a citizen and how people govern themselves. Geography was formerly an accumulation of facts about regions of the world; now it is used to help us understand how man is forced to make adaptations in his living in order to survive and to explain the interdependence of peoples of the world. Reorganization of the content of the former subjects about present-day activities and problems of life has created new and more meaningful concepts in keeping with the basic functions of human life in modern times.

In the opinion of some authorities, *social studies* is a term to describe various subjects, such as history, geography, civics, and economics, in much the same way as *mathematics* applies to arithmetic, algebra, geometry, and the like. Some educators[1] point out that the term can mean either a group of subjects or a fused or correlated area or a program of well-organized experiences utilizing the content of history,

[1] See Edgar B. Wesley, "The Nature and Function of the Social Studies in the Elementary School," *The Social Studies in the Elementary School,* Twelfth Yearbook, National Council for the Social Studies (Washington, D.C.: The Council, 1941), p. 48.

geography, civics, and related subjects as needed. But unless there is a reorganization of the content of subjects about real-life problems and human activities to develop better understanding, more usable skills, better attitudes, and deeper appreciations, the term *social studies* cannot be considered to apply to a broad field of the curriculum. The purpose of the broad-field organization is to give greater flexibility in attacking the areas of living; to use the term as a designation of a group of subjects does not identify a broad field.

The terms *social studies* and *social sciences* have separate and distinct meanings, although they are sometimes used interchangeably. Both terms deal with people and their relationships with one another. But the term *social sciences* refers to the systematic study of the structure and activities of human society. The social sciences are a "compilation of all present knowledge concerning man and society that has been obtained through scholarly research and investigation."[2] They furnish a record of progress and present knowledge in human affairs—in government, economics, social institutions, organizations, international relations, and the like. On the other hand, "social studies are the selected reorganized and simplified portions of social science which are used for instructional purposes," according to Wesley.[3] The social sciences provide a record of the findings of research primarily for the use of adults in the management of human affairs, while the purpose of social studies, as a curriculum area in the school, is to provide a program designed to achieve the sequential growth of the young in an understanding of the problems and activities of modern life and in work skills, appreciations, and attitudes related to human life. The difference seems to be one of purpose and degree of difficulty. Certainly the purposes of the two fields are different, but whether the distinction of difference in difficulty can be

[2] Maurice P. Moffatt, *Social Studies Education* (Englewood Cliffs, N.J.: Prentice-Hall, Inc., 1956), p. 2.

[3] Edgar B. Wesley and Mary A. Adams, *Teaching Social Studies in the Elementary School* (Boston: D. C. Heath & Co., 1952), chap. i.

made will probably depend upon the level of maturity of the children and the nature of the social-studies concepts which they are trying to learn.

An understanding of the place of the social studies in the whole program of the school requires some clarification of the meaning of social education, which many teachers do not distinguish from social studies. The term *social education* can best be described as the "experiences, usually controlled, that improve the individual's ability to participate in group life."[4] It means those activities which help to socialize the child. All areas of the curriculum and school activities provide opportunities for learning to understand other people, develop the skills required for group work, learn how to make friends, develop an appreciation of the rights of others, and behave as good citizens. Social studies, like other areas of the curriculum, make a major contribution toward the social education of the child and perhaps contribute more than most fields to this end, because certain basic understandings of the group process may be derived from the procedure used in the study of social and economic problems.

Social education is more a function of method than of content. Use of the democratic process in science, social studies, and other areas of the curriculum gives meaning to democracy and develops group skills. Social education is learned in the social studies and also in the sciences, language, reading, and club meetings and in many other activities of the school. The distinction between *social education* and *social studies* is further clarified in the following sections of this chapter.

Social education

Social education is a major function of the school. It is directed toward the development of social competence, achievement of cooperation, and improved democratic behavior. Social education permeates the whole school pro-

---

[4] See "Social education" in the *Dictionary of Education,* ed. Carter V. Good (New York: McGraw-Hill Book Co., Inc., 1945), p. 375.

gram from kindergarten through all grades of the school. It is not confined to any one subject, curriculum area, or school activity. It is treated here to help clarify its close relationship to the social studies even though it is not confined to that area of the curriculum.

Man is a social animal. From early infancy onward, his development is facilitated by contacts with those about him. In the early stages of life he is essentially selfish and has to learn that others have rights and privileges and that his greatest rewards come from working with others for the achievement of common goals.

The progress of civilization has been marked by the sharing of the fruits of experience in cooperating to achieve common ends. Modern industry and business are real networks of cooperative endeavors. While competition does exist, progress has been made because man has learned to work with his fellow men. During the many years of the industrial revolution, urban people learned that cooperation would build better living. The businessman marketed the products of the factory. Cooperative research made possible factories to produce the flow of goods needed to satisfy human wants. But progress for the farmer has been slow partly because of his independence and inability to work with his fellow men in the solution of common problems. Disagreements among farm leaders over how to ensure an adequate income for farmers has delayed decision making and experimentation.

Every group of laymen who are considering what the schools should accomplish emphasize "learning to work together." The importance of acquiring group-action skills is recognized by all, but the techniques of learning those skills have not always been understood by teachers. However, progress is being made, as shown by the fact that there is now much more teacher-pupil planning, more use of committees of students, and better organization of learning experiences into units that involve social interaction.

Gradually schools are doing more than giving "lip-service" to education in democratic procedures, but there needs to be a better understanding of the meaning of democracy and how it operates. Lewin points out that the conception of "lack of restraint and maximum freedom" as opposed to "strict authoritarianism" is not correct. Autocracy and democracy both mean leadership as against the absence of leadership, laissez faire; they mean discipline and organization in contrast to chaos. On the other hand, democracy and laissez faire both give freedom to people to the extent that individuals are acting on their own motivation rather than being forced to move under authority. Democracy is neither laissez faire nor lawlessness nor autocracy. In a democracy the leader is no less a leader, although in a different way, than the leader in an autocracy. "The difference between autocracy and democracy is an honest deep difference, and an autocracy with a democratic front is still an autocracy."[5] In a democratic atmosphere the behavior of the individual is changed from hostility to friendliness, from egocentrism to a "we feeling" and to an objective attitude.

If democratic behavior is to be learned in school, teachers must learn to use democratic procedures in the classroom in order to give children an opportunity to learn democratic roles under guidance. In a school which has been autocratic in character, relaxing the standards or releasing the pressure may bring not democracy but laissez faire. A shift from autocracy to democratic action involves a positive change of the type of motivation behind the action—a shift from imposed goals to goals which the group sets for itself.

Confusion often exists regarding the use of discussion as a democratic technique. Discussion may be used to clarify issues and to bring motivation, but democratic practice goes beyond motivation in formulating goals which will carry members of a group through to actual completion of the task. Experiments show that discussion followed by group decisions and the setting up of special goals produces superior results as compared with lectures or requests by a leader.

[5] Kurt Lewin, "The Dynamics of Group Action," *Educational Leadership*, I (January, 1944), pp. 195–200.

Goals are set *by* the group and *for* the group in the group setting, and motivation derived from the group goes far toward achieving execution of decisions.

Democratic procedure must be learned; it does not result from leaving a group of people alone. Absence of knowledge as to how to work together may result in chaos or autocratic control; members of the group should be educated to play the roles of leadership and followership. The follower must have responsibility toward the group and be sensitive to the feelings of others. Interdependence among members has to be learned if positive action is to be taken. The democratic leader also must learn his role, which involves utilizing the contributions of members to help them search for solutions to problems and to guide them to arrive at decisions. He will have a high respect for the worth of each individual in the group and will attempt to help the group members pool their experiences in arriving at decisions. Efficiency in democracy requires organization and leadership of a different kind from that under an autocracy; when achieved, it will dispel the fallacious notion that a democracy is inefficient.

The student who has made progress in learning the methods used in democratic action will be a cooperative individual who:

1. Knows and fulfils the role of leader or follower as needed.
2. Recognizes the authority of the leader and works with him.
3. Carries his share of responsibilities cheerfully.
4. Works well as a committee member.
5. Meets obligations promptly.
6. Volunteers services as needed.
7. Helps develop group objectives and supports those objectives.
8. Manifests a willingness to subordinate personal interests to the interests of the group.
9. Shows respect and courtesy for the ideas of others.
10. Defends the right of others to share in the group process even though they are in disagreement with the majority.

11. Volunteers his own ideas but is willing to pool his ideas with those of others.
12. Seeks to develop personal skills to facilitate group achievement.
13. Senses the effect of his own action on the behavior of others.
14. Manifests group loyalty.

Social education, carried on in connection with the whole school program, develops through experience the concept of democracy and the group skills required for democratic action; and it also provides experiences in problem solving, critical thinking, knowledge of books and other source material, skill in searching for information, and the selectivity to evaluate, organize, and present information. It includes developing a respect for the rights of minorities and behaving as a school citizen. The social studies make a major contribution toward the social education of the child, even though the terms have different meanings.

Goals of the social studies

The specific goals of the social studies in any rural school will be determined by a survey of the problems, institutions, agencies, organizations, and activities of the community; but there are general goals which are common to all areas. It is assumed, of course, that the methods used in the social studies instruction will bring much growth in social education, as just described, but there are definite understandings, skills, attitudes, and appreciations which need to be developed through the social-studies area of the curriculum. The following classification of goals into categories is made for clarification and does not imply any separation in instruction since skills, appreciations, understandings, and behavior are all learned in the same process. Each item involves the development of understanding, correct behavior, appreciations, good attitudes, and skills. The classification is based on the predominant character of expected outcomes.

What the Social Studies Try To Develop

A. Meanings—understandings about
  1. Community institutions, agencies, and organizations
  2. County, state, federal, and world bodies and institutions
  3. Interdependence and customs of people—urban, rural, regional, world. The American way of life is dependent upon coordination of economic activities with distant peoples.
  4. Governments, taxes, political affairs
  5. Social and economic problems—county, state, national, world, such as
      a) Vocations and preparation for work
      b) The cooperative movement
      c) Consumer problems
      d) Conservation
      e) The American economic system
  6. Natural phenomena, such as weather, tides, seasons
  7. Concepts regarding man and his relation to the earth
      a) Adaptations of man to land
      b) Effect of changing technology on land use
      c) Characteristics of land and effect on human affairs
      d) Physical and human differences from place to place on earth
      e) Effect of earth features on human affairs
  8. Social studies concepts, such as time, continuity, location, space, topography, zones, patriotism, and loyalty

B. Behavior pertaining to
  1. Citizenship in school and community
  2. Happiness and security in family life
  3. Friendships among world peoples
  4. Sharing in community and school events
  5. Keeping up to date on current events

C. Appreciations and attitudes regarding
  1. Institutions, agencies, governments, and the like
  2. Contributions of other people, for example, minority groups and other national peoples
  3. Cultural heritage which has a bearing on present-day living

   4. Freedom and democracy as a way of life
   5. Civic rights and responsibilities
   6. Dignity of labor
   7. Travel
D. Skills in
   1. Reading social-studies materials effectively
   2. Use of maps, globes, graphs, charts, tables, and books
   3. Specialized research and problem-solving techniques
   4. Working together—social education phase

These goals as listed are not necessarily complete. In the study of each community, teachers will discover other needs to be met—learnings required if living is to be improved.

Trends in content and procedures in teaching the social studies

In the implementation of the goals of the social studies, teachers are using many procedures and introducing a wide variety of content. An analysis of recent courses of study reveals certain trends and principles of organization and teaching.

1. Social-studies programs are directed more toward improvement of child behavior than toward memorization of facts. Children are taught to use the skills of research and how to think rather than what to think.

2. Efforts are made to organize a program of sequential experiences in keeping with known facts about child development. Because of limited research regarding the relative difficulty of social-studies concepts, teachers encounter some difficulty.

3. Cooperative teacher planning and teacher-pupil planning are being used extensively in the development of the social-studies program.

4. Much attention is being given to aspects of life in the local community, but too often the interrelationships of local living and world affairs have not been included.

5. State history and geography are being given increasing emphasis in the social-studies program.

6. Conservation experiences which utilize content from both social studies and science are being provided rather extensively.

7. In the unified social-studies programs, economic aspects of life are receiving more attention than under the program of separate subjects. How people earn a living is receiving increased emphasis, but more attention needs to be given to how people can spend their money more intelligently.

In some schools children are learning about producer cooperatives, finance cooperatives or credit unions, and consumer cooperatives. Yet learning to be a good consumer involves much more than knowing how to buy or sell cooperatively or how to finance improvements and purchases through cooperatives. It involves knowing something about the relative quality of goods. For example, children can learn to judge the quality of bed sheets, cloth used in clothing, canned foods, insecticides, tooth pastes, soap, tools and machinery, and the like. Citizens should know something about the quality of goods and demand that standard quality be produced. They should have access to information about goods when buying. They should know about government and private agencies which provide protection for the consumer. They should learn about the bulletins dealing with cooperatives and consumer education which may be obtained from the United States Bureau of Labor Statistics, the United States Department of Agriculture, and the Farm Credit Administration. Other sources of information with which the pupils should be familiar are the regional and state leagues and the many farmers' organizations. They can secure information about cooperatives from the Cooperative League of the United States of America (4405 Dearborn Street, Chicago, Ill.).

8. Increasing emphasis is being given to the development of an understanding of other peoples of the world and to the work of the United Nations (UN) and the United Nations Educational, Scientific, and Cultural Organization (UNESCO).

9. Intercultural education and the understanding and support of the rights of minority groups are receiving increased emphasis in the school program.

10. Experience units which utilize the content of several areas of the curriculum are being used more extensively as social-studies units, and subject-matter lines in this area are disappearing. Science, health, art, and the industrial arts are drawn on extensively for information and development of skill.

11. The trend is toward the use of a wide variety of materials rather than a single textbook. Textbooks are tending to become only a part of the source material.

12. Teachers have learned that children must be taught how to read social-studies material. This is due partly to a difference in purpose in reading and partly to vocabulary and concept differences from other kinds of reading.

13. Much more attention should be given to learning such social-studies skills as map reading. Many children do not know how to read maps or how to use globes to find the information they need. Help should be given with the use of keys or legends on a map to find seaports, capital cities, rivers, mountainous areas, swamps, and railroads. Pupils should know how to use the scale of miles to estimate distances and how to use the key on a rainfall map, a population map, or a weather map to interpret the map. They should know how to study a picture map or a pictograph. Study of the globe should help eliminate distortions as to distances and directions. By the end of the sixth grade the children should know latitude and longitude and the zones. A study of a coastline should enable them to pick out the locations of the good harbors. They should be able to recognize the continents by their shape. They should know how to follow the directions on a road map. They should be able to tell the points of the compass on maps and globes.[6]

[6] See Louise Durkee Wagner, "Measuring the Map Reading Ability of Sixth Grade Children," *The Elementary School Journal*, LIII (February, 1953), pp. 338–44.

14. Teachers are giving increased attention to study skills in the instructional program.

15. More extensive use is being made of still pictures, motion pictures, and other visual aids to help children understand distant places and events and to aid in conceptual learning.

16. In the social studies, children are taught how to work as members of a group.

17. Education for citizenship as a major goal of the social studies receives much attention in the program. Citizenship is learned both through practice in the school and through study. An effort is made to tie action and knowledge together.

18. Current events are often used as general lessons to develop habits of keeping up to date in human affairs.

Organizational patterns of the course

When separate subjects such as history, geography, civics, and the like are abandoned in favor of either a broad-fields organization or a core program (see Chapter 6), teachers need some plan of organization to control the scope of the program and to give balance to the learning experiences. In a unified program, educational experiences are often organized about basic functions of life, with some experiences in each life function given at each grade level. A list of basic functions of life might include the following:

1. Protection and conservation of human life—protection against danger, keeping good health, and the like
2. Production, distribution, and consumption of food, clothing, shelter, and other goods and related services. Occupations such as farming, manufacturing, processing of the products of the farm, and business would receive attention under this heading. Consumer education would also fall under this grouping.
3. Transportation of goods and people
4. Communication of ideas. In social studies, this would include the study of the telephone, telegraph, radio, television, and other mass media.

5. Organization and government. Development of understanding of governments and governmental services and of organizations and agencies which provide services would be the objectives of this study. Local, state, national, and international aspects would be considered.
6. Education for children and adults
7. Recreation, sports, theaters, social functions and activities of a similar character
8. Culture activities and materials which deal with art, music, books, and the like
9. Religion. The rural church and its activities would be included here.

Another classification of life processes was suggested in Chapter 6 (see page 95). Other good references for the classification of life processes or the social functions are the following:

Edgar B. Wesley and Mary A. Adams, *Teaching Social Studies in the Elementary School,* Chapter 4. Boston: D. C. Heath & Co., 1952.

John U. Michaelis, *Social Studies for Children in a Democracy,* Chapter 5. Englewood Cliffs, N.J.: Prentice-Hall, Inc., 1950.

Paul R. Hanna, "Social Studies for Today," in the *National Education Association Journal* for January, 1956, pp. 36–38.

Regardless of the pattern used for organization of content, some framework will need to be formulated for guidance in the development of experience units.

There is about as much variation in what is taught at any grade level as there are courses of study. This lack of agreement seems to point to the fact that little is known about the relative difficulty of concepts and experiences. Yet nearly all courses of study provide for the gradation of experiences from the near to the remote.

The gradation of experiences in terms of distance from the learner is not based on the findings of research but on the judgments of teachers and other educators. Under the distance-from-the-learner principle, children learn about family life in the kindergarten and first grade, and about the neighbor or the community the next year. Then, in successive years, come the state, the region, the nation, South

America, Europe, Asia, Africa, and finally Australia and New Zealand, if there is any time left. Apparently this plan is an attempt to get away from the historical or chronological approach and to accept the older geographical organization. Educators were dissatisfied with the older chronological approach because so much time was devoted to the ancient times and not enough to modern life. The regional organization seems to correct that difficulty. But little is known about the advantages to the learner from the gradation of social-studies experience solely on distance from the learner.

The distance-from-the-learner approach has certain disadvantages because it fails to take into consideration known facts about how understanding develops. When the child studies the family and the community early in his school career and distant places years later, there is no relatedness in these experiences because of the intervening years. The study of Asia some years after the study of the community has little meaning for him because Asia is far away and unrelated to his daily life. Yet every aspect of daily living shows the importance of other peoples of the world to the people of the local area. Family welfare and community welfare depend upon the exchange of goods and services throughout the world. The family depends on families in other lands for some of the food on the table and some of the raw materials used to make the telephone, the automobile, and the tractor. Safety and security in modern life are dependent upon the nation's relations with other people. Farm prices are affected by world markets. Numerous other illustrations can be given to show the intimate relation of other people to the welfare of the individual in the local community. Most citizens do not fully appreciate that relation because of the failure to associate local affairs and world affairs in the learning process. If these wider relationships are to be developed, they must be learned in a related fashion at the same time that activities and problems of a local character are being studied.

Many educators agree that the wider approach to the study of local problems and activities is desirable, but they

consider the study of remote peoples and places more difficult for the child than the study of the family and the community. Yet, there are both simple and complex aspects of
life in all regions, and the child can understand how the
members of a family in Peru or Australia or Egypt work
together just as the members of his own family do.[7] Other
aspects of life in other regions can be made simple and
concrete, too. The primary child can be made to realize the
need for warm clothing in Alaska when he learns that Alaska
has a cold climate, and he can understand that by the reverse of the same principle light garments are worn in
Panama. He may not know where Holland is, but he enjoys
seeing what the children there wear and learning the games
they play. He may not be able to find South America on a
map, yet he can enjoy learning Spanish songs and dances.

It is sometimes argued that children understand only what
they can actually see, but it is known that they can make
associations of faraway things with the familiar everyday
objects in their lives. It is chiefly a matter of using technique
to make learning meaningful. Pictures of children at play
in other lands or eating their meals can be directly related
to their own activities at play and at mealtime. Stories about
the work of adults in foreign countries can follow questions
about the work their own parents do. Such magazines as *The
National Geographic Magazine* have a wealth of pictures, and
the film library centers are stocked with lantern slides, film
strips, and motion pictures which show life in other lands.
If the home has a television set, there may be programs
which show scenes in other parts of the world, and the parents may be asked to cooperate with the school in having
the children view these pictures. Also, each community may
have resource people who have visited other countries or
lived abroad for a time and who will tell the children about
the ways of life in those regions. They may have clothing

[7] For a list of activities for nursery, kindergarten, and primary children
to develop international understanding, see *Approaches to an Understanding
of World Affairs*, Twenty-fifth Yearbook, National Council for the Social
Studies, 1954, chap. xvi.

worn in those countries and be glad to wear it to show the class. Children like nothing better than to dress up in clothes that differ from those they wear, and a costume party in which they dress as the children of other lands will help bring an understanding of the fact that differences in dress are only external differences.

Teachers should experiment with an organizational pattern which is designed to develop understanding of life processes or functions based on the difficulty of the concepts rather than on the principle of distance. This would mean the development of a series of experience units to deal with food production, clothing, family life, transportation, and the like at the primary level—experience units which bring out the relatedness of state, regional, national, and international life in the same process. There could well be a cycle of such experiences in the primary grades, and a second cycle covering the same topics in a more complex way in the intermediate grades. In the upper grades there would be a third cycle of a still more complex character.

The whole gamut of life processes need not be covered in a single grade but rather spread over several grades. Evidence is available to show that there is great variation in reading ability and conceptual learning at each grade level —so great as to make a distinction in difficulty between any two grade programs of little importance. Because there is an enormous overlap in abilities of children in any two consecutive grade levels, the cycle organization of experience units may be used to advantage.

A suggestion as to how parallel units may be developed for each grade level is offered on pages 78-81 of the 1956 Yearbook of the Department of Rural Education, *Teaching in the Small Community*. With slight changes in emphasis and attempts to go more deeply into further meaning, essentially the same unit is used in each grade. For example, in the first grade there is a study of foods we get from farms, and from the second through the eighth grades the following topics are to be studied: men that help feed us, how we get our food, how different communities produce their food, how different sections of the United States help us get food, dependence on neighbors and other countries for food, how the industrial world works to feed its people, and how our democratic way of life in a world community is related to food. While this pattern does not correspond with the idea that both the near and the far can be either simple or complex, it does illustrate how the same experience unit can be approached at different levels and provide a more penetrating experience at each higher level.

Constant evaluation of the experimental program would make it possible for the teacher to learn how complex an experience may be for each grade level. From this evidence, a program could emerge which is graded on the basis of difficulty and designed to expand and deepen the understanding of the local community in its relationship to other regions of the nation and the world, and to other occupational groups. Wesley and Adams[8] have suggested a possibility of gradation of social studies on the basis of social experience, and they present a table which begins with concrete experiences with things, individuals, and the like and proceeds to more complex social structures of society. This offers another proposal for experimentation. The best possibility for success in gradation of experiences seems to be a plan which is based on a knowledge of how the individual learns to understand complex processes, first by simple exposure through experience, and then by having additional experiences about the same process or activity. The additional experiences help to uncover previously hidden meanings.

In the development of any organizational plan, the teacher will need to consider not only a wider view to give the topic meaning but also as much of a chronological view as necessary to secure more complete understanding. Starting with the local problem activity or institution being studied, the child will need some historical background to understand why people behave as they do. Institutions and agencies have a history, and they cannot be fully appreciated nor

[8] Edgar B. Wesley and Mary A. Adams, *op. cit.*, p. 203.

understood without digging into their backgrounds to help understand their functions. When each experience unit is being planned, teachers will need to consider both the regional and the chronological relationships.

Any plan of organization which the faculty of a school decides to use will need to be flexible enough to permit the use of materials suited to the maturity, needs, and interests of the students and to allow the exercise of student initiative in exploring for new experiences. Also, it should allow for teacher guidance to help individual children meet their needs. In the process of learning, children should acquire useful information and skills and better attitudes and appreciations. The program should have continuity to provide for gradual growth of the children. Regardless of whether the program is organized in subjects or in the life processes of a broad field, every effort should be made to make learning meaningful in the life of the child. Furthermore, the program must start at the child's level of development and should be of such a character that it helps him get a better understanding of the problems and activities of his immediate environment.

Interests of the rural child

The interests of greatest concern to the rural child are those which arise in the farm or village home, in the neighborhood, or in the community. The rural child lives in a stimulating environment in which he works closely with adults and consequently shares their concerns. He often gathers and sells eggs, helps market the products of the garden, works a corn field, and feeds and waters the livestock. He becomes interested in better feeds for livestock, soil conservation, diseases of poultry, weather, seasons, wild life, home beautification, rural electrification, cooperative marketing, costs of things the family needs to buy, and a host of other aspects of farm life. The farm boy joins the village boy at the community or county fair, at services of the rural church, in use of the community library facilities, in games and social functions, and in school affairs. Life in the country brings the child in contact with rural magazines and newspapers, with radio and television programs of concern to rural people, with modern home and farm equipment, and with the lakes and streams and growing plant and animal life around him.

The social-studies program, like other areas of the curriculum, starts with the interests of the children of the local community and builds an understanding of life problems in such a way as to help them with their solutions. For the rural child, his school and the adults of his home and neighborhood become sources of information needed to develop understanding. The school should help him grow in skill in finding information, interpreting it, and organizing and evaluating it in the solution of life problems.

Community as a learning laboratory

Teachers study rural communities not only to discover the needs and interests of the children but also to familiarize themselves with the resources available to help increase the understanding of the children. Each rural community has an abundance of laboratory facilities for learning in social studies, science, safety, health, and the like. Aspects of the community as a laboratory are discussed in Chapter 3. In one rural community the school children observed voting procedures and visited a butter-making factory, a cheese factory, grain elevators and grain storage facilities, stock yards, the fire department, the post office, a bank, and grocery stores. They attended farm bureau meetings and meetings of the farmers' union. At the county seat, they learned about county courts and found out what the county recorder does. From a visit to the county historical society and the county museum, they learned local history. On other occasions they visited the airport and studied plane schedules and air routes, and they called at the railroad and bus passenger depots to secure information for the study of transportation. As part of a unit dealing with erosion and land formation, the children visited level bottom lands and rough, hilly uplands and studied the effect of water on the soil. In some communities a sawmill, a paper factory, and a lumber yard offer resources for a study of the uses of wood. In a unit dealing with weather, the children of one school visited a nearby weather bureau. In another rural area, the children of the school served on committees to help plan the community fair and exhibit, and they helped with the planning and execution of a county-wide picnic.

In connection with experience units, the community can furnish much practical learning for children. Objects, events, and people will do much to give meaning to learning. But all such experiences call for careful planning so that the field trip makes a definite contribution to the solution of a problem or to an understanding of some life function or process.

World-wide relationships

Even when experience units deal with problems and activities of local concern and utilize the local community as a laboratory for learning, there is a need to show the world-wide relationships of these local problems to world affairs and to the activities of other people. The importance of this relationship has already been discussed, but some additional suggestions are needed to explain aspects of a program to build an understanding of world-wide relationships among people.

The concepts or understandings about other people of the world which can be learned are numerous. Children should learn that all people differ from others in many respects and resemble them in other respects. They should learn that the environment—the land, the weather, and the climate—cause differences in dress, manners, and customs; that the beliefs of people are affected by their traditions and experiences of the past and present; and that there is an increasing interdependence among peoples. Because of this increasing interdependence among peoples, there is a need for channels of communication between people of different nations. Children should realize that other peoples of the world want the same things as the people of this nation, namely, economic independence, happy family life, friends, and security. People in all regions of the world want to live peacefully in the community of nations.

Many opportunities to learn about people of other lands can be utilized. Children can communicate with the children of other lands by an exchange of letters, drawings, pictures, games, songs, stories, food, clothing, and samples of school work. Money may be raised to assist the United Nations International Children's Emergency Fund and the Junior Red Cross. The children can cooperate with the American Friends Service Committee, CARE, Church World Service, UNESCO, and similar groups. They can make Christmas gifts to send abroad and prepare booklets describing school life in the United States to be sent to children in other lands. They can constantly follow current events of an international character. Preparing dramatizations of stories about the children of other lands and presenting assembly programs commemorating special days and events of world significance make the learning real.

Methods of building an understanding of interrelationships among peoples can be learned from some practices carried on in schools of other nations. In an agricultural community in New South Wales, Australia, for example, the children of the sixth grade were studying wool, a major product of the local area. They studied problems of sheep raising and the shearing of sheep. Then they learned how the wool was loaded on a ship and stored on the ship. They examined maps of shipping lanes and traced the ship to the United States where the wool was purchased. They learned that there the wool was made into yarn and clothing. They became interested in the people who purchased the processed wool and wanted to know more about the United States. From books and magazines and from Americans in the area, they sought answers to their many questions.

In some schools of the United States, children take imaginary trips abroad. They secure information from travel agencies and study air routes and shipping lanes. They read about ports or cities where the ships or airlines stop and secure pictures of the area. They spend time learning about the people of the land they plan to visit on their imaginary trip.

The possibilities of building better relations among the children of the world are almost unlimited, but words of caution are needed. There is danger that some unique characteristic or custom of a people will be emphasized instead of their common traits. For instance, if children learn about the Dance of Death or the Devil Dance of Bolivia, they must be made to realize that it is only a part of the folklore handed down from the Spanish conquerors. Originally the priests used such dances to teach the Indians the punishment that would follow wrongdoing, and the dances are now used only rarely for entertainment. Similarly, when children of other countries dress up as Indians or cowboys because they think these costumes are common dress in the United States, they are not getting a true picture of Americans. It should be made clear to the children that distinctive costumes may be worn by people in different countries or even in different parts of the same country, but that these are not always national ways of dressing. Often they are worn only on special occasions.

Children and adults are often critical of practices in other countries because they do not understand the reason for them and judge them by American standards. For example, when the pupils learn that the farmers of the Near East and of parts of South America still use wooden plows drawn by oxen or other animals, they should be made to understand that lack of machinery and of electricity in these regions makes primitive measures necessary. A necessary part of education today should be an understanding of other peoples and other ways of living. This will help our citizens who travel abroad from incurring the dislike of the people in other countries by their criticism of "foreign" ways and methods—a serious fault of Americans.

Both children and adults must learn to avoid emotional indignation toward an entire people. To understand their behavior the student must know how the people live and what their culture, history, and traditions are. Sometimes people are victims of poor leadership, lack of education, or unfavorable environmental conditions.

Citizens need to learn that principles and plans do not become immediate practices. It takes a long time for international agreements to be translated into action. The program of the United Nations has shown that agreements do not immediately transform the relationships among people.

Another word of caution to the teacher is not to attempt to build understanding and relationships with the peoples of too many nations at one time so that there is no real understanding of any. By studying the people of only one land each year, much better understanding can be developed.

Units of social-studies work

Some teachers have raised the question, "How does a social-studies unit differ from any other?" Some educators describe the social-studies unit as one with objectives pertaining to the development of an understanding of human relationships, with its content drawn chiefly from the social sciences. However, in a well-developed social-studies program there are few experience units which utilize exclusively the content of the social studies. The study of food production calls for the use of science, and units on nutrition use much from the health program. Conservation is both a social study and a science; it is discussed in this book under science. Fortunately for the teacher of the self-contained classroom, such as will be found in most rural areas, there is no real need to classify the unit as a social-studies unit or a science unit or any other kind of unit. When the problem or the aspect of living to be studied is developed, as explained in Chapter 6, the questions and the outline define its scope and indicate what information is needed. The children may go to any sources to find answers to their questions.

The following brief descriptions of two work units illustrate many of the desirable characteristics of social-studies
experiences. These samples were selected from a file developed by teachers in rural schools.

A Work Unit on Wheat

In a school near Garrison, North Dakota, the children in a fourth
grade worked with their teacher on a unit on wheat. A study by the
teacher revealed that the chief crop in the community was wheat, that
many resources were available, and that such a unit would contribute
to the division of the program called "food production." The children
from the farms would be able to increase their prestige with the town
children by serving as resource persons, and this was desirable because
the town children tended to look down on the farm children.

It was September and the beginning of school. Harvesting operations were still in progress. While little else was needed to arouse the
children's interest, the teacher posted pictures of wheat farming and
wheat uses on the bulletin board and wrote below them such questions as, "How is this wheat changed to flour?" "Where did the bran
for these muffins come from?"

After some discussion, the children listed such questions as the
following which they wanted to try to answer:

How large is a wheat farm?
When is wheat planted?
Why do we sometimes have crop failures?
Where does the wheat go?
Do they grow wheat in other places?
Why does flour cost more than wheat?
How is flour made?
What foods are made from wheat? Are they good for us?

The activities of the unit were organized around growing wheat,
transportation of wheat, wheat milling and baking, use of wheat for
bread and breakfast foods, and nutrition and health. Problems of
planting, soil preparation, and machinery used were studied. Information was secured on how wheat is carried by truck, rail, and ship.
It was learned that wheat is shipped to milling cities in the state, to
other states, and to ports in Great Britain, Italy, The Netherlands,
France, and Belgium. The children studied maps of the world to locate these countries and the other places where they learned that
wheat is grown.

This unit of work started from the interest of the children in local
events, but it brought in wider relationships. In their study of tools and

machinery, the children used the skills of research to get information about tools used in the past. Understanding of transportation facilities was increased. The interdependence of the farmer and the factory worker was made clear. The pupils used many of the social-studies skills, such as map reading and group work, as they worked together on committees. Source materials included farms, grain elevators, flour mills, geography and history books, and literature furnished by milling companies and shipping concerns. The children consulted encyclopedias and atlases and used motion pictures giving the story of wheat.

At the end of the study of the unit, the experience was evaluated and an exhibit was prepared. Parents were invited to come to the school to hear the children tell what they had learned about wheat and to see the exhibit.

A WORK UNIT ON WOOL

In another community, the children of the fifth grade became interested in wool because many sheep were grown in the community and they wanted to know more about how wool is made into clothing. The objectives were: (1) to understand more about the raising of sheep and the production of wool, (2) to get a broader knowledge of where clothing comes from, (3) to appreciate the different kinds of clothing and their purposes, (4) to know how people are dependent on each other, (5) to develop reading skills, and oral and written expression, and (6) to gain practice in working together. Material was drawn from agriculture to help understand sheep raising; from industrial arts to learn about weaving, clothing, and rugs; from history to learn earlier methods of weaving; from geography to learn about the regions of the world where sheep are raised and textiles manufactured; and from science to learn how to test wool for shrinkage, length of fibers, burning, structure of cloth, and the like.

In addition to studying about breeds of sheep, care of sheep, and the like, the children learned how wool is weighed and marketed. They studied how wool is woven into cloth and learned to recognize the quality of the cloth. This led to the study by each child of clothing for himself, consideration being given to quality, style, and color. The cost of a suit for himself was determined by each child. The relation of clothing to climate was also considered.

The unit of work on wool met many of the characteristics of a good experience. Both vicarious and personal experiences took place. Local resource persons and activities were utilized. Many skills of the social studies and social education were practiced. More meaning was given to local problems of production and consumption because of the wider relationships established between local life and the life of people in other regions of the world.

Summary

The rapidly changing character of society, new objectives of education, and the emergence of crucial social problems have caused much confusion in the social-studies program. Yet, no area of the curriculum can make a bigger contribution to better living in rural areas. Problems of concern to rural people are largely those of relationships at home and with people of other regions and nations. And because learning human relations must start with local people and their problems of living, teachers must carry much of the burden for curriculum organization as well as for execution of the program.

Social studies is a comparatively new term in education and is often misunderstood. It applies to that area of the curriculum which deals with people and their relations with one another. The social studies differ from the social sciences, which are compilations of information obtained through scholarly research to record the present status and progress of man in his interrelationships and used largely to guide the affairs of the adult society. The social studies include the material of the social sciences, but the material is simplified as necessary to help children of varying degrees of maturity to study the processes or functions of society.

While often used synonymously, the terms *social studies* and *social education* also should be distinguished in order to clarify the organization of the school program. *Social studies* can best be used to describe one unified area or broad field of the curriculum, but social education is the process by which the child learns to work as a member of a group. Social education involves not only the group skills needed to operate democratically but also techniques of group problem solving, critical thinking, skill in research, and the like.

Goals of the social studies include understanding and appreciating institutions, agencies, and organizations of the community and wider geographic area; local, social, and economic problems together with wider relationships; relation of natural phenomena and land to problems of life and customs of people; and concepts largely peculiar to social studies. There is also an attempt to improve the behavior of the child as a citizen, as a member of his family, and as a member of a widening circle of friends.

Courses of study and current practices show that attempts are focused on organizing a program with a sequence of experiences designed to improve child behavior as a member of his social group and to acquaint the child with local activities and events and with world affairs. Emphasis is given state history and geography, conservation, and economic affairs. The experience units utilize material from history, geography, civics, science, health, art, and the industrial arts and a wide variety of other sources. The skills of map and globe reading and consumer education need more emphasis.

The most common practice in organizing the program is the classification of learnings about certain social functions or life processes and the grading of experiences in terms of their distance from the learner. Regardless of the plan used, it seems desirable to get not only an understanding of wider geographical relationships but also historical perspective of activities, institutions, and problems. The experiences should utilize materials from the community and capitalize on the interests of the children.

Many school and community activities can be used to develop an understanding of world peoples and events, even when these activities are not part of the organized units of work. The social-education program of the school should attempt to develop this understanding, which is essential in view of modern events and the role the United States plays in world affairs.

Selected references

AMERICAN ASSOCIATION OF SCHOOL ADMINISTRATORS. *Educating for American Citizenship,* Thirty-second Yearbook. Washington, D.C.: The Association, 1954. Parts II and III.

Deals with the role of the school and community in citizenship education, emphasizes local, state, national, and international relations and discusses how to build attitudes and ideals.

HILL, WILHELMINA, and MACKINTOSH, HELEN K. "How Children Learn about Human Rights," *Bulletin No. 9*, Office of Education, Federal Security Agency. Washington, D.C.: United States Government Printing Office, 1951.

Discussion of learning about human rights from the community, books and other sources. Gives list of source materials.

KENWORTHY, LEONARD S. *Introducing Children to the World.* New York: Harper & Bros., 1957. Chaps. ii–xi and appendices A, B, and C.

Discusses appropriate experiences and resources and cultures, modes of living and interdependence of peoples. Good lists of materials for teachers and children will be found in appendices.

KINDER, JAMES S. *Audio-Visual Materials and Techniques.* New York: American Book Co., 1950. Chaps. vi, vii, and xv, and pp. 243–46.

Using flat pictures, diagrams, sketches, drawings, charts, graphs, maps, globes, posters, murals, cartoons, comic strips, motion pictures, and other visual aids to make social studies more meaningful. Sources from which materials may be secured. How to prepare materials.

MICHAELIS, JOHN U. *Social Studies for Children in a Democracy.* Englewood Cliffs, N.J.: Prentice-Hall, Inc., 1950. Chaps. i, ii, iv, v, vi, viii–xiv.

Defines social studies and discusses content and methods of teaching; tells how to plan units of work; and gives criteria for selection of source materials. Discusses construction and use of audio-visual aids.

NATIONAL COUNCIL OF SOCIAL STUDIES. *Approaches to an Understanding of World Affairs*, Twenty-fifth Yearbook. Washington, D.C.: The Council, 1954. Chap. xvi.

Deals with developing international understanding in the elementary school; has description of course of study and a treatment of work in the kindergarten and lower grades and tells how people and materials may be used to educate children to live cooperatively with recent arrivals in this country.

———. *Geographic Approaches to Social Education*, Nineteenth Yearbook. Washington, D.C.: The Council, 1948. Chaps. iii–vii, xi–xvii.

Provides good treatment of significance of land to human life, and the relation of location and climate to man's needs. Tells how to use audio-visual and other source materials in developing concepts of differences from place to place.

———. *Improving the Social Studies Curriculum*, Twenty-sixth Yearbook. Washington, D.C.: The Council, 1955. Chaps. vii and viii.

Reports of experiences of local schools where the social studies curriculum is being improved.

———. *Social Education of Young Children* (2d ed.). Curriculum Series, No. 4. Washington, D.C.: The Council, 1956. Chaps. v, vi, viii, xi, xii, xiii and Part III.

Discusses objectives, intergroup experiences, understandings to be developed, program and units of work from kindergarten through third grade and provides a good book list for young children.

NATIONAL EDUCATION ASSOCIATION, DEPARTMENT OF RURAL EDUCATION. *Teaching in the Small Community.* Washington, D.C.: The Department, 1956. Chaps. ii, iv, and vi.

Provides help for the teacher in rural areas in the development of parallel units, selecting curriculum areas, using the farm as a learning laboratory and choosing source materials.

NATIONAL SOCIETY FOR THE STUDY OF EDUCATION. *Social Studies in the Elementary School,* Fifty-sixth Yearbook. Chicago: University of Chicago Press, 1957. Part I, chaps. v–x.

Chapters by different authors deal with: the organization of the social studies curriculum; relationship to the total school program; providing for individual differences; developing skills of reading, research and reporting; educating for citizenship and teaching international understanding.

PRESTON, RALPH C. *Teaching Social Studies in the Elementary School.* New York: Rinehart & Co., Inc., 1950. Chaps. i, iii, iv, vi–x, and Appendix.

Discusses social studies and social education in the total school program, curriculum organization, types of units and the use of maps. The appendix includes good lists of children's books, audio-visual aids, free and inexpensive materials and resource units.

———. *Teaching World Understanding.* Englewood Cliffs, N.J.: Prentice-Hall, Inc., 1955. Chaps. i, ii, iv–vi.

Excellent treatment of points of emphasis in teaching international understanding, methods of teaching, program, materials for studying, and service activities. Provides good list of children's books about the world.

WESLEY, EDGAR B., and ADAMS, MARY A. *Teaching Social Studies in Elementary Schools* (rev. ed.). Boston: D. C. Heath & Co., 1952. Chaps. i, iv, ix, xi, xiii, xiv, xvii, xviii, xx, xxi.

Offers good definition of social studies, help with selection of materials and program organization and suggests how to plan units by grade levels. Provides fine list of sources of audio-visual aids. (pp. 373–377).

14

ARITHMETIC FOR RURAL AREAS

Arithmetic has always played a more important role in rural life than in urban life. Rural people are constantly required to do quantitative thinking. On the farms, there are problems of farm planning and management which involve acres to be planted in field crops, yields in bushels per acre, number of farm animals, costs of production, and market prices. As pointed out in Chapter 2, farming is a big-business enterprise, and no farmer can be happy and prosperous unless he can keep the margin between costs of operation and market prices great enough to assure an adequate income. And in the village the people work at occupations closely related to agriculture and are concerned with marketing, processing, transporting, trading, and financing—all closely related to farm operations.

So teachers in rural area schools need to know the rural environment and must know how to develop a program suited to the needs of rural people. The teacher in the school serving rural people must recognize the peculiar needs of the rural child for help in quantitative thinking and in number skill. She must recognize that the rural environment develops early in life a readiness for arithmetic beyond that commonly found among urban children. She needs to have clearly defined goals for the arithmetic program and understand how to organize the experiences in school so that work in arithmetic becomes an easy transition from concrete experiences to work with symbols. The teacher will plan the program to develop arithmetic concepts through experience in the school and community. She wants to know what to do about drill on fundamental operations and how to teach children to solve real-life problems. She must understand the experiences the children have on the farm and in the village which create needs for the use of arithmetic.

Special needs of the rural child

Experiences on the farm introduce the young child to many aspects of quantitative thinking and present many problems for him as he continues to develop. The child helps gather the eggs and count them. He needs to learn the concept "dozen" and how many eggs are in a case. He wants to know how to judge the weight of chickens, turkeys, pigs, and cattle. He finds a need for understanding pints, quarts, gallons, and barrels. He needs to tell time by the clock, and he enjoys guessing the time by the sun. There are occasions when he needs to use inches, feet, yards, rods, and miles. He wants to know how to measure boards and build a house and pen for his pets. At a later period he has need for figuring the number of board feet required to build a shed. He wants to know how to tell the cubic contents of a corn crib or a bin of oats and how to compute the number of bushels in a bin or in a truckload of grain. He thinks in terms of acres and sections of land. The child becomes concerned with butterfat content in milk and cream. He has to figure rations for his own pets and the livestock, and he should eventually learn to keep cost and profit records.

The growing boy is often confused about the term *bushel*, which may be considered either a unit of volume or a unit of weight. Yet, weights vary from community to community. He knows that one bushel of corn is not always the same as another bushel of corn because of the difference in size of the ears; the food value, bushel for bushel, is not the same. So, the boy in the intermediate and upper grades will find some advantage in the new term *hundredweight* which is rapidly replacing the bushel as a unit of measure for buying and selling grain. The hundredweight as a unit of measure is favored by many of the large farm organizations, by feed processors, and by the United States Department of Agriculture.

The need for proficiency in the use of weights and measures is the most outstanding distinction between the needs of rural and urban children. Arithmetic textbooks which have been prepared for use in urban schools are not likely to provide sufficient help for the learning needs of rural children. Hence, the teacher in rural schools will need to study the rural environment and be concerned not only with how much emphasis should be given to needs of rural children in general but with the needs in her particular region of the country. In some regions children will be concerned with bales of cotton, pounds of rice, bales or tons of hay, and bushels or hundredweights of flaxseed or soybeans.

Also, children of the town and village need to learn about interest, loans, taxes, insurance, and profit and loss. The need for this information often grows out of the practice of encouraging children to have their own farm animals or small business enterprises. There are also many occasions in the school where clubs and other groups need to handle money. Sometimes the school runs a cooperative store and holds picnics and takes field trips—all requiring the use of money.

Needs for the use of numbers arise before the child starts to school. The teacher will want to know how adequately the child has learned to meet those needs and to understand how to help the child get ready for further learning. She will be concerned with the organization of learning experiences in a sequence which permits the child to advance by easy stages from skill and understanding of simple functions to more complex operations. She must understand the importance of each child's readiness for succeeding operations.

Readiness for arithmetic

The term *readiness* is often used to refer to a background of fundamental skills, understandings, and attitudes needed for success in beginning regular arithmetic instruction. But the child must be ready not only for the first work with abstract numbers but also for each succeeding step in the process of sequential growth. The test of the child's fitness for each new step is his proficiency in the preceding one. Developing readiness for arithmetic is the responsibility not only of pre-school and kindergarten teachers but also of every teacher who is providing the experiences to give meaning to symbols, processes, and generalizations and to activities which develop skill in using symbols. Without this meaning, followed by practice with symbols, succeeding steps would be most difficult, if not impossible, for children.

Since each teacher starts with the child at his level of development, she needs to know the child when he comes to school for the first time, to appraise his growth in quantitative thinking, and to begin building the background needed for work with abstract symbols.

As previously pointed out, the rural child of the pre-school years has had many experiences in the home and community which have led to quantitative thinking. He has learned to count animals, eggs, and apples, and he has often developed a vocabulary to go with his development. He can say the numbers *one, two, three, four, five,* and perhaps *twenty.* He will likely use such words as *later, little, big, near, far, short, long, high, more, less, tall, wide,* and the like. He may have learned to count by tens to 40. He can often group numbers by twos, threes and fours. Sometimes, he may be able to solve simple addition problems if the sum does not exceed ten. And often he can read numbers to ten. He often understands something about money and may even comprehend simple fractions like one-half and one-fourth.

Children of either rural or urban areas do not achieve equal development in quantitative thinking when they enter the first grade. Teachers, therefore, should provide experiences in the kindergarten and primary grades which are designed to develop number concepts, vocabularies, and the use of numbers. Experiences with concrete objects are needed to prevent rote learning—to give meaning to numbers and concepts. This early stage of development is a crucial period, for on this period hinges the whole development of quantitative thinking.

Numerous experiences of the pre-school period and in the kindergarten and first grade provide opportunity to develop readiness for the experiences to follow. Children are doing paper cutting which calls for measurement. They are setting tables for parties and need to count the number of places. They count the number of persons on committees and teams. They learn to group objects and persons and to find pages in the primer. They play games in which they learn to count short steps and long steps. They have occasion to vote to select leaders and to count the votes. They often play store and exchange objects and money. In playing with blocks and other objects, children learn to judge thicknesses, widths, and lengths. They learn to judge the width of a space through which they may ride tricycles. In making valentines and Christmas greetings, children learn to use rulers to measure inches. By other measurements they master the terms *foot* and *yard*. In planting seeds and preparing planting boxes, children have an opportunity to develop such concepts as *square, circle, oblong,* and *triangle.* Children use chickens and eggs to develop number concepts, too. They have learned that chicken eggs hatch in twenty-one days, and they can mark off three weeks on the calendar. They learn about subtraction from the fact that some of the eggs do not hatch.

Throughout the grades, children are acquiring meaning and readiness for arithmetic by working first with concrete materials, then with semiconcrete materials, and finally with abstract or symbolic materials. They learn to count real chickens and use pictures or objects to represent chickens. They group these to learn the concepts of addition, subtraction, multiplication, and division, and they are able then to work problems using numbers to represent the concepts. Addition is observed as putting groups together, subtraction as taking two groups apart, multiplication as combining several groups of the same size, and division as the finding of how many groups of one size are contained in a larger group.

Extent of development of arithmetic readiness in the preschool period and at other stages depends upon mental maturity and the richness of experiences which involve quantitative thinking. Mental maturity helps children see and use relationships and remember information. Experiences provide the information needed and develop an interest in the use of numbers. Experiences lead to the development of meaning, but they do not complete that development, as will be discussed later.

Goals of arithmetic instruction

The organization of a program of experiences which provide sequential development must lead toward the achievement of goals which the faculty of the school have developed and which teachers use as guide lines in planning the total program. Mere drill on abstract numbers does not enable children to solve real-life problems effectively. On the other hand, experiences involving quantities of things do not always lead to skill in the use of abstract symbols. Furthermore, experiences do not always bring the generalizations needed for further work with mathematical processes. To bring systematic development of mathematical ability in children, some goals are needed.

The major goal of arithmetic instruction is to develop in children the ability to use numbers as needed for quantitative thinking in connection with the problems of daily life in such a way as to solve those problems. This involves the skilful use of numbers in the various operations and the use of those skills in the solution of real problems inside and outside the school.

On page 296 is a brief outline of abilities and ideals which an arithmetic program should help children develop.

A. Computational skills

1. Using whole numbers, simple common fractions, per cents, and decimals
2. Using numbers to solve problems in and outside school
3. Estimating and checking work

B. Understanding

1. Concepts of number system, measures, per cents, and the like
2. Arithmetical generalizations
3. Arithmetical relationships
4. Measuring devices, such as footrule, gallon, and scales for weighing
5. Social usages of numbers in connection with banking, trade, building, farm management, and the like
6. The contributions of number to human progress

C. Meaningful vocabularies

1. Technical terms of arithmetic, such as *divisor, sum, denominator,* etc.
2. Units of measure, such as *mile, acre, bushel,* and *hundredweight*

D. Reading skills

1. Ability to read problems involving quantitative thinking and to comprehend their meaning
2. Ability to read graphs, tables, charts, etc.

E. Ideals, such as accuracy and persistence

F. Social sensitivity to numbers and the habit of using numbers as needed in life situations

All goals of arithmetic instruction should emphasize the development of computational skills to a point where operations may be performed automatically in response to thinking, and the development of ability to solve real-life problems. None of these goals will be achieved at one time, but each step in the sequence of experiences should make contributions toward the abilities and ideals which it is desirable to develop.[1]

[1] Another statement of goals is furnished in *The Teaching of Arithmetic,* Fiftieth Yearbook, National Society for the Study of Education, Part II (Chicago: University of Chicago Press, 1951), pp. 6–7.

Experiences in the primary grades

From the experiences of the home and kindergarten, children learn much that leads to quantitative thinking. The development of readiness for further arithmetic is continued in the primary grades in an effort to build understanding and insight rather than skill and speed with numbers. As a subject, arithmetic in the primary grades is not entirely separate from the rest of the school program, since many of the activities of social studies and science call for experiences in measuring, counting, reading numbers, writing numbers, grouping things, and the meaning of numbers. Classes in arithmetic may be held at a separate time of the day, but the motivation for work in those classes is derived from the experiences of the school day and in the home and community.

Considerable differences of opinion exist regarding the grade level at which arithmetic lessons should begin. Some educators would start arithmetic in the first grade because children already show some development in quantitative thinking when they come to school. Others would not begin to teach arithmetic until the third grade because it is "too hard" for young children and because more time is needed for reading in the first two grades. To accept the latter practice is to ignore the basic facts regarding child growth and development as discussed in Chapter 5. Children continuously develop through experience in living, and in that process they cannot avoid using numbers as they handle money, measure objects, construct things, and work with problems which arise. They need to solve their problems and acquire a vocabulary with which to communicate about quantities of things. Real needs for arithmetic arise and must be met; they cannot be postponed for two or three years. But initial instruction in arithmetic in the primary grades is not merely working with abstract numbers. Much emphasis is placed on the development of the meaning of symbols, the processes, the vocabularies, the generalizations, and on insight into problems as the problems come up in the home and at school.

Because arithmetic in the primary grades is not pure rote learning of abstract number facts but rather a series of real experiences linked with other instruction, it must not be considered incidental. A function which is learned in a real-life situation is not incidental. The program which includes experience units involving arithmetical operations should be deliberately planned by the teacher to develop meaning. For example, the children of a first grade who were studying the farm home made a model of a farmyard. This involved measuring, estimating, counting, and grouping objects—all a part of a deliberate plan of the teacher to give meaning to concepts used in arithmetic. Likewise, the children who operated a school store were extending their understanding of trade operations, learning the value of money and how to make change. And the children who built a class museum were learning to count and measure space. In a unit dealing with the post office, children who wrote and mailed letters had to buy stamps, which called for counting, subtracting, and adding. Such experiences are not incidental if they are deliberately planned and if the teacher moves from the use of concrete materials to the use of real numbers in each operation; they are deliberately planned to give meaning to operations, to provide practice in solving real problems, and to develop real purposes for learning. Children are taught to add by putting things together and then to use real numbers in adding. They are taught to subtract by first using real things or substitutes for the real and then using real numbers.

Textbooks in arithmetic and practices in schools show wide variation in what is to be taught in the primary grades.[2] There seems to be common agreement among authorities that primary grade children should learn to count by ones, twos, threes, fives, and tens to 100, to read and write numbers to 100, to understand ordinals to fifth, to do some addition and subtraction, and to have some experience in measuring and simple problem solving. Most leaders in the

[2] See Robert P. Ulrich, "Grade Placement of Computational Topics in Arithmetic," *The Elementary School Journal*, XLII (September, 1941), pp. 50–59.

field agree that by the third grade addition and subtraction of more complex numbers involving carrying and borrowing should be included in the program, and that multiplication, division, and fractions of ½, ⅓, and ¼ should be handled. But teachers realize that the needs of the children and the state of readiness for the next step help determine the operations, understandings, and skills to be learned.

Arithmetic in the middle grades

Arithmetic instruction in the middle grades is focused on provision for experiences which gradually introduce the children to more complex problems and operations. There should be no sudden break in the developmental program from the primary level. The children are expected to enlarge and refine the number concepts learned in the lower grades and to develop greater accuracy in the skills used. Teachers encourage children to participate actively in exploration and discovery and to make an effort to acquire the skills, concepts, and abilities needed for solving problems.

The program of the middle grades usually includes work with decimals, understanding Roman numbers, more complex work in addition, subtraction, multiplication, and division of whole numbers, and use of fractions and mixed numbers. Further work with measures and in problem solving is provided and work in percentage is included.

Classroom teachers usually follow one of two procedures in the arithmetic program: they utilize experiences in daily life to make arithmetic meaningful to children or they use an arithmetic textbook series which includes the essential learnings organized logically and graded according to difficulty. The latter program usually includes much drill and the solution of problems which may not be of vital concern to the local community. The rural teacher may well use a combination of these procedures. Problems may be selected from those arising in local community—life problems which conform to the kinds of operations found in the textbook. A study of the textbooks will help the teacher understand the sequence needed to achieve continued growth in skills and understandings.

Unfortunately, many teachers of the middle grades fail to realize that middle-grade children, as well as primary-grade children, need to understand the meaning of new operations. Such meaning comes from concrete or semiconcrete materials. Middle-grade children will have progressed to a point where they are able to work with symbols, but there are new operations, new concepts, and new generalizations to be learned at every level.

Place of meaning in arithmetic

In the primary grades and at other levels as well, much emphasis needs to be given to meaning. "Meaning is the seeing of reasons for, the import of, or the sense of a process," according to Spitzer.[3] Meaning is, in part, a matter of understanding relationships, such as between addition and subtraction or between dividing by two and multiplying by ½. Van Engen has pointed out that these relationships are important, but he emphasizes that true meaning comes from concrete experiences.[4] The meaning of numbers and concepts comes from concrete experiences, but the meaning of relationships comes from a study of the process of using symbols and generalizations in more complex operations.

It has been emphasized that the meaning of a process may not come from concrete experiences unless the process is abstracted and pointed out. The meaning of "4 eggs plus 3 eggs" is understood as a process, but the concept of "$4 + 3 = 7$" is extracted from such experiences. The child who puts five pencils with four pencils may count nine pencils, but to get the meaning of the process he must also understand the symbolic form $4 + 5 = 9$. Likewise, the generalization of the

[3] Herbert F. Spitzer, *The Teaching of Arithmetic* (Boston: Houghton Mifflin Co., 1948), p. 14.

[4] H. Van Engen, "An Analysis of Meaning in Arithmetic," *The Elementary School Journal*, XLIX (February and March, 1949), pp. 321–29 and 395–400.

operation $6 + 0 = 6$ can best be learned with concrete or semiconcrete objects, but the generalization regarding the operation is divorced from the concrete experience as a further emphasis.

Another illustration of the development of the meaning of a process or a generalization is the situation in which children are learning to add fractions, as in $\frac{1}{2} + \frac{1}{4} = \frac{3}{4}$. The teacher may cut an apple into two halves and then cut one of the halves into two quarters. The children see that the two quarters equal a half. When the half is added to one of the quarters, they realize that a half and a quarter are actually two quarters and one quarter, or three quarters. This process is then written as symbols, $\frac{2}{4} + \frac{1}{4} = \frac{3}{4}$, and the children are led to understand that before fractions can be added, they must be changed to a common denominator. Thus, the meaning developed is the meaning of a process, or a generalization.

Meaning is learned by work with both concrete materials and semiconcrete materials, such as paper money, beads on a string, and bottle tops. These representative materials are used to help children understand operations and develop generalizations. However, the operation with the semiconcrete materials must be related to a similar operation with concrete materials in order to develop the generalization.

Dawson and Ruddell have indicated that the meaning approach to learning "leads to (1) greater retention over periods of time, (2) greater transfer potential, and (3) increased ability to solve new processes independently."[5]

Motivation of drill

After the development of meaning of some mathematical operations, children will see the need of fixing certain processes in mind by using them over and over until the opera-

[5] Dan T. Dawson and Arden K. Ruddell, "The Case of the Meaning Theory in Teaching Arithmetic," *The Elementary School Journal*, LV (March, 1955), pp. 393–99. See also William H. Brownell, "The Place of Meaning in Arithmetic," *The Elementary School Journal*, XLVII (January, 1947), pp. 256–65.

tion can be recalled. Because rote learning by drill methods is frowned upon, many authorities prefer that this process of fixing operations in mind be termed *practice*. Regardless of the term used to describe the process, children need to master certain simple combinations, such as those in addition, multiplication, subtraction, and division, and to learn the combinations so well that the skills operate automatically in more complex operations. Children need to practice not only simple number combinations but also more complex processes. When children have learned the process of adding fractions as previously illustrated, they need to practice adding fractions in a variety of situations.

Drill or practice does not always add to understanding, but it is necessary for accuracy in social situations and also for use in more complex operations. For example, children who play store or post office want to make change, so they need to add without making mistakes. They need to figure bills to determine the total cost, but they cannot do this quickly without the ability to recall certain combinations. Likewise, children who have learned to carry in addition and to borrow in subtraction will need to master the process for other operations as well as for use in social situations.

But practice of the function must not precede the development of its meaning. For example, children will experience the operation of finding how many potatoes they have when they combine three groups of four in each group and find that they have twelve in all. The process is then expressed in numbers, $3 \times 4 = 12$. After learning the meaning of the process and having a need to remember such combinations, children will practice using $3 \times 4 = 12$ until they can remember the product. They soon realize that they cannot work problems of a higher level without a mastery of simpler processes.

In the process of fixing in mind the necessary mathematical operations, the teacher can help to motivate the practice by frequent application to real-life situations. In games and other school activities, the fundamentals which children have practiced are put to use by application in a great variety of situations, and the skills acquired are likely to be more permanent and the motivation greater.

The amount of drill required to master any function will vary with the pupils, with the nature of the material, and with the way in which the teaching is done. Pupils vary in intelligence, interest, and previous experience. Less drill is required by the more intelligent and highly motivated pupils than by the slow and uninterested. Children who see some purpose in mastery will learn in a shorter time. Also, less drill will likely be required for simple skills, such as reducing fractions, than is required for more complex skills, such as division by two-place divisors. Furthermore, if skills to be learned are first encountered in social situations and if frequent application is made during the drill process, children usually require less time to master the skills.

In practicing or drilling children to master mathematical operations, teachers find that the process is most effective if placed on an individual basis, because some children require more time than others. Often children work in pairs to drill each other during the process. However the practice is organized, individual differences must be considered.

Drill does not have therapeutic value. If a phase of arithmetic is not understood by children, drill will not make the operation meaningful. Sometimes teachers discover from a testing program that children cannot add fractions. After telling children how to reduce the fractions to a common denominator, they proceed to drill on that process. Instead, the teachers should go back to work with *things*, such as apples, paper plates, or other material, and develop the meaning of the operation from experiences.

Problem solving

Many children who have been drilled on the fundamental operations and have learned many of the mathematical processes involved still have difficulty in solving problems. This may be due to one or more of the following causes:

1. Problems not real-life problems. No feeling of need to solve the problem is present in the children.
2. Deficiency in computational ability
3. Poor reading ability
4. Mental immaturity
5. Lack of practice in reasoning
6. Inability to apply a sequence in problem solving
7. Inability to estimate answers
8. Poor understanding of relationships in numbers

In most schools, problem-solving experiences are taken from a textbook. These problems do not arise out of real-life situations and many of them are quite foreign to the environment of the rural child. Because the problems are unlike those of daily life, solutions merely give pupils practice in performing the computations needed to get the answers. Authors of arithmetic textbooks have recognized this difficulty, and there has been considerable improvement in the type of problems furnished. Some problems are now organized about centers of interests. However, the teacher will need to make use of situations in the school and in the community to find real opportunities for development of problem-solving ability.

As has already been indicated the activities of the school, home, and community offer real problems for children to solve. In the school, there are paper sales, races which call for a timekeeper, and baseball diamonds to be constructed. In transportation units, costs of travel are computed; in a unit on weather, a thermometer is used and records are kept; in a unit on wool, children are concerned with weight, feeding rations, production costs, and regions of the world where wool is produced, and this may call for the construction of a products map. In 4-H Club work, the boy or girl may borrow money to purchase a calf or a pig, and this calls for a study of interest, cost accounting, record keeping, and the like.

Teachers who know the community and the activities of the children have an inexhaustible supply of real-life problems to be solved. These may be used to replace or supplement those found in the textbook. These problems present real challenges to the children. They are used to give meaning to processes, concepts, and generalizations, and they provide practice by giving children an opportunity to apply generalizations and skills in a rich variety of situations which are important to them.

Summary

Because of the practical character of rural life, there has always been a great need for arithmetic in the lives of rural people. Measuring, weighing, and production-cost accounting play a large part in the lives of rural people and in the lives of the growing boys and girls of the rural area.

To make arithmetic meaningful and useful in the lives of the children, teachers must know the problems which the children face in the local areas. These problems are not the same for rural and urban sections, nor for the various rural regions because of differences in farming operations.

Growing up in an area in which arithmetic is used constantly in daily life, most children of rural areas have considerable development in number concepts, some vocabulary in arithmetic, and may have some familiarity with processes and they are ready for arithmetic in the first grade. Because they need arithmetic in their daily lives, instruction cannot be postponed.

Readiness for arithmetic is conceived as a state of development at any level which is needed for work with the more complex processes to follow. But since children entering school vary widely in development, teachers need to use the activities of the kindergarten and first grade to develop awareness of number and meanings of numbers, concepts, vocabularies, and the like. However, throughout the grades, the experiences of the school and community should be used to bring development needed for further growth in the use of numbers.

The major goal of arithmetic instruction is to develop in children the ability to use numbers as needed for quantitative thinking in connection with the problems which they now face and will continue to face in daily life. This means the development of computational skill and understanding of concepts, relationships, and measuring devices; an understanding of social usages of arithmetic and the contribution which numbers make to human progress; the development of such ideals as accuracy and persistence and the habit of using numbers for communication and problem solving.

Experiences of the primary grades are designed to continue the growth in number concepts, vocabulary, and the like which began in the pre-school period. The major emphasis is on the development of understanding and insight rather than on skill and speed. Children learn some cardinal and ordinal numbers and have some experience with simple fractions, measuring, and simple problem solving.

Middle-grade activities provide continued enlargement and refining of number concepts and processes and the development of greater accuracy in skill. The arithmetic activities suggested in the textbook should be combined with those selected from school and community life.

At all levels of development, children need to develop the meaning of concepts, processes, and generalizations. Meaning is achieved through work with concrete and semiconcrete materials and by study of structural relationships, not by the use of concrete materials alone nor by work with abstract numbers alone. Learning the meaning by beginning with the concrete is needed at all levels when new operations are introduced.

Drill or practice is required to fix in mind certain fundamental processes or generalizations to be used in more complex operations and to acquire accuracy in social situations; but drill must follow the development of meaning, not precede it. Drill is facilitated and made meaningful by the use of skills or functions in a great variety of real-life situations. The amount of drill required will vary with the pupils, the nature of the material, and the teaching methods. Drill is largely a process of trying to achieve permanence in functions already learned in a meaningful situation.

Children often have difficulty with problem solving because the problems are not vital to their welfare, or because they have poor computational ability, poor reading ability, or mental immaturity. The inability to reason or apply a sequence in problem solving may also be sources of difficulty. Difficulties may arise, too, from a lack of understanding of number relationships. Selection of problems from real-life situations and the rebuilding of background skills may be needed by some children.

Selected references

BATHURST, EFFIE. "How Children Use Arithmetic," Bulletin No. 7. United States Department of Health, Education and Welfare. Washington, D.C.: United States Government Printing Office, 1951.

Discusses children's early experiences with arithmetic, methods of teaching, curriculum, and use of materials. Has excellent list of activities.

BRUECKNER, LEO J., and BOND, GUY L. *The Diagnosis and Treatment of Learning Difficulties.* New York: Appleton-Century-Crofts, Inc., 1955. Chaps. viii and ix.

Deals with objectives of arithmetic instruction, characteristics of instructional program, gradation of content, common faults in arithmetical operations, use of tests to diagnose difficulties, case studies of children having difficulties, and treatment of learning difficulties.

BRUECKNER, LEO J., and GROSSNICKLE, FOSTER E. *How to Make Arithmetic Meaningful.* Philadelphia: John C. Winston Co., 1953. Chaps. iv–ix.

Provides good discussion of readiness, curriculum, socially useful skills, individual differences, development of units, place of meaning, role of discovery, perception of relationships, drill, and steps in instruction.

BUCKINGHAM, BURDETTE. *Elementary Arithmetic, Its Meaning and Practice.* New York: Ginn & Co., 1953. Chaps. iii and iv especially.

Helps the teacher with development of number concepts, grouping, abstract and concrete numbers, fractions, and guidance in the generalizing process.

HOLLISTER, GEORGE E., and GUNDERSON, AGNES E. *Teaching Arithmetic in Grades I and II.* Boston: D. C. Heath & Co., 1954. Chaps. i–xii.

Especially good for primary-grade arithmetic. Deals with social and computational aspects, nature of number system, teaching principles and practices, development of number meaning, use of inventory tests, teaching materials, number concepts, the program for grades one and two, and vocabulary development.

MORTON, ROBERT L. *Teaching Children Arithmetic*. New York: Silver Burdette Co., 1953. Chaps. iii–ix.

Helps for the teacher in building understanding of numbers, concept of place value, use of zero, carrying, fundamental operations, insurance, use of money, weights and measures, and how to tell time.

NATIONAL SOCIETY FOR THE STUDY OF EDUCATION. *The Teaching of Arithmetic*, Fiftieth Yearbook. Chicago: University of Chicago Press, 1951. Part II, chaps. iii, iv, v, and vii.

Describes program for the primary and middle grades with emphasis on number thinking, problem solving, sequence of learning, arithmetic readiness, curriculum, and methods of teaching.

SPITZER, HERBERT F. *The Teaching of Arithmetic* (2d ed.). Boston: Houghton Mifflin Co., 1954. Chaps. ii–ix.

Good treatment of instruction in counting, numeration, pre-school and primary work, number experiences, fundamental operations, problem solving, oral problems, fractions, decimals and per cents, weights and measures, and scale drawing.

WHEAT, HARRY GROVE. *How to Teach Arithmetic*. White Plains, N.Y.: Row, Peterson & Co., 1951. Chaps. i–vi, ix, x especially.

Provides help with teaching the numbers by groups, the fundamental operations, and problem solving and offers a comparison of processes in arithmetic.

15

SCIENCE FOR RURAL AREAS

Science in the elementary-school curriculum has been receiving increased emphasis in recent years. This is due in
part to a growing recognition of the importance of science
in human life and to a clearer realization of the need
for better understanding of human affairs—understanding
which is impossible without some information and skills that
can be learned through experiences in science. Also, the
acceptance of the child-development approach in the organization of the curriculum has led to recognition of the
fact that every aspect of learning at the secondary-school
level has its beginning in early childhood. Boys and girls
who are to succeed in science at the secondary school level
should begin the development of scientific generalizations,
methods, and attitudes in the earlier school period. Furthermore, children at the elementary-school level need scientific
information, practice in problem solving, and the thrill of
discovery which science experiences afford. Rural children
are constantly brought in contact with growing plants and
animals and with machines, weather, and land. They want
to know why some foliage changes color in autumn, why
water expands when it freezes, why different plants require

certain kinds of soil, why we have dew and frost and rain, how bees carry nectar, how muskrats build their houses, why green hay when baled produces heat, and how an electric transformer works. Children are always asking "why" and "how," and if their development is to be facilitated, teachers must help them find some answers.

Elementary-school teachers have trouble with science instruction partly because there are so many fields of science and partly because they do not feel competent to teach science unless they know the content well. Yet, because of the broad character of elementary-school teacher-education programs, preparation of such teachers is necessarily limited. So teachers are confused about what science to teach, how to teach it, and what the goals of instruction should be. They do not know where to get help with methods, materials, and content. And they wonder how they can find time to teach science when there are so many other things to be taught.

Place of science in the curriculum

As explained in Chapters 6 and 13, science need not be taught as a separate subject; it may be handled either in the form of experience units of a well-integrated program or as a part of a broad field of study. Science is closely related to social studies, as shown in Chapter 13. For example, a unit on wool calls for the use of science in the study of sheep and in testing woolen cloth. Units on conservation of soil, forests, and animal life involve both social studies and science. The study of weather is a science, but the way in which man is dependent on weather is a social study. The study of food production involves science, social studies, and health. Geography is one of the social studies and is also a science. The problems of living in regions of the world are affected by land, weather, climate, mountains, valleys, and plains.

Science is also closely related to health and safety. Children who are studying milk, for example, will want to know why cows should be tested for tuberculosis and why milk should be pasteurized. In the study of first aid, children want to know why a wound should be disinfected. Safety precautions with reference to fire, traffic, farm machinery, and the like can best be understood with the aid of science.

Much of science involves the use of arithmetic. Scientific experimentation involves record keeping and problem solving. A sixth-grade class which wanted to study the germination of several varieties of wheat seed had to count and plant the seed, make records, and figure the percentage of seed which grew in each plot of ground.

As suggested in Chapter 6, an integrated program may be a series of work units, some primarily scientific in character and others primarily social studies, while still others may deal with health and safety. These work units need to be so organized as to afford a sequence of development from simple generalizations or concepts to more complex ones.

While science may be learned with other content, it should not be taught as merely incidental to other learning. The understandings to be developed, the generalizations to be extracted from experience, and the problem-solving skills to be practiced must be clearly understood by the teacher. Of course, much science is learned incidentally in connection with community experiences and as a part of the school program. Children may bring to school birds' nests, frogs, interesting stones, and the like, and these arouse interests which the teacher may use to induce science learning; but this is not the complete science program. There must also be a well-planned series of experiences designed to bring sequential development, and for many of these experiences the teacher will need to set the stage for learning, as discussed in Chapter 5, since not all of the experience needed will arise incidentally.

Instruction in science may be provided as a series of meaningful work units or experiences in the broad-field type of organization of the curriculum, in which there is a specific period of the school day when science is taught. But the teacher will recognize that many of the science experiences will include some of what are recognized as social studies.

If science is well taught, it will have meaning in the lives of the children, and the work units may cover some content other than science.

Goals of science instruction and their meaning

Regardless of whether the school program is organized as subjects, broad fields of subject matter, or as well-integrated experience units to help children understand the major life functions or processes, some goals are needed to guide the teacher in organization of experiences and in methods of teaching. These goals also help in selection of materials and in guidance of learning. Most of the science goals are the same for rural and urban children; but because science plays a different role in the life of the rural child, the emphasis to be given to aspects of science will not be the same for rural and urban children.

The goals of science instruction for children of rural areas may be stated and explained as follows:

1. To arouse and help satisfy curiosity about the environment and to develop permanent interests in the study of science. Because of constant contacts with the outdoors, life in rural areas can become a series of great adventures for rural children as they increase their understanding of how plants and animals live and grow and how land, weather, and climate are related to growth.
2. To teach the use of science to help solve problems of living. For example, children who own animals or crops of their own become concerned with shelter, food, animal and plant diseases, soil erosion and fertilization, breeding, germination of seeds, and the like. Problems involved in conservation of soil, wild life, minerals, and health have real meaning for children because the problems arise from the activities of daily life.
3. To develop permanent interests in farming and related vocations. Because science becomes the avenue for rich adventure and a means of solving problems, life on the farm can become much more than drudgery and monotony. While it is not expected that all the boys and girls will re-

main in farming areas, those who *do* remain can learn to feel the lure of farm life and find greater enjoyment from adventures in agriculture. Boys and girls who will earn their living in other occupations can profit from an appreciation of farm life and by an understanding of the place of agriculture in human affairs.

While boys and girls do not usually make decisions regarding their vocations at the elementary-school level, permanent interests, developed early in life, are potent influences which lead to choices at a later period. Such interests will lead some to elect vocational agriculture, home economics, agricultural research, food processing, marketing, forest conservation, and the like as their vocations. Without understanding and permanent interests, vocational decisions cannot be made wisely.

4. To help learn the techniques of problem solving and develop a desire to use the scientific method. This involves learning to identify and define the problem, searching for facts while withholding judgment until the facts are secured, experimentation, critical thinking, striving for truth, and learning to generalize from facts and the results of experimentation. Generalizations developed through experimentation and problem solving are then applied to many life situations.

5. To read science material intelligently, develop a science vocabulary, and form permanent interests in the reading and study of science. Science has a specialized vocabulary and the material requires careful reading. Children should learn to read farm and science magazines and books on agriculture and science, and they should develop permanent interests in keeping up to date in new developments.

6. To develop permanent interests in conservation and establish habits of using wisely all natural resources. By practicing conservation and by understanding the need for conservation, permanent interests and habits may be developed.

7. To develop an appreciation of the contribution of science to modern life. Children can learn how science contributes to human welfare and the need for adjustments in social institutions and social practices to keep pace with scientific progress. For example, children can learn how agricultural research has revolutionized farm life, as seen in Chapter 2.

They can appreciate the work done by the Agriculture Extension Service. They can learn to understand how machines and appliances not only add to comfort and enjoyment of rural life but also create problems to be solved. They can appreciate how science aids communication and transportation.

8. To develop a scientific attitude. A person with a scientific attitude is open minded. He respects another person's point of view. He is willing to change his mind if valid evidence indicates that he is wrong. He does not jump to conclusions nor decide on the basis of one observation. He weighs the evidence, looking at it from every angle, and draws his conclusions only when he is sure. He is critical of sources and makes certain that material is reliable. He plans his investigations carefully and makes careful and accurate observations. He reasons from cause to effect and refuses to be swayed by emotion or prejudice.

Science needs of rural children

Because they are brought directly in contact with the outdoors, boys and girls of the farm and village have much interest in science, have many problems to be solved, and have many questions which must be answered if there is to be growth in understanding and continued interest in exploration and experimentation.

Boys and girls of rural areas work around farms feeding the cattle and hogs and chickens, milking cows, running the tractor, helping to harvest the field crops, planting a shelter belt of trees, and doing many other jobs suited to their capabilities. Some of the questions which they ask are the following:

What is the best feed for growing calves?
What is the best feed for fattening cattle?
What kind of food is needed by milk cows?
Is one kind of food better than another for egg-laying hens? for fattening chickens and turkeys?
Is green feed better for the stock than dry feed?
Why do watermelons require a rich sandy soil?
What can be done to keep the soil from washing away?
How can we tell what the soil needs to make plants grow?
Why does salt make ice melt?

What makes the dew and the frost?
What is fog?
Why don't we get more rain?
Can we make it rain if we want to?
Why do plants need sunlight?
What are the stars and the moon?
How do you read an electric meter?
How does an electric clock work?
Why do rabbits girdle the fruit trees?
Why do fruit trees need spraying and pruning?
What is pollen?
How do bees get honey from the flowers?
How do bees make honey?
What is poison ivy?
How can mosquitoes and flies be controlled?
What makes the windmill go?
How does the cream separator work?
How do muskrats build their homes?
Are crows and hawks harmful?
What are the different kinds of birds and how do they build their nests?
Why do leaves come off the trees in the fall?
What trees are best for shade? for lumber and fence posts?

Some questions of children deal with oxidation: the rusting of iron, the decay of food, the discoloration of silverware, the spontaneous combustion from green hay, the heating of green corn in a crib. They want to know why the freezing of water in the car radiator causes it to expand. Some questions are related to atmospheric pressure: how force and suction pumps work, how the vacuum cleaner operates, what makes the windshield wipers turn, how the milking machine gets milk, what makes water run uphill in a siphon. Some questions arise in the home, such as those dealing with fire extinguishers, electric fuses, toasters, lamps, stoves, cream separators, thermometers and barometers.

These and thousands of other questions are asked by children. In finding answers to their questions, children will not only grow in understanding of the environment but will be learning the techniques of problem solving, and they will learn how to set up experiments to help them find the answers. For example, the teacher may lead the children who raise questions about soil fertility to set up an experiment in which they test the different kinds of soil by planting seeds in sample plots of ground. In solving problems, children not only will do some experimentation but also will use books, resource people, and audio-visual aids to help answer their questions.

A good science program is geared to the needs of the boys and girls—needs which vary from one region of the country to another and from one local community to another. Hence, the teacher who would make science instruction meaningful to children must know the local community and its problems, and she must be ready to work with the children to find the answers through reading, research, and experimentation.

Agriculture in the science program

Any good elementary-school science program for schools in rural areas will place special emphasis on the science of agriculture. Unfortunately, most rural schools have neglected to build the understanding needed for agricultural life. This is partly due to the fact that most textbooks have been designed for use in urban centers and there has been a limited amount of teaching and child-study materials developed for agriculture study at the elementary-school level. The neglect of agriculture in the elementary schools has also been due partly to the vocational emphasis given to agriculture at the secondary-school level. Many teachers and school administrators assume that agriculture as a vocational subject should be confined to secondary schools. Yet, any good school program, elementary or secondary, must deal with the problems people face in living, and elementary-school children need to understand the environment in which they live. Boys and girls of farms and villages are concerned with agriculture. They belong to 4-H Clubs and often grow field crops and raise livestock of their own. Consequently, if science is to have real meaning in the lives of these children, the science program of the rural elementary school must include experiences which contribute to growth in the use of science to solve the problems of agriculture.

What problems or topics in agriculture should be included in an instructional program? Hammonds[1] indicates that elementary school instruction in agriculture should deal with such topics as "how farm crops grow," "lower forms of plant life," such as molds and bacteria, and how they live and reproduce, "soil formation and conservation," "identification and control of insects," "birds and how they affect farming and farm life," "trees and shrubs for the farm home," and "farm forestry." Hamlin[2] has suggested that agriculture education in elementary schools should include "improving the appearance of the farm home," "agriculture agencies and the services they provide for farmers," "agriculture occupations and how to prepare for them," "farm safety and accident prevention," "farm fire protection," "weed eradication and control," and "farm conveniences."

What agriculture should be taught will be determined by the character of operations in the particular region. Sometimes the program will need to deal with production of tobacco, cotton, soybeans, fruit, sugar beets, wheat, corn, peanuts, vegetables, cattle, sheep, hogs, or poultry. In each case, soil fertility, plant and animal diseases, and weather and climate will receive emphasis.

In the study of agriculture nearly all of the scientific generalizations and concepts can be developed. In rural areas science means horticulture, field crops, animal husbandry, and forestry, depending upon the region in which the school operates. Study which is related to these areas develops understanding of plant and animal life and their dependence upon water, soil, climate, weather, and control of diseases. And in the processes of planting, cultivating, harvesting, and transporting, all types of machines are used. The study of weather includes air movements, clouds, evapo-

[1] Carsie Hammonds, *Teaching Agriculture*, McGraw-Hill Book Co., Inc., 1950, chap. xii.

[2] Herbert M. Hamlin, *Agricultural Education in Community Schools* (Danville, Ill.: The Interstate Printers and Publishers, 1950), chap. ix.

ration and condensation, and related information. Topography of the land, subsoil moisture, and soil and its origin are related topics. Physical phenomena can have meaning in the lives of children if studied in relation to agriculture. Farm machinery and home appliances can be understood as levers, incline planes, pulleys, electrical and gas engines, and the like.

Complete understanding of these subjects cannot be achieved at the elementary-school level, but problems can be selected to awaken interests, make science meaningful, teach problem-solving techniques, develop good attitudes toward farming, and help the children appreciate the contributions of science to human life. Teachers who have difficulty with the selection of appropriate problems for study can make use of the services of the teacher of vocational agriculture, the county agriculture agent, the personnel of the Soil Conservation Service, and capable farmers of the community.

Conservation in the science program

Any study of science in agriculture will deal with conservation, since rural people are directly involved in using natural resources. Soil, water, and forestry conservation will need to be given much emphasis. And conservation of wild life will be recognized as important to boys and girls of rural areas. In some areas minerals are being extracted from the soil and in all regions such products are being used; consequently, the origin and conservation of mineral resources will be of direct interest to the children. Likewise, the conservation of human life, discussed in Chapter 16, will be very important both to rural and urban people.

Conservation of natural resources should be taught in both rural and urban schools, but the people of rural areas are in a position to practice conservation of these resources to a greater extent than urban people. Rural people recognize that their economic welfare depends directly upon conservation practices. The welfare of urban people is definitely affected by conservation of natural resources, but rural people are the ones who can do most to preserve and develop those resources upon which all human life depends.

While the welfare of man has always been dependent on the soil, man himself has been careless in land use because land has seemed to be so abundant in this country. In earlier days, forests were cleared and crops planted. When the fertility of that land had been expended, man moved on to clear more land and plant more crops. The movement continued, with the wastage of timber, the destruction of nature's method of continuing to fertilize the soil through plant decay, the loss of the moisture-retention features of the forests, the drainage of fertility from the soil, and the exposure of the land to wind and water erosion. The carpet of trees and grass used by nature to preserve the soil and moisture has been removed, and continuous efforts to plant the land have removed much of its fertility. There is no more free land to which man can move. The frontier is gone.

The loss of farm land through waste has been so great that little good farm land remains in the United States. According to reports by the United States Soil Conservation Service, 280,000,000 acres of crop and grazing land have been severely damaged, the equal of the combined areas of Illinois, Iowa, Missouri, Kansas, Nebraska, and Wyoming. Another 775,000,000 acres of crop, grazing, and forest land have eroded to some extent, and there are now only 460,000,000 acres of good land suitable for crops. This includes 85,000,000 acres that need clearing, draining, irrigating, and other improvements to make them productive. All but 95,000,000 acres of the 460,000,000 acres are subject to erosion if care is not taken to check its spread. That is all of the good land that is left; no more can be discovered or created.

The rise and decline of the nations of the world have been determined largely by how the people cared for the land. Some nations have allowed the productivity of the soil to decline and as a result the people have suffered. Ancient Babylon, ancient cities of North Africa, and cities of ancient Rome were depleted of their good soil, and many historians ascribe the decline of these nations to the loss of good land.

Much of the land of India and China has been misused and overplanted, so that many people of these lands cannot be fed from the amount of food produced there. Yet, the people of Japan have demonstrated what can be done with preservation of the soil and wise utilization of the land.

It has been pointed out by specialists in agriculture and medicine that soil erosion starts human erosion. Medical authorities have indicated that the lack of energy of many people can be traced to malnutrition. Poor land brings poor food, indifference, failure to care for the land, and then even poorer land. In areas of the world where there is shallow soil, there will often be found a higher incidence of tuberculosis and other diseases, as well as a general lack of energy.

The cost of replacement of loss in soil fertility in bare land is very great. The University of Georgia translated soil erosion losses into dollars and cents by making a comparison of the cost of replacing with fertilizers the soil washed away from one acre of *woodland* in one year with the cost of replacing with commercial fertilizers the soil washed away from one acre of *bare* land during the same period. Both plots of land received 42 inches of rainfall in the one year. One hundred fifteen pounds of soil were washed away from the acre of woodland. This soil contained a total of three pounds of nitrate of soda, acid phosphate, and muriate of potash. At the time of the study it would have cost five cents to replace with commercial fertilizer the loss of fertility on the acre of woodland. But on the acre of bare land 112,316 pounds, or 56 tons, of soil containing over 3,000 pounds of the ingredients were washed away. The replacement of these ingredients with commercial fertilizer cost $59.15 at 1935 prices. Had the ingredients stayed in the soil, they would have been sufficient to produce 50 bushels of corn for four separate seasons.[3]

Boys and girls can learn how to preserve the land and build up the soil. An explanation of the learning needed by

[3] United States Department of Agriculture, *Soil, The Nation's Basic Heritage* (Washington, D.C.: Superintendent of Documents), pp. 18–19.

children is furnished by Mrs. Henrie Andrews Howell, a Mississippi school teacher, who has written an inexpensive school reader entitled *Muddy Waters*.[4] It tells in fiction form the story of how a worn-out farm was transformed into a paying property with the aid of contour planting and terracing to conserve its topsoil and waterfall. It shows how water can be an indispensable blessing and friend of the farmer or can be his worst enemy through reckless tillage of hilly land. It shows that good drainage, so essential to crops, can be the means of washing away tons of irreplaceable top soil in the course of a single cloudburst. Deforestation and the reckless tillage of soil have destroyed vast areas of farm land, and only the farmer and his family can save the soil upon which human life depends.

In addition to soil conservation, water conservation should also be emphasized. As has been pointed out, denuding the land of forests and grasses has exposed the land so that as the rain falls, instead of being held back, the water rushes quickly to rivers and streams, speeding up soil erosion and creating flood damage. Because little water goes into the soil, the water table underneath the soil falls and there is insufficient water for plants, animals, and man. Measures to prevent the rapid run-off of water include use of cover crops, crop rotation, strip cropping, grassed waterways, pasture improvement, terracing, contour plowing, and the building of dams in gullies and streams.

The wise use of water resources also includes the protection of streams, rivers, and lakes from pollution and the exercise of care in providing a good supply of water on the farm. The health of the people depends upon an adequate supply of pure water.

In most areas of the United States, forest lands have been destroyed and must be rebuilt. Of the original 85,000,000,000 acres of forest land, only approximately 100,000,000 acres now remain. Millions of acres of timber have been cut to secure lumber to build homes and other buildings, and for

[4] Henrie Andrews Howell, *Muddy Water* (New York: Applied Economics, 1949).

many years there were no efforts to provide replacement of lost timber lands. Also, much of the forest area has been destroyed by fire; millions of acres have been burned through carelessness. Now, millions of dollars must be spent to try to protect the remaining forests.

Only after much of the timber has been destroyed have the people of the country come to realize that trees are essential to human welfare. Lumber is needed to build homes, stores, and factories and to make furniture for homes and business establishments. The shortage of pulpwood for making paper has created serious problems for the publishers of newspapers, magazines, and books. Furthermore, the loss of forest areas has destroyed much of the natural beauty of the American landscape.

The wise use of lumber resources includes provision for replacement of timber as cutting is proceeding, as well as the prevention of forest fires. While considerable progress has been made with reforestation, insufficient gains have been made to care for the increasing demands for lumber products. Furthermore, since the program of reforestation was not begun early enough, the trees are still too small to be useful for lumber.

Schools in rural areas can do much by teaching the wise use of forest products, the practice of timber replacement, and the protection of forests from fire. Some schools have developed projects in reforestation which include the planting of trees, the study and treatment of tree diseases, and the care of forests. Boys and girls have learned to be careful with matches and campfires in wooded areas and have used their experiences in school and scouting to help educate adults in the protection and development of timber resources.

In areas where mining is carried on, children are aware of the importance of minerals insofar as mining provides occupations for people; but children are not always aware of how minerals developed in the earth, nor are they aware of the importance of minerals in the life of an industrial society. Minerals cannot be replaced. They are exhaustible natural resources which should be conserved. Iron, coal, copper, zinc, petroleum, and the like are the lifeblood of industry, making possible machinery, automobiles, appliances, and other conveniences of the homes and farms. Yet, the rapid development of industry has brought rapid depletion of many of our minerals.

Children will readily recognize the importance of conservation of wild life, but they do not always know what can be done to help in preservation nor do they always have a desire to conserve wild life. The study of birds and their value to human life will help increase understanding and develop right attitudes. The importance of hunting and fishing as sports will be understood, but will the boys and girls become good sportsmen? In some rural areas fishing is a major occupation which provides food for people; and where fishing is merely a sport, the operation of resorts for recreation is a very significant vocation. Conservation of wild life, therefore, is important in any rural elementary-school curriculum.

Conservation education is not merely the teaching of people to save or hoard natural wealth; it implies the development of natural resources as well as their preservation. Conservation means the far-sighted, judicious use of natural resources without waste, as contrasted with indiscriminate consumption. It means the replacement and restoration of resources rather than consumption without regard for the future. It involves the use of the fruits of scientific research in developing and conserving while still employing the benefits of natural resources. It includes planning for the future as well as for the present. Conservation education requires the use of science to develop understanding and appreciation of natural resources, and it includes practice on specific conservation projects to develop habits in growing boys and girls.

Science program as a whole

Most teachers in rural areas will accept the view that the science program should be organized to bring continuous development of children in the understanding of the problems of living and should help them use the scientific method in problem solving. Teachers recognize the fact that a meaningful science program in rural areas should include topics and problems which involve agriculture and the wise use of natural resources. But they want to know what topics or problems should be included and what should be the nature of a good program. They ask such questions as: "What are the characteristics of a good program?" "How can experiences be graded to bring gradual growth in children?" "What topics or problems are essential?"

A good science program should have the following characteristics:

1. The program has continuity of experience from grade to grade.

From the simple experiences of the primary grade to more complex problems he encounters later, the child continues to develop. Gradation is based on the interest and ability of the child to comprehend.

2. The program has balance and breadth in that there is provision for experiences in a variety of science fields.

Experiences deal with plant and animal life, machines, electricity, magnetism, heat, astronomy, earth science and chemical phenomena, agriculture and conservation. While the science program secures breadth by sampling experiences from the various fields, the teacher realizes that there is more for children to learn than can be mastered in any given year. Some selection must be made, and this selection will be determined largely by the needs of the children in the local community. In planning the program, teachers should try to answer the question, "What science experiences are most needed by these children to help them understand the environment in which they live?"

The organization of experience units to cover three grade levels, as suggested in Chapter 6, offers one procedure for covering a greater scope of material than is possible in any one year.

3. The experiences must have meaning in the daily life of the children.

Problems and materials taken from the local environment make the study of science meaningful to children. Books, magazines, encyclopedias, auditory and visual aids are source material but do not provide the program. Teachers who merely follow a textbook series run the risk of divorcing instruction from the lives of the children and making science only a reading exercise. Topics studied merely from textbooks may be unrelated to the life of the local community. If textbooks are used as the program plan, considerable adaptation to problems of local living may be required to give meaning to science. Some problems of local life not covered by the textbook might be introduced, and some problems in the textbook might be omitted.

4. Teachers take advantage of incidents in daily life to show the children how to find answers to questions.

If curiosity is stimulated, the desire to find answers is encouraged.

5. The program is flexible to permit taking advantage of needs and interests as they arise and to permit the use of community events and seasonal changes.

Children can be interested in planting in the spring, harvesting in the autumn, bird migration in the spring and fall, and frost, ice, and snow in the winter.

6. The science program gives meaning to the rest of the school program.

Whether a completely integrated program, a broad-field program, or a subject organization is used, the work in science must give meaning to social studies, health, and arithmetic, and it must motivate the work in reading, speaking, and writing.

It is little wonder that teachers are confused about what content to include in the science program since authorities in the field do not agree. Analyses of courses of study reveal wide variation in topics recommended for the elementary school by state and local educators. Frank J. Estvan found from 28 to 38 different topics listed for each of the elementary-school grades in various courses of study.[5] Likewise, there seemed to be no agreement as to grade placement of the various topics. An examination of textbook series in science reveals similar variation, although there is evidence of attempts to grade science content and concepts according to difficulty. Simple generalizations are suggested for the primary grades and more complex ones for the upper grades.

The teacher should be free to select content which has high interest value and high utility in the local community. The concepts developed from the experiences should be governed by the maturity of the pupils. From the primary grades on there should be breadth of experience at each grade level. All areas of science may be explored in the primary, middle, and upper grades. Although study in the primary grades develops simple generalizations, and the study of the same topics may appear in the intermediate and upper grades, the study at higher levels should develop deeper meanings and lead to more complex generalizations.

The following is a partial list of general areas of study with a few illustrations of topics for each area. There is nothing sacred about this list of topics nor the lists provided in courses of study or textbook series. Each faculty will need to develop plans and outlines based on local community needs and pupil interest.

Science Areas	Kindergarten and Primary Grades	Middle and Upper Grades
I. Plant life		
Farm crops Grasses	Plant need for water, sunlight, and food	Seed selection, reproduction
Weeds	Seeds, germination	Weed control
Horticulture	Tree recognition, leaves, buds, branches, varieties of wood	Trees, recognition, growth Forest conservation Lumber and other wood products Fruit trees, planting and care, grafting

[5] See Virgil E. Herrick et al., The Elementary School, (Englewood Cliffs, N.J.: Prentice-Hall, Inc., 1956), pp. 223–24.

Science Areas	Kindergarten and Primary Grades	Middle and Upper Grades
II. Animal life		
Pets	Care and feeding of pets	
Livestock	Livestock	Livestock breeds, rations, diseases
Wild life— birds, fish, etc.	Wild life Bees and their work Birds and their homes Saving wild life	Beekeeping Wild life, birds, mammals, hibernation, migration, conservation Rodents
Insects	Recognition of some insects	Helpful and harmful insects
III. Earth, sky, and universe		
Seasons	Seasons and weather, clouds, dew, frost, rain, evaporation, snow	Seasons, climates Weather, prediction, winds, rain, frost, etc.
Weather	Thermometers	Thermometers and barometers
Soil	Soil and uses, rocks, sand	Soil conservation, springs, wells, geysers, hotsprings
Erosion	Streams and rivers	
Minerals Conservation		Minerals, uses, conservation
Earth	Gravity	Earth, topography, volcanoes, earthquakes
Universe	Celestial bodies, sun, moon	Celestial bodies, planets, solar system, milky way, eclipses
IV. Matter and energy		
Magnetism	What magnets do	Magnets and uses, telephone
Electricity	Uses of electricity	Electricity, motors, fuses, appliances, wiring, lightning
Machines	Simple machines	Machinery, levers, pulleys, wheel and axle, friction and greasing
Tools	Airplanes, toys and how they work, how work is made easier	

Science Areas	Kindergarten and Primary Grades	Middle and Upper Grades
Heat	Freezing and melting Fire prevention	Oxidation, rust, spontaneous combustion Heat, fires, refrigeration, pressure cookers, fuel, insulation
Sound	Sources of sounds, music	
Light	Reflection and refraction, mirrors and refraction in water, periscopes	Light, cameras, eye, color, home lights Aviation

More complete lists of topics for study and generalizations to be developed are given in the references at the end of this chapter. However, teachers should learn that the concepts listed are not to be handed out for study as a series of isolated facts. Instead, questions should be asked, plans for study made cooperatively with the children, experiments performed as needed, reading and study carried out to find answers, and, finally, generalizations or principles developed and applied in a variety of situations. For example, the children in a second grade wanted to find out if plants need soil, so they put one pea seed in a jar of soil and one in a jar of pebbles. After watering both, they set the jars aside. In a few days both seeds had sprouted; a few days later the plant in the pebbles was slightly larger; in a few weeks both plants were still growing, but the one in the soil was the more vigorous; and still later only the plant in the soil blossomed. The children did some reading and generalized that "seeds have stored up food to get them started until roots develop" and "plants need soil to get food to continue to grow." Similar experiments led to the concepts that "plants need moisture," "plants need sunlight," "food is manufactured in the leaves from materials in the soil," "the leaves are the food factory for the plant," "roots take in water and materials for food," and "stems carry the water and food materials from the roots to the leaves." These generalizations were then used to help the children in planning and planting a school garden.

Some teaching procedures

How the teacher works with children to bring development in science is perhaps more important than what the children study. The elementary school is not attempting to develop scientists, but, rather, to develop scientific attitudes, techniques of problem solving, and habits which influence better farming and conservation of natural resources. To accomplish these goals the teacher must use procedures which will arouse genuine interest and concern, foster exploration and discovery, encourage cooperative planning, and lead to the use of facts to develop principles or generalizations.

In the study of topics or problems, the teacher must be careful to lead children to find answers to questions and to develop conclusions from experimentation. She tries not to tell the children what the answers should be but to lead them to think and to draw their own conclusions. When children learn to set up problems for study and experimentation, observe carefully, and draw conclusions, they are using scientific methods and developing a scientific attitude. The teacher leads the children to test their beliefs by reading and evaluating what they read, and often to further test their beliefs through experimentation.

In the primary grades, much learning comes through training in observation. Children learn to observe how plants grow and take materials from the soil to make food. They observe water running downhill, eroding the soil. They observe birds building nests. They see buds coming out on the trees in the spring and leaves forming on the trees, and they notice that many leaves change color in the fall. From these observations and from reading and performing simple experiments, they develop principles or generalizations.

Where it is possible, experimenting is one of the best ways of teaching science; but the experimentation must be well done. The children must know the purpose of the experiment. They must participate in the planning, and in planning they must learn to set up proper controls. The plan must be followed carefully and there must be some method of measuring the results. They are cautioned to check results carefully: sometimes by reading and at other times by further experimentation. They learn to avoid hasty conclusions.

Teaching science differs little from other good teaching. The teacher helps to develop interest and leads the children to define their problems, list their questions, find the answers from reliable sources, and study and evaluate their findings before making generalizations.

Source materials

Good teaching is facilitated by having available good source materials for both the teacher and the children. Teachers often need help with both content and methods of teaching; children need resource material to enrich their learning and to verify their findings. There is an abundance of materials for both teachers and children. Every school should have available the *Elementary School Science Bulletin* published by the National Science Teachers Association of the National Education Association. The bulletin is published six times a year and is prepared by leaders in the field. It contains many suggestions for science experiences and for the construction of equipment for the teaching of science. Lists of library books for children and sources of audio-visual materials are frequently given.

Bibliographies, bulletins, and audio-visual aids for agriculture and conservation have been prepared by many departments and agencies of the federal government, such as the United States Department of Agriculture, including the Extension Service and Forest Service, United States Fish and Wild Life Service, and the United States Office of Education, Department of Health, Education and Welfare. Such materials can generally be secured from the Superintendent of Documents, United States Government Printing Office. Issues of *School Life,* published by the Office of Education, contain lists of films available through the federal government. Teachers may also want a copy of *U.S. Government*

Films for Public Educational Use, a 1955 bulletin available through the United States Government Printing Office.

Much material can be secured from state and county sources. These include state agriculture experiment stations, state agriculture colleges, state office of conservation commissions, state departments of education, state branches of the United States Agriculture Extension Service, the United States Soil Conversation Service, and the United States Forest Service, and offices of the county agriculture agent and the home project agent.

Materials and methods of teaching science, science content, and bibliographies of books and audio-visual aids are given in the selected references listed at the end of this chapter. These sources will be helpful to the teacher who wishes to build her own equipment for experimental work.

Reference materials in science for children to read are needed. Several fine series of textbooks in science have been prepared with content and vocabularies suited to different ability levels. Encyclopedias and science readers can also be used. As a part of the experiment in "applied economics," a series of readers using agriculture and science content have been developed and published by the Bureau of School Science of the University of Kentucky. These readers illustrate how science, conservation, and agriculture can be learned as a part of the process of improving skills in reading. Lists of library books and other science materials for children are given in selected references at the end of this chapter.

In some elementary schools, science museums have been developed by teachers and children. These provide a ready supply of source materials for learning in the various aspects of science. Some materials included in these museums are as follows:

rocks	frog eggs	model ships
minerals	moths	handmade toys
shells	snails	weather charts
coral	clams	fossils
sponges	crayfish	petrified wood
tadpoles	turtles	soil samples
toad eggs	model airplanes	goldfish

butterflies	pine cones	pictures of birds
pond insects	machine models	pictures of animals
cocoons	magnets	wood samples
hornets' nests	wood samples	pulpwood and paper display
wasps' nests	mounted leaves	plywood
birds' nests	mounted weeds	model farm
seed samples	pictures of soil erosion	picture exhibit of native
mosses	growing plants	trees and shrubs for
fungi	cross section of tree	landscaping

Sometimes live animals are added to the science museum for short periods of time. Small animals, such as rabbits, chickens, toads, and frogs, are often borrowed from the homes of the children.

As children engage in science experiences, they often find materials which they want to add to the science museum. Over a period of time the museum becomes a storehouse of material and a source of interest to children if it is well organized and properly arranged. Bulletin boards, display cases, cupboards, and shelves are needed to permit storage and displays of materials.

A cooperative science experience

It has been pointed out that science experiences should be selected from the local environment of the children, that the complexity of the experience at various grade levels depends upon the maturity of the children, that the experiences should teach problem solving, and that the experiences should result in the development of generalizations which can be used in the improvement of living and should bring about better attitudes toward science and the local life of the area. Many illustrations showing how teachers and children work together to achieve the goals of science will be found in the references listed at the end of this chapter. A brief description of one cooperative project in landscaping school grounds is given here.

The Guthrie Center school is located in a small Midwest community. It has five teachers, one of whom is a teaching principal, Arnold Sathre. There are 128 children in the five classrooms, with groupings by grades as follows: first, second, third and fourth, fifth and sixth, and seventh and eighth. The school building is a white frame structure located on five acres of land on top of a hill. At the time this account begins, there were no trees or shrubs but many weeds and some grass which had been mowed before school opened in the autumn. One side of the school grounds is part of a hillside, and the water from rains had washed away surface soil at one corner and cut out a small ditch.

At a meeting of the faculty before the opening of school it was decided that the major portion of the science work would center around a single project for the school year of 1954-55. The project selected dealt with "Landscaping the School Grounds." The teachers conceived of many possible units of work which would build the understanding needed for effective landscaping. While they wanted the children to help decide on the units for study, a tentative outline was needed to permit visualization of the possibilities of the project. The outline of work units, developed in the light of past instruction and plans for future years, was as follows:

Landscaping the School Grounds
Units of Work

1. Soils—content and fertility
2. Soil erosion
3. Moisture control
4. Weather
5. Trees
6. Forest conservation
7. Native shrubs
8. Weeds of lawn and fields
9. Grasses
10. Seeds and planting
11. School gardening
12. Insects and control
13. Birds and their relation to gardening and farm life
14. Animals of the woods and prairies
15. Tools and machines used in landscaping
16. Landscaping the school grounds

With the opening of the school year, the children gathered for an assembly to talk about the year's plans and to decide how they could make the school a happier place in which to work. Mr. Sathre talked about the school and the school grounds and showed some pictures of schools he had recently visited which had well-landscaped grounds. He raised questions about what should be done for Guthrie Center. As the children assembled in their respective classrooms, teachers and children talked about the school grounds and raised such questions as these: What kind of trees do we want? Where can we get them? How are they planted? What kind of soil do the trees need? Should we have some shrubs, too? Should there be some grass? Is the baseball diamond in the best place?

Teachers raised questions about things which everyone needed to know before landscaping the school grounds, and representatives were chosen from each room to form an All-school Committee to help coordinate plans and study. Each room developed plans for units of work which would give the background needed to landscape the school grounds. With plans for the year's work completed, study materials were secured by faculty and students.

Detailed planning for each unit was carried on in each classroom. Simple experiences covering a short period of time were planned for the lower grades. More complex learning experiences were planned for the middle and upper grades. Not all of the units could be covered at each grade level, but all units were developed in relation to the major school project, so that near the end of the school year all grades had something to contribute in the form of information which helped with completion of the project in the spring.

The various units of work brought a variety of experiences at the various grade levels. In the upper grades, soil samples were taken and sent to the agriculture experiment station for analysis and the children studied the soils and moisture retention. They secured the help of the county agent, who taught them how to make a miniature soil monolith[6] to put in the museum. This miniature was convenient for the study of subsoils and their relation to moisture control. Children of the middle and upper grades studied fertilization of soil, and all grades gave attention to soil erosion. Several trips were made to farms nearby to study the action of water upon the soil and much reading was done to find answers to questions. The children then decided what to do about the ditch on the school grounds. Units on weather at various grade levels brought the study of clouds, air movements, weather prediction, and the use of thermometers and barometers. The study of trees included identification from leaves, twigs, and bark. The children considered what trees would be most suitable for their project and for the soil on the grounds and the relative value of trees for different purposes. They learned that they could get elm, oak, ash, birch, cedar, spruce, and pine from the woods; that great care is required in the moving of all trees; that the roots of evergreens must not be exposed; and that deciduous trees must be pruned when moved.

The final units led to a sharing of information, in the process of restudying the plans for landscaping, and to actual completion of the landscaping project. Playground space was allocated. Steps were taken to fertilize the soil as shrubs and trees were planted, and responsibilities for keeping shrubs and trees watered were delegated.

Many generalizations, developed in the series of units, were applicable to situations in landscaping and farm operations at the homes.

[6] See H. F. Arneman, *Miniature Soil Monoliths: How to Make Them, How to Use Them* (St. Paul: Agriculture Extension Service, U. S. Department of Agriculture, University of Minnesota).

The children developed generalizations about weeds and weed control, the value of forests, moisture control, gardening, control of insect pests, value of birds, how to protect birds, and how to protect plants against predatory animals.

The units of work were approached in such a way as to arouse and help maintain interest in the project, and many units were developed to teach techniques of problem solving, habits of conservation, and an appreciation of the contributions of science to modern life.

Summary

Science education has been given increased emphasis in elementary schools in recent years. This is partly due to a recognition of the importance of science in human affairs, partly to a recognition that if science is to be learned at the secondary-school level, science learning must begin below that level. It is also recognized that children need science in their daily lives.

Science may be taught either as a subject, a part of a broad-fields program, or a part of a well-integrated curriculum. In any case, if science is to have real meaning, work units will not be pure science but will include much social studies, health and safety, and arithmetic, and will stimulate reading and language development.

While incidental learning in science takes place and is to be encouraged, the program of science should not be incidental to other learning but consist of a well-planned series of experiences.

The goals of science instruction in rural elementary schools include satisfying the curiosity of children, developing permanent interests in science, helping children solve real-life problems, developing permanent interests in farming, and teaching techniques of problem solving. Science instruction should help children learn to read science materials, develop a scientific attitude, and learn to appreciate the contributions of science to modern life.

Boys and girls of rural areas are constantly exposed to the

outdoors and need the development which comes from a program that deals with such areas as plant and animal life, tools and machinery, matter and energy.

In rural areas much of the science program should be built around agriculture and conservation because those are areas of living with which rural people are concerned. Nearly all concepts of science which need to be learned can be developed from experiences in agriculture. Yet, courses of study in science designed for urban centers contain little agriculture for the elementary grades because of an assumption that agriculture is a vocational subject to be taught only in secondary schools. In connection with agriculture, conservation of soil, forests, water, minerals, and wild life should be emphasized. Rural people can do most to accomplish real conservation. Conservation education is not merely learning to hoard natural resources but learning how to use such resources wisely.

The program of science should have continuity, balance, breadth, and flexibility. The experiences should be graded on the basis of the maturity and interest of the children. Science should have meaning in the lives of the children and should be closely related to the rest of the school program. It contributes also to learning in other fields. Teachers should have freedom in the selection of content which has high interest and utility value for their pupils.

How the teacher works with children in science experiences is fully as important as what is studied. Topics or concepts are not to be learned as isolated facts but in the process of problem solving, experimentation, and research. The experimentation must be well done. Children must learn to plan, set up controls, follow plans, measure results, check results, and draw conclusions only on the basis of reliable findings.

Teachers and children need equipment and science materials. Much in the way of such materials can be found in the local community or can be constructed by the teacher and children. Books and magazines dealing with science, agriculture, and conservation should be provided, together with other materials of appropriate difficulty and interest for the various grade levels.

Selected references

ALLEN, SHIRLEY W. *Conserving Natural Resources—Principles and Practices in a Democracy.* New York: McGraw-Hill Book Co., Inc., 1955. Chaps. ii–vi.

Discusses problems of erosion and maintaining nutrient materials in the soil. Deals with uses of water, irrigation, water power, recreation, and navigation. Discusses forest conservation, and conservation of animal and mineral resources.

AMERICAN ASSOCIATION OF SCHOOL ADMINISTRATORS. *Conservation Education in American Schools,* Twenty-ninth Yearbook. Washington, D.C.: The Association. Chaps. i–v and Appendices A and B.

Importance of conservation; land and water problems; conservation of soil, water, forests, wild life and mineral resources; conservation services of the federal government; and school programs, practices and material for teaching. In the appendix will be found bibliographies of materials for primary and intermediate grades.

BATHURST, EFFIE. "Conservation Excursions," *Bulletin No. 13* (1939), Federal Security Agency. Washington, D.C.: United States Government Printing Office, 1940. Entire issue.

Discusses purposes and use of excursions, and discovery and study of industries, minerals, soil, birds and wild flowers. Helps with planning excursions, adaptations to rural areas, follow-up activities and evaluation. Furnishes good bibliography of source material.

———. "Teaching Conservation in Elementary Schools," *Bulletin No. 38* (1938), Federal Security Agency. Washington, D.C.: United States Government Printing Office, 1940. Entire issue.

Presents suggestions for content in conservation program, teaching methods, and units of work and classifies conservation topics. Tells how children may practice conservation and gives good references to source materials.

BLOUGH, GLENN O., and BLACKWOOD, PAUL E. "Science Teaching in Rural and Small Town Schools," *Bulletin No. 5* (1945), Federal Security Agency. Washington, D.C.: United States Government Printing Office, 1949. Entire issue.

Provides an excellent but brief treatment of incidental science experiences in primary grades and planned experiences for intermediate grades. Discusses the meaning and place of science in the elementary school, using science to enrich life, and resources for science. Has fine lists of professional books for teachers, science experience books for children and sources of other printed materials.

BLOUGH, GLENN O., and CAMPBELL, MARJORIE. *Making and Using Science Materials in the Elementary School.* New York: The Dryden Press, Inc., 1954. Entire volume.

Gives excellent suggestions for teachers needing help in preparation and use of materials on science teaching.

BLOUGH, GLENN O., and HUGGETT, ALBERT J. *Elementary School Science and How to Teach It.* New York: The Dryden Press, Inc. Part I, especially.

Gives some trends in elementary-school science, describes the program and methods used in teaching, and suggests an outline of units arranged in sequence, and tells how to find and use resources. Teachers needing help with content will find Parts II, III, and IV very useful. The appendix contains fine bibliography of professional and subject matter materials for teachers, a list of audiovisual aids, and book lists for children.

BURNETT, R. WILL. *Teaching Science in the Elementary School.* New York: Rinehart & Co., 1953. Entire volume.

Elementary-school science programs, science content, and suggestions of many experiences for children.

CRAIG, GERALD S. *Science for the Elementary School Teacher.* Boston: Ginn & Co., 1949. Parts I and VI, especially.

Gives help with program, teaching methods, content, excursion planning; and outlines topics for primary, intermediate, and upper grades. Teachers needing help with science content may wish to read Parts II–V.

HAMMONDS, CARSIE. *Teaching Agriculture.* New York: McGraw-Hill Book Co., Inc., 1950. Chap. xii.

Discussion covers: developing desirable attitudes toward farming, capitalizing on child ownership of livestock or crops, areas of the curriculum where agriculture may be taught, encouraging 4-H Club work and pre-vocational agriculture work.

HATCHER, HALENE. "Better Living Through Wise Use of Resources," *Bulletin No. 15* (1950), Federal Security Agency. Washington, D.C.: United States Government Printing Office, 1950. Entire issue.

Gives an excellent treatment of conservation education. Natural resources are classified; significant concepts listed; and teaching methods discussed. Provides lists of teaching aids, bibliographies, and government agencies where materials may be secured.

JOHNSON, GEORGE D., and KRISTUFEK, DONALD E. *Successful Farming's Soils Book*. Des Moines, Iowa: Meredith Publishing Co., 1954. Entire volume.

Teachers without education in agriculture will find this material helpful as help is given on such topics as soil conservation, soil testing, fertilizing, irrigation, and controlling weeds and crop pests. Children of the upper grades may also use the material.

NATIONAL EDUCATION ASSOCIATION, DEPARTMENT OF ELEMENTARY SCHOOL PRINCIPALS. *Science for Today's Children*, Thirty-second Yearbook. Washington, D.C.: The Department, 1953. Pp. 8–22 and chaps. iii–vi and ix.

Treats the role of science in child development, curriculum, methods of teaching, and use of community resources; gives outlines of units of work; and shows how equipment may be constructed and stored.

PARSONS, RUBEN L. *Conserving American Resources*. Englewood Cliffs, N.J.: Prentice-Hall, Inc., 1956.

Help for the teacher in organizing a comprehensive program. Good source book.

ROBERTS, ROY W., *et al. Modern Farming*. Philadelphia: J. B. Lippincott Co., 1956.

Help for the teacher who has difficulty with content in agriculture. Field crops, livestock, fruit and truck gardening, farm management, and use of power on the farm.

WEAVER, RICHARD L. *Handbook for Teaching of Conservation and Resource Use*. Danville, Ill.: Interstate Printers & Publishers, Inc., 1955.

Helpful source book for the teacher. Deals with all phases of conservation education.

16

CONSERVATION OF
HUMAN RESOURCES

No phase of the educational program for children of rural areas is more important or more difficult to design satisfactorily than that dealing with the conservation of human resources. Without good mental and physical health, safe living, and physical energy, happy and effective living is not possible. Modern life demands healthy, well-adjusted, and intelligent citizens with the energy and willingness to cooperate for the achievement of social, economic, and civic goals. Health, physical vigor, and good leadership are essential to good morale in community life and in national and world relationships. Education in the conservation of human resources is basic education. Some measure of development in this area is indispensable to human life.

While a school and community program of experiences which will lead to the wise use of human resources is necessary, it is difficult to design such a program chiefly because it involves the development of behavior. Good health is not just a matter of knowing facts about the human body; it is a mode of living in which habits and emotions play the dominant role. Taking safety precautions is also a matter of habit, and keeping the body strong is tied in with proper exercise, recreation, rest, and sleep—activities which need to be built into a program of living. A school program which merely leads children to master facts about conservation of human resources is not enough. Some knowledge is needed to understand why and how to conserve, and a good program must develop habits of behavior.

A program in which improved human behavior really determines whether the program is worthwhile cannot be developed by the school alone; it requires the united efforts of the home, institutions and agencies of the community, and the school. In the school, teachers and children can talk about eating wisely, but most of the eating is done in the home. They can talk about rest and sleep, but the talk is of no avail unless the activities of the home are so organized as to provide the necessary relaxation. They can talk about communicable diseases, but vaccination and control of disease are governed by parents. Where services are available in the school, children can be given medical examinations, but the parents have the responsibility of correcting any defects. Teachers can talk about safety in the home and on the farm, but the practice of safety measures requires the cooperative efforts of both parents and children.

Teachers of rural areas have difficulty with teaching the conservation of human resources because of limited facilities and the scarcity of professional assistance. Most schools in rural areas are small schools, even in reorganized school districts. Many of these small schools do not have the services of a doctor, a dentist, a school nurse, a school psychologist, or even a teacher with special preparation in physical education. In many cases supervisory assistance for teachers in planning and executing a school program is not available. And sometimes the school has unsuitable or inadequate toilet facilities, lavatories, gymnasiums, or playgrounds.

It is not possible to present a complete treatment of a program on the conservation of human resources in one chapter, but an effort is made to show the needs of rural people, to provide some assistance in program planning by emphasizing goals and the characteristics of good programs, and by suggesting some sources to which teachers may go for help.

Conservation in any field includes the protection and wise use of resources. It means care in planning for use in the future. It means *development* as well as *protection*. Conservation of human resources means protection against disease and accident, the development of good health habits, and the habit of taking safety measures. It means regular physical examinations with attention to vision, hearing, teeth, heart, and lungs. It means a follow-up on those examinations with provision for needed corrective and protective measures. Conservation of human resources also means the development of desirable attitudes and appreciations pertaining to safety and physical and mental health. It means habits of securing proper recreation, rest, and sleep. It means learning how to provide the food which the body needs and how to eat wisely. It means the provision of pure drinking water and the practice of sanitary measures in the school, the home, and the community. It means play and exercise to provide physical activity, and the development of muscular strength and coordination. And it means the practice of alternating work, rest, and recreation.

In some schools, the program of education for conservation of human resources is too narrow in scope and only helps children learn facts without influencing their behavior. Some teachers think a program is good if there are experiences in physical education, health examinations, or the study of the human body in science classes; but these are only narrow phases of the total program. Physical education does not necessarily develop good health habits. Physical examinations are of little value without a follow-up program that leads to correction of difficulties and immunization against communicable diseases. Mere knowledge of the human body, as it is often studied in science, will not necessarily lead to proper care of the body. A good program must be broad in scope and must lead the children to achieve good mental and physical health habits, protection against disease and accidents, and development of skills, physical strength, vigor, and permanent interests.

Health and health services of rural areas

It has often been assumed that rural life is a healthy life. It is true that the natural conditions of life in the open country are conducive to good health. There is an abundance of fresh air and sunshine, and the long hours of physical labor are conducive to refreshing sleep. Also, rural people are not usually exposed to the tension of high-pressure living so often found in urban sections. Furthermore, people of rural areas have easy access to fresh fruit, milk, meat, and vegetables. The lack of congestion of population would seem to prevent the contraction of communicable diseases.

The facts reveal, however, that rural health has not been good. Reports of physical examinations of boys from rural areas who were considered for induction into the armed forces during World War II showed that their failure to pass the examinations was in a ratio of "41 out of every 100, compared with but 25 rejections per 100 for other groups of the population."[1] A study of the causes for rejection indicate that most defects had appeared during the pre-school or elementary-school period.

Studies of disease and death records for rural areas reveal much about the need for health education and health services. Records show the causes of death, in order of frequency, to be: "heart disease, cancer, intracranial lesions, nephritis, pneumonia and influenza, accidents, tuberculosis, congenital malformations and diseases of the first year of life, diabetes, syphilis, suicide, senility, diarrhea and enteritis, appendicitis, hernia, and intestinal obstruction."[2]

Infectious diseases of childhood take higher tolls in rural districts, despite fewer means of contact. Practically all these

[1] David Lindstrom, *American Rural Life* (New York: The Ronald Press Co., 1948), p. 81.

[2] Frederick Mott and Milton Roemer, *Rural Health and Medical Care* (New York: McGraw-Hill Book Co., 1948), p. 58.

deaths are preventable if there is proper sanitation, immunization, isolation of cases, or proper nutrition. Even after such diseases as measles and scarlet fever are contracted, fatalities can usually be averted through proper medical care.

In rural areas high mortality rates are recorded for infants and mothers in connection with childbirth. Infant mortality is lower in larger urban centers where modern facilities for good obstetrical care and hospitalization are within reach of those who can afford such services. Studies of mortality rates show wide variation between states like Connecticut and Minnesota, where babies have a good chance for survival, and Southern and mountain states, where the rates of survival are low. In general, the death rates are one-fourth higher for rural infants than for infants in urban sections. The chief reason seems to be that "whereas about nine out of ten urban babies are born in hospitals, a much smaller proportion of babies in rural areas are hospital-born."[3]

Reports indicate that certain diseases are associated with particular regions in which rural people live. For example, there seems to be a relationship between goiter and the iodine content of the water; between decayed teeth and the absence of fluorine in the water; between soil composition and the vitamin content in the food; between frequency of tornadoes and accidents; and between dust storms and certain respiratory illnesses.

Association of people with plants and animals often exposes the people to infections and to the danger of accidents. Farm folk are exposed to fungus infections from plants and animals, and infections from animal bites are not uncommon. In some regions danger exists in the bites of poisonous snakes and insects. Some farmers have suffered from the kicks of horses, from being rammed by an angry bull, and from overlong exposure to the sun.

Poor sanitary conditions in rural areas subject the people to a variety of diseases. In some regions of the rural South, carelessness in excreta disposal and lack of a supply of pure

[3] David Lindstrom, *op. cit.*, p. 311.

water have brought on typhoid, paratyphoid, dysentery, and other diseases. Unpasteurized milk can cause undulant fever. In some areas, mosquitoes may bring malaria and rats may transmit typhus.

Several factors seem to account for the poor health record of people in rural areas: (1) poor housing and sanitation, (2) difficulty of communication and transportation, (3) conservative attitudes on the part of many farmers, (4) poor medical and hospital facilities, (5) low income, and (6) poor educational facilities. While new construction and farm building repairs have been effected in some regions, rural housing has not kept pace with urban. Farm homes are older, on the average, than urban homes, and many farm homes have not been completely modernized. While electricity has been made available to rural people, as indicated in Chapter 2, running water and proper sanitary facilities are often lacking in rural homes. In some regions farm homes have windows without screens, improper heating systems, faulty lighting, and lack of refrigeration for food.

Poor communication and transportation interfere with the securing of prompt medical service. Telephones, needed to call for emergency service, are not as common in rural homes as in urban homes. In some regions lack of transportation prevents getting an ill member of the family to a doctor. The mechanically defective automobiles and unpaved roads of some rural regions seriously interfere with prompt medical service.

While the farmer is becoming more urbanized, there is still a large measure of conservatism among farmers and a disinclination to seek medical service for what is believed to be a minor illness or to secure regular physical examinations. Farmers' organizations are now carrying on health educational programs which should do much to change the attitudes of many farm people.

Health records of people in rural areas are unfavorable partly because medical and hospital facilities are not so numerous as in urban areas. In 1955 roughly 70 per cent of the nation's 218,000 doctors lived in metropolitan areas which comprise only half of the total population. The roster of the Arkansas Medical Society lists "1,208 doctors in the state, only 230 of whom live in communities of 2,500 people or smaller; but 67 per cent of the 1,909,511 people who live in Arkansas make their homes in such small communities."[4]

The shortage of dentists in rural areas is fully as great as the shortage of doctors. The scarcity of both has doubtless been affected by the fluctuating income of rural people and by the inadequacies and scarcity of hospital facilities in rural regions. When farm income drops, doctors and dentists are the last to be paid for their services; and doctors and dentists like the conveniences of hospitals and clinics which are to be found in urban areas. Furthermore, many doctors prefer to specialize rather than to follow general practice, and specialists usually work in clinics.

While there is a shortage of nursing personnel in urban sections, the shortage is much greater in rural areas. Nurses want to work where there are doctors and hospitals. Usually, too, very little provision is made for nurses' training in rural regions, and nurses tend to work in areas where they receive their preparation.

Physical facilities for rural health services are as deficient as the personnel. Hospital facilities are lacking in both quantity and quality. "There should be 4.5 hospital beds per 1,000 persons, yet hundreds of counties have less than one bed per 1,000 persons, and over 1,200 counties are without any type of hospital."[5] The quantity and quality of hospital facilities have improved somewhat since that was written, but there is still a serious shortage of physical facilities as well as personnel to render the health services needed by rural people.

Organizing for service

Through efforts of the federal government, farmers' organizations, and other groups, progress is being made in

[4] "Rural Clinic, Can It Cure Doctor Shortage," *Business Week*, August 20, 1955, p. 156.

[5] David Lindstrom, *op. cit.*, p. 318.

improvement of medical services and in health education of rural people. Extensive research has been conducted by the United States Department of Agriculture and Public Health Service and, through the activities of the various state branches of federal departments, educational programs are being organized and carried out. Medical service is being improved through the organization of group-practice clinics. These clinics, organized by physicians, make available the services of specialists and the use of technical equipment. Also, medical schools are now offering short courses for doctors from rural areas and voluntary health group membership is growing among rural people.

Since a really effective program in conservation of human resources requires the united efforts of many people to achieve desired goals, some organization—such as a health council—needs to be effected. Local circumstances and resources will always determine the form which the organization should take. In rural areas councils may be developed, either on the local community level, the county level, or both. In larger community areas local councils have been very effective in working with the school and community agencies. Small schools have often found the county organization the most effective.

In sparsely settled areas where schools outside the county center are one- or two-teacher schools, the county health council has proved to be an effective instrument in developing a program that includes improved health services and an educational program for adults and children. This council often consists of the county superintendents of schools and representatives of the medical and dental associations, the county nurse and representatives of local schools, churches, commercial, and service clubs, and farmers' organizations. Such councils have studied the needs of the children and adults, made plans to develop programs, and sought the cooperation of institutions, agencies, and individuals in carrying out plans. Under the sponsorship of such councils, various projects have been developed and executed. These projects have included the following: (1) health education programs for schools, (2) countywide immunization programs, (3) dental clinics, (4) circulating libraries of health-instruction materials, (5) tuberculosis testing of cattle and milk pasteurization programs, (6) testing of wells to insure good water supply, (7) adult health education programs, and (8) improvement of hospital and medical services.

In larger consolidated or reorganized school districts, local health committees or councils have been formed. Projects similar to those of the county health councils have been planned and carried on. Local councils, working with the school faculty, have arranged for physical examinations, have helped develop educational plans for the school, and have carried on active educational programs with parents. This has often been accomplished with the cooperation of the local parents' and teachers' associations. Local health councils have also worked with school administrators and local boards of education to secure nursing service and regular physical examinations for children in the school.

Goals of the school and the community

The conservation goals of the community school and those of the people and interested agencies are the same. The cooperating agencies, as well as the school, have roles to play in a program of service and education. Goals are developed cooperatively and all share in their achievement. These goals may be as follows:

A. Physical examinations at regular intervals for each school child

B. Contacts with parents to secure corrective measures as needed

C. Immunization against communicable diseases

D. Promotion of sanitation in the school and community and in the homes

E. Removal of hazards to health and safety

F. Organization and conduction of an educational program for adults

G. Procurement of personnel and facilities for the school and community to help maintain health of children and adults

H. Development of a safety, health, and physical education program for children which would help them

1. Form good health habits, such as eating wisely, keeping clean, and getting proper exercise, rest, and sleep
2. Understand the need of good health and how to maintain it
3. Acquire good attitudes toward health and sanitation
4. Attain self-sufficiency in health matters—ability and willingness to guard health of self and others
5. Take safety measures in the school, on the playground, on the highway, in the home, on the farm, and in the community
    a) Have a feeling of responsibility for their own safety and the safety of others
    b) Develop a safety conscience and consciousness
    c) Acquire confidence in themselves in times of emergency by knowing what to do
    d) Refuse to take foolish chances
    e) Use safely the products of a mechanical age
    f) Form habits of conduct that enable them to meet the situations of daily life without accidents
    g) Form habits of obedience to all safety rules and regulations
    h) Work with others to remove hazards to safe living and to build protective devices against danger
    i) Be conscious of the dangers from uncontrolled emotions and antisocial attitudes
6. Achieve and maintain good mental health—make satisfactory social adjustments, face problems objectively, learn the function of emotions, and alternate work and play
7. Achieve permanent interests in recreational pursuits to secure release from emotional tension
8. Engage in active games which develop physical strength and vigor, endurance, coordination, sense of balance, and good posture
9. Understand the importance of rules and accept success or defeat in a sportsmanlike way
10. Read material on health, safety, and physical education

Planning health and safety programs

The health and safety programs of the rural school should deal with the following: (1) food and nutrition; (2) water; (3) rest, relaxation, and sleep; (4) fresh air and sunshine; (5) elimination; (6) the body and proper clothing; (7) cleanliness and care of the teeth; (8) control of infection; (9) care of eyes and ears; (10) posture; (11) heat and light; (12) medical and dental services; (13) safety at school, at home, on the farm, on highways, and in the community; (14) emotional development and mental health.

The program of education for health and safety is not separated from the total program of the school but is made an integral part of the total plan of education for child development. As suggested in Chapter 6 and elsewhere in this text, activities need not be carried on under subject headings or even under broad fields of study. Learning may take place through well-integrated experience units designed to help children gradually achieve increased understanding and better attitudes that lead to habit formation.

Points for the teacher to consider may be listed as follows:

1. The health, safety, and sanitation problems of the school and the community should be selected by the teacher and the pupils for study.

The over-all plan of the program may be drawn up by the faculty, but it is the students who will work on the problems and seek the answers to the questions that arise. When the children have a part in planning the program, the work will be geared to their interests and needs.

2. The experience units in health and safety should be drawn from the other areas of the curriculum, where possible.

In one sixth-grade class the problem of securing a good supply of clean drinking water on the farm was selected for study because the water on one farm had been found to be impure and the farm needed a new well. The children wanted to know how people can tell whether the water is safe to use, how water can be located, and why it becomes impure. They expressed a desire to know where a well should be located. Under the direction of the teacher, they listed their questions and secured source material for study: bulletins from the Agriculture Extension Service and from the State Department of Public Health. They found much information in agriculture, science, and social-studies books and health readers. They secured the help of the teachers of vocational agriculture and science in the high school. They visited several farms and studied the location of the wells with reference to the barns, houses, privies, sheds, and other buildings. From science books they learned about underground streams and how water is tested. From health and social studies material they discovered how water becomes polluted.

3. If the study of conservation of human life is to be more than a study of facts from a textbook, the problems for study must be selected from life situations in the school, the homes, the farms, and the community.

Problems selected from real life have meaning for the children, and the study of such problems is more likely to result in improved behavior.

Many events in the school can set the stage for experiences in health and safety. When dental examinations were made in one school under a program sponsored by the Parent-Teacher's Association, the children studied tooth decay and care of the teeth. In another school, where one hot dish was served at noon to supplement the lunches brought by the children, a study of nutrition and eating habits was made. If some children are absent from school because of illness, the stage may be set for a study of communicable diseases, common colds, and the like. If some children have to get glasses, units of work on the eyes and the care of the eyes can be developed. The matter of disposing of the garbage from the school lunches can lead to a study of sanitation measures.

Many events in the home arouse interests which may lead to the development of work units. When cattle are being tested for tuberculosis, the children want to know why. If someone is injured in a fall, units on safety are developed.

In the community there occur fires and highway accidents. Fluorine is placed in the water system of the town. The handling of garbage presents problems. The town dump harbors rats and may be a health menace. The boys and girls of Petersburg, West Virginia[6] using the community for learning and practice in their health program, listed problems on garbage disposal, sewage disposal, street cleanliness, water supply, city dump, animal pests, school health, food handling, insect pests, poultry and livestock within city limits, control of contagious diseases, recreation, and public parks and rest rooms. They studied the problems and proceeded to get help in improvement of living in the community.

4. Children can be taught to take pride in good health.

No children should be made to feel conspicuous or inferior because of ill health, of physical defects, or of being overweight or underweight, but much can be done to develop a desire to correct these conditions.

5. Each aspect of the health and safety program should receive some attention at each level of development.

Primary children may learn how to care for their teeth; middle-grade children may study tooth decay as well as dental care. Primary children may learn how to keep clean; middle-grade children may learn about diseases which come from lack of cleanliness. Primary children may learn what foods are best to eat and develop good eating habits; middle-grade children may study food content for body building or good nutrition.

6. Experiences should be graded on the basis of the interest and maturity of the pupils.

7. In the study of diseases and accidents, teachers should avoid emphasis on morbid phases of situations.

8. Teachers and children should concern themselves with maintenance of a healthy and safe school environment.

[6] See Effie Bathurst, "Petersburg Builds a Health Program," *Bulletin No. 9* (1949), Federal Security Agency (Washington: U.S. Government Printing Office).

Ventilation, lighting, seating, and cleanliness of toilets, lavatories, lunch rooms, classrooms, and hallways can be their concern. Clean, safe, cool drinking water should be available. The social atmosphere of the classroom and playground should be conducive to good mental health.

9. Children should develop individual health habits.

These include such niceties and safeguards as having a clean handkerchief and using it properly, keeping hands and face clean, washing hands before eating and handling food, after going to the toilet, and after handling playground and other equipment. Good health habits include getting a drink and going to toilet when necessary, being properly clothed, eating in a calm and leisurely fashion, brushing teeth regularly, and keeping the body clean. School schedules should facilitate the formation of good individual health habits.

10. Schedules of work and play should be developed to facilitate health practices.

Classroom activities should be varied so as to avoid the strain of sitting still for long periods. There should be periods for rest and relaxation and for play.

11. Children should learn the importance of having regular physical examinations.

Where facilities permit, medical and dental examinations should be conducted regularly.

12. Teachers should learn to detect illness of children under their care and should refer the children to medical personnel for examination and diagnosis.

References at the end of this chapter suggest symptoms of illnesses which may be detected by observation.

Fostering mental health

Studies of pupil adjustment in schools of rural areas reveal that about one in every five children shows evidence of poor mental health of a varying degree of seriousness. A study of third- and sixth-grade children in one county in Ohio indicated that the percentage of maladjusted children was higher in the sixth grade than in the third grade, that maladjustment was much greater among boys than girls, and that maladjustment was greater among children who were retarded in school work than among those who made normal progress.[7] Tendencies toward maladjustment seemed to develop and become more pronounced at the sixth-grade level than at the third. Whether retardation in school work was a cause of maladjustment or the result of maladjustment or whether there is no cause-and-effect relationship was not revealed in the study. However, Greenblatt[8] found no relationship between mental-health status and grade-level expectancy. These and other studies fail to reveal any one cause of mental maladjustment. But Greenblatt's findings do show that children of good mental health and those of poor mental health tend to be friends with other children of like mental-health status.

While the causes of mental maladjustment have not been traced to any one source, we do know that failure of a child to meet his basic social needs, as described in Chapter 4, will cause him to be unhappy and often seriously maladjusted. Causes may be traced to lack of security in the child's family, low social status of his family in the community, failure of the child to achieve success in any personal endeavor, and the absence of friends. Whatever the cause, the maladjusted child is mentally ill and needs the help of the school in solving his personal problems.

Efforts of the school should be directed toward helping those children who are maladjusted to solve their problems and providing a good social climate which will keep children happy and well adjusted. Helping the maladjusted child to solve his problems is possible only by learning to know the child, the environment in which he lives, and the activities which occupy his time. Children must learn to face their own problems and understand themselves. Mal-

[7] *Mental Health Problems Among School Children in Miami County, Ohio* (Columbus, Ohio: Bureau of Prevention and Education, Division of Mental Hygiene, Ohio State Department of Public Welfare, September 1946).

[8] E. L. Greenblatt, "Relationship of Mental Health and Social Status," *Journal of Educational Research,* XLIV (November, 1950), pp. 193–204.

adjusted children need careful counseling by parents and teachers and guidance in activities of the school to help them achieve personal and social security.

For all children, a good social climate is conducive to mental health, and recreation is needed by all. Group activities in the classroom help children work with others and make friends. Warm friendly relationships between the children and the teacher and within the group of children contribute to the happiness of individuals and to a satisfying emotional life. Children who learn to play and to like games find such activities good outlets for the frustrations of other aspects of living. Likewise, freedom to choose the activities in which the child can express himself by creating something has therapeutic value. In some schools these activities take the form of a hobby hour when the children may draw, paint, carve, write, practice photography, do craftwork, conduct experiments, and the like. All are the means of doing things for fun, but they help children find themselves by discovering their talents and giving expression to their ideas and emotions.

Recreation and physical education

All children—the maladjusted as well as the adjusted—need physical activity. When children sit for long hours at a time, they become restless and need physical activity. The program in conservation of human resources must make provision for such activity at certain periods of the school day.

The phase of the program in conservation of human resources called "physical education" is both developmental and recreational in character. It has both therapeutic and educational value. It helps children develop strength and agility, provides exercise, and enables children to acquire many physical skills. It helps many children find enjoyment and social acceptance. It helps all children secure needed recreation and learn games and sports which they can play outside school and after school days are over.

Because boys and girls differ in needs and interests, the activities should have variety. Some children will meet their needs for development and satisfy their interests through rhythm activities of an individual character, such as running, leaping, skipping, and swinging, or through those of a group character, such as folk dancing, square dancing, and social dancing. Other children's needs and interests will be reached through active games of many kinds. Some games involve team play and not only provide the needed physical activity but also develop loyalties, respect for rules, and good sportsmanship.

The following principles may serve as guide lines for the physical education program:

1. The kind and amount of activity should be determined by periodic physical examinations.
2. Needs, interests, and capacities of particular children should influence the selection of activities.
3. Teachers and children should plan together. The children should be encouraged to create games and furnish leadership.
4. Activities should be suited to developmental levels of children and be progressive in character, proceeding from individual activities and simple games at the primary level to more highly organized activities in the middle and upper grades.
5. Activities should be organized to protect the health of the children.
   Children of the intermediate and upper grades often take part in an intra-mural program of competition. However, since the circulatory system has not attained its full development at this age, activity should be intermittent rather than sustained over long periods of time. The strain of competition among representative teams from several schools should be avoided.
6. All activities should be conducted in a safe and healthful environment.

Safety education

There is a great need for safety education in schools of rural areas, as shown by accident records for the nation as a whole and for farmers in particular. Over the past twenty years nearly 100,000 people have lost their lives each year through accidents and four times as many were disabled. During World War II more lives were lost at home than were lost in the military service abroad. Only three diseases —heart disease, cancer, and cerebral hemorrhage—cause more deaths than accidents. Fatality accidents are connected most frequently with homes, motor vehicles, and occupations, with frequency of occurrence in the order mentioned. Among the occupational groups, more deaths occurred in agriculture than in any other group, as shown in Table 5. Agriculture accounted for 25 per cent of all worker deaths, although agriculture workers represent but 16 per cent of the total labor force. Farming is less safe than manufacturing, service, trade, and public utilities. That the farm is less safe than the factory is shown by the fact that deaths per 100,000 farm workers is four times that of workers in manufacturing occupations.

Studies of causes of accidental deaths on farms reveal that the most frequent cause arises in connection with farm machinery, but many accidents are associated with the han-

TABLE 5

ACCIDENTAL DEATHS AND DEATH RATES OF WORKERS AND PER CENTS OF FATALITIES BY INDUSTRIES, 1955[9]

| | Deaths | | |
Industry	Total	Per 100,000 Workers	Per Cent of Total Worker Deaths
Agriculture	3,700	55	25.1
Construction	2,400	76	16.9
Service	2,300	15	16.2
Manufacturing	2,100	13	14.8
Trade	1,400	11	9.9
Transportation	1,300	44	9.2
Mining, quarrying, oil and gas wells	800	104	5.6
Public Utilities	200	14	1.4
Total	14,200	24	100.0

[9] Adapted from *Accident Facts* (Chicago: National Safety Council, Annual Report, 1956), p. 23.

dling of farm animals or with falls. In order of frequency of fatal injuries, the following farm machines seem to offer the greatest hazards: tractors, circular saws, combines, discs, plows, corn binders, hay rakes, and mowing machines. Accidental falls in the barn, barn lot, or field, or from the barn loft have been frequent causes of fatalities; other falls have been from trucks, windmills, ladders, roofs of barns or houses, haystacks, trees, and silos. Excessive heat while working in the field has accounted for many fatalities each year, and lightning also has claimed the lives of agriculture workers.

Other accidents give clues to dangers to be avoided. Fatal accidents in homes over a ten-year period were caused by falls, burns from explosions or fire, poisonings, firearms, mechanical suffocations, and poison gas. Drownings account for 6,000 to 8,000 deaths in a typical year, while motor vehicles took the lives of 37,800 United States citizens in 1955. An analysis of motor-vehicle accidents by the National Safety Council shows that two thirds of the mortalities occur in rural areas, that about one third of traffic accident victims are pedestrians, that the death rate is considerably greater at night than in the daytime, and that a large number of pedestrian deaths in rural areas come from "walking along the highway." Tables compiled by the National Safety Council reveal that in a single year, traffic accidents account for nearly 8,000 deaths and 175,000 injuries to children of 14 years of age and under.

Experience units for study in the safety program should be developed cooperatively by the teacher and children, and the topics and problems should be based on a study of the hazards to human life in the community. The following is a sample of experiences which may be developed as work units for various grade levels. Of course, the character of the content and the generalizations developed would be determined by the maturity of the pupils.

1. Fires and explosions—may deal with matches, removing rubbish in which fires can start, and other prevention measures, with ways of protecting against fires and with methods of extinguishing fires

2. Burns—may include burns from fires, electric appliances, stoves, fireworks, and the like
3. Water—will lead to taking swimming precautions and first-aid measures
4. Highways and streets—will deal with walking, bicycle riding, crossing the streets, etc.
5. Falls about the home—will include removing hazards such as toys on steps, broken furniture, ice on walks, and falls from trees, ladders, roofs, etc.
6. Falls about the farm
7. Tools and machinery
8. Farm animals
9. Foods—may include care of foods and food poisonings
10. Gas—may lead to care with bottle gas, gas stoves, etc.
11. First aid—will cover care of cuts, bruises, scratches, and broken bones
12. Lightning
13. Bus riding—would include getting on and off buses and behavior in the bus
14. School safety

Source materials

There is an abundance of source material available to teach health, physical education, and safety. Children should have reading material with vocabulary and concept difficulty suited to their abilities; teachers need information to help them in program planning and execution. Most state departments of education have issued course-of-study and content material dealing with health, physical education, and safety. The State Department of Public Health and the State Safety Council publish materials for use by teachers and children. Many state branches of the United States Agriculture Extension Service publish bulletins dealing with safety on the farm.

Federal departments and agencies have prepared much material to help teachers with content, curriculum, and methods of teaching many subjects. The list given on page 360 is especially helpful.

Let's Have Clean Water, Public Health Service Publication No. 264, Department of Health Education and Welfare, 1952.
A kit of materials for community leaders to help in efforts to solve local water pollution problems. Contains the following:

> *Chairman's Guide*
>
> Program suggestions and sources of information.
>
> *Clean Water is Everybody's Business*
> *The Fight to Save America's Waters*
> A Mark Trail adventure in Public Health and Conservation.
>
> *The Living Waters*
>
> Background readings on uses of water and the importance of pollution control.
>
> *Washing Our Water: Your Job and Mine,* by Helen Beal Woodward (Pamphlet No. 193)
> *Water Pollution in the United States*

Rural Health: Annotated List of Selected References, by Helen Johnston and Elsie S. Manny, Library List No. 60. United States Department of Agriculture, 1953.
This is a selected list of publications which present an over-all view of rural health in the national setting.

The Public Health Service and the Office of Education in the Department of Health, Education and Welfare and the United States Department of Agriculture have all published material dealing with nutrition, school lunches, health, safety, and physical education. If the school library or the local library is unable to supply lists of the materials, a letter to the department in Washington will bring the information desired.

The National Educational Association has several annotated bibliographies which give sources from which the teacher may secure much help. Among these bibliographies are *Safety and Safety Education, Problems and Topics on Safety Education, Dramatizations in Safety Education,* and *Visual Aids in Safety Education.*

Professional associations of doctors and dentists have available materials for distribution. The American Dental Association provides some fine pamphlets, such as *Diet and Dental Health* and *Your Child's Teeth.* From the National

Dental Hygiene Association may be secured *Facts about Teeth and Their Care* and other materials. The American Medical Association will furnish such teaching materials as "Health for the Rural Child," prepared by J. P. Hubbard.

Life insurance companies and manufacturers of food products have material on health and nutrition, and The National Safety Council's annual report provides help in safety instruction. Other sources are the American Automobile Association, the American Legion, the American Red Cross, Automobile Manufacturers Association, Boy Scouts of America, Girl Scouts, and National Congress of Parents and Teachers. (See list of addresses at the end of this chapter.)

Textbooks for children serve as one resource in health education. Some schools provide a basic text for each grade. Many schools have available a variety of such materials, including texts from each of several series. Such material should vary in content, style, and reading level.

The publications listed at the end of this chapter provide lists of other source material for the health, physical education, and safety programs.

Summary

Conservation of human resources deals with an important but difficult part of the elementary-school program, vital to human life. Organization and teaching of conservation programs is difficult because the improvement of behavior is involved.

Conservation of human resources includes both protection and development. In health, safety, and physical education, children learn to protect themselves and others from danger, to develop physical strength and skills, and to form good habits. They also learn to make satisfactory adjustments in social relationships.

A successful program that involves the improvement of child behavior requires the cooperative action of the school, community agencies and institutions, and individuals in the community.

Teachers of small schools in rural areas have limited facilities. The organization of county and local area health councils can help provide better facilities and improve the programs in health, safety, and physical education.

The records of rejections of young men for service in the armed forces indicate that, despite the advantage of fresh air, sunshine, and availability of fresh food, other conditions have aversely affected the health of rural people. The scarcity of doctors, dentists, nurses, and other personnel has handicapped rural people in the prevention and control of disease. Deficiencies in quantity and quality of hospital and clinical facilities are other handicaps. Factors which seem to explain the poor health record of rural areas may be listed as follows: (1) poor housing and sanitation, (2) difficulty of communication and transportation, (3) conservative attitudes of rural people, (4) poor medical, dental, and hospital facilities, (5) low income, and (6) inadequate educational facilities.

Through the efforts of federal and state agriculture, health, and educational agencies, considerable progress is being made in the education of rural people and in the provision of personnel and facilities for medical and dental services.

The goals of the school and community program in the conservation of human resources include the following: (1) physical examinations and follow-up procedures, (2) immunization, (3) sanitation, (4) removal of health and safety hazards, (5) procurement of medical and dental facilities, and (6) educational programs for adults and children. The educational programs for children include the development of understanding and good habits and attitudes toward health, sanitation, and safety, leading children to take safety measures in homes, schools, and communities and on the highways. It also includes achievement and maintenance of good mental health and the development of permanent interests in recreation and physical education.

A good program in health and safety education has the following characteristics:

1. It is a part of the total educational program of the school.
2. Teachers and children cooperatively select, develop, and

execute plans based on problems of the school, the home, and the community.

3. Instructional material is drawn from science, social studies, and other areas of the curriculum.
4. Events in the school, home, and community provide the motivation and setting for units of work.
5. Children learn to take pride in good health, but no child is made conspicuous because of deficiencies.
6. Experiences are graded on the basis of the interest and maturity of the pupils.
7. Each aspect of the health and safety program receives some attention at each level of development.
8. Morbid phases of disease and accidents are not emphasized.
9. A healthy and safe school environment is maintained.
10. Children are led to develop individual health and safety habits.
11. School schedules are arranged so as to facilitate good health practices.
12. Children learn the importance of regular physical examinations.
13. Teachers learn to detect evidence of illness in children and to refer such children for complete examinations.

Many rural children show tendencies toward poor mental health and need assistance. Maladjustments of the early school period often become greater as the children advance through the grades. Efforts of the school are directed toward helping maladjusted children solve their problems, maintaining a good social climate in the school, and developing recreational interests for all the children.

The program in physical education is both developmental and recreational. It should develop strength, coordination, agility, and physical skill and help children form permanent interests in play. Activities should be varied to meet the different needs of the children. Needs, interests, and capacities determine the selection of activities, which are conducted in a safe and healthful environment and are organized to protect the health of the boys and girls.

Accident records show that people of rural areas need

safety education. Only three diseases account for more deaths than accidents. Records reveal that: (1) Most accidents on the farm are caused by work with farm machinery; (2) falls about farm buildings or in the field are frequent causes of deaths; (3) many accidents of rural areas come from activities in the home and from walking along the highways; (4) two-thirds of motor-vehicle accidents occur in rural areas; and (5) many children of elementary school age and under are involved in accidents.

Problems for study in safety education should be based on studies of hazards to life and limb in the school, the home, and the community, and content and generalizations should be graded according to the maturity levels of the pupils.

Materials for the various phases of the program in conservation of human resources may be secured from many sources, such as state and federal agencies, professional associations, and private commercial concerns.

Selected references

AMERICAN ASSOCIATION OF SCHOOL ADMINISTRATORS. *Safety Education*, Eighteenth Yearbook. Washington, D.C.: The Association, 1940. Chaps. iii, iv, and vii.

Deals with objectives, curriculum and teaching methods in safety education and shows how the work may be integrated with the rest of the school program. Presents sample work units, safety guides, and a check list of hazards in the home and on the farm. Discusses school safety councils and bus patrols.

AMIDON, EDNA P. "School Lunch and Nutrition Education," *Bulletin No. 14* (1951), Federal Security Agency. Washington, D.C.: United States Government Printing Office, 1951. Entire issue.

Shows the relation of the school lunch program to health and to eating habits at home; discusses dietary needs of children and gives references bearing on the school lunch.

BATHURST, EFFIE G. "Petersburg Builds a Health Program," *Bulletin No. 9* (1949), Federal Security Agency. Washington, D.C.: United States Government Printing Office, 1949. Entire issue.

Tells the story of how children in one school improved health and sanitary conditions in the school and community; how the children planned, collected facts, made decisions and took action.

FEDERAL SECURITY AGENCY. "Nutrition Education in the Elementary School," *Nutrition Education Series*, Pamphlet No. 1. Washington, D.C.: United States Government Printing Office, 1943. Entire issue.

Discusses how teachers may check the nutrition of children, plan school lunches, cooperate with parents, and conduct experiments in nutrition by using animals. Gives sources of information on materials and methods.

GROUT, RUTH. *Health Teaching in Schools* (2d ed.). Philadelphia: W. B. Saunders Co., 1953. Chaps. i–iii, v, vi, x and Appendices B and C.

Describes the characteristics of the healthy child, his health needs, how to organize the education program, how to coordinate school and community health programs, and how to teach health at the various grade levels. Shows how to get help from organizations and agencies. The appendix contains a list of free and inexpensive material and a good check list on school sanitation.

McNEELY, SIMON A., and SCHNEIDER, ELSA. "Physical Education in the School Child's Day," *Bulletin No. 14* (1950), United States Department of Health Education and Welfare. Washington, D.C.: United States Government Printing Office, 1953. Entire issue.

Gives characteristics and needs of children at various age levels and describes the program, methods of teaching, and facilities and materials needed. Describes what children do in the way of activities after school hours and furnishes bibliographies of source materials for games and rhythms.

NATIONAL EDUCATION ASSOCIATION, DEPARTMENT OF RURAL EDUCATION AND AMERICAN ASSOCIATION OF HEALTH, PHYSICAL EDUCATION AND RECREATION. *Health, Physical Education and Recreation in Small Schools*. Washington, D.C.: The Department, 1948. Entire issue.

Describes how the small school can organize a program of health, physical education, and recreation to meet the needs of children and explains how to discover needs and how to use resources. Gives a check list for planning, a list of equipment, and a scheme for evaluation.

NATIONAL SOCIETY FOR THE STUDY OF EDUCATION. *Mental Health in Modern Education*, Fifty-fourth Yearbook. Chicago: University of Chicago Press, 1955. Chaps. viii and ix especially.

Provides discussion of mental health practices in primary and intermediate grades, personalities of children, factors which impede progress in growth, causal relationships, and what parents and teachers can do to help children.

ROGERS, JAMES FREDERICK. "What Every Teacher Should Know about the Physical Condition of Her Pupils," *Pamphlet No. 68*, Federal Security Agency. Washington, D.C.: United States Government Printing Office, 1945.

Helps for the classroom teacher in detecting common diseases through observation. Holds the view that teachers can often tell if the child is unhealthy. Gives some common symptoms of disease. Furnishes summary of important points for observation. Tells what to do after inspection of the child.

SEHON, ELIZABETH L., *et al. Physical Education Methods for Elementary Schools.* Philadelphia: W. B. Saunders Co., 1953. Chaps. ii–x.

A methods book of practical value in planning a meaningful physical education program. A helpful guide in organizing and adapting a suitable program for any grade level. Gives suggestions and descriptions of games, creative rhythms, folk-singing games and folk dances, social and tap dancing. Useful bibliography at the end of each chapter.

STACK, HERBERT J., SIEBRECHT, ELMER B., and ELKOW, J. DUKE (eds.). *Education for Safe Living* (2d ed.). Englewood Cliffs, N.J.: Prentice-Hall, Inc., 1949. Chaps. iii–ix, xv and xvi.

Discusses causes of accidents, bicycle safety, school patrols, home, farm and school safety, fire prevention and protection, first aid treatment, and teaching units and methods.

VANNIER, MARYHELEN, and FOSTER, MILDRED. *Teaching Physical Education in Elementary Schools.* Philadelphia: W. B. Saunders Co., 1954. Chaps. vi–xiv.

A very good source book of activities for children in grades one through six and a suggestion of how to teach children through these activities. Provides a list of activities and games suitable and recommended for each grade level, with explanations for playing these games.

List of addresses of sources for material

Aetna Life Insurance Company
Hartford, Connecticut

American Association for Health Physical Education and Recreation
Washington, D.C.

American Automobile Association (AAA)
Washington, D.C.

American Dental Association
Chicago, Illinois

American Dietetics Association
Chicago, Illinois

American Heart Association
New York, New York

American Home Economics Association
Washington, D.C.

American Medical Association
Chicago, Illinois

American Public Health Association
New York, New York

(The) American Red Cross
Washington, D.C.

(The) American Social Hygiene Association Inc.
New York, New York

Automobile Manufacturers Association
New York, New York

Boy Scouts of America
New York, New York

Girl Scouts
New York, New York

Metropolitan Life Insurance Company
New York, New York

National Committee for Mental Hygiene
New York, New York

National Congress of Parents and Teachers
Chicago, Illinois

National Dairy Council
Chicago, Illinois

National Dental Hygiene Association
Washington, D.C.

National Education Association
Washington, D.C.

(The) National Foundation for Infantile Paralysis
New York, New York

National Health Council
New York, New York

National Life Stock and Meat Board
Chicago, Illinois

National Safety Council
Chicago, Illinois

National Tuberculosis Association
New York, New York

17

THE PRACTICAL ARTS
AND THE FINE ARTS

Teachers who wish to improve the living of rural people must be concerned with enriching the culture of farm and village folk through the development of the practical arts and the fine arts. These arts have always played a major role in rural life, and with proper guidance the children of rural areas may learn to make their lives even more enjoyable and profitable through their experiences in the arts. To guide the development of children teachers need to have a vision of the potentialities of the arts in the enrichment of life, to understand the goals of a good instructional program, and to have a good comprehension of the scope and nature of a program which will lead to the children's development.

The arts in rural life

In rural areas the arts have been the means of relieving the monotony of farm life by providing a means of recreation for individuals and groups. In many rural areas art groups and community events of various kinds have been organized to foster the development of creativeness and to enrich the social life of adults and children. These groups and activities include clubs for painting and handicrafts, rural weaver clubs, sewing and fancywork groups, dramatic clubs, lyceums, folk-dancing clubs, choruses, orchestras, bands, community fairs and festivals, picnics, celebrations, art exhibits, and tournaments. Good illustrations of state movements and statewide events are the Little Country Theatre Movement in North Dakota, the Farm and Home Week and Rural Art Exhibit in Minnesota, the Carolina Folk Movement, the New York State rural drama movement, the Illinois Rural Chorus, and the Wisconsin Music and Drama Tournaments.

The arts are expressed by rural people through activities of the home, as when a farm or village family makes designs for a layout of buildings and landscaping to achieve beauty and utility. On the farm, the architecture and placement of houses, barns, sheds, silos, hen houses, driveways, and the like can be part of a plan created by the farmer and his family. A desire for beauty is further expressed through the placement of trees, bushes, and flowers and the painting of the buildings. All may be planned to fit in with the landscape in such a way as to add to a pleasing picture which gives joy to living. Floor plans, interior decorating, choice and location of pictures and furniture, and arrangement of the kitchen can express art in the home. Concepts of balance and utility can be expressed by the farmer in planning the interiors of barns and sheds and places for the storage and repair of tools and equipment. Family orchestras, group singing, individual hobbies, selection of radio and television programs, and the games played all reveal the development of the arts among members of the rural family.

The arts have real economic value for rural people. The farmer or villager who develops a well-planned and beautifully landscaped home not only experiences the joy of creation and the daily satisfaction that comes from harmonious surroundings but also adds real economic value to his property. What are mere hobbies to rural people of some regions have become full- or part-time vocations in other areas. The art products of the weavers and pottery and jewelry makers of the Navajo and Pueblo people provide the entire income for many of them. The weavers of Kentucky and the wood craftsmen of several other regions have found that art can have real economic value.

Art as a way of life

Art is a way of living, and it is important in the lives of both rural and urban people. A feeling for order and arrangement, a thirst for beauty and cleanliness, a desire to surround oneself with objects and events which have meaning and comfort and enjoyment—all these are manifestations of art and expressions of ways of living.

Man cannot separate his wants, his needs, his whole physical and emotional world from art. The caveman did not call the carved handle of a weapon, art, neither does the contemporary man call a well-arranged garden or an attractively kept place of business, art, for the reason that the weapon to the caveman and the garden or place of business to the contemporary is such an integral part of life. Art, then, is not something limited to certain aspects of life or to a few. Every phase of life illustrates the use of art, the effort to produce order and to understand form and function.[1]

Art forms

While a study of human life reveals manifestations of art in every phase of human endeavor, teachers' conceptions of the arts for children are often limited. Art is not just painting or drawing or woodwork. Broadly conceived, art takes many forms and represents individual attempts to express ideas and emotions through such activities as painting, sculpturing, carving, modeling, acting, dancing, singing, playing a musical instrument, writing poetry, constructing a bird house, landscaping the school grounds, arranging exhibits, beautifying the schoolroom, and so on. Art also in-

[1] From "Art in the Total School Program," *Bulletin No. 9,* Wisconsin Cooperative Educational Planning Program (Madison: State Superintendent of Public Instruction, 1947).

cludes the appreciation of the beautiful in nature and in the works and activities of man. Art means making or creating, but it also means the appreciation of the efforts of others.

Teachers ask, "What is creative art and how does it differ from any other kind?" Webster's *New International Dictionary* defines *create* as "to cause or occasion; to form . . ." and "to produce as a work of thought or imagination, especially as a work of art or dramatic interpretation along new or unconventional lines." Munro indicates that there are broad and narrow views:

In a broad sense, any sort of production, or making, is creation, and thus all student art can be so described, whatever its quality. In the narrow sense, the term implies novelty or originality, as contrasted with the imitation of earlier products. In addition, it suggests that the work is somehow important and valuable; it would not be applied to something that was new in a merely freakish, trivial way.[2]

Munro questions the teacher's practice of calling the "spontaneously conceived and executed" work of children "creative." From his viewpoint the work of children is spontaneous in that it is not directly influenced by the teacher, but "it is rarely original, in the sense of being new." While he recognizes child art as a contribution to human culture, he emphasizes the improbability of children's being creative or even completely spontaneous in their work for the reason that children have been exposed to pictures, cartoons, and other material and merely imitate to a large degree. "The most that can be claimed is a relatively high degree of freedom from definite influence during the immediate process of production."[3]

But does the creation of a work of art by a famous artist or of a machine by an inventor mean that the product is entirely new? The answer must be "no," for the artist draws on the experience of other artists for color, balance, and

2 From Thomas Munro, "Creative Ability in Art and Its Educational Fostering," *Art in American Life and Education,* Fortieth yearbook, The National Society for The Study of Education (Bloomington, Ill.: Public School Publishing Co., 1941), p. 290.

3 *Ibid.*

other qualities of his work, even though his work is new in the sense that it has never been done by others and new in the sense of revealing the use of different techniques from those commonly used. Also, no one man ever built a machine alone; he utilizes the fruits of the labor of many people, and he creates his machine by using the achievements of others. The product is new, but the materials or devices out of which the machine is built are old. The child who expresses his ideas in a painting or a drawing, no matter where he acquired them, is creating. Those are his ideas now and he expresses them in his own way.

All work in the arts need not be creative in the sense that it results in a new product. The child may transfer his own design or the design of another to a booklet he is making. He may enjoy singing songs and giving his interpretation of poetry which someone else has written. He enjoys a folk dance which he has not created. He acts the character in a play which he has not written; the interpretation of the part may be his own, but there is little actual creativeness in the action. But all these activities do bring development of appreciation and build permanent interests in the arts.

Much of the work in school may be called practical arts in the sense that the child is using his ability to produce something for the school or for his home. In school he mounts pictures for an exhibit or builds a cage for white rats; at home he decorates the walls of his shack or makes a nest for the chickens or a rack for his tools. These activities may not be creative in a narrow sense but they do involve a sense of proportion, harmony, and orderliness—important artistic qualities.

How can teachers distinguish between the practical arts, the fine arts, and the industrial arts? As already indicated, practical arts refers to the application of art principles to the affairs of daily life. For example, the child makes a gift for his mother or he helps decorate the schoolroom. He may be creating designs or he may merely apply his concepts of harmony. Practical arts are functional activities, but they may also include some fine arts. However, when the child paints a picture for fun or merely to express an idea, he engages in a fine arts activity and the product may serve no utilitarian purpose except to satisfy him. That activity would be fine arts. So the practical arts involve the use of fine arts, but some fine arts are not used to render service.

How do the industrial arts differ from the practical and the fine arts? Industrial arts may be thought of as those experiences which develop fundamental skills and understandings which are basic to further experiences in education for industry. Leaders in the field of the industrial arts emphasize such pupil goals as "good workmanship and design," "pride and interest in doing useful things," "fundamental skills," "leisure and avocational pursuits," and "creative expression."[4] These are also goals of learning in the fine arts. Much of the work in the industrial arts is creative, and some of the work in the fine arts is not creative art. For example, when the boy making a chair or a table uses his own original design, he is doing creative work in art; when the child uses block printing, he may be doing creative work; the make-up of a school paper involves using balance and harmony in design; and, as already indicated, some of the work in the fine arts involves merely the application of designs and forms and other experiences to develop appreciation. In the elementary school, teachers usually deal with all phases of the school curriculum and need not concern themselves with whether the children are using fine arts, practical arts, or industrial arts. Rather, they will be more concerned with experiences which will bring well-rounded development in children and the achievement of goals in learning.

Goals of instruction in the arts

Goals of instruction in the fine arts and the practical arts have been stated in many ways. In sixteen courses of study

[4] "Philosophy and Objectives of Industrial Arts in the Wisconsin Schools," *Curriculum Bulletin No. 19*, Wisconsin Cooperative Educational Planning Program (Madison: State Superintendent of Public Instruction, 1953), p. 21.

analyzed by Lawson,[5] thirty-eight objectives of art teaching were listed. In general, these objectives dealt with developing appreciation and creative ability or power of expression, improving the socioeconomic life, home life, and leisure enjoyment, and making other subjects of study more meaningful. In most lists of goals or objectives, curriculum makers reflect concern for the development of the child rather than for the achievement of art products.

School faculties in rural areas, need to consider the needs of the children and the character of life in the homes and the community. The goals should be directed toward both the development of the boys and girls and the improvement of community life. The goals of instruction in the fine arts and the practical arts may be as follows:

1. To stimulate children to express their ideas and emotions freely and to provide opportunities for undirected expression through a great variety of art media.

   For some children, experiences in art will merely provide opportunities to have fun, to find a release for the emotions, and to secure recreation. For other children of superior ability, art activities provide opportunities to develop special talents and may require intense concentration of effort. The stimulation of a child to express himself may grow out of the experiences in the social studies or science. Sometimes reading a good story may stimulate children to paint a picture or to express their ideas in the making of a movie or the construction of puppets for dramatic expression. Stimulation may also come from experiences in the home or community. Then art becomes a means of expression of thought and feeling.

2. To reinforce learning in the whole school program. While activities of the school day provide the stimulation for expression, the act of interpretation and expression gives greater meaning to experiences in science, the social studies, speech, and the like. The various arts also reinforce each other in the learning process.

---

[5] Douglas Lawson, "Objectives and Organization in Elementary School Art Programs," *The Elementary School Journal*, XLIV (January, 1944), pp. 274–78.

3. To help children solve problems and make things for the school, the home, and the community. Children may make Christmas and birthday gifts, design Christmas cards, make scenery and costumes and programs for plays, design and construct clothing, rabbit pens, and the like. They are thus learning to do better the things they will do anyway.

4. To develop appreciation of art in its various forms. This includes appreciation of nature and art products, a love and awareness of orderliness, cleanliness, and beauty, and enjoyment of good music and drama.

5. To develop permanent interests in the arts for recreation and social purposes. Many children will find that hobbies and other activities enrich life and add to the enjoyment of living. Art interests can help children make use of leisure time through activities which develop their personalities and help them establish enduring friendships.

6. To develop abilities and interests which contribute to the economic welfare of rural people. While dressmaking, cooking, furniture and tool repair, good housekeeping, and home beautification have economic value in all areas, certain handicrafts such as weaving, ceramics, and carving have economic values in special regions.

Experiences in art

Art as a form of expression grows out of the experiences and activities of the children. Rural areas abound in possibilities for stimulation. Circuses, fairs, festivals, harvesting, planting, fishing, and hunting are just a few of the activities which can offer incentives to expression. The natural surroundings of rural children can offer stimulation to those who are sensitive to the changing character of the seasons; but children must be sensitized to the beauty in life; they must learn to use the senses of sight, hearing, smell, taste, and touch. When attention is directed to familiar phenomena, reactions are provoked from which expression emerges through the use of such media as drawing, painting, rhythmics, singing, poetry writing, and craftwork. The rural teacher who is sensitive to surroundings need never let a day pass without utilizing opportunities to develop art experiences which enrich the lives of the children; but this can never be accomplished by the teacher who considers art as only drawing and painting or cutting and pasting.

Practical or functional art should begin in the environment of the classroom. No child should spend his school hours in a dismal, forbidding atmosphere. The building may be bleak and depressing on the first day of school, but after that negative conditions are unnecessary. With cooperative planning between the children and the teacher, a transformation which is highly enjoyable can take place. Children are fertile with ideas and they love the activity of changing the familiar. They acquire the feeling of belonging if each one has a part in creating an atmosphere that is truly theirs. They cherish the help they get from a teacher sensitive to appropriateness when they are perplexed by a problem in artistic endeavor. Nothing creates cohesiveness, morale, and good emotional climate as does the sharing in arranging and decorating a classroom. Children respond to color and good arrangement, and they are quick to reject the ugly or the inappropriate. In general, their judgment improves with guidance.

Next, the school grounds and surroundings may need consideration. In the absence of landscaping, art lessons can prepare the way for a cleanup day and a planting day in the spring or for an Arbor Day activity. When plans are made well in advance, the school has an opportunity to feel out community willingness to participate in beautification of the grounds. A landscaping activity in the school often has far-reaching effects on the neighborhood to the extent that families become yard-conscious and improve their own yards. Children, too, are often good ambassadors and spread the news of change in their immediate surroundings at school, showing that they are stimulated by the new look in a familiar environment.

Art activities should be extended beyond the activities in the school, however. Field trips are enriching if they are well planned with definite goals to be attained. A trip may be arranged to visit a farm home or a town home that offers possibility in the study of architecture or appropriate interior decorating and furniture arrangement or well-planned landscaping. Other trips may be made to museums to study paintings, sculptures, crafts, or weaving. Other possibilities are visits to a store to study what constitutes a well-arranged window display; trips to places where skilled men or women work in crafts; visits to places where art materials are made; and trips to nearby places of natural beauty. Field trips offer opportunities to explore the world of living things: plants and animals of all kinds—animals that swim, animals that fly, animals that walk or crawl. Planned trips arouse awareness of that which is ugly as well as of that which is beautiful, and they provide the opportunity for learning through all the senses.

Further art experiences in rural areas may come from poster making in art classes to promote participation in community events. Appropriate colorful posters created by the children convey a positive message of school accomplishment. Child-created posters which promote interest in Education Week, PTA meetings, and school exhibit days motivate increased attendance at school functions. Poster making can be fun and, if not carried to excess, will offer rich experiences in learning; but some teachers do not realize that while some poster making is desirable, so much time may be devoted to the activity that little opportunity for other art experiences is left.

Experiences in music

As one of the fine arts music shares a large part of the esthetic life of a people. This is especially true of rural people because music is an art form which a family or a group can share as a unit. From the lullabies of early childhood to the musical enjoyment of old age, music plays on all human emotions, and the school should meet the needs of children for its development. Every child has a need to learn the religious and secular songs of his culture, but he should go beyond this. Participation in group singing, choral singing, and instrument playing further develop musical training and satisfy needs for expression. Playing the piano or the organ or other instruments offers the child an opportunity to become a part of a band or an orchestra which provides him with music participation as well as the chance to be included in school and community functions. The public has come to appreciate school bands, and even in small communities people are usually willing to support such school activities. The public may overlook the more subtle and personal values of music to the individual, but the personal recognition and self-realization that come from being able to perform on an instrument are well identified by the school.

Public interest in music has been greatly stimulated recently by the cinema, radio, and television and by concert groups that travel to smaller towns and cities. These media of communication have boosted the sale of records to people who previously have felt that they could not afford them and have created new needs for music.

The school has a service to perform in the cultivation and refinement of musical tastes. Listening to well-selected music influences tastes and appreciation. Radio programs and records of instrumental music have not been fully explored as a learning medium in the schools, and these are neglected in many rural areas where economic conditions make their use prohibitive. These media can be used before school starts in the morning and at noon as well as during study periods; but the music must be properly selected and softly played. Many music records can be purchased or borrowed from libraries. These can do more to improve the quality of music appreciation than hours of talking about better music.

The following quotation illustrates how one group of twelve teachers in an elementary school enriched the music experiences for children of their school:

In the primary classrooms where only rote-singing had been practiced, the program was enriched by introducing a rhythm band. Children and teachers together talked about instruments which could be made. Once children got the idea that they could use their own initiative in experimenting with the use of objects which could produce pleasing sounds they began looking for things to bring from home. Tin tops, horseshoes, nails, coffee cans, combs, wood blocks, bottles, toy drums, and rattles of different kinds were found and youngsters began trying their skill at constructing instruments which could be used for making music. The first try-outs resulted in more noise than music. At this point the teachers thought it helpful to introduce some commercially-made rhythm band instruments. An electric record player and a variety of suitable records were bought. In a short time every youngster had some instrument of his own and the groups began playing together by following rhythm band arrangements. The individuals in the groups began to develop skills through frequent opportunities for band playing. Some found it easy to sing while playing. Those whose first movements were hit-or-miss developed a feeling for rhythm. The drummer used several different beats. By the end of the year the children were making arrangements of their own and no longer following solely the ready-made rhythm band arrangements.

Singing was a major activity in all the grades. At first one group visited another group to share songs. Finally the entire school began coming together for combined group singing. Many singing games, in and out of school, were enjoyed. In some classrooms children often had opportunity to listen to recordings of music by well-known composers and to a variety of types of music. Gradually children began to recognize differences in voices and the fact that some children had more skill than others in singing. They suggested that some of the best singers form a glee club.

The enjoyment of these activities inspired children to put words to familiar tunes and later to create tunes of their own. The children were given many opportunities to respond to music through creative dancing. The value of this activity was evidenced at a spring music festival during the second year of emphasis on music. All participants were given an opportunity to engage in a creative interpretation of a musical selection. They were, for the time, seemingly unaware of the huge audience. Parents and teachers noted the grace, poise, rhythm, and creativeness of the children.

Through this music program which included listening, singing, dancing, creating, and the playing of instruments, each child was helped to find a way through which he could enjoy participating in some music activity.[6]

6 "The Characteristics of a Good Elementary School, A Guide to Better Schools," *Bulletin No. 5*, Vol. XXI, State Department of Education (Richmond, Va.: The Department, March, 1949), pp. 9–10.

Teaching the arts

There are no set rules for teaching the arts. Certain things are basic and fundamental in good art work, but the instruction is an individual matter and each child should develop his own art products in accordance with his feelings and ideas, so far as possible. The teacher should have some knowledge of design and color harmony and tone value, of course, and should be able to recognize artistic quality, but the child must learn to develop these qualities for himself and not have them imposed upon him.

Certain principles which may be used to guide the teacher in art instruction are listed below.

1. The teaching of art is an individual matter and each child should develop his own art products in accordance with his feelings and ideas.

2. The art products of children should not be judged by adult standards.

Standards of taste are the outgrowths of experience. Primary children are proud of their work and are satisfied with what they do. The teacher should be concerned with the development of the children and not with superior products.

3. Teachers will have their own conceptions of art quality, but they should realize that even experts disagree on art standards.

Some believe that there is an absolute standard by which the merits of art products may be judged and that the greater the development of skill among judges, the closer will be the agreement on merit. Others, called subjectivists, hold that art quality is purely a personal matter. The viewer's tastes determine what he likes and there really is no universal standard. The advocates of the relativistic theory believe that there is a plurality of standards, with each culture group having its own standard. Persons of similar background and attitudes usually have about the same standards. Gordon[7] found that experts disagree more among

---

[7] Donald A. Gordon, "Individual Differences in the Evaluation of Art and the Nature of Art Standards," *Journal of Educational Research*, L (September, 1956), pp. 17–29.

themselves than a group of laymen do; the latter reveal a more simple and uniform point of view when judging art products. Experts who judge paintings are influenced by their tendency to approve or disapprove of modern art and by their interest in technique, craftsmanship, style, and originality.

4. Teachers should not expect every child to become an artist.

Every child will become a consumer, a home builder, and a citizen of the community, however, and he can use and enjoy art.

5. Instruction in the arts should permeate the whole school program and not be confined to an hour or a period of the school day.

Industrial arts and fine arts should be unified insofar as possible, and all art should function in the life of the school. Art form cannot be divorced from function nor feeling from good workmanship nor social values in fine arts from social values in the practical and industrial arts. When children read stories, they often want to express their ideas and emotional reactions through painting, drawing, dramatizations, writing, or the preparation of booklets of stories. In the assembly of stories written by children into booklet form, art design and bookbinding may be practiced. Also, in many social-studies units, singing adds to the understanding of the way of life among the pioneers and among the people of other regions. Music is a part of the folklore of all people and, together with art, adds to the understanding of a culture.

Although the arts should permeate the whole school program, the teacher will probably wish to have some specific time on the school schedule for lessons or units in art and music. How much time should be allocated for this instruction can only be determined at the time of planning the whole schedule. If a separate period is provided on the time schedule, the activities of the special period should be motivated by experiences in the rest of the school program.

6. The teacher should exemplify art in her own life and activities.

Dress and grooming, harmony in the classroom, mount-ings on bulletin boards, and flower arrangements can repre-sent the teacher's expression of art. The teacher who has a feeling for form, color, and balance can lead children to be-come aware of these qualities.

7. Teachers may use resource people from the community to serve as art consultants.

The dressmaker, the architect, the landscape gardener, the homemaker, and the store window decorator may help chil-dren to learn how to use art in daily life. In many rural areas there are artists who can help with the instruction in paint-ing, ceramics, and weaving. Many teachers have been able to bring to school representatives of people from other lands who have displayed and explained works of art and shown costumes and crafts of their country.

8. Teachers must learn to improvise because many schools do not have special workrooms and equipment and often art materials are limited.

The teacher may need to use the regular classroom and improvised equipment. Many of the art supplies available include scrap and waste materials, gunny sacks, straw, orange crates, empty tin cans, newspapers, wood from trees on the farms, and sometimes local clay.

9. The work in music should include such a wide variety of experiences that each child may discover some phase of musical activity in which he finds enjoyment.

It is not expected that musical artists will be produced, but it is hoped that all children will enjoy participation in music making or listening.

10. Every music experience and other art experience pro-vides learning in appreciation.

Appreciation, negative or positive, develops through acquaintance and through activities. Children can learn to dislike an experience as well as to enjoy it.

11. Rhythms are valuable aids to development in music appreciation as well as in dancing.

Rhythms are physical motions that are motivated and controlled by music. Children who have a well-developed sense for rhythm are sensitive to the regular recurring pulsation of music.

12. Appreciation of the culture of people of other lands may be developed by using the art, music, and dances of those countries.

By using these arts from abroad, the program is enriched for children and their understanding of other people becomes greater. When these arts are used in connection with appropriate social-studies work units, children develop more kindred feelings with the Spanish, Norwegians, Italians, Latin Americans, and other foreign cultures they learn to know. Music and the other arts have often been called the universal languages.

13. Music, art, dancing, and dramatics can be used to build better relationships with minority groups.

Negro music and Mexican music, ceramics and weaving will not only enrich the lives of the children but also help them recognize how diversity among peoples can enrich the lives of all.

14. Teachers should recognize that in art and music the programs should be organized to bring gradual development.

In art, kindergarten and primary grade children develop preferences for art media through much experimentation with a variety of materials. The teacher should make available charcoal, pencils, colored chalk, crayons, modeling clay, and craft materials. As the children draw and paint, they express their own conceptions of the world about them. As they develop, they strive for beauty of proportion and spacing; but the teacher must wait for this growth.

In music, young children begin with activities which help them discover their own voices. Through experience they learn that voices go up and down. Through singsong playtime activities children gain the use of singing voices. They acquire a feeling for rhythm by responding to rhythmic movements. They learn to recognize sadness and happiness in music and fast, slow, and moderate tempos. From such experiences, children are introduced to the reading of music, perhaps by using familiar songs to help them learn time lengths and the respective pitch levels of the tones. Continued work with rhythms, folk songs, and a variety of materials extend musical development and help children develop tastes for music.

Summary

The practical arts and the fine arts have always played a major role in the cultural and social lives of rural people, bringing enrichment and making life on farms and in villages enjoyable and profitable. Landscaping the farm or town home, interior decorating, family musical activities, and hobbies have contributed to individual enjoyment and family solidarity.

The arts have real economic value, as shown by increased valuations of improved property and by the income of people of some rural regions where markets for art products are available.

Art as a way of life for all rural people should become a way of life for the children in school. Art is more than painting and drawing. It includes the development of orderliness, cleanliness, a sense of balance, and making, creating, and appreciating.

No fine distinctions can be drawn between the fine arts, the practical arts, and the industrial arts. When the principles of the fine arts are applied to useful things in the affairs of life, they become practical. Many of the industrial art activities are creative, while some of the experiences in the fine arts are not creative but are designed to develop appreciation.

Although the ability of children to do creative work is sometimes questioned, children do use past experiences to build products new to them. All creativity involves the utilization of the experience of others in the development of the new.

The goals of instruction in the fine arts and the practical arts include the stimulation of children to express their ideas and emotions freely and to provide opportunities for expression. The arts reinforce learning in the rest of the school program and much of the stimulation for art work is derived from other subjects. Development of appreciation of the arts is an important goal of instruction, and the program in the arts is designed to help children use the arts for social and recreational purposes and develop interests and abilities in the arts as a contribution to their economic life.

Rural areas abound in opportunities for experiences which stimulate children to express themselves, but children must be led to become sensitive to beauty in the environment.

Functional art begins in the classroom where children may work to make their school attractive. Children then extend their art experience to the schoolgrounds and into the community. Through field trips children develop appreciation of art and become aware of the beautiful in nature. Community activities offer a stimulus to do work in the practical arts.

Experiences which provide musical development include singing songs and playing in bands and orchestras. Experiences with radio and television programs and concerts aid in the cultivation of musical tastes. Recorded music may be used at intervals during the school day to provide both relaxation and development of appreciation of good music.

Some principles which may be used to guide the teacher in art instruction are the following:

1. There are no set rules for the teaching of art.
2. Art products of children should not be judged by adult standards.
3. Teachers should recognize that even experts disagree about art standards.
4. Teachers should not expect each child to become an artist.
5. Instruction in the arts should permeate the whole school program.
6. The teacher should exemplify art in his own life and activities.
7. Resource persons from the community may serve as art consultants.

8. Teachers must learn to improvise where workrooms, equipment, and materials are not available.
9. The work in music should include such a wide variety of experiences that each child may discover some phase of musical activity in which he can find enjoyment.
10. Every art experience provides learning in appreciation.
11. Rhythms are valuable aids to development in music as well as in dancing.
12. Appreciation of the culture of the people of other lands may be developed through use of their art, music, and dances.
13. The various arts can be used to build better relationships with minority groups.
14. The art programs should be organized to bring about the gradual development of the children.

Selected references

ANDREWS, GLADYS. *Creative Rhythmic Movement for Children.* Englewood Cliffs, N.J.: Prentice-Hall, Inc., 1954. Chaps. iii–x.

A guide for teaching creative rhythmic movements to children in the elementary school. Suggested resources and bibliography.

CARABO-CONE, MADELEINE, and ROYT, BEATRICE. *How to Help Children Learn Music.* New York: Harper & Bros., 1955. Chap. i.

Begins with simple games and activities and progresses toward the more complex. In each game the focus is on the isolation of one learning process. For each learning process, related variations are presented. Very good.

COLE, NATALIE ROBINSON. *The Arts in the Classroom.* New York: The John Day Co., 1953. Entire volume.

Shows how a teacher, through encouragement, understanding, and guidance, released the creative spirit in her fourth- and fifth-grade pupils with satisfying results. Tells of the techniques used in teaching creative painting, creative clay work, design and block work, free rhythmic dancing, and creative writing.

ERDT, MARGARET HAMILTON. *Teaching Art in the Elementary School.* New York: Rinehart & Co., Inc., 1955. Chaps. iii, iv, vi, and viii especially.

A guide to teaching art in the elementary grades. Shows the role of the teacher in helping the child to realize his potential creative and esthetic strengths. Suggests the various stages of child development and the types of art to fit the needs at these stages. Provides source materials and ideas for art activities.

GRANT, PARKS. *Music for Elementary Teachers.* New York: Appleton-Century-Crofts, Inc., 1951. Chaps. ii, iv, xi–xiv, xvi.

Gives the aims of school music and methods of teaching songs, rhythms, and music appreciation. Especially helpful to the classroom teacher with a limited background in music.

HOOD, MARGUERITE V., and SCHULTZ, E. J. *Learning Music Through Rhythm.* Boston: Ginn & Co., 1949. Chap. i.

A good introduction to teaching rhythms, including action songs, free rhythmic activity with instrumental music, the use of rhythm instruments, folk games and dances.

KRONE, BEATRICE, and KRONE, MAX. *Music Participation in the Elementary School.* Chicago: Neil A. Kjos Music Co., 1952. Chaps. ii–vii.

Suggested activities for singing and for playing instruments which will make familiar songs more interesting to elementary-school girls and boys.

MADDEN, IRA C. *Creative Handicraft.* Chicago: The Goodheart-Willcox Co., Inc., 1955. Entire volume.

Deals primarily with the craft of woodworking. Provides information on kinds of woods, useful tools, wood finishing, patterns and designs. Provides instructions for making patterns and a variety of project material in the form of detailed drawings and photos, design suggestions, and variations.

MOORE, FRANK C., *et al. Handcrafts for Elementary Schools.* Boston: D. C. Heath & Co., 1955. Chaps. i–xii.

Provides a discussion of how to organize and teach handicrafts. Deals with specific crafts: paper, novelty, ceramic, wood, metal, textile, graphic arts, and leather. Has many pictured designs and patterns with information telling what materials and tools are needed, what skills are needed, and the procedure to be used.

MYERS, LOUISE KIFER. *Teaching Children Music in the Elementary School* (2d ed.). Englewood Cliffs, N.J.: Prentice-Hall, Inc., 1956. Entire volume.

Provides much help for teachers in the development of musical appreciation and musical ability in the elementary school. Includes: teaching singing, using rhythms, developing muscular coordination and control, creating music, reading music, listening, outline of a program to bring development, teaching aids, and the role of music in better human relations. Bibliography and list of source materials provided.

NEWKIRK, LOUIS VEST. *Integrated Handwork for Elementary Schools.* New York: Silver Burdett Co., 1940. Part I especially.

Excellent source book for the elementary-school teacher. Deals with handwork as an integral part of educational method in the elementary school. Part II is a guide in handwork techniques, giving suggestions for a great variety of suitable handwork activities for grades 1–8.

NEWKIRK, LOUIS VEST, and ZUTTER, LA VADA. *Crafts for Everyone.* Scranton, Pa.: International Textbook Co., 1950. Vol. I and II.

Volume I provides a guide in working with craft projects made from wood, metal, and leather. Volume II includes projects to be made from plastics, textiles, paper, and many native materials which may be available in or near the community. The projects range from simple to difficult. The appendix gives a list of supply houses where supplies may be purchased.

POWERS, MARGARET. *A Book of Little Crafts.* Peoria, Ill.: The Manual Arts Press, 1942. Entire volume.

A good source book of arts and crafts in the lower elementary grades. Discusses experimenting with color and design, shapes, sound, and dramatics. Especially helpful to the inexperienced teacher because the materials needed and procedures for each art activity and craft are given.

18

EVALUATION AND IMPROVEMENT
OF SCHOOLS IN RURAL AREAS

Elementary and secondary schools of rural areas derive their functions from the ideals, aspirations, and problems of living of the people in the region where the schools operate, and these are constantly changing. The most effective program of education becomes obsolete in time unless continual adjustments are made in accordance with the needs of the children in the changing society. Adaptations of the educational program cannot be made unless there are constant appraisals of the effectiveness of the program. Furthermore, even if the living conditions did not change, frequent evaluation would be needed because procedures and curriculum practices do not always lead to the achievement of the outcomes anticipated by the program planners. So parents, teachers, and children should share in a continuous appraisal of the effectiveness of the educational program.

Instruments of evaluation

The term *evaluation* refers to the process of determining the extent to which goals set by the social group are being achieved. Evaluation involves a search for changes in the learner as a result of experiences provided, but the search should be made in terms of evaluative criteria set up by the social group. Evaluation is not testing, although tests may be used as one of the techniques for gathering data to be used in evaluation.

In the evaluation of the school program, parents and teachers may first set up criteria involving statements of what a good school for the community should be. They can then proceed to gather evidence concerning abilities, status, appreciations, problems, and behavior patterns. This evidence can then be used to make an assessment of the effectiveness of the educational program. Tests and other devices are used merely to assemble data which need to be interpreted in the light of the criteria set up. These devices are the instruments of the evaluation, not the evaluation itself.

Evaluation varied in scope

Evaluation varies in scope with the purposes and the nature of the social group concerned. The following areas of evaluation and personnel participating show the varied character of evaluation:

1. *Evaluation of the total educational services of the community.* This represents a study of all educational influences and services provided by the various institutions and agencies of the community. It includes the evaluation of development which comes from the school, of the activities of the library, churches, Boy Scouts, Girl Scouts, 4-H Clubs, recreation centers, health centers, adult education programs, farmers and homemakers clubs, service clubs, community fairs and festivals, lecture and concert activities, and the like.

The evaluators include all of the people—teachers, ministers, lawyers, doctors, farmers, businessmen, and housewives. These people are concerned with a community-wide educational program which involves creating a good environment and activities for development of all of the people. A study of community-wide educational facilities enables leaders to discover omissions, duplications of effort, overemphasis, and underemphasis and to make improvements in the neglected areas or weaknesses in community life.

As pointed out in Chapter 4, the school does not provide all of the educational development opportunities for children and certainly only a small part of the opportunities for adults. As indicated in Chapter 3, community planning to meet the educational, social, and religious needs of all of the people is needed. And successful community planning depends on evaluation.

2. *Evaluation of the school program to determine the extent of achievement of the general goals of education.* This involves the study of improved behavior of children in the school, homes, and community. The school is the major educational institution which provides learning opportunities and guidance in learning for the young, and the achievements of children should be cooperatively studied by parents, teachers, and young people. Such a study should reveal strengths and deficiencies and lead to improvement in facilities and personnel, and it may lead also to changes in goals.

3. *Evaluation of curricular practices, procedures, materials, and organization of the school.* This is a professional task and should be carried forward by professional educators. General goals of education can be developed cooperatively with laymen, but the evaluation of achievement of goals should be the joint responsibility of all concerned. Some clues as to weaknesses in methods, content, and organization may come from the general evaluation with parents, but the evaluation of ways and means to achieve goals must be the responsibility of professional people who have a knowledge of child development and learning and an understanding of the techniques which have proved to be most effective.

4. *Evaluation of pupil progress.* This should be a continuous program in which teachers and children share the responsibility. Parents are concerned with the progress of their

children and they should share in decisions as to what method shall be used to report progress to the parents, but only the teacher and the individual child can make a fair assessment of his development. Various techniques can be used to help both the teacher and the child study progress and discover learning areas which need more attention.

5. *Evaluation of each educational experience.* In connection with each act of learning, teachers and children need to make an appraisal of the extent to which the special purposes of the unit of work have been achieved. The teacher should be concerned with the contribution which each experience makes toward achievement of the general goals of education.

Parents, teachers, and children have somewhat different purposes in the evaluative process. Adults of the community are concerned with the over-all effectiveness of the school in helping youth achieve a better life. They are vitally interested in the achievement of major purposes for which the school is established. But teachers are concerned not alone with the achievement of major goals but with the testing of methods, the materials used, and the organization of the curriculum. Children are most concerned with the achievement of specific understandings and skills, with personal adjustment to the social group, and with enjoyment of experiences which appear to them to be worthwhile.

The school staff will need to recognize the fact that the kind of evaluative techniques to be used will depend upon who is doing the evaluating and what the purpose of the evaluation is.

Evaluation of the total educational program

Any evaluation which is designed to study the effectiveness of the school must be broad in scope and must cover the full time devoted to schooling. What development takes place through experiences from the time the child starts to school until he has completed all of the years of study provided by the community? What development comes from the total program of activities in which he engages?

Throughout this book the interrelationships of all aspects of instruction have been emphasized. The child does not learn to use English solely in reading and language classes. Much art development comes through social-studies activities. Much science is learned in connection with social studies. And good citizenship is practiced throughout the school day. Furthermore, the guidance in development which is begun by teachers in kindergarten or first grade is continued throughout the secondary school in those communities where education through grade twelve is provided. This education should be a continuous developmental program, so a comprehensive evaluation of the work of the school should be made cooperatively by all teachers at all levels. This evaluation can be shared with parents when achievement of major goals is the chief concern.

Any evaluation of the total school program should be based on the goals of education which have been developed cooperatively by the people and the professional staff. (See Chapter 6.) Questions like the following may be asked:

Is there evidence that the children understand the meaning of democracy and that they practice it in group activities?

Do the children understand the American economic system, and do they comprehend the interdependence of rural and urban people?

Do the children see the relationship of local welfare to the welfare of people in other lands?

Do the children practice conservation of human and natural resources?

Have the children developed the basic skills of communication and the use of numbers?

Have the children learned to work together to achieve common goals?

Do the children have the skills, attitudes, and knowledge needed for a happy home life?

Have the children acquired permanent interests in wholesome recreational activities?

Are the activities acquired by the children contributing to the rural culture as well as to recreation?

Any attempt to evaluate the effectiveness of a school program without a framework of goals will likely result in confusion and bickering. Successes, failures, omissions, and overemphases cannot be determined except in the light of goals which have been set for the school. The starting point for evaluation is a review of the goals. Teachers and laymen can then proceed to gather evidence with which to determine the success or failure of the school program.

Having clarified the goals of the school program, a procedure may be outlined as a guide in assembling evidence needed for judgments. A great variety of techniques may be used, some objective and some subjective. Most objective techniques provide evidence regarding only narrow aspects of child development. For example, standard tests of achievement in reading reveal evidence of ability to comprehend the content used in the test but do not measure ability to comprehend other material nor do they give evidence of extent of reader interest. Most standard tests of achievement in English usage give some measure of the child's knowledge of the mechanics of English but do not give any measure of his ability and confidence in expression. Where objective techniques are available or can be developed, they should be used, however, since evidence from this source is likely to be reliable. But teachers and parents will be seriously in error if the evidence for evaluation is derived solely from that which is furnished by published standardized tests. Teachers must know what each test measures and must find other means of collecting evidence regarding development which is not adequately measured by the published test.

The following is a brief outline of the techniques often used to assemble evidence for interpretation in the light of established goals:

    A. Community surveys covering such items as
        1. Changes in community life
        2. Occupations and problems of graduates

  3. Conservation practices
  4. Recreation activities
  5. Health and safety conditions
  6. Leadership roles of graduates
  7. Home and family life
  8. Adult education
  9. Institutions, organizations, and agencies
 10. Delinquency
 11. Mobility of population
 12. Cultural, religious, and social life
 13. Public opinions relating to the school and community

B. Behavior of children at work and play

C. Conferences
  1. Pupil-teacher
  2. Parent-teacher
  3. Adult groups
  4. School staff
  5. Class-teacher

D. Records
  1. Cumulative
  2. Anecdotal
  3. Health
  4. Out-of-school activities

E. Classroom activities
  1. Creative writing, including autobiographies
  2. Free oral expression
  3. Art expression

F. Social contacts
  1. Pupil-teacher
  2. Parent-teacher

G. Home visits

H. Parent-teacher correspondence

 I. Sociometric techniques

 J. Teacher made objective and subjective tests

K. Standardized objective tests and scales[1]

[1] Complete lists of published tests and scales are given in references at the end of this chapter.

1. Mental ability test
   a) Group intelligence tests, such as Otis Quick Scoring Mental Ability Test, Pintner General Ability Tests, California Test of Mental Maturity, and Cornell-Coxe Performance Ability Scale
   b) Individual tests of mental ability, such as the Terman-Merrill Revision of the Stanford-Binet Scale
2. Achievement tests
   a) General survey tests, such as the Stanford Achievement Tests, the Iowa Every Pupil Test of Basic Skills, California Achievement Test, Metropolitan Achievement Test, and Coordinated Scales of Attainment
   b) Diagnostic tests
3. Personality and social behavior scales
   a) Self-rating
   b) Teacher-rating

L. Check lists of interests and behavior

It is obvious that some of these techniques are more suitable as data-gathering devices for evaluation of the over-all effectiveness of the program and that others are more suitable as measures of pupil progress or of the suitability of curriculum organization and content methods of teaching. It will also be recognized that correct interpretation of findings in the light of the goals of the school and the purposes of the evaluation will be of great importance.

In his survey of evaluative techniques used by teachers, Fickles found that in the evaluation of pupil progress, teachers most frequently used "class-teacher conferences, cumulative pupil records, parent-teacher conferences, teacher-teacher conference and unrecorded observation," but that the teachers believed the most beneficial techniques to be "anecdotal record, class-teacher conference, home visiting, pupil-teacher conference and unrecorded observation."[2]

The techniques which teachers use to gather data for evaluation will depend upon the characteristic or factor to

[2] James A. Fickles, "Deciding How to Evaluate," *Journal of Educational Research*, XLVI (October, 1952), pp. 133–39.

be studied, the familiarity of the teacher with measuring instruments, the adequacy of funds for purchasing published materials, and the time and assistance available for administration, and scoring the tests and interpreting the results.

Organization of evaluation programs

A large variety of approaches have been used by local and state groups in organizing their plans for study and evaluation of the effectiveness of school programs. These may be classified under the following four headings:

1. *The rating of aspects of educational programs.* This procedure involves the evaluation of educational practices, equipment, buildings, instruction, and so on by the group as a whole, by committees, or by individuals. The basis of the rating is an estimate of how well standards that have been set up are met by local practices. The ratings are usually expressed numerically and are based on defined levels ranging from poor to excellent. The application of some procedures yields a numerical rating of the total educational program.

The evaluation is ordinarily carried out as a cooperative self-survey by the staff and by citizens of the community. In this way strengths and weaknesses of existing programs are identified. Steps can then be taken to plan an improvement program. This procedure is illustrated in the following publications:

Elementary Evaluative Criteria. Boston: Boston University, 1953.

Handbook for Self Appraisal and Improvement of Elementary Schools, by E. Wilson and H. J. Otto, Austin, Texas: State Department of Education, 1948.

2. *The systematic analysis of local educational practices to discover needs and to establish a basis for improvement programs.* This approach does not involve ratings but leads the faculty to look for examples of desirable practice. It is well illustrated in the cooperative study of elementary education sponsored by the Southern Association of Colleges

and Secondary Schools.[3] Through the cooperative activities of many Southern educators, sets of criteria were set up for studying important aspects of the educational program, including the various curriculum areas, the instruction, and the organization of the school. When these criteria are used to evaluate the educational program of some school, the members of the faculty are called on to give illustrations showing how each of the criteria is being applied in the school. This is done cooperatively in meetings or in study groups. For some items excellent examples can be given, while for others it becomes evident to the staff that there is a deficiency. After a systematic consideration of all of the criteria for some curriculum area—for instance, the social studies—the faculty lists problems that the school faces in this area. Then the group considers immediate steps and long-term steps that should be taken to bring about an improvement. This self-survey of existing practices thus becomes the basis of an improvement program. In many communities, interested citizens participate in this study. Thus emphasis is placed on the value of cooperative study and action by school and community.

3. *Consensus studies or subjective appraisals.* By *consensus studies* is meant the cooperative study of any aspect of the educational program by the citizens of a community and the educational staff to arrive at a common understanding as to the situation and to decide on the steps to be taken by school and community to bring about needed changes. This approach has been extensively applied in Illinois in connection with the state-wide study of the curriculum. To guide the discussion of particular problems of concern to a community, study guides have been developed and tried out in selected centers, thus making it certain that all aspects of the selected problems being considered are systematically examined. Provision is made for securing the judgments of the interested participants about various aspects of the particular problem involved. After an extended discussion of the issues and of

[3] See *Evaluating the Elementary School*. Atlanta, Ga.: Southern Association of Colleges and Secondary Schools, 1951.

possible solutions, an attempt is made to arrive at a consensus of opinion. This procedure involves the use of prepared study guides which focus the attention of the group on a problem and assure that it will be canvassed carefully. Thus, each locality is given guidance in the study of problems which are of concern to it. As new problems arise, new guides are prepared by state committees.[4]

A similar scheme of study and evaluation was used in Wisconsin as a part of the curriculum-planning program. Six major purposes of the cooperative state program, as given in the study guide, were:

1. To coordinate the efforts of educators and lay citizens in defining the task of the school today and tomorrow.
2. To stimulate widespread study of public education in relation to preschool and school age children, older youth, and society so that the educational program may be continuously improved.
3. To work with local schools in conducting continuous curriculum studies, to aid teachers in finding solutions to present and emerging curriculum and guidance problems, and to coordinate the preparation of curriculum guides.
4. To help teachers and pupils in cooperatively planning, executing, and evaluating those experiences which will lead most effectively to the attainment of the purposes of education.
5. To aid and stimulate the development of such statewide conditions as will facilitate continued curriculum improvements; for example, teacher education and parent education, certification, finance and administration.
6. To promote such interaction with other community groups and agencies as will more fully utilize the total educational resources of the community for the best growth of the child.[5]

[4] An illustration of the study guides used in Illinois is given in *What Do You Think About Our School's Music Education Program?* Consensus Study No. 7, Springfield, Ill.: Illinois Curriculum Program, 1952.

[5] From "The Task of the School: A Study Guide for Use of Professional and Lay Groups," *Bulletin No. 1*, Wisconsin Curriculum Guiding Committee (Madison, Wis.: State Superintendent of Public Instruction, 1950).

4. *The identification and study of specific areas of instruction or problems of concern to particular schools or groups.* In many communities the school and citizens have undertaken the study of specific problems in curriculum and instruction and other areas on a less formal basis than is implied by the three types of systematic procedures previously described. The study of methods of dealing with problems informally identified by the staff may be undertaken according to plans devised by the local group. Illustrations of such areas of study are: conservation, citizenship, safety, health, grading and promotion, report cards, reading, language, and arithmetic. Sometimes the outcomes expected from educational development in the particular area are listed and an effort is made to secure evidence of improved behavior of children.

Teachers in rural areas are concerned with the evaluation of the whole educational program and will wish to study special fields of the curriculum in some detail in order to discover areas which need improvement. A guide for the study of the various curriculum areas is provided in the Appendix (see page 408). This guide consists of a series of questions regarding pupil behavior and curriculum practices. Teachers should try to think of specific examples of child behavior to substantiate answers to the various questions. Data from tests, check lists, and similar sources may be used as evidence of increased understanding and better attitudes and appreciations. Teachers should also cite illustrations of curriculum procedures in the study of the school program.

The purpose of the guide is to stimulate group thinking about the instructional program. The faculty should work as a team to develop curriculum plans and therefore should work together in the evaluation. A study of present practices will often lead to the consideration of how the program may be improved. Neglected areas may be discovered; better procedures may be found; and more suitable instructional materials may be secured.

When parents and teachers study the effectiveness of the school in helping children to achieve the goals of education, they may discover unmet needs of children and deficiencies in buildings, equipment, supplies, organization, and school personnel, as well as in the organization of the school curriculum. People of the community will then want to consider how deficiencies can be corrected to achieve desired goals for the school.

Improvement of rural education

Building an educational program to meet the needs of rural people depends on the improvement of many factors which facilitate or impede educational efforts. The evaluation of community and school programs will reveal some of the changes which must be made if education is to fulfil its proper role in creating a better life in a changing rural society.

The factors to be considered may be listed as follows:

1. *Years of schooling available to children.* In many rural areas of the United States only eight years of elementary school education has been provided for boys and girls, but they also need secondary school education which is geared to their needs. Recent figures reveal that opportunities for additional schooling have been increasing. Over three fourths of rural boys and girls now receive some high school education, but there are many still to be served. Kindergartens and two-year community colleges should also be available to the children of rural areas. Under the guidance of a well-educated teacher, children of kindergarten age can receive educational development on a par with that provided at any other age level. Children who have not attended good kindergartens have missed much of the pre-school development needed for successful learning in the first grade. Regional community colleges can provide opportunities for rural youth to solve some of the complex problems of modern rural life.

2. *Quality and quantity of professional workers.* Generally speaking, the rural areas have been short-changed in quantity if not in quality of professional workers. Teachers of rural areas have been improving their professional qualifi-

cations, but on the average they do not match the years of schooling of urban teachers. Extensive in-service educational programs conducted by local school districts and by state and county officials have helped teachers of rural areas improve their qualifications; but, partly because of limited financial resources, many schools of rural areas do not have adequate personnel for supervision, guidance, health, and library service and for service to exceptional children.

Professional personnel for rural educational service not only need good preparation in terms of years of schooling but need to understand and love rural life. They should have a vision of the possibilities inherent in the education of children in a rural environment.

The procurement and retention of a good professional staff depends, to quite an extent, upon good salary schedules and good living and working conditions. Teachers like to work in a school system where teaching materials and equipment are good and where there are opportunities for good teamwork and professional development.

3. *Length of the school year.* Teachers need time to plan and develop good instructional programs and time to guide children in development. In most communities teachers are employed only for nine or ten months of the year and devote most of this time to working directly with children. There is little time for cooperative teacher planning, for conferences with parents, and for out-of-school activities with children. In some school districts, teachers are employed by the calendar year and spread the work with children over a ten-month period. These teachers have a one-month vacation and use the time before school opens and some time each month for consultations with parents, faculty meetings, and curriculum planning.

4. *Teaching supplies, equipment, and school housing.* Poor housing can defeat the purposes of a good health program, and inadequate reading and resource materials will decrease the opportunities for child development.

5. *Financial support for education.* In many rural areas funds are not sufficient to provide the educational services

needed for the people. Increased support from federal, state, and county governments will be needed to ensure good education for many rural boys and girls. Records reveal a growing tendency for larger governmental units to carry a share of the costs of education. The development of larger school district units has also provided funds with which to increase educational services.

6. *Administrative and supervisory service.* Most rural school districts are small, whether the district operates a one- or two-teacher school or a larger twelve-grade school system. And in small school districts the people cannot procure all of the educational services needed. The problem is being solved by two rapidly growing movements: (1) the reorganization of school districts to form larger districts and (2) the development of intermediate school administrative and supervisory units.

School districts are being enlarged by combining small districts into larger ones. Such districts have one administrative office but any number of school attendance units. Such larger school districts have advantages in procurement of good teachers, more adequate supplies and equipment, and supervisory personnel.

This is not intended as an argument for large school attendance units nor to discount the advantages of even the one- or two-teacher school. But such schools should be administered as a part of a large administrative unit to permit the utilization of supervisory and health services, to secure better financial support, and to provide good secondary school education for all rural boys and girls.

The second movement—that of development of effective intermediate school administrative units—is growing because of the need for educational services which cannot be supplied fully even by most reorganized school districts. The intermediate unit of administration is the unit which is larger than the *local* unit and smaller than the *state* unit. It may have boundaries equal to a county or to several counties. Such units have been operating in some states for many years, but they represent a recent development in such states as Iowa and Ohio. With adequate funds for operation, the office of the intermediate school unit can provide general supervisory service, library service, health service, and many other services, according to the needs of the local school district.

7. *The educational program.* The educational program should be distinctively rural and not a copy of urban programs. It should be geared to change and should help improve the social, recreational, religious, and economic life of rural people. It will be the program of a community school developed by the people for service to the people.

Summary

School people and citizens of the community need to carry forward a continuous program of evaluation because curriculum practices do not always help children achieve the goals anticipated and because changing conditions in society make curricular adjustments desirable.

Evaluation is the process of determining the extent to which experiences result in the behavior of the learner in accordance with goals established. Evaluation should not be confused with testing and the use of a great variety of data-gathering devices used to assemble evidence; it involves the subjective interpretation of evidence and an appraisal of the effectiveness of a program.

Evaluation varies in scope according to the area of concern of the social group. Citizens and professional people may evaluate the effectiveness of the whole community-wide educational program; teachers and parents may limit evaluation to the school program and the general goals of education. The evaluation of curricular practices, procedures, materials, and organization is a professional task which should be carried forward by the school. Assessments of pupil progress are continually made by teachers and children to help uncover areas of learning which need to be strengthened. A still further area of evaluation is that made by teachers and children in connection with each unit of work.

Evaluation of the total school programs should represent a complete appraisal of all experiences of children from the beginning of the school period to the end.

Steps in evaluation include a review of goals and the development of criteria for evaluation. Many instruments are then used to gather evidence for study, such as surveys of community living of graduates, pupil-teacher and parent-teacher conferences, observation of behavior, scores on standardized and teacher-made tests, cumulative records, autobiographies, and the like.

A wide variety of schemes have been used in the organization of evaluation plans. These include the following: (1) attempts to rate aspects of educational programs on a rating scale; (2) a systematic analysis of local educational practices to discover needs and to establish a basis for improvement; (3) consensus studies or the subjective appraisal of the school program with the aid of study guides; and (4) the identification and study of areas of instruction or specific problems of concern to particular schools or groups.

The study and evaluation of a school program will likely reveal the need for improvement not only in curriculum practices but also in the school administrative and financial structure.

Among the factors which facilitate or handicap rural schools in the achievement of desirable goals of instruction in rural areas are: (1) the years of schooling available; (2) the quantity and quality of professional workers; (3) the length of the school year; (4) teaching supplies, equipment, and housing; (5) financial support; (6) administrative and supervisory service; and (7) suitability of the educational program for rural areas. The trend is in the direction of providing a longer school year to give teachers time for planning with each other and with parents. There is also a trend toward increasing the financial support of local school districts through federal, state, and county governmental units. Education services in many places are being increased without undue cost to taxpayers through school district reorganization and the development of intermediate school units.

While progress is being made by teachers in rural areas, greater efforts need to be expended to increase teacher qualifications and to secure people who understand and love rural life and who will help develop a school program that contributes to a better life for people of the farms and villages.

Selected references

BECK, ROBERT H., COOK, WALTER H., and KEARNEY, NOLAN C. *Curriculum of the Modern Elementary School*. Englewood Cliffs, N.J.: Prentice-Hall, Inc., 1953. Chap. x.

Deals with levels of evaluation, techniques of evaluation, and the measurement of pupil progress.

HANNA, LAVONNE A., POTTER, GLADYS L., and HAGAMAN, NEVA. *Unit Teaching in the Elementary School*. New York: Rinehart & Co., 1955. Chap. xv.

How to evaluate changes in behavior, including criteria for selecting techniques and the use of various techniques by teachers and pupils.

HAND, HAROLD C. *What People Think about Their Schools*. Yonkers, N.Y.: World Book Co., 1948.

Descriptions of procedures used for studying and evaluating school programs by citizens of the community.

RAGAN, WILLIAM B. *Modern Elementary Curriculum*. New York: The Dryden Press, Inc., 1953. Chaps. xiv and xv.

Evaluating pupil progress and the program of the elementary school.

SHANE, HAROLD G., and McSWAIN, E. T. *Evaluation and the Elementary School Curriculum*. New York: Henry Holt & Co., 1951. Chaps. iii, v, vi especially.

Excellent treatment of the nature of evaluation and its function in improving elementary education. Appendix B gives criteria of good citizenship in behavioristic terms. Appendix C has a bibliography of evaluative instruments.

SUMPTON, M. R. *How to Conduct a Citizen's School Survey*. Englewood Cliffs, N.J.: Prentice-Hall, Inc., 1952.

Detailed discussion of possible survey procedures.

TORGERSON, THEODORE L., and ADAMS, GEORGIA SACHS. *Measurement and Evaluation for the Elementary School Teacher*. New York: The Dryden Press, Inc., 1954. Chaps. i and iii and Appendix A.

Discusses purpose, meaning and instruments of evaluation, and relationship of evaluation to goals. Gives criteria for judging the merit of evaluation instruments. Appendix A is a selected list of tests and scales for use in elementary schools and a list of publishers of standardized tests.

WRIGHTSTONE, J. WAYNE, JUSTMAN, JOSEPH, and ROBBINS, IRVING. *Evaluation in Modern Education.* New York: American Book Co., 1956. Chaps. ii and iii especially.

Deals with principles, scope, and methods of evaluation, steps in the evaluation process, characteristics of an evaluation program, and types, uses, and qualities of evaluation techniques. Excellent treatment of procedures and techniques. Directory of publishers of tests in appendix.

YAUCH, W. A. *How Good Is Your School?* New York: Harper & Bros., 1951.

Handbook to help parents judge the quality of local schools.

APPENDIX

GUIDE FOR THE STUDY AND EVALUATION OF INSTRUCTION IN CURRICULUM AREAS OF THE ELEMENTARY SCHOOL

In the study of the school program teachers should attempt to determine whether desirable outcomes result from the educational experiences and to record specific instances of pupil behavior as evidence of achievement of each suggested outcome. In answering the questions, teachers should write specific statements as to what is being done regarding curricular practices, methods of instruction, and materials. It is recommended that teachers work as a group or in committees to pass judgment upon the effectiveness of the school program at all levels rather than attempt to evaluate the work at any single grade level.

In the study of each curriculum area the following questions may be considered:

1. What are the most effective ways of evaluating the outcomes of instruction?
2. What are the strengths of the present program?
3. What are the weaknesses of the curriculum offerings?
4. What is needed to improve instructional practices?
5. What should be done to improve instructional materials?
6. What plans for immediate action should be made?
7. What should be the long-range plans for improvement of the program?

The following guide is divided into curriculum areas so that one area at a time can be studied. Analyses of school programs by the use of this guide have helped local school faculties to discover strengths and needs for improvement.

I. The Language Arts of Speaking, Listening, Writing, Spelling, Handwriting

    A. Outcomes

        Are most of the children

1. Growing in comprehension when listening to talks, directions, and discussions and forming good listening habits?
2. Gaining increased confidence and fluency in speaking situations?
3. Showing growth in their speaking and writing vocabularies?
4. Growing in ability to organize thinking for speech and writing?
5. Showing increased ability to work in groups in problem-solving situations?
6. Giving evidence of ability to do research in problem solving, including the use of books?
7. Showing good taste in choice of radio, television, and motion picture programs and using critical thinking about them?
8. Growing in enjoyment and proficiency in creative writing?
9. Developing pride and proficiency in spelling and handwriting in all written work?
10. Growing in awareness of appropriateness of language for specific situations?
11. Developing a higher sense of values, personal interests, and greater maturity in standards of accomplishment?
12. Showing evidence of growth in English usage and in complexity and organization of sentence structure?
13. Giving evidence of growth in self-help and self-evaluation?

    B. Curriculum

1. Is the program based on the premise that language grows only through the process of group living, and are frequent opportunities provided for the children to speak and write in the various social situations in which the language is used?
2. Is the program designed to capitalize on personal experience and to develop interesting experiences about which to speak and write?

3. Do activities include group work in problem solving that calls for search for information, reporting, discussion, and decision on findings?

4. Is instruction provided in listening—developing comprehension and good listening habits?

5. Are there satisfying language-arts experiences which are close to the children's everyday living, and do the experiences make use of natural settings and community resources?

6. Is there a systematic year-to-year developmental program in speaking, listening, and writing?

7. Does English instruction permeate the whole school program of the child or is it confined to certain periods of the day?

C. Methods of Instruction

1. Are the children living in a wholesome, friendly classroom atmosphere where they feel free to express their real thoughts and are assured of genuinely friendly and sympathetic interest?

2. Is the program designed to accept the child at his level of development and to help him grow rather than to meet any specific grade standard?

3. Does the faculty recognize the relationship between growth in communication and the emotional and social development of the child?

4. Is instruction individualized within class organization through flexible grouping and differentiated tasks, and is it developing leadership?

5. Is help given to small groups and/or individuals in overcoming difficulties of expression?

6. Are basic skills taught in relation to use?

7. Is instruction in better English usage given as need arises for it in connection with speaking and writing?

8. Does the program include help in more effective communication in the total school day?

9. Is a record kept of each child's work to show progress?

10. Is the child conscious of progress in communication ability?

11. Is legibility in handwriting emphasized in the whole school program?

12. Do spelling lists for study include words needed by the children in their daily writing? Does spelling grow out of a need for expression?

D. Materials of Instruction

 1. Is the textbook used primarily as a source book of directions and information for learning?
 2. Are workbooks organized to permit use on only those portions needed by the individual child?
 3. Is there available a rich quantity of good stories, visual and auditory aids, or other interesting material which can be used to give new and rich experiences?
 4. Are the materials varied as to difficulty and appeal for each grade level?

II. The Language Arts of Reading

A. Outcomes

Are most of the children

 1. Developing independence in work recognition?
 2. Acquiring ability in comprehension?
 3. Growing in ability to read for facts?
 4. Learning to organize, evaluate, and interpret?
 5. Showing enjoyment in reading?
 6. Gaining in ability to use reading in problem solving?
 7. Developing skill in using books and general references to find information?
 8. Giving evidence of ability to read orally and interpret the meaning for others?
 9. Showing discrimination in choice of books and development of appreciation of good books?

B. Curriculum

 1. Does the program provide for the development of reading readiness?
 2. Does the program provide for sequential development of reading skills?
 3. Is reading instruction confined to one period of the day or is reading taught in all subjects where children use reading?
 4. Are the reading activities sufficiently varied to give the children opportunity to read for different purposes?
 5. Does the program provide for the development of independence in word recognition and for a gradual growth in reading vocabularies?
 6. Is time provided in the school schedule for recreational reading?
 7. Do the children have opportunities to read orally to appreciative audiences made up of other pupils?

C. Methods of Instruction
    1. Is there provision for checking physical and educational readiness for reading?
    2. Is the physical and social climate of the classroom conducive to growth in reading?
    3. Are a variety of teaching methods used in beginning reading?
    4. Is there a systematic plan for development of basic skills in word recognition and comprehension?
    5. Is independence in word recognition developed by use of a variety of methods, such as context clues, phonics, and the use of pictures?
    6. Do teachers set the stage for reading by developing interest in stories to be read?
    7. Is there provision for the children to enjoy good books while learning to read?
    8. Is there provision for individual differences through flexible grouping or other means?
    9. Is attention given to reading in all areas of the curriculum?
    10. Do teachers and children recognize that speed of reading is governed by the purpose in reading and the difficulty of the reading content?
    11. Are the children made conscious of progress in reading ability?
    12. Do teachers enlist the help of parents in encouragement of extensive reading?
    13. Are the children encouraged to use their initiative in choosing and reading books?
    14. Is there provision for extra help for children with special disabilities?

D. Materials of Instruction
    1. Is there a good basal series of readers so graded as to ensure a gradual development of reading skills?
    2. Is the basal reader series considered as a step-by-step series rather than a grade-by-grade series?
    3. Is one basal series used throughout the elementary school?
    4. Is there a wide variety of reading materials varying in difficulty and reader appeal?
    5. Are test materials available to help determine readiness for reading and to help diagnose difficulties in learning to read?

III. The Social Studies and Social Education

  A. Outcomes

    Are most of the children

1. Increasing their understanding and appreciation of
   a) Institutions, agencies, and governmental units?
   b) The interdependence of rural and urban people and peoples of the world?
   c) Social and economic problems?
   d) Man and his relationship to the earth?
   e) Natural phenomena?
   f) Cultural heritage?
   g) Freedom and democracy?
   h) The local community?
   i) The changing character of society?
2. Developing social studies concepts such as time, location, and loyalty?
3. Acquiring skill in problem solving?
4. Improving skill in reading social-studies materials?
5. Growing in skill in using maps, globes, charts, books, and reference materials?
6. Showing the ability to work effectively as members of groups?
7. Practicing good citizenship in the school and community?
8. Carrying responsibilities for school and community events?
9. Showing interest in current events?
10. Learning to make friends easily?
11. Learning the roles of leadership and followership?
12. Acquiring good attitudes toward minority groups and toward the people of other nations?
13. Showing evidence of good relationships in family life?
14. Demonstrating ability in critical thinking?

  B. Curriculum

1. Are the experiences in social studies organized as meaningful units of work?
2. Are experience units a part of the total curriculum plan developed by the whole school faculty?
3. Does the curriculum plan provide for continuity of experiences and gradual growth in conceptual learning?
4. Does the program have balance in that experiences lead to both historical and geographic perspectives?
5. Are educational experiences organized to give breadth of experience—economic, social, and political?

6. Are all the activities of the school used to develop good citizenship and the ability to solve problems cooperatively?
7. Are the conditions and needs of the community included in the program?
8. Are the needs, interests, and abilities of the children considered in the organization of the curriculum?
9. Is there provision for regular attention to current events?
10. Do experience units often deal with local and world relationships?
11. Does the curriculum plan provide for the solving of problems of the school and community?
12. Are experience units organized to permit utilization of content from other curriculum areas as needed?

C. Methods of Instruction

1. Are methods of work designed to give children practice in use of social-studies skills?
2. Is the problem-solving approach used extensively?
3. Do problem-solving experiences begin with the study of concrete situations and lead to generalizations?
4. Do learning experiences develop awareness of time and space relations?
5. Do the children have help in reading social-studies materials?
6. Do the children participate in planning, executing, and evaluating the learning activities?
7. Is the daily class schedule sufficiently flexible to allow for varied blocks of time for new features needing special emphasis?
8. Do teaching procedures make provision for individual differences in the abilities, interests, and educational backgrounds of the pupils?
9. Are social-studies skills learned through practice in meaningful situations?
10. Are children encouraged to assume responsibilities for activities of the school, home, and community?
11. Is the atmosphere of the classroom democratic?
12. Do the children feel that they share in decisions?
13. Are the children given opportunities to learn the roles of leaders and followers?
14. Are the children encouraged to form friendships with people of other cultures?

D. Materials of Instruction

1. Are the resources of the community used extensively in the learning experiences?
2. Is there a good supply of maps, globes, charts, and the like?
3. Is there a rich variety of source material in the form of books and visual aids?
4. Are textbooks used as resource material rather than as the curriculum pattern?
5. Are visual and auditory aids used extensively to give meaning to distant places and peoples and to events of the past?

IV. Arithmetic

A. Outcomes

Are most of the children

1. Developing desirable interests and attitudes toward arithmetic?
2. Developing competence in using measurements and quantitative procedures when dealing with problems of daily living?
3. Acquiring meaningful concepts of numbers and of the number system?
4. Becoming increasingly skilful in the fundamental operations and in ability to apply them to life situations?
5. Acquiring a vocabulary of common numerical terms needed for communication?
6. Developing skill in reading and interpreting material involving quantitative concepts?
7. Increasing in precision and respect for accuracy?
8. Learning budgetary procedures, simple accounting, and other procedures frequently used in real life?

B. Curriculum

1. Is the program organized in such a sequence as to bring gradual development in number concepts and the use of numbers?
2. Is there a conscious effort to develop number concepts and understanding of simple operations in the primary grades?
3. Are experiences in arithmetic adapted to pupil readiness, needs, and abilities?

4. Is the program in arithmetic developed cooperatively by the faculty of the school?

5. Are problems selected from life situations in the school, home, and community?

6. Does the program have balance in that provision is made for the learning concepts and operations needed in the affairs of life?

7. Does the classroom schedule allow adequate time for systematic practice and the development of skill in the use of numbers?

C. Methods of Instruction

1. Are all number concepts and operations with numbers introduced in meaningful concrete situations?

2. Are generalizations developed from work with concrete materials and from meaningful experiences?

3. Do drills follow, rather than precede, the use of number facts or processes in real-life situations?

4. Are activities so organized as to permit the children to work in accordance with their maturity and interests?

5. Is problem solving taught in such a way as to develop reasoning and reflective thinking?

6. Is there variety in the media used to develop basic concepts?

7. Are the children taught to use self-evaluation devices and to make plans for self-improvement?

8. Are the children conscious of their own progress?

9. Are diagnostic instruments used to determine types and cause of difficulties in learning?

10. Is remedial instruction adapted to the needs of individual pupils?

11. Is arithmetic used to strengthen and reinforce learning in the rest of the school program?

D. Materials of Instruction

1. Is there a good supply of manipulative materials and objects, and are these used to make numbers and number operations meaningful?

2. Are there measuring devices and instruments commonly used in daily life?

3. Are the resources of the community used to help the children learn the uses of arithmetic in daily life?

4. Are practice materials prepared and used to develop and maintain basic knowledges and skills?

5. Does the school use the same textbook series throughout the grades?

V. Science

  A. Outcomes

    Are most of the children
    1. Displaying curiosity and interest in science?
    2. Learning to use the scientific method in solving problems arising in the home, the school, and the community?
    3. Showing interest in agriculture because of science used in farming?
    4. Learning to read science material and acquiring a science vocabulary?
    5. Giving evidence of using science and studying science of their own volition?
    6. Practicing conservation of soil, forests, and other natural resources?
    7. Showing appreciation of the contributions of science to modern life?
    8. Displaying a scientific attitude in thinking and behavior?
    9. Developing generalizations in science and applying generalizations in new problem situations?
    10. Acquiring an understanding of the relationships of man and his physical environment?
    11. Giving evidence of increasing skill in observation, experimentation, manipulation, and reasoning?
    12. Forming habits of observing natural phenomena and other science manifestations in daily life?
    13. Learning to do critical thinking and to distinguish between scientific facts, prejudice, and superstition?

  B. Curriculum
    1. Does the program have such continuity that experiences from the lower grades forward provide for progressive development in ability, attitudes, and appreciations?
    2. Does the program have sufficient flexibility to permit adaptation to the needs and interests of the children, to changing conditions, and to the local environment?
    3. To what extent does the learning in science reinforce the learning in other curriculum areas?
    4. Are the problems and content of science largely drawn from the rural environment in which the children live?
    5. Is definite provision made in the school program for planned science experiences as contrasted with incidental experiences only?
    6. Is the program in science well balanced in that there are experiences in the various fields?

7. Are scientific facts and generalizations learned through well-organized and meaningful work units?

C. Methods of Instruction

1. Are problem-solving techniques and the experimental approach used in the teaching of science?
2. Does learning proceed from the use of concrete materials and phenomena of science to generalizations and to wider vicarious experiences, such as reading in science?
3. Are the children given opportunities to use generalizations in observation and study?
4. Are the children encouraged individually to explore the field of science beyond the regular classroom activities?
5. Are the children led to realize that exploration in science has no limit?
6. Are incidents used to awaken interest in science?
7. Are efforts made to use science to develop interest in agriculture and conservation of natural resources?
8. Is the help of resource persons in the school and community sought?

D. Materials of Instruction

1. Are there adequate facilities, such as water, heat, light, and electricity?
2. Is there suitable storage space for materials to be used in science?
3. Are there facilities for displaying science materials and for posting items of interest?
4. Do the teachers and children use the community as a laboratory for learning?
5. Do teachers and children construct materials for experimentation?
6. Are textbooks used primarily as source materials?
7. Is there an adequate supply of library science books, bulletins, pamphlets, and magazines of varying degrees of reading difficulty and interest appeal?

VI. Health, Physical Education, and Safety

A. Outcomes
Are most of the children

1. Practicing good health habits, such as brushing teeth, covering the mouth when coughing, and eating wisely?
2. Developing responsibility for their own health, such as seeking periodic health appraisals?
3. Immunized against communicable diseases?

4. Practicing sanitation in the school, home, and community?
5. Being careful to protect themselves and others from injury?
6. Taking safety precautions in handling tools and equipment?
7. Refusing to take risks in such activities as bicycle riding, walking on highways, and the like?
8. Obeying safety rules and regulations?
9. Growing in ability to use first aid in emergency situations?
10. Eager to help remove hazards to safe living?
11. Developing an understanding of the relation of foods and nutrition to body building?
12. Participating in active games of their own volition?
13. Increasing in physical strength, coordination, and sense of balance?
14. Learning to know the meaning, values, and age-level limitations of strength, endurance, and body skill?
15. Showing good posture when sitting, standing, and walking?
16. Growing in appreciation and understanding of good health and physical fitness?
17. Becoming good sportsmen in both success and defeat?
18. Showing increased tendencies to obey the rules of games and increased understanding of the need for rules?
19. Giving evidence of good mental health as shown by their social and emotional reactions?
20. Learning the techniques of solving personal problems?
21. Acquiring interests in recreational activities?

B. Curriculum
1. Do the children have periodic health examinations? Are there follow-up contacts with parents?
2. Are all of the activities of the school used to develop good health and sanitation habits and habits of taking safety precautions?
3. Are other content areas of the curriculum used to develop understandings, attitudes, and appreciations of good health and safety?
4. Are problems of health and safety in life outside the school included in the curriculum plans?
5. Does the curriculum have both breadth and balance in that all important aspects of health, physical education, and safety receive attention at all levels?

6. Does the curriculum provide for progressive learning and habit formation throughout all grades of the school?

7. If periodic physical examinations are handled under school auspices, do teachers provide appropriate instruction to accompany the examinations?

8. Is the program flexible enough to permit adaptation to the needs, interests, and capacities of the children?

9. Is the physical education program organized to progress from simple games, rhythms, and individual activities in the primary grades to more highly organized activities in the upper grades?

10. Are the children taught games to be used in activities outside the school?

11. Are the various activities of art, music, handicrafts, and physical education used to develop recreational interests?

12. Is the school health and safety program considered as a definite part of a community plan?

C. Methods of Instruction

1. Do the children participate in planning, executing, and evaluating the health and physical education programs?

2. Do teachers avoid making the ill or physically defective child conspicuous?

3. Are teachers alert to health conditions among pupils, and do they know enough about symptoms of common diseases to refer children to nurses and doctors when necessary?

4. Does the school schedule provide adequate time for eating and intervals of time for rest, relaxation, and physical activity?

5. Are activities so organized as to give each child opportunities to meet his needs for status, a feeling of belonging, and success in his work and play?

6. Are units of work designed to go beyond the development of understanding in efforts to secure good action and habit formation?

7. Are the children encouraged to create games and activities?

8. Are intramural games, if used at all, carried on only for brief periods of time because of the danger to the health of children of the elementary-school level?

9. Do teachers recognize that behavior is most likely to be improved by a combination of knowledge, group decision making, and practice?

10. Are pupils given definite responsibilities for leading and helping others when working in small groups?

11. Are people of the community asked to share in the instructional program?

D. Materials of Instruction

1. Is the school environment of such a nature as to contribute to healthful and safe living?

2. Is the school building properly lighted and heated?

3. Are the school buildings and grounds sanitary?

4. Is there adequate space for indoor and outdoor physical activity?

5. Is there a good supply of books, bulletins, and pamphlets for use as source material for units of instruction?

6. Are health readers considered as source materials rather than as guides for the whole health-instruction program?

7. Are children permitted to use physical education equipment for self-directed activities?

8. Are such institutions as health centers, clinics, and hospitals used to increase understanding and appreciation?

VII. The Practical Arts and the Fine Arts

A. Outcomes
Are most of the children

1. Showing freedom and enjoyment in some form of artistic expression?

2. Becoming increasingly effective in expression of ideas and feelings in an original manner?

3. Developing competence in problem solving through exploration and experimentation with a variety of materials?

4. Growing in appreciation of the beautiful in nature and in human works of art?

5. Learning to use music and art for social and recreational purposes?

6. Developing ability to apply functional and esthetic criteria in the choice and use of goods, performances, and services?

7. Learning to use art values and art judgment in practical affairs of the school, home, and community?

8. Revealing richer and happier experiences in their homes through experiences in art and music?

9. Developing love for order, balance, and symmetry in the affairs of daily life?

10. Showing growth in discrimination in choice of programs for televiewing and radio listening?
11. Demonstrating preferences in choice of musical records?

B. Curriculum

1. Are experiences and activities of children in the school, home, and community utilized to stimulate expression?
2. Does the program provide for experiences in the community to develop powers of observation and art values?
3. Are the needs for art in the home and school being met through the experiences of the curriculum?
4. Are opportunities provided for children to participate in art and music activities of the community?
5. Is music used at intervals during the school day to contribute to enjoyment and relaxation?
6. Does the program of musical development begin with learning to use the voice in simple tunes and with rhythmic activities and extend to more complex experiences in vocal and instrumental music?
7. Is there sufficient variety in music and art activities to permit the gifted to identify their abilities and to explore possibilities for the future and to permit all children to find areas of maximum enjoyment?
8. Is art used in functional relationships with other areas of the curriculum?
9. Is the musical program well balanced in terms of vocal and instrumental activities?
10. Do the music activities emphasize understanding and enjoyment as well as skill development?

C. Methods of Instruction

1. Are the children permitted to experiment with a wide variety of art media to find their most satisfying means of expression?
2. Are the children encouraged to develop their own art standards through experience and observation?
3. Are the activities of the whole school day used to stimulate the children in functional art?
4. Are the children encouraged to apply learning in art to the affairs of the home?
5. Does the program in art have such balance and breadth that the children will have opportunities both for free expression and for acquisition of the art values needed by the consumer?

6. Are children with special talents encouraged to continue their development in art, crafts, and music?
7. Do teachers exemplify art tastes in the classrooms?
8. Are the arts used to develop appreciation of the other cultures?

D. Materials of Instruction
   1. Are the children taken on excursions into the community to study art in nature, in the homes, and in buildings?
   2. Are people of the community used as consultants in the arts and crafts?
   3. Does the supply of art materials permit the children to explore and experiment with different modes of expression?
   4. Is there a good supply of visual and auditory aids for use in art and music?

INDEX OF NAMES

INDEX OF SUBJECTS